Deconstructing
Will Smith

Deconstructing Will Smith

Race, Masculinity and Global Stardom

WILLIE TOLLIVER

McFarland & Company, Inc., Publishers

Jefferson, North Carolina

This book has undergone peer review.

ISBN (print) 978-1-4766-7569-5
ISBN (ebook) 978-1-4766-4745-6

Library of Congress and British Library
cataloguing data are available

Library of Congress Control Number 2021059017

Front cover: Will Smith stars in *Hancock* (2008),
directed by Peter Berg (RGR Collection/Alamy Stock Photo).

Printed in the United States of America

McFarland & Company, Inc., Publishers
Box 611, Jefferson, North Carolina 28640
www.mcfarlandpub.com

To Lenell

Acknowledgments

This project began as a Gladden Public Lecture under the auspices of Joseph Gladden, Jr., the former chair of the Agnes Scott College Board of Trustees. The lecture was introduced by President Mary Brown Bullock and Dean Rosemary Levy-Zumwalt, during an evening I will always remember. Other support from the administration has been a generous grant by the Holder Fund for Faculty Innovation.

I must give deep thanks to Lisa Camp, Gary Mitchem, and especially Layla Milholen at McFarland for their faith in my proposal and for their forbearance.

For their abiding friendship and support at every possible level, I must express my appreciation of my colleagues in the Agnes Scott English Department, both individually and collectively, both past and present: Christopher Ames, Christine Cozzens, Jim Diedrick, Alan Grostephan, Melissa Fay Greene, the late Steve Guthrie, Linda Hubert, Waqas Khwaja, Bobby Meyer-Lee, the late Kamilah Aisha Moon, Jamie Stamant, Nicole Stamant, Peggy Thompson, and Rachel Trousdale. I must also recognize my other essential colleagues outside the department: Yvonne Newsome, Tina Pippin, Beth Hackett, Julia Knowlton, and Michael Schlig. There are several former students who have become colleagues and valuable sounding boards for my ideas: Fredrick Holloman, Monica Gresham, and Chesya Burke.

I would also like to acknowledge the contributions of my students over the years to this work. Sarah Dooley of Oberlin College spent a memorable January semester providing me with crucial research assistance. I cannot praise highly enough the devotion and enthusiasm of the Agnes Scott students who have worked with me and have shared their critical insights: Aziza Taylor, Taji Okolo, Saleema Mustafa, Trisha Manns, Kate Whitney, Jamila Pitts, Emily Ly, Avanti Lemons, Elizabeth Kell, Julia Dwyer, Gabby Shepard, and Summer Robinson.

I must also thank my family for their encouragement and support: Lenell Shelby, Lillie Shelby, Lenell Shelby, Jr., and Sele M'Poko.

Finally, I must express special gratitude to Heino Nurk, who has given me so much, including a little room of my own.

Table of Contents

Prologue

A Slap Heard Round the World

On May 18, 2012, at the Moscow premiere of his film *Men in Black 3*, Will Smith slapped Ukrainian journalist Vitalii Sediuk who evidently attempted to kiss him during an interview on the red carpet (fig. 0.1). The video went viral, and the story was reported by the international and American news media. The responses on the blogosphere predominantly expressed support for Smith's actions. According to the commentators, the journalist had invaded Smith's personal space and had, in effect, assaulted the actor. Therefore, Smith's physical reaction was both understandable and justified. This event lends itself to much more scrutiny because of its larger, multiple, and complex meanings. This confrontation over a kiss is revelatory of the nature of Smith's star persona, the crisis of masculinity that informs that star identity, the

Fig. 0.1. Will Smith poses with Russian fans at the 2012 premiere of *Men in Black 3* in Moscow (Zuma Press, Inc./Alamy Stock Photo).

global implications of African American celebrity, and the historical development of Black male images both on and off the screen.

What occurred during this incident? There are varying accounts as well as different interpretations of the meaning of this encounter.[1] Some viewers of the video saw the journalist greet Smith with a hug and then an attempt at a traditional European double cheek kiss. During the interaction, Smith seemed suddenly surprised and created an awkward moment during which the kiss got off track. It did seem as though his mouth was the target. Why did Smith suddenly panic at the prospect of a male kiss? Even more importantly, why did Smith feel compelled to slap the writer in reaction? In some versions of the scene, Smith pushes the perpetrator away and then gently slaps him. The slap was both instinctive and deliberate. What the public witnessed was a clash of cultures, the spectacle of what happens when an African American star performs on the international stage. Through a misunderstanding of motive and a misreading of gesture, Smith may have struck a defensive posture drawing upon a cultural code of masculinity. The slap could be a response to an affront to his manhood, an action that might be a manifestation of gender conditioning within a specific racial and cultural context. Some commentators have noted that Smith's behavior in its excess replicates a kind of Black male macho posturing. His act assures his audience and himself of his authentic heterosexual Black manhood. This behavior may be at odds with less rigid concepts of masculinity that circulate in European culture. For instance, during the coverage of past Olympic Games, it was not unusual to witness Russian male gymnasts congratulate their teammates for their performances with kisses to the mouth (Clarey B15). Again, what this kiss-and-slap incident may underscore are the tensions that exist, even in the world of international film and red carpets, when cultures come together in global spaces.

What if the kiss were not a muddle, but intentional? What could have been the motive? In a similar and earlier situation, Sediuk presented Madonna with a bouquet of hydrangeas, a flower she hates, which forced an outraged response. Although he has been characterized as an opportunistic prankster, he can also be construed as a brilliant provocateur, with a specific agenda: to uncover the contradictions of celebrity. In these acts of guerrilla theater he deconstructs the protocol of the red carpet, a constructed media event that supports the star system and the Hollywood industrial machine. His confrontations with stars and their shocked and unrehearsed reactions break the surface of the illusion rendered by the processes of publicity and offers up eruptions of reality. Will Smith's slap reveals a real identity behind the star image. His reaction is an authentic act within an artificial context. What marks this momentary dropping of his public face is his conscious effort to restore his mask. In the video, we can see him resuming his identity as "Will Smith." This sight elicits sympathy because we get a glimpse of how difficult it is for him to maintain his characteristic charm and affability. There is a vulnerability there that goes beyond having his private space invaded; we get a glimpse of his private self.

Not only did Sediuk deconstruct the red carpet; he deconstructed Smith as well. Just as he carefully did his research to know how to devise an encounter to reveal Madonna, he chose exactly the right tactic for Smith. On subsequent appearances on talk shows, Smith admitted that the journalist had a schtick, but he said that when he slapped him his "ass got schtuck" (Loinaz). The joke, however, is on Smith. In attempting to kiss him, Sediuk referenced the controversy over Smith's refusal to kiss a man in his first serious film, *Six Degrees of Separation*. In effect, the journalist restaged that moment which was one of the lowest points in Smith's career in terms of negative reactions to his performance and his just developing star persona. He was charged with immaturity and homophobia. The role in that film provided a challenging test for him, his ability to do what the role required, and he failed it. The moment on the red carpet in a sense offered a retake of that test, which Smith symbolically failed again. His action was a defense of a personal affront, but on another level, it revealed a homophobic element that emerged from an authentic private place. Smith's act unintentionally also set up a contradiction within his attitudes about homosexuality. In the week before this incident in which he slapped a man for attempting to kiss him, he publicly announced his support of same sex marriage (Valby).

Smith's slap of Sediuk resonates with another slap heard around the world. In the 1967 film *In the Heat of the Night*, Sidney Poitier's character, Virgil Tibbs, is slapped by a white man whom he is questioning in relation to a murder investigation. Tibbs draws up and returns the slap with force and defiance. This moment was galvanizing, fueling Black revolutionary spirit during the Civil Rights movement. The spectacle of a Black man slapping a white man, standing up and asserting his authority and equality, had a transformative meaning in a deeply racially conflicted society. Compare this iconic moment to Smith's encounter on the red carpet in Moscow. The former confrontation resonates against a political movement and social change. The contemporary parallel circulates as part of the publicity apparatus of an individual celebrity, and its most salient meaning can be best understood not within racial discourse but within the economic logics of the film industry. Notice also how none of the commentary notes the races of the two men. Does this omission describe an advance in racial discourse? Race here seems to be displaced onto another form of difference. The commentary emphasizes Sediuk's "foreignness" as opposed to Smith's identity as an American. Even more, Smith is described as the "hero" in the narrative of this incident. His Blackness becomes elided with his nationality. Is this what happens when African American star identities become globalized? Will Smith's kiss on the red carpet provides a rich opportunity to engage in a number of issues that are germane to a larger analysis of contemporary Black male celebrity: the construction of the star image; the intersection or racial, gender and sexual identity anxieties; the displacement of race onto other forces; and the intertextual relationships of film representations of Black male masculinity. These are a few of the important perspectives upon which I will draw in reading Will Smith as a cultural icon.

Introduction

Deconstructing Will Smith

Will Smith, the celebrated actor and rap artist, has reached a level of Hollywood success that is unprecedented for a Black star. His presence guarantees that his film will "open large" in terms of ticket sales on its given premiere weekend and will garner subsequent huge box-office returns. After the summer triumphs of *Independence Day* and *Men in Black*, Smith was considered to "own" the July 4 weekend. This kind of clout has earned him a position among Hollywood's elite. His salary, over $20 million per picture, places him in the exclusive inner circle of preeminent male stars. Even more than this, his success and his movement to a place of high visibility and cultural centrality renders him iconic in significant ways. As he himself would concur, even fame and celebrity are inevitably racialized. A spectacularly successful Black actor carries with him cultural baggage in such a way that his success has a meaning that goes beyond the personal. For instance, Smith's entry into the top echelon of Hollywood male stars constitutes assimilation at an extremely high level. Why has Smith specifically been able to experience this breakthrough, and what are the benefits and costs for him and for Black America? This indeed is the central issue of this study: What are the larger meanings of Smith's celebrity? What does it say about the state of Hollywood and about the racial climate of society in general, especially in the era of Obama and after? How does Smith's racial profile intersect with issues of class, gender and sexuality that inform recent discourses concerning the Black male? These are the ideas explored in eight chapters that analyze different aspects of Smith's films: "Reading Will Smith," "Culturally Mulatto," "A Slave to Fashion," "Hottentot Adonis," "A Postlude to a Kiss," "Science Fictions and Racial Facts," "Dynamic Duos and Magical Negroes," and "Genre, Interrupted." The focuses of these analyses will be his films: *Where the Day Takes You* (1992), *Made in America* (1993), *Six Degrees of Separation* (1993), *Bad Boys* I and II (1995, 2003), *Independence Day* (1996), *Men in Black I, II and III* (1997, 2002, 2012), *Enemy of the State* (1998), *Wild, Wild West* (1999), *The Legend of Bagger Vance* (2000), *I, Robot* (2004), *Hitch* (2005), *The Pursuit of Happyness* (2006), *I Am Legend* (2007), *Hancock* (2008), *Seven Pounds* (2008), *After Earth* (2013), *Focus* (2015), *Concussion* (2015), *Suicide Squad* (2016), *Collateral Beauty* (2016), *Bright* (2017), *Aladdin* (2019), *Gemini Man* (2019), and *Bad Boys for Life* (2020). In my analysis, I will also draw upon critical works concerning the history of Blacks in the movies, the evolution of Black identities, film genres, and theories of fame and celebrity as well as race and masculinity.

In Chapter One, "Reading Will Smith: Floating Signs and the Semiotics of Stardom," I examine the racial implications of Will Smith's broad-based appeal. His rise within the film industry power structure could be construed as symbolic of general racial progress, or as merely exceptional or emblematic. It is significant that Smith's career should have its ascendancy at an historical moment of marked racial division. Perhaps there is a sense that Smith fulfills a need in the popular consciousness, a cultural wish for racial rapprochement. There is also the sense that like Bill Cosby's in the '80s, Smith's popularity masks the real problems of Black America in the '90s. Another important aspect of Smith's cross-over appeal is the nature of the Blackness that is engaged and negotiated. Smith offers to his mainstream audience a Blackness that is almost voided of its cultural and historical content. This assertion is based upon essentialist notions of Blackness, and the argument articulates the ways in which Smith's persona and characterizations recognize and refute these notions. In opposition, it could also be argued that Smith's image does not deny but instead complicates, extends, and transforms what it means to be Black. This chapter performs two specific tasks: to read Smith against theories of stardom by Richard Dyer, Paul McDonald, and P. David Marshall, and to ascertain the nature of his signifying power as a Black male star by comparisons to the global public personas of Paul Robeson and Michael Jordan.

Chapter Two, "Culturally Mulatto," reads Smith against the concept of the New Black Aesthetic as formulated by Trey Ellis in his 1986 essay published in the journal *Callaloo*. Ellis sets forth a manifesto for a new sensibility in Black expression, one that has been forged in the years after the Civil Rights movement. This new generation of African Americans claims a different kind of Black identity that recognizes and embraces all their cultural influences, not just those that have been traditionally characterized as essentially Black. These new young artists come from the Black middle class and have graduated from elite colleges and universities. They also have global experience and are able to move comfortably in multiple social worlds. Many are biracial, but all are what might be termed "cultural mulattoes." Examples of members of the New Black Aesthetic (NBA) would include Vernon Reid of the Black rock group Living Color or Lenny Kravitz whose music is also an amalgam of Black influences as well as mainstream rock. Zadie Smith offers a thorough anatomization of this phenomenon in her 2000 novel *On Beauty*. Other writers who can be so categorized include Paul Beatty (*White Boy Shuffle, The Sellout*), Colson Whitehead (*Sag Harbor, The Underground Railroad*), and Andrea Lee (*Sarah Phillips*). Scholars who have focused on this topic include Mark Anthony Neal (*Soul Babies: Black Popular Culture and the Post-Soul Aesthetic*). Most recently, Touré has taken up this hybridized Black identity in his book *Who's Afraid of Post-Blackness? What It Means to Be Black Now*. This post-racial identity as manifested in the cinematic field was noted in the September 3, 2000, issue of *the New York Times Magazine*. In a celebrity profile, actor Chris Tucker of the *Rush Hour* films declared that he is the first post-racial movie star because his film characters do not depend on traditional notions of race and because his films are globally successful. Tucker is incorrect in his own self-assessment in that his characterizations depend quite heavily on racial stereotypes, but he is correct in perceiving a new post-racial era of Black filmic representation. I would argue that it is Will Smith who marks the establishment of this new racial identity.

"A Slave to Fashion" explores Smith's star persona through the discourse of fashion. I examine Smith's public fashion statements through his appearances over the years on the red carpet, singly and in tandem with his wife Jada Pinkett Smith. My two arguments here are that his public dress is fundamental in the construction of his stardom which elides the public and the private and that he contests the codes of masculine dress by exercising the sartorial license extended to men of color. In an analysis of his costuming in key music videos, I note the recurrence of black and white visual themes, and I read the storylines of these clips as narratives of assimilation, one of the central issues attached to Smith's film characters as well as his own career. A focus on *Wild, Wild West* and Smith's performance of female impersonation will provide an opportunity to explore the debated issue of drag among Black male actors and comedians in Hollywood. His costuming in films such as *Six Degrees of Separation*, *Men in Black*, and *Enemy of the State* serves to address cultural anxieties about Black masculinity and find resolution in Smith's post-racial, fashioned body.

In the chapter titled "Hottentot Adonis" I read Smith against theories concerning the representation of the Black male body. I take my cue from David Marriott who claims in his book *On Black Men* that the two most powerful modes of the visual representation of the bodies of Black men can be found in the iconography of lynching and pornography. Here I take a second look at *Men in Black* and its play upon the anxiety over the Black phallus. Fear of the Black male member is invoked in certain scenes in *Wild Wild West* and *I, Robot*. Upon the release of the latter film, Smith discussed during talk show appearances his much-analyzed nude scene. Evidently, there were frontal nude shots, but he joked that his "willie" had to be digitally removed. The implications concerning the general emasculation of Black men on screen are clear. *I, Robot* raises another issue as Smith's character possesses a bionic arm. The construction of a cybernetic science fiction hero becomes another way of cinematically containing and controlling the Black male body. The imagery of lynching can be read into two of Smith's films *Wild Wild West* and *Seven Pounds*. In the former, his character narrowly escapes lynching through a combination of the quick timing of his rescuers as well as his own quick wit. When juxtaposed to actual accounts of lynching, even of victims who attempted to talk their way out their situation, this scene takes on an irresponsible ahistoricality that even a postmodern interpretation cannot redeem. In *Seven Pounds*, Smith's character atones for his accidental role in the deaths of seven people by sacrificing parts of his body. The disassembling of his Black male body replicates the ritual harvesting of body parts during acts of lynching. The difference here is that the victim feels he is truly guilty of his crimes and in effect lynches himself.

Quite often in his films, Smith's characters enter homoerotic spaces. Perhaps the most pertinent example of this phenomenon is in *Six Degrees of Separation* in which Smith essays the role of a young, gay Black man. The fifth chapter, "Postlude to a Kiss," examines the controversy surrounding Smith's well-publicized failure or refusal to kiss another male actor for this film. Examined is the extent of Smith's homophobia and resistance to portraying the role of "Paul Poitier" as written and the effect upon the finished film will also be discussed. Elsewhere in his oeuvre, Smith relies upon homosexual reference and parody to achieve some of his comic effects. This can be seen not as a point of weakness in Smith, but as a strength. His willingness to associate his image with homosexual subject matter, even in passing, allows him to negotiate the highly charged area of the perceived threat of Black male sexuality. These associations, in addition to other factors, permit Smith to circumvent the negative stereotypical associations of Black males with hypermasculinity and hypersexuality. The result for Smith is a Black male image that is consumable by mainstream audiences. Smith thus is engaged in the significant cultural work of the reconstruction of the Black male image in the popular imagination.

The sixth chapter, "Science Fictions and Racial Facts," begins an examination of Smith's films in terms of their conformity to and subversion of the norms of genre. This chapter addresses the fact that so many of Smith's films are science fictions. In these films he is positioned as the hero who saves the world or survives as the last man on Earth. This alone is remarkable given the history of science fiction films in which that narrative privilege is reserved for white men. Smith's presence in these films complicates the way race is usually treated in this genre: as a metaphor for other issues or in terms that reinforce the racial binaries and dynamics of present-day American society. When Smith is the central figure who confronts the enemy aliens, his Blackness is mitigated because the aliens become the other. Smith then represents not a specific racial identity, but the entirety of the human race. In this chapter, I also offer readings of individual films. For instance, I see the robot rebellion in *I, Robot* as an allegory of resistance under the slave system and *Bright* as a prime example of the racial reversal strategy employed in several of Smith's science fiction films.

The seventh chapter, "Dynamic Duos and Magical Negroes," considers Smith's contributions to the interracial buddy film and the related Magical Negro film. One of the remarkable facts about Smith's film career is that he has almost always been paired with a white male: Harry Connick, Jr., Jeff Goldblum, Tommy Lee Jones, Gene Hackman and Kevin Kline. It is the nature of the buddy film to reflect in some way the state of American racial relations. Smith's addition to this equation makes the interracial pairing self-conscious and parodic. The effect is that the customary racial conflict is defused and deflated. The unique configuration of the personal and ideological in the deracialized Smith has this effect. At this point, it is instructive to compare Smith to Eddie Murphy whose stardom precedes and prepares for Smith's. There are fascinating differences in the racial messages to be found in their films and characters. One point to be made is that Murphy's personae are situated within conventional definitions of Blackness, whereas Smith easily transcends these definitions. The succession from Murphy to Smith is culturally significant, revealing either real social progress or simply its illusion. This chapter also reads Smith against the stereotype of the Magical African American Friend or the Magical Negro. This Black archetype in recent film is characterized by his otherworldliness, loyalty, and wisdom. He functions either to educate or to sacrifice his life for the white protagonist. Examples of this screen phenomenon include Morgan Freeman in *Driving Miss Daisy*, Mykelti Williamson in *Forrest Gump*, or Michael Clarke Duncan in *The Green Mile*. Another example is Will Smith's performance in *The Legend of Bagger Vance* as the mysterious stranger who aids an amateur golfer in reclaiming his game. Instead of complicating or countering the stereotype, Smith's character raises it to a new problematic level.

"Genre, Interrupted," Chapter Eight, investigates Smith's interventions into the genres of the superhero film, the romantic comedy, and the biopic. In *Hancock*, Smith plays a down on his luck superhero whose reputation is rehabilitated with the help of a public relations friend so that he can better serve and save humanity. This is perhaps Smith's "Blackest" role in that for once his character touches the real experiences of Black men. Hancock's transformation invokes the cases of scandal compromised Black male sports stars whose redemptions have been facilitated by public atonement and effected by the machinery of the celebrity system. Smith's career trajectory from rapper to global film star parallels this metamorphic narrative which also occurs in his other films. In the romantic comedy, *Hitch*, Smith becomes another kind of magical negro or superhero, a relationship expert who saves the love lives of white men whose affections are unrequited. Of interest here is how the film reconfigures the logic of the romantic comedy genre to avoid the pairing of a Black leading man with either a white female to avoid audience racial discomfort or with a Black actress to avoid feared losses at the box office. In each case, Smith invokes the racial stereotypes and anxieties of the past while advancing his star image and rendering himself unthreatening and safe for mainstream audiences.

The last section of Chapter Eight focuses not on Smith's attributes as a star, but his achievement as a film actor. It is curious that his most notable performances are those in which he portrays real people. He received critical acclaim for *Six Degrees of Separation* in which he captures the essence of David Hampton, the tragic dreamer and con artist who captured the imagination of playwright John Guare. Smith was nominated for a Best Actor Oscar for Michael Mann's *Ali* (2001), a film which presented Smith with several challenges beyond the physical and mental training required for the role. Although Smith received general praise for his performance, there were complications in his inhabitation of the boxing legend who also was an icon of the Civil Rights struggle. Within Smith's performance is a contest between two kinds of identities: one post-racial and the other racially transformative. Ali was a part of the vanguard who won the rights and privileges enjoyed by the younger generation. Smith's post-racial, Post-Black identity can be seen in the interviews he gave upon the film's release in which he confessed his struggle to completely understand Ali's situation. I argue that we have arrived at a remarkable historic point when a Black actor cannot identify with the suffering and struggles of his forebears. It is a testament to Smith's hard work and skill that he overcame this difficulty to register a creditable performance.

Smith's fully felt and invested work in 2006's *The Pursuit of Happyness*, however, is arguably his best. As Chris Gardner, a rags-to-riches success story from homelessness to high finance, Smith exhibits impressive range, hitting notes of both the lows of despair and emotional highs. In 2015's *Concussion*, he plays Dr. Bennet Omalu, the Nigerian-born forensic pathologist who confronts the National Football League with his discovery of CTE, or chronic traumatic encephalopathy, in professional football players. Not only does Smith take on an African accent, he does something extraordinary with the role, registering the effects of racism on a proud Black man of great intellectual achievement and a lofty sense of personal integrity. In these roles Smith transcends his star status by breaking the acting code or giving performances that are true feats of acting rather than reiterations of his usual screen enactments of the "Will Smith" type. According to David P. Marshall in *Celebrity and Power*, the third stage in the development of the movie star is a transgressive movement outside the star persona to achieve an identity beyond the constructed public and private self. Not only does he fully engage the subjectivity of real persons, he also connects with their social, cultural, and racial realities. In the process, he takes steps to free himself from the restrictions of his stardom.

The Conclusion, "The Biggest Movie Star in the World," poses once again this study's fundamental question: If Will Smith is indeed the quintessential global movie star, exactly how has he accomplished this? It retraces the sources of Smith's ingenious manipulations of image and race. Just as his star persona is intentional, so is the arc of his career. At the beginning of his ascendancy, Smith proclaimed that his goal was to be the biggest movie star in the world. Certainly, he has realized his dream through the implementation of a master plan formulated with his business partner Jim Lassiter. Together they have shaped business strategies, film narratives, and a star persona that have assured Smith box office dominance at home and abroad. Even more than this, Smith has had a significant cultural impact and must be recognized for what he has achieved beyond merely being successful: the formation of a self, a career, and a cinema that expands what it means to be Black and male and a vision of a global stardom that suggests the perfectible post-racial world he wants to bring into being.

ONE

Reading Will Smith

Floating Signs and the Semiotics of Stardom

Will Smith has attained a level of achievement in Hollywood that is unparalleled and unprecedented. From his debut as a rap artist in 1986, he has moved from success to success, breaking new ground and scoring numerous firsts. In 1988 he was the first rapper to receive a Grammy. This award was for the song "Parents Just Don't Understand," which exemplified Smith's innovative brand of positive rap. After he moved on from his subsequent television career as the star of the situation comedy *The Fresh Prince of Bel-Air* (1990–1994) into feature films, he continued to make entertainment industry history. The box-office record set by his film *Independence Day*, released on July 3, 1996, set a pattern that was repeated the next year by *Men in Black*, released on July 2, 1997. As a result, Smith earned the reputation of being the box-office king of the Fourth of July weekend, a reputation solidified by the openings of *Wild Wild West* (June 30, 1999), *Men in Black II* (July 3, 2002), *I, Robot* (July 16, 2004), and *Hancock* (July 2, 2008) (Corliss). He was also recognized as a dependable box-office attraction. Any film that he headlined would be sure to make money. At this juncture, he moved onto the A-list of film actors commanding a $20 million per film salary. During the '90s Smith was the only Black star operating at this level.

In 2007 *Newsweek* anointed Smith "The $4 Billion Man." Sean Smith, who reported the story, concluded: "With a worldwide career box office of $4.4 billion, Will Smith is now the most powerful actor in Hollywood" (S. Smith). In the years since then, Smith's position has shifted somewhat in the wake of new trends in films and newer stars (such as Dwayne Johnson whose records rival and even surpass Smith's and who is discussed specifically in the *Conclusion*), but he has maintained his ranking near the top of the highest-earning stars. Among Black actors, Smith's position is essentially uncontested. In terms of aggregate worldwide box-office earnings, both Eddie Murphy ($6.695 billion) and Samuel L. Jackson ($4.287 billion) approximate his record ($6.529 billion).[1] This is the result of both men having had longer careers and having made more films. Compare Murphy's forty-two films in a leading role and Jackson's fifty films to Smith's twenty-eight. Given his output, it is remarkable that Smith's overall numbers are in the same range as theirs. When his career earnings are averaged with his overall number of films, Smith eclipses them both.[2]

Smith's power resides in his economic clout as *Forbes* magazine confirmed in 2009 asserting that Smith is peerless in terms of his financial value (Singh). He is able not only to garner huge box-office receipts but also to guarantee financing

11

and distribution for any film project to which he attaches his name. The magazine reported that "'Will Smith stands alone as the only actor to score a perfect ten among industry voters in the Star Currency survey'" (Singh). Richard Corliss observes that Smith's bankability is an anomaly in today's Hollywood. In general, stars no longer can guarantee box-office success—with the sole exception of Will Smith. He is "the last movie star" in a "post-movie-star era" (Corliss).

Will Smith's standing in the world of entertainment and in the world is clear. He is an African American star whose appeal goes deep into the national and international imaginations and reaches across boundaries of race, ethnicity, class, age, class, gender, and nation. His achievement has historic dimensions but has not received the serious analysis it deserves. What are the reasons for his universal popularity? How exactly is his stardom constituted? What price has been paid for his success? What are the larger meanings of his ascendency? Indeed, the implications of his stardom are so far-ranging that they extend beyond his individual identity and render his status iconic. For this discussion, iconicity has two meanings. In general, iconicity refers to the ability of a symbol to refer to or stand in for something else, such as a value, quality, or subject that it resembles (Chandler). Smith's stardom tells us something about American society, its evolving identity, its issues, and its relation to the world. One of the central issues that define the nation is race. Will Smith functions as an icon or sign of race in a semiotic sense, semiotics referring to the study of the relationship between material things or signs and their non-literal meanings. What makes his success so extraordinary is how he excels despite the barrier of race. Maryann Erigha articulates the underlying reason that African American actors have found Hollywood acceptance historically so challenging: "Refashioning the stigma that Black Americans face in the larger U.S. society, Hollywood likewise brands Blackness as problematic" (142). Economic imperatives render Blackness a problem, compromising the full potential of box-office profit: "At the stage of commercially lucrative blockbuster movies, Black worldviews, ideologies, and identities are, in large part, systematically, consciously, and symbolically excluded from the screen" (21). In order to function and survive in the industry, the Black performer must accommodate the demands of white corporate interests and the expectations of white general audiences by mitigating their "stigma":

> The idea of "doing Hollywood movies," of Black people, more or less, shedding Blackness for mainstream success, is embodied in the phenomenon of the crossover star, a concept first used to describe screen actors who appeal to multiracial audiences. In crossing over to mainstream movies, actors seemingly "transcend race" by drawing viewership from multiracial audiences, and especially large white audiences, in addition to attracting audiences from their racial group [Erigha 151].

Smith is the prime example of a crossover star for his time. The reason most often invoked to explain Smith's preeminence is that he "transcends race." A *Newsweek* reporter writes the following about Smith's charisma: "His appeal is so universal that it transcends race" (S. Smith). Corliss adds: "It's good to be the King of Hollywood— of the entertainment world. Smith is above and apart, leaping national borders, transcending race" (Corliss).

The assumption behind these statements is that Blackness carries an inherent negativity that must be overcome, an essential insight of critical race theory whose tenets inform the racial analysis of this study. The specific problem beyond industrial considerations is the preponderance of negative perceptions about Black males the circulate in our society (criminal, irresponsible, violent, hypersexual). Philippa Gates writes: "Black masculinity is regarded as a threat to white mainstream culture because of its potential to be hypersexual" (21). Smith defies these stereotypes and thus can project an image of Blackness that is "safe" for consumption by the white mainstream. He contests received notions of Blackness by the way his film performances avoid the issue or by engendering a new racial discourse. He signifies race differently, or he initiates an alternative code of interpreting racial meaning. These variations are characteristic of the complexity of racial signification. Not only does Smith convey messages at different registers, he expresses oppositions to be read differently by white and Black audiences. These oppositional messages can cancel each other, and what remains is the triumphal iconic image of Will Smith.

The idea of the star having the ability to contain contradictory meanings and messages is central to the influential theory of stardom formulated by Richard Dyer in his seminal study *Stars*, wherein he elaborates upon the connection between the meaning of stars and ideology, the star containing the ideological contradictions circulating within specific social and cultural spheres. Dyer credits Charles Eckert's work "for its linking of the produced image to the specific ideological realities of its time" (28). Those ideological realities are multiple and often conflicting and oppositional, which is reflected in the polysemic nature of the stars who symbolize those historical moments. Stars variously accommodate these oppositions within ideology through displacement, concealment, privileging one side over the other, or holding both in tension. There is one other mode of managing these contradictions: "the star effects a 'magic' reconciliation of the apparently incompatible terms" (26). Will Smith's capacity for signifying race and containing contradictions, such as embodying Blackness and also its effacement; such as signaling the possible transcendence of race through his individual star image and success while masking the continuing social and economic realities of the Black population, is a paradigmatic example of an ideological "magical synthesis" (26).

Claire Sisco King also bases her theory of Smith's stardom upon the concept of the negotiation of conflicting significations, terming her approach metonymic criticism. In her interpretive scheme, celebrity personae function as examples of metonymy or "a figure of speech that substitutes one word or phrase for another with which it is associated" ("Hitching" 84). Thus, a female star, according to Barthes, becomes synonymous with ideals, ideologies, and values such as "beauty, sexuality, and femininity" ("Hitching" 84). More importantly, stars stand in for the cultural discourses that metonymic associations attach to them, and they allow audiences to deal with these cultural issues and their complexities and contradictions through the distance provided by their star images. In King's analysis, Smith serves as a metonym for American attitudes and ideologies about race and gender, and, as such, he also embodies ambivalences carried within those logics. She writes: "Smith also matters for critical considerations of race and gender in U.S. culture because his persona has become a site of contestation. Some frame Smith as a trailblazer paving the way for other men and women of color. Yet, others consider him a 'sell out' whose success relies primarily on his assimilation into white culture" ("Hitching" 88). Smith thus conveys two conflicting messages simultaneously, positive and negative, and this ability to hold two ideas in tension or in synthesis, as has been articulated as this study's overview, is constitutive of his singular star power.

The formulations of Dyer and King that help to describe the complex composition of Smith's stardom also suggest that he possesses a kind of "difference" that sets him apart and permits ascendance. His star identity is different from that of other comparable Black actors such as Denzel Washington and Eddie Murphy. Washington's Oscars and film directing credits extend to him a power position that approximates Smith's. What distinguishes Washington from Smith is that he is a superlative actor who disappears into his roles while still maintaining his identity as a star. Smith is not primarily a paragon of the acting craft. Consequently, he does not often reach a complete unity with the roles he plays. There is always some uncontained aura of personality that hovers around his performances. Paul McDonald delineates the difference between acting styles, between "impersonation," whereby the actor differently embodies the characters he plays, and "personification," whereby the actor "foregrounds the continuities of the star's image over and above differences of character" ("Reconceptualising Stardom" 185). For the most part, Smith's performances belong to the latter category. He is recognized and valued as a star whose brand is synonymous with success, whereas Washington is primarily distinguished for the quality of his acting. Cynthia Baron is explicit about this: "Washington is a star performer and prestige star whose public image, financial success, critical acclaim, cultural significance and industry position are linked in some way to public recognition of his acting ability" (*Denzel* 5). Stephanie Larrieux underscores the difference between Smith and Washington:

> Smith's crossover success could not have been possible, however, had it not been for the trailblazing efforts of Black male leads such as Sidney Poitier, Harry Belafonte, and Denzel Washington. Washington in particular was initially looked upon to become the great break-out crossover Black star of the post–Civil Rights era. He possessed the talent to do so, but despite having made a variety of movies including one in the science fiction genre, Washington was unsuccessful in producing a major blockbuster or, "one of those films that becomes the all-time top ten money-makers and embeds itself and its stars (for better or worse) in the national consciousness" ... the way Will Smith has [Larrieux 209; Nickson, *Will Smith* 1].

The difference between Washington and Smith hinges upon Smith's ability to transcend not only race, but any film he headlines or any character he plays. In a sense, he becomes his own auteur. Dyer observes that it is rare when "the totality of a film can be laid at the door of a star" (*Stars* 153). This is what happens again and again with Smith's films which in certain ways constitute their own genre.

Smith is also distinct from Murphy (and Washington) in that his portrayals do not rely upon conventional notions of Black identity. Both Murphy and Washington's characters inhabit the world of racial difference in a way that Smith's do not. Smith's characterizations move the Black male figure into new and unexpected spaces, and to the extent that he does this, he has cultural import and achieves iconicity. Aside from the previously discussed semiotic meanings, the term iconicity describes, for this inquiry, the phenomenon of Black men who rise to prominence in such a way as to symbolize a historical moment. It is a condition these figures do not chose, but one that is thrust upon them. Most often these icons are athletes or entertainers: Jack Johnson, Jesse Owens, Joe Louis, Jackie Robinson, Muhammad Ali. (It is particularly interesting that Smith stars in a film biography of Ali, a film in which two different kinds of racial and cultural icons, from different eras and distinct modes of Blackness, confront each other.) In the world of entertainment, a line of descent can be drawn from Paul Robeson to Sidney Poitier to Bill Cosby. The practice of reading Black male celebrities as cultural icons enjoys a current popularity. There are numerous studies of the racial and cultural implications of such iconic figures, for example: David Halberstam's *Playing for Keeps: Michael Jordan and the World He Made* (2000), Orin Starn's *The Passion of Tiger Woods: An Anthropologist Reports on Golf, Race, and Celebrity Scandal* (2011), Michael Eric Dyson's *Making Malcolm: The Myth and the Meaning of Malcolm X* (1996), or McQuillar and Johnson's *Tupac Shakur: The Life and Times of an American Icon* (2010). Hazel Carby's *Race Men* (1998) focuses on Black male icons from Du Bois to Paul Robeson to Miles Davis to Danny Glover, reading them all as representative men symbolizing the aspirations of Black men and Black America. The intention of this book is to do the same for Will Smith. What exactly does he represent? I claim that his star persona represents a compelling intersection of issues of race and masculinity that have arisen over the last three decades. Claire Sisco King concurs that Smith's "public image has unique probative value for studying the intersecting discourses of race and gender in US culture" ("Hitching" 83). To read and interpret him through the lenses of these two issues is to approach a sense of how and why he occupies the position of the world's most preeminent Black male star.

Will Smith and the Requirements of Stardom

Will Smith's iconic status warrants analysis in terms of its social, cultural, and historic dimensions, and some key strategies in star theory provide the critical tools for such a project. Paul McDonald in *The Star System* explores the spectacle of the movie star within the contexts of the history and development of Hollywood as an industry. It would be difficult to understand the nature of Smith's stardom without reading it against the era of Hollywood history out which he emerges. During the '90s, when Smith rose to stardom, the making of movies underwent a transformation because of the conglomeration of studios and corporations and the gigantification of production which resulted in bigger films, bigger budgets, and higher margins of profit. With this growth in the size of production came a concomitant minimalization of risk. Certain kinds of films tended to get made: safe bets, sequels, genres with transnational appeal (science-fiction, action, animation). Films with "high concepts," or marketable stories summarized in a few words, were green-lighted as were "event films," or big-budget spectacles with the promise of a huge payoff. Genres began to merge into each other forming hybrid genres with broader appeal to larger and wider audiences. Schatz terms this transformation of genres a part of the horizontal integration of film production. He goes on to describe this hybridization of Hollywood story-telling as "purposeful incoherence" wherein stories are "open" thus lending themselves to multiple readings and audiences (Schatz 23). This loss of control on the part of Hollywood narrative during this stage of its evolution creates the possibility for new kinds of characters to slip through, such as Black men who become central characters, even heroes who save the world. Will Smith steps in to fill this space. Like the new "open" Hollywood narratives, he is an "open" star text available to different audiences and interpretations.

Another factor in Smith's pre-eminence in the Hollywood of the '90s was his ability to function "synergistically." Synergy within the film economic system describes a "synchronization of promotional energies" (McDonald, *Star System* 80). In this case, the above the title star, through multiple talents, can advertise a film from several platforms. A classic example is Will Smith in the release of *Men in Black* in 1997. The film itself is a hybrid of genres (science fiction, action, comedy, conspiracy thriller), perfectly constructed for numerous and variant constituencies. The publicity campaign for the film capitalized on Smith's careers as a rap star and television personality on the series *The Fresh Prince of Bel-Air*. He brought to the film two pre-existing audiences. Both a music single of his title song from the film and video were used strategically to popularize the film. The film was also promoted through manipulations of Smith's style and race. His Blackness was associated with a coolness and hipness, which played to white and Black audiences simultaneously but on different registers. However, other aspects of his racial identity, which might be perceived as threatening or problematic to mainstream audiences, were neutralized. The flexibility of Smith's racial profile contributes to his synergistic power, which is almost unique among contemporary stars. In this characteristic, Smith most resembles earlier stars such as Frank Sinatra or Elvis Presley as Julie Lobalzo Wright argues in her study of male crossover stars (5–6). His stardom breaks the rules on several levels. As Richard Corliss has observed, Will Smith is the only current star who does not prove the axiom that a high-powered star does not necessarily mean big box-office returns. Smith unfailingly generates profit. Even in 2012 he proved his value; *Men in Black 3* in the May weekend of its release overtook *The Avengers*, then the fourth biggest grossing film of all-time (Ryan). Smith breaks the rules of Hollywood, not only for Black actors; he redefines the nature of stardom in general.

While he acknowledges that star identity is comprised of screen performances and the image that is constructed from the processes of publicity, McDonald still maintains that star image is ultimately produced and consumed in commercial terms. The movie star is a "form of capital" (50). Will Smith as a star within the economy of Hollywood has a specific function. He is an investment to the studios who seek to reduce risk and to maximize profit. As a hedge against the variations of a supply-and-demand market, the studios seek to create "inelastic" demand, or a demand for their product that is consistent and independent of price and supply. A reliable star does this by guaranteeing profit despite all mitigating factors. This is what Smith does so well. He generates money regardless of his films' genre or even critical reception, and this is his value and the source of his power within the industry.

This economic necessity determines the nature of the star persona as much as audience response and identification. So much is at stake at the high levels of risk and profit at which Smith functions, there can be no elements left to chance or the possibility of alienating that audience. Consequently, as a Black male star, his two defining features, race and masculinity, must be managed: "In Hollywood film, the Black male body is offered as heroic only when it is contained" (Gates 21). Ultimately, he must serve an ideological function as well as economic, which is to affirm the values that underpin Hollywood narratives, which are synonymous with traditional American beliefs: positivism, meritocracy, heterosexual marriage, the family, an ethic of hard work, good over evil. Also within this mythos is the conviction that race is no longer a problem in an idealized colorblind American society. These are some of the ideas that circulate in mainstream filmmaking, and ideas that Smith as one of its biggest stars must validate. He may break many of the rules of contemporary stardom, but this one requirement he meets again and again in virtually every performance.

P. David Marshall offers another theoretical model of stardom in *Celebrity and Power*. He gives an account of the construction of star identity by outlining the three stages of its development. These stages are derived from the historical emergence of the individual film star from the situation of screen performers in the early days of the film industry being identified only by type. The first manifestation of star identity is "the physical performer," who is distinguished from mere type by the prominence of a single physical feature. This physical performer then must recognize his precedents, stars who have exemplified this type, and then differentiate him or herself from his or her peers. It is important to have a unique variation of the type: "If the type is replicable by other performers, then the inherent value of the emerging screen star is limited" (99). Marshall's example is Tom Cruise who belongs to the "youth" type, in a line of succession with James Dean and Marlon Brando but is instantly and universally physically recognized because of his trademark smile. As he matured, Cruise's type becomes the all-American hero which includes Paul Newman and Robert Redford of an earlier generation as opposed to the anti-heroic Dustin Hoffman or Al Pacino.

Will Smith likewise at the beginning of his career was categorized as a "youth" type, but a Black youth whose defining attributes were his coolness and hipness. At this stage of his evolution race was integral to his individual star identity. Unlike Tom Cruise, who fits into a tradition of male stars, Smith's relationship to his Black male predecessors is more complicated. There is not a substantial coherent tradition of Black male stars for there to be a construction to which he can conform. There were such stars as Sidney Poitier, Harry Belafonte, Richard Roundtree, and Billy Dee Williams, but there is little that Smith's image draws from them other than the attribute of "safeness." Here Smith is more aligned with Poitier than the more politically committed Belafonte. If anything, he contests and revises the Black male star images of the past. As his star ascended in big-budget blockbusters, his persona aligned itself more with the traditional white mainstream movie hero. Again, in this case, the individual characteristic that distinguished him was his Blackness.

The "picture personality" is the second stage in the development of the star identity, and it is "a new variation on the male film celebrity, one that builds on previous constructions but provides markers of distinction and differentiation"

(Marshall 101). This stage indicates a transformation of the film actor from a physical type with a signature feature to an individual star with a public profile that is separate from a persona created by a sum of film performances. These two identities, personal and professional, though distinct, still support each other, and this mutuality allows the picture personality to achieve a sense of unity. Tom Cruise separates himself from his physical type and achieves individuation by a series of film roles that redefine the rebellious youth persona. His film characters move from outsider status into positions of success and power, and in the process affirm the status quo. Will Smith makes this transition as well. As he grows out of his hip youthful phase, elements of which he never completely leaves behind, he becomes the all-American hero who happens to be Black. In doing so, he revises this hero type through the addition of his one differentiating trait, his Blackness. While he revises the hero type, he revises film representations of Blackness. His image argues against prevailing racial stereotypes and makes the case for courage, ingenuity, intelligence, and patriotism being qualities that are also inherent in Black men. For his transformative virtue, the Smith film persona is welcomed into the mainstream, integrated and assimilated, just as the Cruise persona becomes upwardly mobile. Smith's characters, even though their Blackness is registered and because that Blackness is basically regulated, do not disrupt the existing structures of power, and Smith's reward is universal acceptance and superstardom.

The connection between the Smith film persona and his public image is also an index of his having achieved a picture personality. There is a consistency and unity between that nature of his characters and what he seems to be off-screen. Smith's stardom does not exhibit the customary tension between private and public. He does not withhold his "real" self whose surface the viewers wish to penetrate, to understand, and to possess. Instead, he conflates the private and public into a single star spectacle, and he does this better than anyone else in the business.

Transgression is the final stage in the development of the film star, and this is done either by contradicting the established star profile or by flouting social and moral norms. In the first case, Marshall writes, "the celebrity must break the filmic code of his or her personality" (106). This is done in the attempt to achieve "autonomous subjectivity" or freedom from a fixed identity. The star must create greater distance between the private self and the film persona in order to enhance his or her mystery and star power. One method of creating this distance is through the acting code whereby the actor or actress is cast or performs against type. Serious acting signals a separation between a private identity and a star image. When an actor performs against type, the audience becomes aware of the performativity of the performance. The actor has made a transition from being a star ("personification") to being an actor ("impersonation"). Tom Cruise in *Interview with the Vampire* achieves a transgression by playing against type. The role of the vampire Lestat with its violence and homoeroticism posed a great risk for Cruise and his clean-cut image. He risked compromising his star power, his relationship with the audience, and his earning ability. It was a gamble that paid off because the film elevated him to a higher level of stardom where he earned even greater professional respect and he was free from the limitations of type and personality.

This liberation through transgression can also be accomplished through a violation of the moral code. The private self enters a space outside conventional and acceptable behavior. Often the star's private life overshadows his or her work but does create a clear distinction between the role and the libertine. Marshall points to Elizabeth Taylor as an example of a star whose actual professional achievements became overshadowed by a very public private life. She achieved an "autonomous subjectivity" by this means. Fatty Arbuckle is an example of a transgressing star who, because of the scandal surrounding him and the accusations of murder, was ruined. There is a limit beyond which even a star cannot go. How can Will Smith be construed as being transgressive? He does not often utilize the acting code. Once his star persona was established, there was no real variation. Smith is never cast against type. One could not imagine Smith doing what Denzel Washington does in *Training Day* or *American Gangster*. The closest approximation is *Hancock* in which he plays a reprobate superhero whose misdirected heroics do more harm than good. Yet, the narrative arc of the film is toward rehabilitation and redemption, and in the end, the character reaffirms Smith's heroic star persona. *Six Degrees of Separation* is transgressive in the sense that playing a gay character so early in his career was truly risky. This role came chronologically before his star identity was fully constructed and, as will be discussed in detail in a later chapter, was not a risk at all because he hedged his bet and did not perform the character's sexuality. *The Legend of Bagger Vance* could also be transgressive because it is an unexpected choice of role, a deliberate taking on of a racial stereotype that opposes the empowered all-American heroic star profile he assumes in most of his other roles. The role does offer him the opportunity to invoke the acting code to distance his private identity from the film and to signal that he is indeed giving a performance as Bagger Vance.

Smith's performances overall do not utilize the acting code to add depth and seriousness to his professional reputation. For the most part he is not an actor operating in the impersonation mode, one who disappears into a role. He does operate in this mode when he plays real-life characters, such as Muhammad Ali in *Ali* or Chris Gardner in *The Pursuit of Happyness*. In these cases, he does give fully dimensional performances. Generally, he functions as an actor of personification, one whose screen persona is carried over from film to film and is not distinct from his off-screen identity. He does not create a brand of himself based on high artistic achievement, separating himself from his roles as Cruise does. Smith does not quite evolve into this highest level of stardom. He does not guarantee quality, but he does have a brand which delivers entertainment and dependable big box office.

As for achieving a distinct personal private identity through moral or social transgression, Smith would be challenged to find a way to alienate his audience. There was the incident in 2007 when Smith made a comment about Hitler that was misconstrued and caused a firestorm of comment. The *Huffington Post* published the following report: "Will Smith found himself in hot water last week after making a statement to a Scottish newspaper that Adolf Hitler 'didn't wake up going "let me do the most evil thing I can do today."' I think he woke up in the morning and using a twisted, backwards logic, he set out to do what he thought was good" (Rotello). This was in answer to a reporter's comment about how Smith believes that everyone is basically good. He was able to rectify the situation immediately by making a public response clarifying his intended meaning and winning an apology from the news service that promoted the story. There was no harm done to his reputation. Smith has been the subject of gay rumors throughout his career. Most actors receive this kind of scrutiny, and most expect it as a rite of passage on the road to stardom. In the spring of 2012, there were tabloid reports of a relationship between Smith and actor Duane Martin, but nothing was substantiated (Cronin et al.). What would it mean if Smith were gay? Would he lose his international star status? What would such a revelation cost him? It is hard to predict. Perhaps there might be some decline at the box office, but would it destroy his career? This probably would not happen, but it is dubious that the studio power structure would continue to invest so heavily in him if his new situation were to create vulnerabilities in his value. More problematic would be the dissolution of his marriage to Jada Pinkett Smith. Their marriage is one of the most iconic in Hollywood, certainly an institution within the African American community. Again, there might be disappointment on the part of the public, but not a backlash. Infidelity would not destabilize the structure of his celebrity. There have been in circulation stories about the couple's open marriage and a sanctioned infidelity with a female co-star in one of his films (Simpson). However, an onscreen pairing of Smith with a white actress might prove more troublesome. Objections might come from multiple audiences. Certain factions of the mainstream audience might be offended by an interracial couple. Black women were outraged by Smith's co-starring with Charlize Theron in *Hancock* (Watson). The issue was the failure to hire a Black actress for the part. This casting in *Hancock* is highly unusual in Smith's body of work. Most often interraciality is avoided, as in *I, Robot* wherein the anticipated a romantic/sexual connection between Smith and the character played by Bridget Moynahan never materializes. Although some might resist an interracial relationship in a mainstream film, many more would not. Given their overall acceptance and embrace of Smith, most audiences would have no problem with seeing Smith paired with a white actress (Carson). It seems Smith himself and his creative team are reluctant to cross that line. So great are the financial stakes in Smith's films that even the possibility of transgression cannot be allowed.

Marshall's theory of stardom rests upon the connection between stardom and freedom. The goal of the star is to represent for the public an ideal of personal freedom: "the film star has been constructed to represent the ultimate independence of the individual in contemporary culture" (118). Historically, as screen players became stars and maximized their value as the industry grew, they reaped financial benefits, which constituted one kind of autonomy. The audience vicariously experiences this economic freedom through their star gazing. Stars establish their identities through type and personality, then claim a subjective autonomy by separating their performing personae from their public personalities. Smith does progress from type to personality but does not quite meet the final requirement of stardom which is to separate his public and film images. Somehow, he reaches the highest level of his profession without liberating himself from certain constraints connected to his condition of being a Black male star. Given his remarkable success and the extent of his power, Smith should have attained the subjective autonomy that accrues to his stature, but in important ways that will be examined, he remains a star who is not free.

Paul's Case

The relationship between race and stardom that Will Smith illustrates is not unique. Paul Robeson, who enjoyed an international career as an athlete, singer, and actor during the '20s and '30s, was a precursor of Smith. Stuart Hall suggests that Robeson was the one Black star who was able to transcend racialized representation ("Spectacle" 243). This is a quality that Smith also appears to possess. A comparison of the two icons in their historical moments serves to define Smith's specific star identity. Richard Dyer is the foremost theorist of stardom, and "one of the first to examine the complex and contradictory nature of African American celebrity" (Mask 7). His analysis of the meaning of Paul Robeson's career in *Heavenly Bodies: Film Stars and Society* provides perspectives and insights that can be applied to a reading of the social and cultural meaning of Will Smith.

Dyer poses the question: How did Robeson achieve crossover success? His status as an international phenomenon was unprecedented and unrivaled by other Black entertainers of the time. Other questions are generated by his unique iconic position: "How did the period permit Black stardom? ... What was the fit between the parameters of what Black images the society could tolerate and the qualities Robeson could be taken to embody? Where was the give in the ideological system?" (65). An even greater issue is the price that had to paid for such a degree of stardom. The obvious answer is that Robeson had to strike a Faustian bargain; he was a sell-out, betraying both himself and his race. Donald Bogle is pointed in his characterization of Robeson as essentially self-interested: "No matter how much producers tried to make Robeson a symbol of Black humanity, he always came across as a man more interested in himself" (70). Interestingly, Sidney Poitier, who would achieve a similar iconicity in the '60s, also received this criticism for the integrationist nature of his films (Bogle 195–196). Smith has not escaped the same charge for many reasons ranging from the mainstream focus of his rap to his espousing of conservative political positions.

Selling out to the white power structure of the entertainment industry may not offer a full explanation for crossover success. Equally significant are the ways these Black actors found to negotiate with that power. Robeson's star image spoke to both white and Black audiences. For whites Robeson represented Blackness and Black people; for Blacks he was a symbol of possibility. His roles ranged from Black folk heroes to stereotypes generated by the white racial imaginary (Sambo, the brute). All these images were viewed positively by the white audience because they captured its idea of Black essence which was comprised of primitivism, emotion, intuition, naturalness, and a lack of self-consciousness. These qualities were set against essential characteristics of whiteness which were rationality and intellectualism. To the white audience, the Black qualities were superior to the white in a racially romantic way, and they wanted to keep those qualities pure and contained. Black audiences of the time alternatively saw Black primitivism as a complement to white culture, a force that could make great contributions to the transformation of general culture.

Will Smith also speaks to Black and white constituencies in different ways. One way by which he bridges the racial gap is by accepting scripts that were originally conceived and written for white actors. When he inhabits these roles, he performs the intended narrative functions of his characters, which are not raced, at the same time he inflects his performance with his racial signature (his humor, his line readings). In this way he addresses the mainstream audience while signaling his racial authenticity to his Black viewership. Although Smith avoids Black stereotypes in his film characters, he nonetheless presents a form of Black essentialism. Analogous to Robeson's primitivism is Smith's "cool," which is received positively by both white and Black audiences. For the former, his coolness contributes to his humor and provides a masculine style that contains Black male threat. For the latter, his "cool" testifies to his racial "realness." Smith's cool has another function that works similarly to Robeson's primitivism; it also works as a foil to white logic. In the *Men in Black* series the tension and counterpoint between Agent K (Tommy Lee Jones) and Smith as Agent J is based upon the opposition between repressed systematism and hip intuitiveness. On the other hand, Smith's characters do not go so far as to valorize naturalness to the exclusion of self-consciousness. His cool is predicated upon a heightened ironical awareness of the nuances and contradictions of racial discourse.

Atavism was an important aspect of Robeson's film characters, atavism being the belief that "within the civilised Black man there is the trace of savage ancestry" (Dyer 89). At any point, there might be an eruption of elemental wildness. In his films, Robeson's characters incorporated aspects of this notion in portrayals that approximated one specific stereotype associated with Black men, the brute. Again, Black and white audiences interpreted this stereotype differently. Although this image was not positive for Black viewers, it still had its uses. Bogle notes that Black audiences, despite the problems with Robeson's films, were enthralled by his larger-than-life image. Bogle reports that despite the fact Robeson "was often a Black brute figure, Black audiences saw a Black male completely unlike the servile characters of most American movies" (Bogle 98).

For white audiences, the brute figure was problematic in another way. The spectacle of a strong, assertive, physically imposing Black man was threatening. Consequently, the brute character was "eliminated gradually from his work, as a disturbing undertone that could either be ignored or seen as something that is contained or withheld" (Dyer 99). The brute is a character type that Smith has not enacted (except perhaps for some aspects of *Hancock*). His characters operate on the side of right and serve to restore and maintain general safety and security. It is curious that even though the idea of atavistic reversion has no applicability to how Smith is read today, his image is still in other aspects subject to the same strategies of containment as Robeson's.

The Emperor Jones (1933), an adaptation of Eugene O'Neill's play which was written with Robeson in mind, is one of Robeson's most significant films and serves as a paradigm of how his image signifies. The trajectory of the narrative has Brutus Jones (Robeson) making a transition from Pullman Porter, to libertine to murderer to convict. He escapes to a Caribbean island where he becomes the business partner of an exploitative white trader and eventually the ruler or Emperor of the island. He abuses his power, and the people turn against him. The final sequence has the Emperor Jones fleeing into the jungle where he encounters visions of his personal and of the racial past. As he loses his mind, he is killed by the islanders. In the original play, Jones's vision is a retrospective of his life but then includes memories of slave auctions, the middle passage, and finally of Africa. The film version omits the references to slavery, the terror of American history, and in the process "empties the play of its historical dimension" (Dyer 98). The referencing of slavery as an aspect of Robeson's atavism was eliminated to avoid alienating both white and Black audiences. Its inclusion would have foreclosed the possibility of Robeson's crossover success. The price of Robeson's ascendency was the erasure of Black history from the screen.

Robeson's singing of Black spirituals is another example of this kind of elision. Dyer writes:

> The simple pure distillation of the Negro essence in the development of the spirituals and Robeson's singing of them purges Blackness of the scars of slavery, of the recognition of racism. At most these elements are marginalized or rendered invisible. None of Robeson's films confronts slavery or racism directly [83].

The same can be said about the films of Will Smith. One exception is *Ali* wherein Smith plays a real-life figure whose story defines race in Civil Rights–era America. On the other hand, *The Pursuit of Happyness*, in which he portrays the homeless-to-stockbroker American dream of Chris Gardner, dramatizes his rise as a capitalist fable without full and serious attention to the forces of racism that worked against his progress. Most often in his fictional films, Smith's characters exist in the future worlds of science fiction, where race is not an issue or is displaced onto aliens. *Men in Black III* diverges from this pattern. Here Smith as Agent J time travels back to 1969 to assist a younger version of his partner Agent K. During these exploits J encounters several racially charged situations which he finesses with charm and wit. The reality of racism is reduced to a punchline.

In films with contemporary settings such as *Enemy of the State* or *Hitch*, Smith's characters do not directly confront racism; they are protected to a degree by their upper middle-class status or by the conventions of the genre of the film (conspiracy spy thriller, romantic comedy). Rarely does a Smith character exist entirely or believably within the context of the past. Two examples are *The Legend of Bagger Vance*, set in the 1930s, and *Wild Wild West*, set in the post–Civil War era. Bagger Vance is a magical figure who appears out of the night to guide and support a failing golfer as he seeks to regain mastery of his game and of his life. Captain James West is a special agent to President Ulysses S. Grant who sends him on a special mission. Neither of these characters could have existed; the former is a mystical figment while the latter is an anachronism. Each are, to quote Daniel Webster about slavery and the Civil War, "an imaginary negro in an improbable place" (Jefferson). Will Smith's crossover success is attributable in part to an avoidance of race and racism, and this omission can be read into the construction of his characters as ahistorical.

Throughout his career Robeson moved in white realms of power: "The sense of being a Black presence in a white space marks every stage of Robeson's career" (Dyer 103). This was particularly true when Robeson appeared not in films but on the concert stage which historically was overcoded as white. Dyer goes on to assert that Robeson's precarious position in the limelight amounted to his "sacrificing his specifically Black cultural heritage to the codes and conventions of white culture" (103). He cites the 1942 layout in *Look* magazine of Robeson and his family posed before the façade of his white-columned Connecticut mansion (fig. 1.1). Robeson's material success could be read as aspirational by certain members of the Black public. Yet, the house referenced the plantation, and for some Black readers Robeson was compromised by the image, signaling assimilation and accommodation at the highest level. White audiences, alternatively, might have been offended by the spectacle of a Black man who had risen too far. Either way, Robeson was caught in a difficult place.

Will Smith also inhabits white spaces—on the list of Hollywood's highest-paid actors and on the screen within the narratives of his films. As has been stated before, many of the roles Smith accepts were conceived for or first offered to white actors. As a result, he moves through the world within the film where he is the only Black person. His race is not emphasized, and he is able to function within the story without disrupting the surface of the narrative. Nonetheless, there are racial counterforces at

Fig. 1.1. Paul Robeson, his wife Eslanda Goode Robeson, and their son, Paul Robeson, Jr., at home in Enfield, Connecticut, in 1942 (Everett Collection Historical/Alamy Stock Photo).

play in all his films, which will be discussed throughout this study. Robeson's characters, in contrast, always operate within Black or African environments. Race is central to his meaning. The erasure of race in Smith's performances is offset by his off-screen image. In his private life as a Black star, he is exemplary. His marriage to Jada Pinkett Smith is a Hollywood institution and a source of pride for his African American public (fig. 1.2). He has supported Black causes and, in his role as producer, has provided work and showcases for Black artists. He has never been involved

Fig. 1.2. Will Smith (center) and family (wife Jada Pinkett Smith, daughter Willow and sons Jaden [next to Willow] and Trey) at the 2008 premiere of *Hancock* at Grauman's Chinese Theatre in Hollywood (©Phil Roach/Globe Photos/ZUMA Press, Inc./Alamy Stock Photo)

in a scandal. This impeccable public identity is on display in a story on Smith and his family that appeared in *Architectural Digest*. He is posed with his wife and three children in front of the adobe style house on their California estate. The warm and colorful interiors are replete with architectural details taken from "Persian, Moroccan, Spanish, as well as Southwest American cultures" (Rus). The private life inferred from the photographs is above reproach and serves as model that is beyond aspiration for most readers, Black or white. This domicile stands in stark contrast to that of Robeson, and in the difference between the two might be gauged the development of the condition of Black stars as well as racial attitudes over the decades, a progression from the white neo-classical home an integrated and co-opted Black star of the '40s to the serene multicultural home of a contemporary global celebrity.

Even though Robeson enjoyed fame and affluence off screen albeit in vexed and ambivalent ways, his screen persona continued to be praised but at the same time controlled and contained. This was accomplished through several practices: the attempted erasure of his sexuality, the diminishment of his narrative agency, and the proscription of his narrative function. Dyer writes: "In the context of Robeson's functioning within white discourses, the gradual elimination of this sexuality from his image can be understood as a further aspect of the need to deactivate, lessen the threat of, his image" (107). The example Dyer uses to illustrate this point is Robeson's performances in *Body and Soul*, directed in 1924 by Oscar Micheaux, in which he portrays two roles: a corrupt and seductive fake minister and an honest and upstanding inventor. Although the film is the work of a Black director, it still demonstrates the general cultural anxiety over the representation of Black male sexuality. In the film the minister's sensual appeal to the female protagonist and to the women of his congregation is dramatized by an act of rape and is punished by banishment. The respectable Black man on the other hand is basically de-sexed by his virtue. In neither case is a full, healthy sexuality permitted to be expressed on screen.

Will Smith's characters experience the same regulation of sexuality. Although Smith is an attractive Black male with an increasingly imposing physique, his screen characters rarely are depicted in sustained romantic relationships or scenes of intimacy. As will be discussed in more detail later, he is not often paired with a female co-star, and when he is, she either dies or otherwise disappears from the film. There is one sexual encounter in *Bad Boys* and one lovemaking scene in *Seven Pounds*, which is staged as demurely as a 1940s melodrama, with the camera pulling back and fading out. There is a sex scene in *Ali* involving Ali's wife, played by Smith's own wife, Jada Pinkett Smith. In more recent films, Smith's characters engage in a sexual liaison in *Focus* and sustained marriages in *Concussion* and *Collateral Beauty*. This reluctance to confront Black male sexuality throughout his career may be a calculation on Smith's part. He may be unwilling to risk the discomfort of his audiences who have elevated him to the level of superstardom. The difference here between his position and Robeson's is that Smith now has more power within the film system to make this kind of decision. It does raise the question as to why Smith does not feel he can utilize his power, which he does indeed have, to take his audiences with him, challenge them, and to open up possibilities for Black representation.

Another method of containment is what Dyer terms deactivation whereby

Robeson is denied an active role in the film's narrative. This is borne out physically in Robeson's static acting style. When he is on screen with other actors, he is the still center, but not the source of animation. This tendency toward passivity is even more pronounced in photographs whether studio publicity stills or the artistic studies by such photographers as Carl Van Vechten and Nickolas Muray. The series of nudes taken by the latter in 1925 have generated much critical interest and analysis. The camera captures Robeson in an objectifying gaze that renders him powerless, the way women are reduced to domination by the eye of the beholding male artist and viewer. The photographic and filmic gaze effectively puts Robeson in his place. This kind of optic transaction never happens to Smith. The camera never lingers over his body in an appreciating regard. There are moments in *Bad Boys*, for instance, when he is seen in body-fitting clothing, or in *I Am Legend* when his character is filmed during a physical workout. The difference here is that he is seen in motion, which is the traditional way that (white) male bodies are photographed. The body in motion breaks the gaze and maintains a subjectivity and agency. That Smith can avoid the compromised positions that Robeson could not argues for a certain degree of progression for the Black male star in Hollywood.

The last mode of containment that Dyer describes is achieved through the construction of the narrative function of Robeson's roles. In specifying the actions and motives of Robeson's character in the 1940 film *The Proud Valley*, Dyer could also be detailing those of several Smith's characters. In this film, Robeson plays a Black sailor who finds himself in a Welsh mining village where he is accepted by the townspeople whom he helps in their various struggles. In his analysis Dyer makes the following observation: "In domestic terms, David/Robeson's role in *The Proud Valley* is again purely as helper, sorting out the problems of the whites around him" (127). This description applies equally to Smith's role in *The Legend of Bagger Vance*. Dyer continues: "In one sequence, he [David/Robeson] acts, on his own initiative as go-between for Emlyn and his girlfriend Gwen who have fallen out" (127). Similarly, in *Hitch* Smith serves as a facilitator and intermediary in the courtship of the characters played by Kevin James and Amber Valletta. Dyer concludes: "Despite being the star of the film, there is no question of him being a lover" (127). This situation does not appear universally Smith's films, but the evasion or absence of a love interest for his characters is not unnoticeable in such blockbusters as *I, Robot*; *I Am Legend* and *Men in Black III*.

Hazel Carby sees another pattern in Robeson's screen persona in *The Proud Valley*: "Robeson helps the community through a crisis, exercises leadership, and, ultimately, sacrifices his life so that others will survive" (Carby 81). The willingness of the Black hero to sacrifice his life is a character trait that appeases white audiences, and Smith's characters are not immune to this propensity, witness the conclusions of both *I Am Legend* and *Seven Pounds*. In terms of meeting the requirements of mainstream narrative logic that subordinates them even in films in which they are stars, Smith and Robeson, across time, share an identity.

Dyer concludes by giving an overall account of Robeson's crossover appeal. He claims that the spectacle of a great artist reduced to a stereotype resonated with the public. Robeson was perhaps never fully able to express the power of his genius because the vehicles provided by cultural institutions and industries were too small. Inevitably he was constrained and reduced. Dyer makes the following assessment: "whether contained by the compositional or narrative structures of the text he appears in or held back by his own performance technique—but the fact of it, the moving affect of it, may be the emotional heart of Robeson's cross-over appeal" (134). This appeal, which approximates pity, can only be to white audiences who, in a sense, feel an ennobling liberal frisson at the victimization of this Black man who signifies race for them. How did Black people interpret and process Robeson's artistic enslavement? This is a perspective that gets lost. Again, if this is the price he had to pay for stardom, the perpetuation of the spectacle of Black suffering and the silencing of Black responses, it was too high. As Robeson's career developed, so did his social and political consciousness. When he dared to seize his personal and artistic power, to speak out for social justice and to refuse demeaning roles on and off the screen and stage, his crossover career predictably came to an end.

Such a fate seems incomprehensible for Smith. Is there a political position that he could take or a public statement that he could make that would effectively end his career? His stardom appears to transcend these concerns, and he is indestructible, as he has stated in interviews (Cornelius). In fact, his confidence and positivism are the qualities that have won for him the good will of both Black and white American audiences as well as audiences around the world. Instead of being moved by his plight, they are inspired and buoyed by his persona onscreen and by the private celebrity they decode through the various platforms of publicity. He is the opposite of Robeson, and this may be attributable to the changes over the last half century in society's attitudes about race as well as the growth and transformation of the entertainment industry. Smith as a star phenomenon can exist only within a certain context; he is the product of his historical moment, as was Robeson. Both stars reached extremely high levels of success in a difficult field, and both were subject to limitations because of the perceptions of their race and sexuality. Most importantly, both fulfilled the needs of their audiences to such a degree (and at such cost) that it seems that had they not come along when they did, they would have had to have been, and in large part actually were, invented.

Like Mike

Michael Jordan, the legendary NBA superstar, reflecting upon his own experience explicitly expresses this idea of a coming together of man and zeitgeist: "Society was looking for something positive and I fit the bill" (Denzin 6). Jordan is another Black male celebrity whose public identity warrants critique, and his star status has indeed generated a growth industry of social and cultural commentary. Jordan and Smith occupy similar positions: one the highest paid athlete of his time, and the other the highest paid Black actor of his time. Although their fields are different, sports and film, they intersect in terms of how their successes involve corporate agendas, international markets, and the commercial commodification of their images. It is fascinating to note that the corporate and television pressures and influences that had an impact on Jordan's public persona were at the same time being exerted upon Smith by Hollywood. Both men also pay the price for their high iconic status with the necessity of negotiating their race and masculinity in order to be rendered safe for global audiences and consumers. In defining the terms of Smith's iconicity, the components and requirements of Jordan's success are relevant and instructive. The language and descriptions used to delineate Jordan's status and situation can be equally well applied to Smith. The similarities between the two specify the nature of stardom for Black men at the highest level.

Michael Jordan's rise to prominence coincided with the revitalization and internationalization of the National Basketball League, in which he was instrumental, and the globalization of the Nike brand, for which he served as spokesman. In his Black male body was a perfect example of the social and historical forces at play during the '90s: the construction of American racial discourse through the spectacle of sport; the creation of the illusion of racial harmony through advertising images; "the normalization of exceptional Blackness" (Denzin 7); and the shaping of American Blackness for consumers around the world in an "emerging international racial order" (Denzin 7). Jordan represented all these things in addition to becoming a celebrity sign signifying himself: "this sign of MJ was one that would sell globally, the gentle, kind, warm, dependable, wholesome, authentic, family man, the man for all seasons" (Denzin 6). These adjectives also describe Smith and his universal appeal.

The Jordan star persona carries many meanings and can be read from multiple perspectives. He is a polysemic signifier "who encodes conflicting meanings and values" (Kellner 48). Kellner continues:

> As a Black superstar, he presents the fantasy that anyone can make it in a society of competition and status, that one can climb the class ladder and overcome the limitations of race and class. As a national and global superstar, he represents different things to different people in different countries.... Indeed ... different individuals and audiences are going to receive and appropriate the text of Michael Jordan in different ways according to their own race, gender, class, region, and other subject positions [Kellner 48].

On the same terms, Will Smith circulates within various cultures as a sign for a proliferation of discourses. As a result, the exact meaning of that star sign resists final definition. This quality of indeterminacy is shared by both Jordan and Smith, particularly in their functioning as racial signs. Andrews's characterization of Jordan's racial signification also reflects that of Smith:

> As a cultural construct, Jordan's mediated racial identity is neither stable, essential, nor consistent; it is dynamic, complex, and contradictory. Thus, it is perhaps more accurate to refer to the facts of Michael Jordan's Blackness, and to assert his status as a floating racial signifier who, in Derridean terms, is constantly under erasure [Andrews 108].

Within the many racial meanings that Jordan and, by distribution, Smith carry, there are four narratives that, as outlined by Andrews, are most distinctive: the shaping of the image into an All-American ideal; the transcendence of race; the erasure of Blackness and sexuality; and the fall from grace. Jordan became the All-American hero of the Reagan era, a deliberate corporate creation of a "hard body" masculinity. The term "hard body" refers to the Reagan ideal of the (white, privileged) men who embody "strength, labor, determination, loyalty and courage" (Jeffords 24–25 qtd. in Andrews 124). This type opposed the "soft body" which belonged to the "irresponsible, indolent, deviant, promiscuous … nonwhite urbanite" (Andrews 115). This categorization of national identities rested upon a racial politics informed by a "doctrine of conservative egalitarianism and colorblind bigotry" that opposed welfare and affirmative action (Andrews 115). Proponents of this ideology pointed to the success of Black stars in sports and entertainment to rebuke the rest of the Black population for not taking advantage of the opportunities that America offers. Jordan was one such example who was celebrated by the New Right for being proof of an "'open class structure, racial tolerance, economic mobility, the sanctity of individualism, and the availability of the American dream for Black Americans'" (Gray 376 qtd. in Andrews 125–126). He was fashioned as a "Reaganite racial replicant; a Black version of a white cultural model" (Andrews 125).

This description resonates with Smith's star identity. He, too, in both his public and screen personas inhabits the space of the representative American hero. Even though his career has sustained itself from the '90s to the present, that career interestingly is anchored on Reaganite values. In his interviews, Smith extols the efficacy of hard work and the attainability of the American dream. In addition, he literally is a "Black version of a white cultural model" when he takes on roles that were originally written for white actors.

Jim Naughton, in *Taking to the Air: The Rise of Michael Jordan*, writes: "Jordan is the figure who transcended the Black identity of professional basketball, and thus garnered a widespread and inclusive simulated appeal that resulted in his becoming America's favorite athlete; a status no Black man before him had achieved" (Naughton 137 qtd. in Andrews 137). In order to become an American hero Jordan had to transcend race, which means an avoidance of Blackness, an eradication of specific racial markers from his public identity:

> Although the media could not escape the fact that Jordan is of African American descent, his identity has been shrewdly severed from any vestiges of African American culture. Some Black superstars, the most prominent being Jordan, have been able to pander to the racial insecurities and paranoia of the white majority primarily because of their ability to shed their Black identities in promotional contexts [Andrews 127].

The Jordan image projected in commercials and visuals was wrapped in the iconography and symbolism of the mainstream and the global. The latter dimension is particularly demanding. Denzin concludes that erasure of race is a primary demand of global capitalism: "The universal human nature [Jordan] announces is one … that erases race. And this seems to be the last requirement of global capitalism: cultural differences disappear, to be replaced by a universal, circumspect human nature that knows its place in the order of things" (Denzin 11).

Even though these cultural forces may work against the assertion of difference or of group identity, race cannot be transcended; it always returns. Andrews asserts that race is "*always already there*" (Andrews 128). He goes on to observe that "Jordan is not an example of racial transcendence, rather, he is an agent of racial displacement. Jordan's valorized, racially neutered image displaces racial codes onto other Black bodies" (Andrews 128). Michael Jordan could be the exceptional Michael Jordan as long as other basketball players (Charles Barkley, Dennis Rodman) and indeed all other Black men were seen to be Black. The problem is that their Blackness reinforces prevailing racial stereotypes.

The erasure of Blackness is central to Will Smith's star identity as well. He inhabits his white-conceived screen roles (*Independence Day, Men in Black, Enemy of the State, I, Robot, I Am Legend, Seven Pounds*) with almost seamless ease. There are markers of race in his performances, such as the code switching in his line readings. There are even self-conscious insertions into the narratives that signal the character's Blackness as a way of racializing the original role. For example, in *I, Robot* there are references to Del Spooner's grandmother and her sweet potato pies, which is an anachronism given that the story is set in the future. The only reason this detail is in the film is to remind the audience that Will Smith is Black. This is just one example of the curious racial undertow in Smith's films which are produced to mitigate or erase the signs of Blackness.

In many of these roles, his character is also exceptional in the sense of being the sole Black person in the world of the film or not being connected to a contextualizing Black culture or community. In his existence as a star, he also experiences the only-one syndrome. His essentially de-racialized screen persona is distanced from the boyz in the hood typos that was established in the Hollywood of the '90s. His transcendent position also allows him to displace Blackness onto other Black male stars such as Denzel Washington, Eddie Murphy, and Wesley Snipes, all of whom in their roles signify race in familiar terms.

From the beginning of his career, Michael Jordan's Black male athletic body has been the subject of intense scrutiny from every possible perspective. Given the way racial discourse sexualizes and objectifies the Black body, it is fascinating how Jordan's body has escaped this kind of gaze. The emphasis is on his strength, power, speed, rather than on his sexual appeal. His body has been turned into a commodity for consumption, but only in the marketplace. There are no nude studies of his form. As Mary McDonald notes, other athletes such as Olympians Carl Lewis and Robert Johnson posed nude for the June 1996 issue of *Life* magazine, which is unimaginable for Jordan. Even in his Hanes underwear ads, when he is viewed appreciatively by women, the moment is curtailed by humor and coyness. The potential representation of Jordan not only as a sexual object but as a sexual actor is forestalled. In this way, the sexuality of Jordan's image is consistently and firmly contained.

Another mode of containment is through domestication. Jordan's heterosexual masculinity is always framed within the narrative of family values. McDonald writes: "Placed within the nuclear family as a devoted son, father, and husband, Jordan is a 'safe sex symbol' who counters historical and contemporary stereotypes of Black masculinity as threatening, irresponsible, and hypersexual" (M. McDonald 123–125). Smith's persona functions in the same way. He certainly has an imposing body, but it is deployed in athletic stunts. It has a hard-martial aspect, much like the bodies of such action stars as Schwarzenegger and Stallone. He is never seen in repose with an aura of sensuality and open to an erotic gaze. Even in his one nude scene in *I, Robot*, his body is filmed as his character showers, and the point of the scene is to convey his vulnerability and constant paranoid vigilance. Black women, however, as evidenced by blogosphere testimony, do respond to him counter to the efforts to desexualize his image by appreciating his physique and virility (Palmer 32).

Smith also is subject to the containment of his sexuality through the nature of his films' narratives. In many of his films, he fails to make a romantic or sexual connection with his putative leading lady. One can point to Linda Fiorentino in *Men in Black* and Bridget Moynahan in *I, Robot*. Smith is almost never shown engaged in sexual activity on screen. Offscreen, he is committed to the long-term (though unconventional) married life he has shared with Jada Pinkett Smith since 1997.

The possibility of risk to the Black star image means that there are limits even for those celebrities who transcend race. The standard for crossover status is rigorously monitored, and any shortcoming is swiftly prosecuted. Andrews anatomizes this phenomenon:

> African Americas are tolerated, and even valued, if they abdicate their race and are seen to successfully assimilate into the practices, value system, and hence identity, of white America. Moreover, African American membership in this exclusive club requires constant affirmative renewal. Any fall from grace (ranging from the judicial severity of a criminal misdemeanor, to the tabloidic scandal of sexual impropriety, to even the supposed democratic right of asserting one's racial identity) cancels membership, and re-casts the hitherto American person as a criminally deviant, sexually promiscuous or simply threatening racial Other [Andrews, "Fact(s)" 228].

This fall from grace is exactly what Jordan experienced at one point in his career. His heroic virtue and membership in the white mainstream came under intense scrutiny upon the dissemination of rumors concerning his gambling. The censure reached a critical point with the death of Jordan's father. The media tried to link the death with Jordan's gambling habits, and his public reputation reached its lowest point.

Once the murderers were apprehended, there followed a process of rehabilitation for him. Jordan retired from basketball, started over by pursuing a minor league baseball career, and finally returned to the NBA as a corrective representative of traditional and conservative American values that opposed the excesses, unruliness, materialism, and arrogance of the new generation of players. He was again embraced by the public and the press just as quickly as he was brought under suspicion. This fickle elevation and demotion cycle is the habitual mode of operation of the hegemonic forces that regulate Black bodies in American society. These manifestations of that power underscore the precariousness of the positions of Black men, even when they are global stars.

So far Will Smith has not been victimized by a coalescence of ideological and institutional powers. He has not been compromised or discredited by the media which create and destroy cultural idols. He has been able to do what Paul Robeson and Michael Jordan were not. He remains steadfastly upon his pedestal, and this may be his genius.

How has he been able to survive and prevail? Clearly, he negotiates the complex and difficult field of racial politics and celebrity identity with infinitely greater sophistication, subtlety and finesse. He may benefit from developments in racial attitudes and celebrity culture. He has been able to secure a measure of personal power that allows him to be a self-creation, one that as a racial signifier represents something new.

Reading Will Smith against the economics of contemporary Hollywood, the principles of star theory, the semiotics of celebrity, and critical race discourse begins to offer answers as to the nature of his appeal, his success and his larger cultural meaning. Reading him against a Black male star precursor such as Paul Robeson and against a global sport star such as Michael Jordan yields themes (assimilation, accommodation, containment, emasculation, infantilization, objectification, narrative marginalization) that will be traced through the various permutations of his signification, through his individual performances, through the film genres that provide the context for those performances, and through the complex relationship between the history of Black male images and his unique star persona.

Two

Culturally Mulatto

Another perspective through which to view Will Smith's star ascendency and his adroit negotiation of race is generational. His success is dependent upon the coalescence of forces at a specific historical and cultural moment. This generation is composed of those who were born after the Civil Rights Movement and benefited from the fruits of that struggle and thus inhabit and experience Blackness differently from their parents. Born in 1968, around the time of the passage of the Civil Rights Acts, Smith became a star during the early '90s, and his star power reached an apogee by the end of the decade. During those years a special sensibility emerged among young Black artists seeking to define themselves and their work in terms free of the racial past but at the same time inspired and always beholden to it. The rise of Will Smith's star and the development of this Black artistic voice are parallel phenomena which resonate with each other and at certain points intersect.

From New Black Aesthetic to Post-Black

In 1987 Trey Ellis published in the journal *Callaloo* the seminal essay "The New Black Aesthetic" which heralded a new age of Black consciousness and artistic production. The product of private prep schools and Stanford and the author of the novel *Platitudes*, he articulated this artistic tendency and named it The New Black Aesthetic, or the NBA. Although not a formal manifesto, the essay still sets out a definite description and definition of this group of young artists. Ellis terms them "cultural mulattos … who grew up as the first generation of African Americans not to have their lives defined by legalized segregation" (Ellis qtd. in Baron 4). The cultural mulattoes, most often the college-educated children of college graduates, have more social mobility than previous generations, effortlessly moving between the Black and white worlds. Ellis writes:

> a cultural mulatto, educated by a multi-racial mix of cultures, can also navigate easily the white world. And it is by and large this rapidly growing group of cultural mulattoes that fuels the NBA. We no longer need to deny or suppress any part of our complicated and sometimes contradictory cultural baggage to please either white people or black [Ellis 235].

While the members of this group are well-versed in Black history and culture and take pride in their Blackness, they nonetheless feel liberated from the strictures of an essential Black identity or "superblackness." At the same time, they feel free to create and to exist outside of the white gaze.

Concomitant with this ability to resist both racial worlds is an almost contradictory embrace and inclusion of all cultural influences within their own artistic productions: "All the voices we hear around us form our post-modern character" (Favor 695). This reliance on multiple models is predicated on the practices of earlier Black artists because this new generation has "inherited an open-ended New Black Aesthetic from a few Seventies pioneers that shamelessly borrows and reassembles across both race and class lines" (Ellis 234). As the NBA breaks down the barriers between white and Black culture, it also extends what it means to be Black. The subject of the work of the New Black Aesthetician "is the investigation of Blackness in America with the goal of 'expand[ing] or explod[ing] the old definitions of blackness'" (Ellis 237 qtd. in Favor 697). Favor concludes: "The New Black Aesthetic, then, is liberating in that it allows many different types of blackness to be seen/heard" (Favor 697).

One significant aspect of this expansion of Blackness is the freedom of the NBA artists to critique those existing definitions of Blackness. Having grown up after the Civil Rights Movement, they feel a distance from the racial struggles of the past, a distance that engenders parody and irony (Lott, "Response" 245). The object of parody here is the Black nationalist movement. Although they convey an irreverence toward the past, the NBA generation sees itself as indebted to Black nationalism, even as an extension of it: "Nationalistic pride continues to be one of the strongest forces in the black community and the New Black Aesthetic stems straight from that tradition" (Ellis 239). The NBA seeks to define itself beyond that ideology, but not beyond race. The New Black Aesthetic is emphatically not post-racial: "As a cultural mulatto, Ellis refuses to define his art solely in terms of the 'economics of slavery.' But neither does he retreat into a 'world of make-believe' in which 'race' has no significance" (Favor 697). The function of NBA parody is racially affirmative. Favor writes: "the Afro-centric nature of Ellis' post-modernist parody is an essential part of his New Black Aesthetic" (696). Bertram Ashe goes on to elaborate upon the NBA's role as a critic of received notions of Blackness:

> These artists and texts trouble blackness, they worry blackness; they stir it up, touch it, feel it out, and hold it up for examination in ways that depart significantly from previous—and necessary—preoccupations with struggling for political freedom, or with an attempt to establish and sustain a coherent black identity. Still, from my vantage point, this "troubling" of blackness by post-soul writers is ultimately done in service to black people [Ashe 614].

The New Black Aesthetic defines an artistic tendency and sensibility that was articulated in the late 1980s and continues to the present day. Its attributes and objectives can be seen in artistic productions ranging across literature, film, media, and music. What their creators have in common is the critical perspective of the cultural mulatto which focuses on "the peculiar pains, pleasures, and problems of race in the post–Civil Rights movement United States; the use of nontraditionally black cultural influences in their work; and the resultant exploration of the boundaries of blackness" (Ashe 611).

The next significant iteration of the New Black Aesthetic appeared in the

Introduction of the catalogue for the Studio Museum of Harlem's 2001 exhibition *Freestyle*. Here museum director Thelma Golden terms this artistic trend "post-black." She formulated this idea with conceptual artist Glenn Ligon. This term immediately stirred controversy—and still does—because it is confused with "post-racial" with its implication of the existence of an evolved American society that is colorblind and free of racism. According to Golden, "post-black" only describes the work of a specific group of artists at a specific time. Cameron Leader-Picone clarifies this point: "'post-black' refers to contemporary shifts in how blackness is redefined, rather than to labeling individuals as holding a 'post-black' racial identity" (428). These artists resisted being labeled as "black" artists expected to create out of a "responsibility to a certain history and to certain kinds of images" (Copeland 4). Golden elaborates upon this point:

> When I started looking at the artists for *Freestyle*, I felt that many artists, particularly Glenn's generation, felt burdened by this thing called "black art." They always had to talk themselves out of that in order to begin to talk about their work. So, we began to talk about how I was seeing all these artists from *Freestyle* who didn't even feel they had to address this [Sussler].

She goes into more detail in interview with Susan Muchnic:

> We also talked about all these young artists we saw who didn't live through multiculturalism and didn't have all the angst we had about it. They didn't even feel apologetic abut making work that didn't have to do with black culture. At the same time, we realized that globalism has changed the dialogue and opened up African identity. Black artists were no longer these people in the United States working out of a history that began with slavery. Post-Black was a shorthand term we used to refer to all that [Muchnic].

While the Post-Black artists reject a "normative racial identity," they do not seek freedom "from race itself" (Leader-Picone). They find that Blackness remains at the center of their project: these were "artists who were adamant about not being labeled as 'black' artists, though their work was steeped, in fact deeply interested in redefining complex notions of blackness" (Golden 14 qtd. in Ashe 612). Darryl Pinckney offers the following summation: "Black culture is a subject matter, but the new black artists don't treat it as 'specific to them.' It is not autobiographical. It is an interest, not a weapon" (Pinckney).

The most recent expression of the Post-Black idea is *Who's Afraid of Post-Blackness: What It Means to Be Black Now* by journalist Touré. His articulation of the concept restates, refines, and extends definitions set out earlier by Trey Ellis and Thelma Golden. What remains constant is the insistence on Post-Blackness as an emanation of a post–Civil Rights generation as an attempt to expand the boundaries of "authentic" Black identity and representation, as a sensibility and position distinct from post-raciality, as a claim for a unique individual and not group expression, and as a perspective that is both critical of and contributory to Black history and culture. The core of the argument made by Touré is as follows:

> The definitions and boundaries of Blackness are expanding in forty million directions—or really, into infinity. It does not mean that we are leaving Blackness behind, it means we're leaving behind the vision of Blackness as something narrowly definable and we're embracing every conception of Blackness as legitimate. Let me be clear: Post-Black does not mean "post-racial."

Post-racial posits that race does not exist or that we're somehow beyond race and suggests colorblindness: It's a bankrupt concept that reflects a naive understanding of race in America. Post-Black means we are like Obama: rooted in but not restricted by Blackness [Touré 12].

One idea that gets special treatment is the independent individuality and the multiple Black identities that are possible with Post-Blackness. In his Introduction to Touré, Michael Eric Dyson articulates this sense of a liberated, post–Civil Rights Post-Blackness: "It made sense for Blacks to unify against oppressive forces as a strategy of racial combat, but it made less sense to adopt that strategy as a means to define the race. What it means to be Black will always be richer than our response to oppression at any point in our history" (Dyson xiv). He adds: "The point of fighting for freedom is for Black folk to define Blackness however we see fit" (Dyson xiv). Touré contributes to the idea of a Blackness beyond essentialist definitions: "As the artist William Pope.L says, 'Blackness is limited only by the courage to imagine it differently'" (Touré 7). Then he elaborates:

The cult of the individual is something that is going to be a rescuing point for Black people. I think in order to do good for your community you have to do good for yourself and you have to stop thinking about being down and what everyone's gonna think about you. You have to see the whole field of options and professions and fields of inquiry that exist in the world like one big buffet court [Touré 8].

Perhaps the most eloquent description of this new Black identity is offered by Wahneema Lubiano:

Post-Black is what it looks like when you're no longer caught by your own trauma about racism and the history of Black people in the United States. Then everything is up for grabs as a possibility. Because you're not wearing the trauma anymore. You get to use something that produced all that trauma and do something else with it. So that's how I'm thinking about how post–Blackness can operate. It's not a disavowal of history, it's just the determination that you're not wearing all that trauma anymore and you're not waiting for the world to be different to live your life in more interesting ways [Touré 22].

Post-Blackness manifests itself in one of the three dimensions of Blackness, according to Dyson. The three modes of Blackness are: Introverted, Ambiverted, and Intentional. The first category includes those Blacks who see themselves as Black accidentally. They just happen to be Black. Dyson includes figures such as Clarence Thomas and Condoleeza Rice in this group. Intentional or extroverted Blackness is exhibited by figures such as Malcolm X, Martin Luther King, Jr., and Jay-Z, for whom Blackness is their cause or mission. Post-Blackness resides within the Ambiverted identity which floats between the other two. Dyson clarifies this definition:

[Ambiverted] Blackness refers to having a more fluid relationship with it: Blackness is an important part of them but does not necessarily dominate their persona. Dyson says it's "people who more completely embrace Blackness—they aren't trying to avoid it—but that ain't the whole of their existence. I love it but it doesn't exhaust me." In this group he places Barack Obama, Colin Powell, and Will Smith [Touré 9].

The most significant characteristic of the Ambiverted Black identity is a "multi-linguality," the ability to codeswitch or the ability to switch between the modes of Blackness. Again, Dyson elucidates:

Black people have different modes of Blackness and when we need to be each of those variet-
ies of Blackness, we exercise them. We vacillate among the modes depending on what we need.
When you deal with multiple audiences you have to pivot around different presentations of
Blackness. The ability to maneuver within white society—and how high you can rise within
white power structures—is often tied to your ability to modulate. Black success requires Black
multi-linguality—the ability to know how and when to move among the different languages of
Blackness. A prime example is Oprah Winfrey, who will switch modes in a matter of seconds
and can sometimes convey multiple modes at one time [Touré 11].

The same could be said of Will Smith who in several ways is the perfect embodiment
of Post-Blackness and the New Black Aesthetic. Ashe has conceptualized the New
Black Post Soul Aesthetic as a matrix or net and asserts that a true Post-Black text
either must "fit" into the matrix or bounce off it. The post-soul, Post-Black matrix
features three points of possible contact for the potential Post-Black text: "the cultural mulatto archetype; the execution of an exploration of Blackness; and, lastly, the
signal allusion-disruption gestures that many of these texts perform" (Ashe 613). If
Will Smith can be construed as a post-soul, Post-Black text, then it is easy to see how
he fits into this matrix.

The cultural mulatto is the product of class privilege which allows for an easy
assumption of Black pride and a personal distance from historic Black struggles. Ellis
emphasizes how this middle-class status affords access to elite education and greater
social mobility, particularly movement between white and Black worlds. The cultural mulatto is comfortable in white contexts and is readily trusted by and trustful
of whites. Additionally, the Black middle class is the source of many artists: "being
a middle class artist, black or white, has always been the rule rather than the exception" (Ellis, "Response" 251). Ellis asserts that this has been true in one area of creative endeavor where the New Black Aesthetic sensibility often manifests itself: rap.
He claims that "most of the big-name rappers are middle-class black kids" (Ellis 241).
Smith's biography bears this out. His first rise to fame was as part of the duo DJ Jazzy
Jeff and the Fresh Prince whose work was distinct from gangsta rap because of its
family-oriented, middle-class subject matter reflective of his own upbringing in Philadelphia. Even as his career developed and took shape, Smith carried with him a
class imprint. In role after role, from Paul in *Six Degrees of Separation* to Robert Dean
in *Enemy of the State* to Alex Hitchens in *Hitch* to Ben Thomas in *Seven Pounds* to
Howard Inlet in *Collateral Beauty*, Smith embodied a cultural mulatto archetype, a
stereotype-defying professional Black man operating successfully in a white world.

Although most of Smith's screen characters would not necessarily find themselves the protagonists of narratives created by such NBA, Post-Black authors as Colson Whitehead or Paul Beatty, he nonetheless fits into the matrix because of the way
his screen characters expand the representations of Blackness. At the height of his
star power during the '90s in film after film he portrayed the heroes of Hollywood
blockbusters, figures who were in the position of saving the world within the contexts
of science fiction (*Independence Day, Men in Black*). Later, he would play the last man
on a post-apocalyptic Earth in *I Am Legend*. These kinds of roles inhabited by a Black
man were unprecedented in Hollywood, and Smith taking on such roles and having
these performances widely accepted around the world, was doing revolutionary work

in altering the images of Black men and the meaning of being Black. The reframing of definitions of Blackness and the questioning of the existence of essential and authentic Black identities are key to the NBA, Post-Black idea.

Another of the prerequisites of the NBA Post-Black artist is freedom of influence, the ability to claim all influences, not just Black, as personal capital. Trey Ellis points to musician Vernon Reid of the band Living Colour as example. Reid's work draws upon hard rock as much as from R&B and blues. This is not what would be expected of an African American artist. Other examples of this hybridity would include Lenny Kravitz and Fishbone. Touré would include "Kanye West, Andre 3000, Drake and Pharrell" (Touré 6). These performers project "personae … filled with middle-class and/or culturally avant-garde signifiers" (Touré 6). Artists like these are fortunately positioned through class, education, and privilege to benefit from the full range of culture: "It has always been impossible to have been educated in America without having been greatly influenced by non-black artists" (Ellis, "Response" 251). Ashe develops this anatomization of the Post-Black artist further when he explains that they focus on "the peculiar pains, pleasures, and problems of race in the post–Civil Rights movement United States; the use of nontraditionally black cultural influences in their work; and the resultant exploration of the boundaries of blackness" (Ashe 611).

Drawing upon multicultural influences has another effect: allowing these Black artists entrée to the mainstream. Black art becomes assimilated, and American culture becomes enriched and transformed by a stream of Blackness. Touré even argues that the contributions of Black art to the mainstream are so significant that it is difficult to draw a fine line between Black and white culture. Using rap as his example, he asserts that rap, once established, was embraced by consumers beyond the Black community, by the white suburbs and the world beyond. It has taken over the culture with incalculable impacts and repercussions. He writes: "It is the lingua franca—the common language. Now the minutiae of Black culture is [sic] on wide display and Black artists and people can no longer honestly think Black Culture is some private space that we alone know about" (Touré 41). Pointing to the career of an actress such as Halle Berry, Touré observes that such a Black actress moves beyond race to become a signifier of American popular culture. Certainly, the same could be said of Will Smith. He embodies the movement of Black culture into the mainstream. Blackness is not unknowable but a part of the social and artistic fabric. Notice how in the first stages of his career, he took rap to multiple audiences through the broad appeal of his middle-class subject matter (parents and girls as opposed to bling and banging). Emblematic of his advancement of rap is the acceptance of his work by the musical industry establishment in the form of the first Grammy awarded to a rap artist. Smith at first refused the award but then accepted the next year when the rap award was presented not during a subsidiary event but during the main ceremony. This is representative of moving Black art into a position central to popular culture. Smith completed the same progressive move in his film career when he attained superstar status integrating the top echelon of actors with $20 million paychecks and $100 million first-weekend box office receipts. He is synonymous with the stardom of the '90s and a globalized Hollywood. Again, Smith becomes a Black artist whose impact renders him a symbol of American popular culture in general. If a Black artist represents American culture, what then is the nature of his or her relation to Blackness? This condition of ambivalence that someone like Smith inhabits, as he represents two worlds simultaneously, signifying race and the mainstream, is the essence of the New Black Aesthetic and Post-Blackness.

The last point of contact in the NBA, Post-Black matrix is the artist's interrogation of Blackness and recognition of the historical experiences of Black people. Touré emphasizes that Post-Blackness is not a blithe denial of the past. Leader-Picone confirms this: "Touré does not present a definition of Post-Blackness that imagines a blackness detached entirely from the history and culture of African Americans" (Leader-Picone 433). Favor seconds this perception: "As a cultural mulatto, Ellis refuses to define his art solely in terms of the 'economics of slavery.' But neither does he retreat into a 'world of make-believe' in which 'race' has no significance" (Favor 697). Post-Blackness thus rests upon a contradiction: "the twin attempt conceptualized in Post-Blackness to argue for the individual liberation of the African American subject while remaining focused on the 'serious race issues'" (Leader-Picone 424). On one hand, these artists feel free to incorporate multiple influences in their work and to flout the expectations of Black art by not focusing on social justice and "the soul-killing consequences of racism" (Leader-Picone 423). On the other hand, these artists remain true to their Black predecessors, even though they may mock and parody them: "the Afro-centric nature of Ellis' post-modern parody is an essential part of his New Black Aesthetic" (Favor 696). The Post-Black artist and his or her "parodic impulses … both critique and keep alive the cultural nationalism they inherited" through a "recombinant historical irony" (Lott, "Response" 245).

Ultimately, the highest loyalty of the Post-Black artist is to the race itself:

> These artists and texts trouble blackness, they worry blackness; they stir it up, touch it, feel it out, and hold it up for examination in ways that depart significantly from previous—and necessary—preoccupations with struggling for political freedom, or with an attempt to establish and sustain a coherent black identity. Still, from my vantage point, this "troubling" of blackness by post-soul writers is ultimately done in service to black people [Ashe 614].

Will Smith may fit into the Post-Black matrix because he expands representation of Blackness in his screen personae and because he moves Blackness into the center of popular culture. He certainly is a figure who contests the concept of authentic Black identities. This is an issue that has concerned him from the beginning of his career: "The commercial success of the second album did not silence the critics who felt Will Smith had betrayed rap. If the songs were not hard-hitting stories about drugs and deprivation or life on the streets, then it wasn't real" (Robb 28). Smith responded by arguing that there is no final authority that determines what is legitimately Black. Even though his background is middle-class suburban, he still comes from a Black background and that his music is just as "real" or authentic as any other iteration of rap. He goes on to assert that appealing to a white audience is not a failing, especially as all rap reaches and speaks to white audiences. Smith's defense of diversity within Blackness is consistent with NBA Post-Black ideology.

The most problematic connection between Smith and Post-Blackness is the tenet about "troubling blackness." How does Smith "trouble blackness"? Troubling Blackness means interrogating it through irreverence, parody, and irony, and from a position of self-conscious perspectival hybridity. Kara Walker, the conceptual artist and her controversial silhouette images depicting the perversities of slavery, would be an example of an artist who troubles Blackness:

> It's difficult for me to imagine an artist from a previous generation presenting images from slavery with the crude, in-your-face irreverence that Walker brings to them. But one of the generational shifts that the post–Black era brings us is the impact of emotional distance from the past struggles: These are not Blacks who grew up in a time of organized battles for rights in the street and that leads to a different perspective on Blackness. Walker's freedom to immerse us in difficult slavery images and to inject into them the comedic force of a madcap Andy Kaufmanesque carnival at which you're not sure if you're supposed to laugh comes only with the distance of time. She's leaning hard on the math of tragedy plus time equals comedy. And yet we know she is not irreverent or disrespectful of slaves and slavery. She is diving into our subconscious blood memories and fears and mixed-up dreams about slavery. Walker said, "A lot of the work isn't really even about slavery. It's just kind of using it as a way into a conversation that nobody would have in any other context" [Touré 37–38].

In fiction, one could cite Paul Beatty (*The Sellout*) and Colson Whitehead (*The Underground Railroad*). In the realm of comedy and performance, Touré points to Dave Chappelle and his sendups of slavery on his legendary and brilliant television show as the epitome of a Post-Black sensibility and links him with Walker: "Walker and Chappelle approach slavery with a bit of impudence or even cheekiness that would not have been previously possible, because they have a general sense of removal from the sacredness of history that inspires a feeling of independence and individuality. This is work that is emblematic of this post–Black era" (Touré 39).

Smith's humor does not have a satirical edge that offers insights into the Black condition and that speak to all audiences and specially to Black audiences. His humor does not operate through twists of logic and altered subversive perspectives. Although he invokes Eddie Murphy and Richard Pryor as role models in the shaping of his approach to comedy, their edginess and topicality do not appear in his performances in music, television, or film. They both dig deep to tell fearlessly uncomfortable truths about being Black in America. Smith, on the other hand, takes a much lighter approach, less confrontational, less boldly inventive. He describes his comic vision as he formulated it at the beginning of his career: "'I have a great understanding of what Black people think is funny and what white people think is funny. I'm able to find the joke that everyone thinks is hilarious … walking that line where it's very specific to everyone, but universal at the same time'" (Robb 14). Smith continues to explain his choice to cross racial boundaries: "'I think that transition is what helped me bridge the gap, because that's what my success has really been about: bridging the gap between the Black community and the white community'" (Robb 14). Smith's artistic mission is conciliatory, to appeal to both white and Black audiences, but to what end? Is his goal to promote racial accord and harmony, or to broaden his appeal to enhance his stardom? He sees his work as providing audiences with entertainment. There is no indication that he offers a critique of Blackness or racism. For him, Blackness is something that is incidental. This is borne out by his attitude toward colorblind casting. Many of his film roles in the '90s were originally conceived for and offered to white actors, and Smith was eager to take on these parts: "Will sees the racial interchangeability of his movie roles—all originally written for white actors— as the foundation of his 'everyman' appeal" (Robb 114). He saw it as a challenge and a victory for himself when he was able to pull off the feat of inhabiting these roles as a Black actor without his race making a difference.

Smith's ability to evade race is what Hollywood producers and directors found appealing about him. Witness this commentary about his being cast in 1998's *Enemy of the State* directed by Ridley Scott: "as with his two previous SF-adventure movies, Will's role had not been written specifically as a black character. Once again, the producers hoped his audience appeal would transcend any issues of race" (Robb 110). In terms of the racial implications of his role choices and their effects, Smith does feel has a responsibility: "I want to play positive characters. I want to play characters that represent really strong, positive black images. So that's the thing I consider when I'm taking a role after I decide if it's something I want to do" (Robb 119). His investment in positive images summons up a racial uplift or respectability ideology which contributes to traditional civil rights conversations and not a liberated, individualistic Post-Black discourse.

Another putative area of overlap between Smith's screen personae and Post-Blackness is a diffidence about the depiction of racism. His films, with few exceptions (*Ali*, for example), do not directly deal with race or racism, as will be discussed at length in later chapters. If they do, it is only tangentially. The avoidance of race, of course, is a deliberate calculation to advance his career. This absence in his onscreen personae and the thematic concerns of his films is not the result of naiveté. Smith was well aware of racism growing up and negotiating the power structure of Hollywood and the realities of Los Angeles:

> It was the fast cars which brought Will face-to-face with the institutionalized racism of the police force, his stardom offering no immunity. "In the two years I had my Corvette, I probably got stopped 35 or 40 times," he claimed…. "All through life growing up as a young Black man, you see that happen to everybody around you. The cops killing someone and getting away with it. So probably from the time you can understand race, seven or eight years old, there's a weight that you carry" [Robb 37–38].

His consciousness of racism is a constant even after his ascent in Hollywood:

> Far from seeing his colour as an obstacle to overcome he sees it as truly irrelevant to his success. "It's not any more of a hindrance than it is doing anything else," said Will of being Black in Hollywood. "Racism is an unfortunate part of American culture. It's something you don't accept but something you know is going to exist" [Robb 114].

His acknowledgment of racism does not translate into his performances or his films, and by choice. This choice is not quite the same reason Post-Black artists who do not focus on racism and historical oppression in order to explore other dimensions of Blackness. Smith's diffidence in his work is more of a career consideration than an aesthetic imperative.

As has been suggested, Smith does fit into the Post-Black matrix to a certain extent as he expands the representation of Blackness and moves Black artistic production into the mainstream. However, he does not seem to have a Post-Black project of "troubling Blackness," nor a principled, artistic distancing from historical Black struggle and the effects of racism. His commitment is not to a critique of Blackness for Black people, but instead to a universality that reaches beyond race. His audience seems to be everyone. His address to Black audiences is not about the ironies and absurdities of Black existence, but about his success. As a race figure, his function is inspiration and aspirational, not corrective or instructional or subversive as would be the case a Post-Black actor like Donald Glover or Lakeith Stanfield. Smith is more post-racial than Post-Black, and this is yet another tension in his image and personae that makes his unprecedented stardom possible.

Will Smith Transcendent

Smith's star persona rests upon a tension between Post-Black and post-racial tendencies. Yet, the latter seems to hold sway. Throughout his career, commentators have observed that his success is predicated upon his ability to circumvent the pitfalls of being Black in Hollywood. *Newsweek* proclaims: "His appeal is so universal that it transcends race" (S. Smith). Producer Dawn Taubin has said, "'You'd be hard-pressed to find anybody with this kind of appeal. He transcends race" (Uschan 87). Pulitzer Prize winning columnist Eugene Robinson includes Smith among "'a small but growing cohort with the kind of power, wealth, and influence that previous generations of African Americans could never have imagined'" (qtd. In Pinckney). These high achievers have overcome the barriers of race. Robinson terms Smith a "Transcendent." As such, part of the work that Smith does is to embody the possibility of a society where Black people can fully realize themselves and where race doesn't matter. This post-racial position finds expression in different ways throughout Smith's career.

The September 3, 2000, issue of *The New York Times Magazine* features an interview by Lynn Hirschberg with the actor and standup comic Chris Tucker, whose success in the *Rush Hour* series in the '90s nearly rivaled Smith's.[1] These films were the top-grossing interracial kung-fu action comedies Tucker starred in with Hong Kong star Jackie Chan. This article is one of the first usages of the term "post-raciality" in popular journalism to describe the sensibility under discussion. Tucker makes the following statement about his role as an entertainer: "I want to speak for everybody" (37). In other words, he does not feel it is necessary for him to represent Blackness on screen, unlike Black actors in the past, nor to speak specifically to Black audiences. He implies that for Hollywood and the audiences it reaches, it is now possible for Black actors and actresses not to claim and defend their race in order to have viable careers. When Tucker claims that his films have nothing to do with race, he is either completely disingenuous or naively lacking in historical perspective. His characters in the *Rush Hour* films exist so far within a racial stereotype that he does not seem to be aware of it. Certainly, scholars of race and media have noticed. For instance, Geoff King singles out "the enactment of racist stereotypes, particularly that of the 'coon,' by Black comedians, such as Eddie Murphy, Martin Lawrence, and Chris Tucker, and notes that their performances are uncomfortably reminiscent of racist ideologies that have been used to justify racial discrimination in the past" (Park et al. 159). In *Rush Hour 2* Tucker plays Carter, a police detective from Los Angeles, who gets involved in solving a case involving a bomb attack and the Triad crime gang while visiting Police Chief Lee (Jackie Chan) in Hong Kong. Although Carter is a Black character in a position of authority and one who operates with some degree of competence, a hero/protagonist within the film narrative (and not a typical Black criminal), the development of this character devolves into stereotype:

> Carter is a loud, impulsive, hypersexual yet childish Black man who is often portrayed as ignorant and causing trouble. He constantly reinforces stereotypes associated with his own race. He tells a Chinese woman that he likes his chicken "dead and deep fried," as if it is natural that a Black man likes fried chicken. He also furthers the African American stereotype in his manner of speaking, such as "she's the bomb," "mack out," and "look fly" [Park et al. 163].

Tucker's performance as Carter does not move racial representation into a post-racial space where race does not matter; instead, it is a performance that depends on race as it is commonly constructed and rendered into stereotype.

Tucker's observation about the increasing irrelevance of race in Hollywood is not entirely invalidated. There is truth in the idea that race, to a certain extent and in certain cases, is becoming increasingly invisible in ways that either mark social progress or the re-inscription of the narratives of the film past. The problem is that he is not accurate in applying this new appellation to himself. The biggest omission of the Lynn Hirschberg article on Tucker is the failure to acknowledge Will Smith's role in the establishment of the idea of post-raciality in the films of that era. Smith can be taken as a signifier of post-raciality, his screen personae managing to circumvent the trap of racial stereotype and accomplishing the Post-Black task of moving Black representation into new positions. If this is so, then this permits a more nuanced understanding of the dynamics of so much of his work.

To illustrate the contradictions and tensions inherent in Smith's image and signifying power, one can point to the beginning of his acting career and his character in the television show *Fresh Prince of Bel-Air*, which ran on NBC from 1990 to 1996. This show is poised upon the conflict between classes within the Black community. Will, the nephew from the inner-city, is removed to the household of his wealthy lawyer uncle who lives in Beverly Hills. The conflict between the generations and the classes is brought to a climactic moment at the end of the series' first episode. After Will has disrupted a dinner party hosted by Uncle Phil, they have a confrontation (fig. 2.1). Will accuses his uncle of bourgeois hypocrisy, of being a sell-out. His uncle counters with his testimony of having known Malcolm X and dismisses Will as an ignorant ne'er-do-well. Uncle Phil leaves the room, but he returns to discover, to his surprise, Will at the piano playing Beethoven's "Für Elise." Uncle Phil is wrong in his reductive assessment of Will, who demonstrates potentialities that seemingly contradict his public image. Also implicit is an interrogation even of the concept of contradiction: is it not possible that the sensibility that Will exhibits can be an integral part of his identity, that oppositions can be held and sustained simultaneously within a single signifying figure? The composite identity of the Fresh Prince is also shared by Smith himself.

Fig. 2.1. In the NBC show *The Fresh Prince of Bel-Air*, Uncle Phil (James Avery) and Will often clashed from opposing class and generational viewpoints, bourgeois vs. street (NBC/Stuffed Dog/Quincy Jones Ent/Kobal/Shutterstock).

The Fresh Prince show began with a smart and sharp premise of the clash of classes within a Black home, but very quickly devolved into broad comedy without focus or clear social point. Robin Means Coleman refers to the show as a "neominstrelsy" sitcom (qtd. in Park et al. 159). In fact, the portrayal of the Black middle and upper classes did nothing to put it on a continuum with the cultural work done by *The Cosby Show* of the 1980s in expanding classed images of Blacks. Instead, the Black bourgeois, particularly in the portrayals of the children, was subject to ridicule, which has been the usual practice in literature and film over the years. In fact, one of the cultural projects of the new century will be the reflection of this new Black prosperity in serious art. What *The Fresh Prince* did accomplish was to put Smith and his character Will into an environment of affluence and possibility, thus changing the terms of his own Black identity. This social and cultural mobility is central to Smith's racial significance, and this will become evident again and again; he moves the image of the Black male into unaccustomed spaces just as Smith himself was in the process of conquering Hollywood.

Another more recent post-racial moment for Smith was the election of Barack Obama as president in 2008. The connections and similarities between Smith and Obama are many and distinct, both being among the most famous Black men on the planet. This is acknowledged by Smith himself who, jokingly, claimed that he always expected that he would be the first Black man to be president of the United States. He adds that he doesn't mind that it was Obama who beat him to it. Smith also jokes that he should portray Obama in the film version of the president's life. He says there is something about the ears (Denham). It is interesting that Smith sees himself in alignment with Obama because in certain ways it was Smith who paved the way for Obama. For instance, in the period before the 2008 election, Obama had to be introduced to world audiences. In Irish newspapers, Obama was described in terms of a known quantity: Will Smith. As one editorial writer noted: "voters have been checking out Obama and liking what they see. An African-American man in a suit who's not too dark-skinned or radical; intelligent and wholesome in the Will Smith … pattern" (M. Devlin 33). Readers were asked to see Obama as the Will Smith of the political realm. At that time Will Smith's sci-fi thriller, *I Am Legend*, opened globally to record box-office, just as Barack Obama was a frontrunner in the primary race to become the Democratic nominee for president of the United States. In one case, Smith portrays the last man on earth while Obama was on his way to become the first Black president. Perhaps there is a sense in which the last and the first come together. Much was written about how Obama represents a new concept of race and can communicate his message across racial borders, attracting voters both Black and white. Smith has achieved a level of stardom that complicates our received notions of identity politics. His appeal transcends racial and national categories to reach truly global dimensions. Smith and Obama could be seen as indicators of a social and cultural transition, with Smith setting the precedent. What Obama accomplished in the political sphere, Smith had been doing in Hollywood for the previous twenty years.

There are specific similarities between Smith and Obama in terms of the debates they generate. Obama's biraciality, educational background, and class status raise questions about the authenticity of his Blackness. Likewise, Smith has had to withstand charges of inauthenticity from the beginning of his career as a middle-class rapper who crossed over to the mainstream. The power of his fame and success turn this charge on its head. Smith's persistence forces us to see that his iconic status does not so much represent inauthentic Blackness as a new definition of Blackness. In performance after performance, role after role, he resists stereotype and asks us to extend our ideas of what a Black man can be. To save the world, to be a devoted father, to be the last man on earth, all these possibilities are contained in his film persona. Just as Barack Obama is changing what national leadership can be, Smith is also doing considerable cultural work in reshaping the meaning of Blackness and manhood.

The key to Smith's appeal is his ability to contain within his image many contradictory messages. As a result, he can speak to a wide range of audiences. The most important example of this is the way his film images embody and, at the same time, do not embody race. Smith is a perfect example of the post-racial movie star, in the same way that Barack Obama is an example of a post-racial political candidate. Smith represents a Black identity that has been formed as a result of the Civil Rights movement, a beneficiary of the dream. These "post-racials" are not just Black, but feel free to claim all their other identities. Smith perhaps is the one Black performer who consistently switches his racial messages, and this is the basis of his unparalleled success. This dexterity allows all audiences to extend to him their good will and to get from him exactly what they need.

The template for Smith's star power and his transformation of race can be found in his first serious performance in the 1991 film *Six Degrees of Separation*. In this film he plays a young man who pretends to be the son of Sidney Poitier in order to enter the world of wealth and privilege on Manhattan's Fifth Avenue. Smith has said that the reason he was cast is that the qualities he possesses make it believable that these people would invite him into their living rooms. Critical commentary concurs: "Of course rich white folk would let this strange black guy into their living room— hadn't America already done so?" (Portwood). Senator Joe Biden, in his controversial comments during the spring of 2007, claimed the same thing about Obama: "'I mean you got the first mainstream African-American who is articulate and bright and clean and a nice-looking guy'" (Thai and Barrett). He is the kind of Black presidential candidate with whom America feels comfortable and are willing to invite into the national living room.

Contrarian film critic Armond White takes a more skeptical view of the Smith-Obama connection. He does admit that Smith is a political figure as are all actors, but particularly for him as a Black public figure, Smith reflects "the way we think about race, masculinity, humor, violence, and fantasy" (White, "Crappyness"). He sees Smith and Obama aligned in the way they negotiate race in their respective realms:

> His pop-culture ascension syncs with Barack Obama's superhero feat as the first Black male to become a major party presidential candidate. Both these events can be described as Triumphs of the Will, decades-late endorsement of African-American aspiration. If one thing is certain in this life, it's that no modest person becomes a movie star or a politician. Smith and Obama, first rate egotists, share a smooth, casual approach to popularity. Both accept racial identification but not in any polarizing way; their Black, white, and in-between appeal has a beige complexion. Asserting or rescinding racial identity at will, Smith has mastered the game that Obama is just learning [White, "Crappyness"].

White continues:

> It matters that Smith and Obama—the most popular Anglo surname and an immediately, recognizably exotic surname—both are seen as inoffensive and associated with non-threatening ideology. It is the basis of the public confidence each man seeks. Smith's distance from gangster rap (remember the disses he received as the first Grammy-winning—i.e., "safe"—rap artist?) parallels Obama's distance from radical, upstart Black nationalism, liberation theology and prophetic Christianity.... Despite Smith and Obama's casual, presidential demeanor, the ease with which they carry their opportunity and success reflects a willed

triumph over adversity—a whispered pact to leave the audience's enthusiasm undisturbed. This electability is not so different from box-office charisma. They are stars who charm rather than challenge; and their public image is interchangeable [White, "Crappyness"].

White reserves his most pointed pejoration for Smith:

> White argues that Smith's status alone means he's no longer a lawn jockey, this being a garden-gnome-like statuette, usually Black, symbolizing tameness and docility. His failure to show, as White puts it, "any social consciousness at all," does not lessen his impact. If anything, it enhances it. A silent Black man without social consciousness … has made it possible for Americans to identify with him. They not only admire, but like and perhaps even respect him. Or, at least they respect his silence [Cashmore 134].

This is a negative and reductive account of the essence of Smith's post-racial appeal, and not entirely fair because Smith in his private life has been exemplary in exhibiting social consciousness in his support of many causes and of other minorities in the film business. His screen personae, on the other hand, do not reflect or engage with social issues or historical Black experience. It also is not true that Smith is silent because he does speak, but his positions have often proven to be problematic.

Smith was not silent upon the occasion of Obama's election to the presidency (fig. 2.2). Smith had supported Obama from the beginning and would be a significant bundler for the re-election campaign off 2012. He had not been noted as politically engaged before this: "Smith stated in 2008 that Obama is only the second political figure he has ever thrown his support behind—the first being Nelson Mandela"

Fig. 2.2. Will Smith wrote an editorial about America transcending racism upon the election of Barack Obama in 2008. From left: Barack Obama, Sasha Obama, Malia Obama, and Michelle Obama (Shawn Thew/EPA/Shutterstock).

(Bonilla-Silva 74). Still, it was November 4, 2008, that held a special magic for Smith. His reaction to this historic event is revelatory of his attitudes about race. After the election, Smith's reaction was published in *USA Today*, the content of which also appeared in articles related to the release of his film *Seven Pounds*. In his statement, he says several remarkable things:

> For me, it was something that I've always believed. I've read the Declaration of Independence. I've read the Constitution. I have the preamble memorized. It's something I've always believed in, and when Barack Obama won, it validated a piece of me that I wasn't allowed to say out loud—that America is not a racist nation.
>
> I love that all of our excuses have been removed. African-American excuses have been removed. There's no white man trying to keep you down, because if he were really trying to keep you down, he would have done everything he could to keep Obama down. Yes, there are racist people who live here, absolutely. But they're not the majority anymore.
>
> I'm an African American, and I was able to climb to a certain point in Hollywood. On that journey, I realized people weren't trying to stop me. Most people were trying to help me. Before Obama won the presidency, it was like, I'm the exception. Tiger is the exception. Michael Jordan is the exception. Bill Cosby is the exception. But there's something about being the leader of the free world, with every other position on earth below that. You can't argue with that. If Barack Obama can win the presidency of the United States, you can absolutely be the manager at Saks.
>
> Come on. It was such a fantastic experience for me to be able to say out loud that I love America and not be called an Uncle Tom. That I can stand out, and I can say out loud that I love this country and not get funny looks.
>
> I don't think we are African Americans, Irish Americans or Japanese Americans anymore. I think Americans are a new race of people. We are Americans of African descent. We are Americans of Irish descent.
>
> It's a whole new world [W. Smith].

In an article in *The Toronto Star* Smith goes on to assert: "America, to me, is the most fantastic nation that has ever existed in the history of the planet. 'We hold these truths to be self-evident that all men are created equal.' There's nothing ever been written better than that, ever! Now we just have to live up to it. A cycle of African-American citizenship has been completed with this. I'm just hyped" (Howell). Smith's euphoria is consistent with a conviction that was widespread during the time of Obama's victory: the election of the first African American president heralded the arrival of a new post-racial America.

Of course, the outraged criticism of Smith's statements appeared immediately. He anticipated the backlash himself, admitting that his perspective could be coming from a place of celebrity privilege: "I don't think America as a whole is a racist nation. Before Obama won the presidency I wasn't allowed to say that out loud because people would say: 'Oh yeah, of course for you, Mr. Hollywood'" (O'Toole). Annette John-Hall of *The Philadelphia Inquirer* seconds his jocular self-assessment: "But let's face it, when you're perched on top of the box office, your perspective on racial attitudes may not be the same as those of someone worn down by the worst of inequality" (John-Hall). She takes him to task for his exuberance in an article titled "Race Still Matters in Obama's Post-Racial America," Smith being described as "often lauded as a symbol of Hollywood's 'post-racial' change of heart" (Squires 48). She refutes Smith with a recitation of the realities of institutional racism: "Fact is, before we skip into post-racial wonderland together, we still have some institutional dismantling to do. Disproportionate red-lining, lack of equality in pay and lending. Inferior education. One Black senator in Congress, a dearth of professionals of color in every segment, from boardrooms to newsroom" (John-Hall).

Reed and Louis in their article "'No More Excuses': Problematic Responses to Barack Obama's Election" take the criticism of Smith's position to a higher, more scholarly level of discourse. They cite Smith's appearance on *The Oprah Winfrey Show* two days after Obama's election and his assertion that this historic event removed all obstacles to Black progress and that Black people can no longer claim victimhood: "'The history of African Americans is such that you want to be a part of America, but we've been rejected so much it's hard to take ownership and take responsibility for ourselves and this country. It was like, at that second, at that moment, all of our excuses were gone'" (Moore qtd. in Reed and Louis 99). Reed and Louis systematically invalidate this attitude of blaming the victims and denying the far-reaching effects of racism. They cite the public commentary of right-wing conservatives, Black conservatives such as John McWhorter, and prominent African American entertainers other than Smith such as Wanda Sykes and Bill Cosby. Cosby is well-known for his criticism of Black communities for their lack of self-policing and lax work ethics. About Cosby they write: "Comedian and actor Bill Cosby considers anti-intellectualism, poor parenting and a pathological youth culture hold back the African American poor from full inclusion in American society" (Reed and Louis 101).

Reed and Louis counter this attitude with data from William Ryan's seminal 1971 study *Blaming the Victim*. They point to systematic racism as the cause of African American struggle as manifested in discrimination in economics, criminal justice, housing, and medical care (Reed and Louis 104–7). They conclude that "the apparently widespread belief that systemic racism does not exist is an ominous development, which undoubtedly mitigates efforts to eliminate or reduce racism." They critique the idea that with the election of Obama Black youth can now achieve anything they desire because of the underlying assumption that what has held Blacks back is their own psychological self-doubt or self-defeating negativity. Reed and Louis finally assert: "Of course, to some degree, personal ambitions and beliefs may limit many youth; however, to suggest that this psychological factor is the major cause of racial inequality in America is to deny facts as presented not only by scholars, but by the federal government and governmental commissions" (107).

Despite the evidence, Smith persists in believing that the Black community must be held responsible for its conditions. In an interview in *Esquire* in 2015, seven years into the Obama presidency, he makes the following statement:

> I've always been telling my sons, We have to separate fault from responsibility—whose fault it is that Black men are in this situation, whose fault it is doesn't matter. It's our responsibility to make it go right. It's our responsibility. It's a lot of people's fault, systemic racism, and it's a lot of people's fault that the Black community is in the situation that we're in, but it's our responsibility to clean up the mess [Raab].

Among the most powerful and eloquent critiques of Smith's denial of racism is expressed by Ewuare X. Osayande in "An Open Letter to Will Smith." He reminds

Smith of how his celebrity status carries added responsibility to the Black community because of the influence he consequently exerts. He also warns of the danger in aspects of Smith's election response:

> It was truly the most historic event in our generation. But for us to now profess that this one act was so compelling as to turn a country that owned and sold Africans as slaves for almost one hundred years since it declared itself a nation, that fought a Civil War to determine if it would keep them enslaved, that then rendered them second-class citizens and sanctioned segregation and the terrorism that came with it for another hundred years, and that spent the last forty years fighting against their advancement through every sphere of American life, into a nation that is not racist is a thing of fantasy like your films [Osayande].

Osayande is withering about Smith's lack of historical understanding of the history of racism:

> World-famous Black actors before you, such as Paul Robeson, Sidney Poitier, and Harry Belafonte, couldn't separate themselves as easily due to the legislative and social constraints of Jim Crow. But now, because of their struggle and the blood sacrifice of Black people, you can have separated yourself from the very Black community that nurtured you and supported you, only to turn around and make a statement that only works to soothe the guilt-ridden conscience of a nation that continues to downplay its legacy of racism and the toll that legacy has taken on those of us who are Black, Brown, and poor. To use the platform bequeathed to you by the Civil Rights Movement to deny the legacy of racism and its continued persistence amounts to a slap in the face to each and every Black person that died and continues to die due the reality of racism [Osayande].

The critique of Smith reaches a crescendo as he denounces Smith's alliance with conservatives who aver that the problems of Black America are self-generated. The following is included in Osayande's concluding statements:

> Taken at face value, your remarks defend the racist proposition that any problem Black people experience in this nation must be of our own making and doing. America remains in denial as to the actual state of racial progress. Your comments only work to rock this nation into a deeper slumber.... No, Will, unlike the characters you portray in your films, people of color in this country do not have the privilege or luxury to exist without a walking [sic] awareness of race and what that means in a country that at any given moment and without any warning can remind us of racism's truth in all its cruelty and brutality. No, we cannot afford to pretend or play make-believe. In our world the bullets are real as is the racism [Osayande].

Aside from the clarity he provides about the racial implications of Smith's public utterances upon Obama's election, Osayande reveals several aspects of Smith's star identity. He perceives a continuum between the post-racial postures of Smith's political assertions and the persona created by his screen performances. He describes Smith's thinking about racism as being worthy of the fantasy fictions of his films, worlds wherein colorblindness prevails, his Blackness is nearly erased, and racism does not exist. Osayande makes an important elision between Smith's public image and his screen persona. In other words, the two identities seem to converge. This is unusual for major Hollywood stars who maintain a distance between their identities on and off screen. This confluence may contribute to Smith's "difference" and the uniqueness that allows him as a Black exception to attain the highest realms of stardom.

Osayande also underscores Smith's denial of the past and his predecessors in his Obama proclamations. He sees these attitudes as clearly separative from the Black past, which is not a Post-Black perspective, one that signifies upon the past for the benefit of Black people. Smith is less associated with a Post-Black identity because of his lack of connection to the reality of racism and his stronger embrace of Obama-era post-racial hope. Yet in these same performances Smith expands the range of young, Black male representation in film, clearly a Post-Black victory. If his hip and "cool" performances do not affect the ironic, self-conscious, and parodic deconstruction of Blackness that Post-Blackness aims for, he does speak to Black people in other ways: through the inspiration provided by the example of his success.

Smith exists within an ambiguous space between the Post-Black and post-racial views of American society. Similarly, as elaborated in the previous chapter, Smith can carry and then cast off the racial sign at will, the way other Black global stars like Oprah Winfrey and Barack Obama have taken the ease and effectiveness of racial identity code-switching to the highest level. Smith's ability to incorporate elements of evolving Black identities over the course of his career through the '80s and the '90s, from Post-Blackness to post-racial and back, and still appeal to the audiences of the world is a powerful testament to his unique brand of racially transcendent stardom.

THREE

A Slave to Fashion

The significance of Will Smith's status as Post-Black, post-racial global movie star can be seen by reading his image through the prism of fashion. Certainly, his dexterous negotiation of race and Black manhood renders him "safe" for the widest swath of film audiences, transcending the negative stereotype of the Black male as threatening, violent, and hypersexual, a stereotype that does not translate into Hollywood profit. The themes that thread through his and any Black actor's career entail the mitigation of a perceived alienating Blackness and of a sexually potent masculinity. These themes are woven into the fabric of a Black actor's performance and costuming, and this is especially true for Smith. In his every performance, there are moments when the meanings of Smith's iconicity are registered through the language of the body and costume.

Starring in Black and White

Although Adrienne Kennedy's 1976 play *A Movie Star Must Star in Black and White* has its own specific concerns with racial identity and oppression, the very title is suggestive in general for Black representation and performance. The title highlights the necessity of the Black public performer to confront the issue of race, the binary opposition between Black and white. This is especially true for Black icons of popular culture who must maintain a delicate balance between racial consciousness and mainstream acceptance. To understand Will Smith's unique negotiation of this tension, one might compare his work to that of Michael Jackson whose transcendence of race surpasses even Smith's. It is instructive to look at their music and video work to see how they explore the ideological opposition of Black and white using black and white imagery in their most significant music videos. The music video form has been the subject of a body of scholarly analysis, its three-and-a-half minutes combining music and movement to go beyond its promotional, aesthetic, and technological potentialities to impact representation and to challenge and subvert the status quo. Carol Vernallis notes that music video's "interaction among music, lyrics, and image creates complex social meanings" (xiii). Burns and Hawkins also remark upon the form's communicative power: "As music videos animate our social and cultural spaces, they shape significant representations of gendered, sexualized, raced, and class identities" (3). Music video theory affords the tools and perspectives to excavate its larger meanings. The scrutiny of formal elements, such as mise-en-scène (costuming and color), contributes to the focus of this study, the racial discourse signified by the video star.

Michael Jackson's "Black or White" video is among his greatest achievement in the form. As it premiered on November 14, 1991, on MTV, BET, VHS, and Fox in the United States, it also debuted in twenty-seven countries around the world reaching 500 million viewers, the largest audience in history for a music video. The first broadcasts created a swell of controversy for its violent and sexually suggestive concluding segment. Since then, critics have debated Jackson's racial politics as conveyed by the song's lyrics and the video's innovative and provocative visuals.

The introduction of "Black or White" features child actor Macaulay Culkin in a battle of wills with his father played by George Wendt. Culkin is playing rock music at high volume to which his father objects. In protest, Culkin cranks up the sound of his music and the amplifier of his electric guitar, and he literally blasts his father out of the house, propelling him half-way around the world to crash land in Africa. At this point, Jackson appears, and the song begins. Jackson performs the song in a series of vignettes featuring various world cultures. He dances with a group of Zulu warriors, Thai women in traditional dress, then against a battle scene involving Native Americans, then with an Indian woman in the middle of a city street, and finally with Russian dancers performing a Cossack dance. This sequence conveys the larger import of the video. Tamara Roberts writes: "Jackson … is able to move freely between these groups, phenotypically ambiguous and able to perform all of their dances, channeling them through his personal vocabulary. His ability to flow between categories showcases the artifice of racial categories" (35). The scene changes, and Jackson walks through raging flames exclaiming his defiance of the forces of hate and oppression, particularly the Ku Klux Klan. At this point, Culkin lip syncs the rap interlude of the song along with Jackson, enunciating the message of the piece, that he refuses to be reduced to a color.

Jackson next appears atop the torch of the Statue of Liberty. As he sings, other major world monuments appear: the Sphinx, the Eiffel Tower, Big Ben, Hagia Sophia, the Parthenon, the Kremlin, the Taj Mahal, the Golden Gate Bridge. As this part of the song ends, the video's most famous scene begins in which thirteen people of different races dance, repeating the words of the song's title and visually transform from one into the another. This was one of the first uses of the special effect of "morphing" created by Pacific Data Images. The scene effectively projects the song's meaning that everyone may look different but also share a common humanity, and thus race does not matter. At the end of the scene, the camera pulls back, in a moment of cinematic self-consciousness, to reveal the sound stage on which the previous scene has been filmed. A Black panther appears on the set and wanders down into a back street and morphs into Michael Jackson.

What follows is one of the most extraordinary sequences in a music video. As Elizabeth Chin writes:

> The final portion of the film has come to be known as the "panther dance," and it is in this section of *Black or White* that I am most interested. Set in stark contrast to what has come before it, the "panther dance" includes no recorded music, no singing, and rather than an upbeat

anthem to multiculturalism, it is a dark and gritty exploration of the ugly racial reality in a society in which people assert that they do not see race. Whereas in the song-based portion of the film Jackson and a host of professional dancers had happily traded trademark moves, here Jackson danced alone in a darkly lit alley, grabbed his crotch, zipped his fly, jumped on a car and smashed its windshield, screamed, threw a garbage can through a window, fell to his knees in a puddle of water, and screamed some more [58].

The video concludes with the cartoon character Bart Simpson watching the video we have just viewed, only to have his father, Homer, scream out a command for him to turn it off, which Bart does with resentment.

The video "Black or White" effectively illustrates Jackson's utopian post-racial vision: "it espouses a comfortable, optimistic notion of harmony and multiculturalism" (Manghani 34). The song itself is successful at expressing a Post-Black aesthetic at the very level of the music. Being a fusion of rock, R&B, and rap, the song rests upon multiple cultural influences, one of the prime characteristics of Post-Black art. Yet, the video presents challenges to interpretation. For instance, there is some criticism of its imagery in terms of stereotyping (Brackett 176). Chin takes exception to several of the video's representations of diversity. The African dancers are not culturally authentic but are dancers trained in Western ballet and modern dance. The Native American scene is not a dance sequence, but an attack right out of a Hollywood western. His international dance sequence is so blatantly essentialist and fetishizing that it must be intended as an ironic critique of multiculturalism (Chin 66). If this so, then a subsidiary assertion of the video is that these images of culture are mere constructs and have no power to define or constrain individuals.

The problem with this reading is that it attributes too much sophistication to the rhetoric of the piece. This reading also obscures the obvious meaning of the video, that real cultural differences can be overcome through the universal force of music and dance. Yet, even this declaration of racial transcendence is problematic. David Brackett offers the following analysis:

> Yet the yearning for a world beyond racial and economic oppression comes to rest on the unrestricted agency of individuals.... Such dreams ignore the futility of individual action in a world where such actions are constrained by institutional and discursive forces beyond the power of any single social actor to change him- or herself or, indeed, the world. This emphasis, in fact, has the paradoxical effect of reinforcing individualistic ideals that work against concerted social action that might intervene at institutional levels [176–177].

If the ostensible message of *Black or White* is that race is irrelevant, it is contradicted by elements both within and outside the video-text. Burnett and Deivert point to Jackson's album covers and his physical evolution. His facial features, through serial plastic surgery, become increasingly Caucasian, and his skin becomes whiter and whiter (Burnett and Deivert 34–35). This extratextual detail refutes the video's racial claim because for Jackson in the private sphere of his behavior and personal choices evinces the belief that race, especially whiteness, does make a difference.

The other contradiction of the video's message resides in its controversial ending section, the panther dance scene. As Roberts points out: "Rather end on a happy note, Jackson chose to punctuate the song with a vision of unresolved angst and the sense that interracial and multicultural happiness is a façade" (35). When the video premiered, this scene of seemingly unmotivated violence provoked reactions of shock and bewilderment. The video was censored in that it was pulled and reedited. In the new version, the one most frequently shown now, Jackson's destructive behavior has specific targets. He now smashes windows bearing graffiti of bigotry and hatred, including the racial epithet and the swastika. This change renders the violence more readable in conventional socio-political terms. Jackson's unique artistic vision and voice hereby was distorted and suppressed. The original meaning of the panther dance scene was disturbing, incomprehensible, and unacceptable to mainstream audiences. This four-minute virtuosic performance was nothing less than a pure expression of Black rage. Both Chin and Lott offer perceptive and forceful interpretations:

> The dominant and digitally altered version argues that violence like Jackson's can be understood only if it comes as a response to overt racism (rather than, as in the original, a response to structural racism)—and in this case Jackson is now taking action against a racism that makes no sense—except to a white audience unprepared to confront Black anger. In substituting the racial epithet for structural racism as the object of Jackson's violence, this version also rectifies the original uncanniness of Jackson's unaltered performance. For it is structural violence that hegemonic forces seek to avoid recognizing, and it is the specter of structural racism that makes Jackson's rage and anger so oddly unintelligible to audiences who cannot decipher Black rage even when it is spelled out in the most direct terms. Replacing the reality of structural racism with digitally rendered racist graffiti neatly contains the problem as one of overt racism practiced by those who identify as racists, eliminating the need to look further or more carefully... [Chin 70–71].

Chin continues:

> ...the panther dance rejected the demands of white audiences for "Black entertainment" and instead offered a statement about Black identity. No jungle wiggles, no titillating jiggles. Jackson's panther dance is a taking off of the mask, a revelation of the abiding rage and anger that whites both fear and suppress: a truth that cannot be morphed into something palatable either in dreams or in reality [72].

Lott comes to the following conclusion:

> No wonder nobody wanted to see the end of "Black or White"! It reveals the underside of the urge to transcendence the video depicts: a recognition of violent racist suppression, an inwardness with violent resistance, and, in the very final moments, an acknowledgment of the mutilations (including plastic surgery?) suffered by Black bodies in the act of self-liberation. Taken as a whole, "Black or White" conjures an incredible depth and complexity of responsiveness to the ongoing predicaments of racial demarcation in America ["Aesthetic" 553].

The panther dance gives the lie to the rest of the video's point about racial harmony, the video becoming "an example of discomfort and a collapse in regular discourse that music video seems well placed to affect" (Manghani 35). As Chin points out, this ending "serves only to underscore what Jackson has been saying all along: this 'it doesn't matter stuff' is a charade. 'It' is the *only* thing that matters" (68). One wonders why Jackson allows this contradiction. Perhaps he is asserting that racial identity is essentially contradictory. Despite the racially transcendent aspects of his star image, the Post-Black hybridity of his music, and the denials of race in his lyrics, Jackson in "Black or White" assumes a voice that is neither post-racial or Post-Black, but hyper-racial, or pure Black. Jackson is both sexual and violent, appropriating Black male stereotypes not to reject them but instead to speak through them. He takes the kind of political and artistic risk that Smith, in his identity as just an entertainer, never dares.[1]

Even at the level of costuming, Jackson consistently registers a racial consciousness. Throughout the video, his clothing reflects the play of ideas about the contradictions of race in American society. During the first part of the film, Jackson's body is bifurcated representing racial opposition. He is Black on the bottom half of his body and white on top. He is wearing black leather jeans with silver studs around the crotch and a low-riding metallic belt. As he dances among the various ethnic groups, this black and white habiliment remains the same enunciating his connection to world cultures and his role as a unifying figure. Roberts notes that "wearing a nondescript black-and-white costume, Jackson becomes an Everyman for the late twentieth century—a global citizen" (33). In the scene in which he bursts through flames declaring his defiance of racial hatred, he wears a billowing oversized white shirt over a T-shirt with a deep V-neck. On his right arm is a black band and a laced-up white glove and wrist guard. Over his black pants he wears elaborate knee pads and leg armor. At every point, his dress reinforces the song and video's message about how the lines between the races can be bridged. However, in the last scene, Jackson undergoes a sartorial transformation to all-black costuming, which, along with his explosive dance movements, expresses something different, a Black rage that is existential and cannot be contained.

Smith's costuming in his earlier video work also engages issues of race and identity, and the system of color symbolism provides ways of interpreting them. It is notable how often Smith resorts to white costuming in his music videos. This trend begins in the 1988 clip of "Parents Just Don't Understand" at the beginning of his career. Here, Smith, the Fresh Prince, comically cavorts in various domestic settings in a white union suit which accentuates his youth and blameless high spirits. This persona contrasts with the hard gansta image of other rappers of the time. Smith in his white underwear, which infantilizes him, allows him, accompanied by his clean and innocent lyrics, to make rap safe for the mainstream. An appeal to purity and wholesomeness is still operative in his later video of "Just the Two of Us" from 1997. This song, from the album *Big Willie Style*, is a celebration of fatherhood as he sings to his son to convey lessons about manhood, tears, knowledge, and discipline. He also promises his protection, support, and love. In the video he appears with both of his sons as well as his own father. There are also quickly edited inserts of famous fathers with their sons, celebrities and legends such as Sean Combs, Magic Johnson, and Muhammad Ali. The video is an affecting celebration of Black fatherhood and an affirmation of the Black family. Smith and his son are both dressed in white casual clothes. Smith wears a ribbed white sweater, a silver chain around his neck, and white jeans. The whiteness of the vestments here makes a statement about the purity and power of Black paternal love and about its universality.

Smith's 1998 video of "Gettin' Jiggy Wit It," directed by Hype Williams and styled by June Ambrose, is notable for its visual and sartorial flair. It won the MTV Music Video Award that year for Best Rap Video. The video marked Smith's return to rap after years of his success on television in the series *The Fresh Prince of Bel-Air* and on the big screen in *Independence Day, Men in Black, and Wild Wild West*. What's even more critically compelling is its signifying on Jackson's "Black or White." The clip is focused on the power of dancing in different cultural contexts. The storyline begins with Smith in a darkened studio with bands of swirling metallic lights in the background. He sports a Black suede jacket and a hot pink shirt. This footage is intercut with Smith and dancers in electric blue Adidas Puffa tracksuits. The scene changes to ancient Egypt with Smith outfitted as a pharaoh fronting lines of dancers including Black muscle men. This sequence, shot at the Luxor Casino in Las Vegas, references Jackson's Egyptian concept in his 1992 video "Remember the Time." Then, there is a shift to the Pacific and South Pacific with Hawaiian and Polynesian dancers against a volcano backdrop and Smith in a multi-color suit of vivid red, blue, and green on black. Finally, Smith, in a flowing white coat over more white costuming, dances beneath the Statue of Liberty at the New York, New York Casino. The transitions of the video through various geographical locations with Smith dancing in the foreground echoes Jackson's cultural transitions in "Black or White." Even Smith's reversion to black clothing in the closing moments is not unlike Jackson's complete embrace of Blackness in the panther dance. However, the messages are not the same. The Jackson video argues for the bridging of real racial and cultural divisions while the Smith video operates within a Post-Black space. His immersion in and movement through a series of cultural vignettes do not have a rhetorical impact. It assumes that Smith and the Black female dancers, the Egyptian and Polynesian dancers, as well as the briefly seen Bollywood actress are already united as if the power of rap has become a part of all cultures. Halifu Osumare theorizes: "Black hip-hop's contemporary musical/visual sampling often appropriates elements of other cultures, even as it is being appropriated by youth from various cultures around the world" (108). Osumare then notes the ease with which, for example, a group of male ninth grade students in Hawaii can absorb the mélange of cultural references in "Gettin' Jiggy Wit It," signaling a deep global postmodern sensibility (108). Smith's video transcends race without having to recognize the lines, which have been elided in any case.

In these Smith videos, the symbolism of the color white as visualized through the costuming follows conventional interpretations, but in other instances the persistence of white costuming generates different meanings. Instead of expressing the complexities of racial identity or the profundities of the Black experience, Smith videos can be read as narratives of assimilation. This interpretation of color coding does not apply in isolation as evidenced by the 1997 video "Can't Nobody Hold Me Down" by Puff Daddy (Sean Combs) and Mase, which visualizes the rap artist/mogul's fear of being overwhelmed by his success. Greg de Cuir, Jr., notates the connection between the star's internal state and the video's art direction: "The second sequence of the video takes place in a sterile white chamber suffused with bright light. This is yet another abstract dreamscape in which materialist fantasies are played out" (63). In the clips "Miami," "Wild Wild West," and "Will 2K" the showcasing of white clothing similarly dramatizes a persistent crisis of identity for aspiring Blacks and here the specific dilemma of a young Black performer negotiating his entrée into the mainstream.

The video "Miami" signally treats an aspect of Black bourgeois existence: an anxiety over identity and assimilation. This is understandable given Smith's own middle-class background. In doing so, the video aligns itself with a trend within Black artistic production during the '80s and '90s. This was a period when debates over Affirmative Action were in circulation and when Blacks were making advances into professional hierarchies. The experiences of this rising Black middle class, some of whom and their children inhabit the space of Post-Blackness, were narra-tivized in such novels as *Company Man*; such memoirs as Jake Lamar's *Bourgeois Blues*, Stephen Carter's *Confessions of an Affirmative Action Baby*, and Lorene Cary's *Black Ice*; and such films as *Strictly Business* and *The Inkwell*. This pattern of upward mobility and crossing over was reproduced in the music world as rap artists like Ice-T and Queen Latifah made transitions into mainstream entertainment. Smith made this migration as well and did so to spectacular effect, and it is interesting how the story of this rise and its attendant issues replicates itself in the storylines of his music videos.

The "Miami" video was released on November 23, 1998, in conjunction with the release of the single from the album *Big Willie Style*. Directed by Wayne Isham, the short film went on to win the MTV Video Music Award for Best Male Video that year. The video follows Smith on a spur of the moment flight from freezing Philadel-phia to sunny Miami. From the Philly diner to the private plane to the red carpet to a hip lounge to a cool convertible to Ocean Drive at night to a strip of South Beach to a speedboat, the camera and its precisely executed digital morphing effects allows Smith to make these transitions with swaggering ease. Carol Vernallis observes that this sense of "a trajectory through space while following along with the music" is "one of music video's pleasures" (109). She effectively captures the themes of "Miami" when she refers to "the unfolding spaces of music video—conveying possibility, autonomy, and prowess" (109). The lyrics celebrate a multi-ethnic mix as Smith addresses his audience composed of people of all ages, races, and nations (Haiti, Jamaica, India, Cuba). Smith here recognizes the broad base of his appeal that crosses boundaries of race, age, and nationality. The imagery of this clip is also steeped in the mate-rialistic accouterments of celebrity and success (the private jet, the exclusive club, the cool convertible, the racing speedboat) which are staples of the rap video idiom. The visual motif of costuming as an aspect of this mise-en-scène tells a specific story about racial identity and success: the journey from Black to white. Smith's costuming changes throughout the video, from a black athletic suit to a sleek black designer club outfit to black jeans and sweater to shorts. While speeding along in a white convert-ible, Smith tears off his black sweater to reveal a white tank top. When Smith's jour-ney of liberation escalates as he strides across a beach, he rips off his jeans and strides across a beach in white shorts. His attire is instantaneously transformed from black to gleaming white, and the implication is that he has finally arrived.

In its meaning and its setting, "Miami" has correspondences with a video from an unexpected musical genre: post–New Romantic British yacht pop. The video in question is George Michael's "Careless Whisper" which also features leisure boats and a Miami background. "Miami" shares with yacht pop a desire for social ascendance: "What unifies such lifestyle music videos is that the protagonists all capitalize on a sense of autonomy to make headway into new landscapes of pleasure ... pleasure becomes the orientation of the moment, taking in new locations, new women, a new look, and an escape" (Halligan 106). The definition of yacht pop resonates with attitudes animating Smith's trajectory in his video: freedom and aspiration. The difference is that for the post–New Romantics the objective is class elevation while for Smith it is transcendence of both class and race. The last segment of the video has Smith in a speedboat approaching a party at a club with a dance floor extending out over the water. Smith docks the boat and runs along the pier to join the revelers. The constant throughout this transition is the costuming. Smith recounts the production of the video: "We changed the fighting a shark plot into a riding a boat to go to a Latin-themed dance number plot. I still got to wear the white pants" (Siquig). His comment underscores the significance of the white clothing trope. The video continues with Smith singing and dancing in white pants and a hot pink silk shirt in front of a multicultural crowd, all to the tune of a driving Latin beat. Like the concept of the "Gettin' Jiggy Wit It" film, this musical number also echoes Michael Jackson's theme in "Black or White" of music and dance transcending cultural and national boundaries. The message here does not register racial difference and conflict as forces to be overcome. Instead, it celebrates a post-racial world where racial and cultural differences have already been assimilated into the norm.

This pattern of transformation from black to white is continued in another video, "Wild Wild West," which was released in May 1999 in concert with the film's release the same month. The song itself was taken from Smith's album *Willennium* and reached the number one spot on the Billboard chart. The extravagantly produced video (featuring a roster of guest stars including Stevie Wonder, "Babyface" Edmonds, Dru Hill, Kool Moe Dee, MC Lyte, Larenz Tate, Shari Headley, and Enrique Iglesias) was directed by Paul Hunter with cinematography by Thomas Kloss and special effects by Jeff Doron. The video is structured as a counterpoint between a narrative extension of the feature film (with intercut inserts of the film's stars Kenneth Branagh, Kevin Kline, and Salma Hayek) and a musical production interlude. The clip begins against the background of a burning town. The setting replicates the mise-en-scène of standard westerns, but also, in an effort perhaps toward historical realism, the filmmakers' attempt to reference the scourging of free Black communities after the Civil War. In the film the Black town is destroyed not by an avenging Confederate general but by the mad scientist Dr. Loveless. Before the conflagration (like the fire Michael Jackson walks through in "Black and White"), Smith engages in a gunfight as well as performing the song. The action continues in a cavernous science laboratory equipped with futuristic machinery and wheels. The performance amps up with Sisqo, bare-chested, but dressed in Black leather pants and vest, giving a virtuosic dance performance and nearly stealing the show. The music stops, and the scene shifts again to a dance hall where Smith takes center stage wearing the black nineteenth-century costume he wears as his character in the film: a black suit, a long duster, leather vest, gun holster slung around his hips, and a black gambler hat. As the musical number resumes, to the astonishment of characters in the ballroom, an ensemble composed of dancers of every possible race and ethnicity, he takes the stage. He throws his hat above the crowd, and it swerves through the air like a boomerang. Changing color from black to white in mid-air, the hat returns to its original position on his head. Just as suddenly, his suit is transformed into a luminous white.

Continuing this pattern of costume transitions from black to white and its susceptibility to racial interpretation is the "Will 2K" video directed by Robert Caruso and choreographed by Fatima Robinson. This clip visualizes the song which also appears on the *Willennium* album. Released in October 1999, this video has proven not among Smith's most widely viewed, but holds interest, nonetheless. The plot involves Smith time traveling during the course of a turn of the twenty-first-century party. The theme centers on a general cultural anxiety about the transition into a new century but is resolved with the attitude that the beat must go on. Will is late for his own party. As he arrives the room transforms into a globe, and he is transported back to the 1930s with him presiding over the festivities as a Cab Calloway figure—notably in a white tuxedo and top hat. The cinematography replicates the black and white tonalities of Hollywood films of the era. His other costuming includes a white track suit and space suit of silver lame. During the 1980s segment, including a *Soul Train* Line, he sports an Afro and sunglasses with frames in the form of white stars. At the end of the video, Smith returns to the present with the crowd staring at him in astonishment. Somehow his image remains in the past and does not return to the colors of the present. As the video ends, he complains, "I hate being black and white." The joke registers, but so does a subtext, a statement resisting racial categorizing which is not dissimilar to Michael Jackson's colorblind vision wherein one's color doesn't matter.

It is surprising that there hasn't been more commentary on this trend in some of Smith's music videos, but these visualizations contain within them, at one level of signification, a recognition of the meaning of Black success and the price that must be paid. Whatever anxiety there might be about assimilation into the mainstream is quite neatly resolved in these narratives in an effortless and unself-conscious crossing over into a white mainstream. This resolution is contradictory to Smith's other racial messages and problematic in other respects. Yet, it cannot be denied that this transition is a journey that many Black artists have taken, for good or ill, and certainly this describes the trajectory of Smith's career.

"I Make This Look Good"

Speaking in retrospect about the production of *Wild Wild West*, Smith recalls his enthusiasm about the film's art design, its melding of mid-nineteenth-century America and a science fictional mise-en-scène, as well as its costuming. He was eager to conjoin his 1990s sensibility with the need for historical accuracy. He enthused over the period waistcoats and his anachronistic 1869 sunglasses. He was inspired even to comment on the connection between his approach to acting and the costumes that clothe his characters: "'That's the great thing about being an actor—as soon as you get the wardrobe on, you really start to feel the thing'" (Robb 120). For many of his films, an examination of fashion lends additional meaning to his performances, to aspects of his star persona, and to the films themselves.

In *Six Degrees of Separation* (1993), for example, Smith as the young con artist protagonist poses as the son of Sidney Poitier in a campaign of social ascendancy. His project is to gain entry to the American Dream in the form of the Fifth Avenue apartment of the parents of the prep school students he claims to be his classmates. When he succeeds in gaining the trust of the art dealer and his wife, he is invited to spend the evening and is rewarded with the pink shirt of their son. This shirt represents not only Paul's desire for an elevated class and status, but also a transcendence out of his race, a deliverance effected by his adoption by his chosen white father and mother. In this performance, Smith expertly moves the image of the Black male screen image into unaccustomed classed spaces and argues for the legitimacy of more fluid Black identities.

In another scene, an imagined flashback to a speculated narration about Paul "Poitier's" origins, he learns about the habits of the rich people he eventually cons from Trent, a friend of their children. Trent has sexual designs on Paul who uses to advantage the other young man's desire for his body. The deal that they strike is that for each piece of information Trent provides, Paul will remove an article of clothing. As he learns about the gifting habits of the very rich, Paul takes off his sneakers. Trent wants to continue: "I'd like to try for the shirt" (*Six Degrees of Separation* 1:04:53). In both scenes so far under discussion, the shirt becomes a marker of class aspiration, but here the shirt conveys different messages. It is the removal of the shirt and the revelation of the Black male body that is significant. The request for a chance at the acquisition of Paul's shirt is a ploy to gain access to Paul's body in a process of objectification and sexualization. He becomes fetishized in the way the Black male body often is in popular representations. Elsewhere in the film, when he first appears at the Kittredge apartment, he claims to have been stabbed and is bleeding. Flan takes him into the bathroom, has him remove his shirt, and then administers first aid. There is a charged moment between Flan and the shirtless Paul. A gaze passes between Paul and Ouisa as well. This pattern of attention to Paul's body continues in the scene in which Ouisa discovers Paul in flagrante with the hustler he has picked up for the night. Here Paul's body, divest of every garment and the meanings attached to them, is exposed in its entirety.

One of the most invoked scenes in history and film of Black male nakedness is the slave auction block, male slaves stripped for inspection and commercial transaction. The body in this situation is not just objectified but commodified as well. The Trent/Paul scene replicates this scenario. The difference is that it is the young Black man who is himself selling his body and stands to profit from the exchange. This puts a twist on the historical dynamic. Yet, what remains incontrovertible is that, in terms of sexualization and the body as capital, Paul (and by extension, Smith) is racialized. The character whose project is social transcendency is brought to earth in these moments as is Smith. For an actor whose screen persona is predicated upon racial transcendence, these instances of clear subsumption under racial stereotype are rare, but not so rare as one would suspect.

A similar class message is carried in the scene in which Dr. Fine recalls his encounter with Paul who has been successful, as with the Kittredge's, in gaining entry to his home and enjoying his hospitality. When Dr. Fine calls the police after discovering Paul's duplicity, for all his outrage, he cannot accuse him of anything, neither theft nor breaking and entering. He has willingly given Paul the keys to his brownstone. Paul admits that the only thing he has taken is a bit of brandy, and he has taken the liberty of listening to classical music on the stereo. The other key element of Paul's social climbing ruse is his donning of the doctor's silk robe during his stolen afternoon. The silk dressing gown or smoking jacket is a signifier of male social status, luxury, and leisure and has a history of such associations going back to the seventeenth century (Schneider).

Wearing that classic robe of burgundy silk jacquard with the black shawl collar and waistband, Paul summons up other associations. In Anthony Minghella's film adaptation of Patricia Highsmith's *The Talented Mr. Ripley*, one of recent cinema's most notable examples of a fashion film, there is a scene in which Tom Ripley (Matt Damon), who has killed and assumed the identity of the heir Dickie Greenleaf, is enjoying the material spoils of his crimes. He is ensconced in an over-decorated rented Roman apartment, celebrating a solitary Christmas. Seated on the floor before a fire, he is dressed in red print silk pajamas and an olive-green paisley silk dressing gown. The costuming and mise-en-scène echoes a scene in Lamont Johnson's 1980 television film version of Willa Cather's classic 1912 short story, "Paul's Case." Eric Roberts as Paul has absconded with the bank roll of his Pittsburgh employer and has escaped to New York where he books a suite at the Waldorf and orders a wardrobe from Brooks Brothers, including a burgundy foulard dressing gown. Paul Poitier's donning of the gentleman's robe puts him in intertextual relation to these two other dreamer imposters, and this relation gives him an elevation. It assures him a place as an example of a fictional archetype, the con-artist or trickster that resides at the heart of the American literary imagination. Paul Poitier in that elegant dressing gown is also elevated and distanced from the racial stereotype invoked by Dr. Fine when he exclaims: "This fucking Black kid crack addict" (*Six Degrees of Separation* 0:53:37). Paul resists this kind of reduction; he negates and surpasses it. Similarly, Will Smith's own distancing act in his choice of roles and performances and in his deliberate and careful construction of his screen persona and public star image, separates him from prevailing cultural and cinematic constructions of Black men.[2] In the instance of *Six Degrees of Separation* and others his putative transcendence is effected by a crucial choice of costume.

About Smith's various identities, Sarah Gilligan writes the following: "Central to Smith's cross-media representation is the blurring of his on-screen characters, star-celebrity persona, and the illusion of an off-screen persona that is grounded in an allegedly 'authentic' and possibly stereotypical Black identity" (179). I would argue that these identities are not blurred, but distinct. For instance, Smith's appearances on the red carpet create a tension between the public and private aspects that comprise his star persona. According to D. Paul Marshall in *Celebrity and Power*, in the stages of the development of a film star there is a necessary construction of a public celebrity persona to offset the aggregate image comprised of his/her screen performances. For Smith as a screen star, there is a distinct opposition between these two identities. If his film performances deemphasize his Blackness, off-screen his identity is one of exemplary Black masculinity—as a paterfamilias and upstanding member of the Hollywood and the Hollywood Black establishment. His marriage to Jada Pinkett Smith is a revered institution within the Black celebrity community. His support of other Black artists and causes is above reproach. His conventional Blackness is nowhere more apparent than in his performances on the red carpet, one of the significant elements of the mise-en-scène of the public star persona.

C.S. King observes that most images of Smith, whether in movie posters or magazine covers or social media, feature him wearing a suit. The suit has a multiplicity of meanings, and particularly vexed ones for Black men. King notes that "this recurrent wardrobe choice matters because of its particularly racialized and classed history. Typically, the business suit metonymically signifies professional success, hard work, and responsibility. The iterations of the suit seen in these images of Smith—dark, simple, and conservative—connote centuries-old bourgeois norms of respectability" ("Hitching" 94). In other words, these business suits signify conformity, contain Smith's Blackness, and render him safe for mainstream viewers. David Magill writes: "Smith presents a fantasy of Black identity that ambivalently challenges the colour line through a liberally racial vision of Black masculinity that calms white cultural fears" (127). However, this is not always the case. Witness the spectacles of Smith on the red carpet. On these occasions, he chooses to inflect men's formal wear with swagger and flair, a posture often taken by minority male subgroups in response to or defiance of male norms in fashion history. Despite the tendency of his image to uphold these norms, Smith's wearing of the suit in a particularly raced way in these celebrity events connects him deeply to the sartorial practice of Black dandyism. The Black dandy is "a gentleman who intentionally appropriates classical European fashion, but with an African diasporan aesthetic and sensibility" (Lewis 8). These are Black men around the world who dress in colorful tailored suits with all the accouterments, raising the level of male display to the highest level. Yet, behind the extreme style is an ideology:

> Dandyism is much more than dressing up and following the politics of respectability. Dandy Lions craft an identity for themselves outside of so-called norms rather than conforming to mainstream, white values. The Black dandy is a social engineer who employs sartorial instruments to articulate his own masculinity and, in essence, his own humanity. By appropriating the outward and highly specific signs of class, culture, wealth, education, and status, the dandy cleverly manipulates clothing and attitude to make his own statement [Lewis 13].

Lewis continues her definition of this Black male fashion philosophy:

> The Black dandy embodies the idea that when a body is encased within a "suit," the masked or "suited" individual exceeds ordinary human expectations. The dandy is deliberate in his use of the Black body to express not only his individualism, but also his relationship to his own community and to mainstream culture, challenging negative perceptions of what he is capable of doing or being. His bright, colorful style and positivity resist stereotypes, categories, boxes, or ideas that society has about Black men. He confronts, amazes, and confounds… [Lewis 12].

This is exactly what Smith does in his public appearances as well as in his career. Gilligan refers to his "endless red carpet 'stylin out' performances of his slick and stylish, yet ever playful and self-reverential Black dandy persona" (177). His choice of bespoke suits and tuxedos by Afro-Anglo designer Ozwald Boateng, known for his provocative cuts and use of color, is telling. In these instances, Smith expresses his Post-Black self, rooted in Blackness, free to question it, but also free to embrace it.

While his self-fashioning may express a contemporary racial and gendered sensibility, Smith nonetheless is in conversation with the past and with an African American and global Black tradition wherein the wearing of the suit becomes a political act. The three-piece suit becomes an iconic form of dress for the Black public intellectual. Witness the sartorial preference of Cornel West. This preference goes back to the turn of the century and the stylistic choices of W.E.B. Du Bois for whom fashion was a statement expressing humanity, manhood, and equality. Smith stands in relation to figures like Du Bois, responding to the call, when, for instance, he appears at the premiere of *Concussion* wearing a plaid Bespoke suit that evokes the style of Du Bois (figs. 3.1 and 3.2).

Transitioning back from Smith's public image to his screen persona, one sees an opposite deployment of the meaning of the suit. In Smith's box office hit *Men in Black,* the narrative trajectory of the film's protagonist, as he taken from his position

Fig. 3.1. W.E.B. Du Bois assumed a posture as a public intellectual dandy in the early twentieth century (Science History Images/Alamy Stock Photo).

Fig. 3.2. Will Smith styles on the red carpet in a plaid bespoke suit at the 2015 New York premiere of *Concussion.* Directed by Peter Landesman (Mediapunch/Shutterstock).

as a cop and transformed into a Black-suited government functionary or Man in Black, echoes Smith's transformation from a rap artist into a Hollywood superstar. The film's arc echoes Smith's assimilative trajectories in his video work. Once again the meanings of the suit as a sign of masculinity and power and Black men's relationship to those meanings offer a rich opportunity for interpretation, this time of *Men in Black*. At the beginning of the film, there is a crucial sequence that tracks Smith's character's initiation into the MIB, and it is a remarkable example of "a process of containment through costume" (Wong). King details the costuming transformation of Smith's character:

> James Darrel Edwards III [Smith], enters MIB headquarters to begin his career as a secret agent. Upon arrival, Edwards wears a colorful striped T-shirt and track pants, which ... connote a street sensibility [and cultural Blackness]. The MIB director, a white man, forcefully instructs him to put on "the last suit you'll ever wear." As the recruit officially enters the MIB program, the director, speaking in voice-of-God narration, proclaims the erasure of Edwards's former identity and his complete transformation into Agent J, explaining, "You will conform to the identity we give you" ["Hitching" 95].

The assimilationist journey is reenacted here: the price of admission to the mainstream is the total erasure of identity, but at the same time notice Smith's subversive insistence on style within conformity, a marker of irrepressible Blackness when he says to his partner, Agent K, as he puts on a pair of wayfarer sunglasses, "'You know what the difference is between you and me? I make this [suit] look good'" (King, "Hitching" 95). At this moment, Smith conveys two messages simultaneously, the subjugation of Blackness to white hegemonic patriarchal power and the assertion of Black male cool.

One of the most powerful images of Smith as a signifier of cool is to be found in his 1995 film *Bad Boys*, co-starring Martin Lawrence and directed by Michael Bay. As one of a Black detective team, toward the end of the film, he is shot running with a gun toward the camera. The moment is iconic. Smith is captured torso bare, with his dark-colored shirt flying behind him (fig. 3.3). He is an object of desire in motion. Gilligan refers to "the now familiar 'Will Smith running' shot ... [that] is ... commodified" (Gilligan 177). After viewing the rushes of this scene, director Bay said to Smith: "'Will, come look at this! This is what a movie star looks like!'" (Iannucci 41).

In concert with the meanings of Smith's white costuming in his music videos, the fashion discourse of the black clothing in his films also signifies. Gilligan cites as meaningful the implications of the strategically placed branded articles of clothing in Smith's films: the Belstaff Trailmaster leather jacket in *I Am Legend*, the Converse Chuck Taylor All Star shoes in *I, Robot*, and the Ray-Ban sunglasses in *Men in Black* (Gilligan 185–86). The black suit in *Men in Black* might also be mentioned, specially tailored for Smith by costume designer John David Ridge with custom made shirts by Anto of Beverly Hills. Gilligan argues that these iconic fashion pieces facilitate Smith's embodiment of his characters' world-saving heroism, and, as such, allows for him to attain a status that transcends race. Through the language of fashion, Smith speaks to his legions of audiences not so differently, bypassing the considerations and complications of race. He is speaking the universal language of consumption. Gilligan concludes: "Black style thus functions as a commodity—as the antidote

Fig. 3.3. In the look that made him a star, Will Smith headlines as Mike Lowery with Martin Lawrence as Marcus Burnett in *Bad Boys* (1995). Directed by Michael Bay (Columbia Pictures/ Photofest).

to racism" (187). The commercial appeal of Black style supersedes other aspects of Smith's star identity. His Blackness is rendered as an attitude, a wardrobe choice, a purchase, or even as an accessory. Despite exuberant eruptions of Black pride and cool, Smith's fashionable expressions ultimately are coopted by the larger forces of society, culture, and industry and are shaped and reshaped in their interests.

Wearing the Dress

Toward the end of *Wild Wild West*, a film that continually asserts itself in any project of interpreting his screen persona, Smith performs in drag. The scene was contested between producer Jon Peters and director Barry Sonnenfeld as it did not make narrative sense. Sonnenfeld says, "'I never wanted to see Will in drag.... I thought it was prurient, unnecessary, silly and in there only because Peters loved it and refused to let us take it out'" (Jones). The scene stops the movie cold, derailing the story, and the film never recovers from Will Smith's drag moment (Weiss). The film, described as a steampunk science-fiction Western, is an adaptation of the popular 1960s television show headlining Robert Conrad. Smith stars as a Black version of Captain James West who is involved in foiling the plot of a mad scientist, Dr. Loveless to take over the United States after the Civil War. At a meeting between Dr. Loveless (Kenneth Branagh) and President Ulysses S. Grant (Kevin Kline) over an agreement to surrender the United States to Loveless and a contingent of foreign governments, Smith appears disguised as a belly dancer named Ebonia, a name evocative of stereotypes of Black women. His appearance has a comic frisson because earlier in the film West protests that he doesn't wear costumes, even if necessitated by his undercover missions, thus asserting his heterosexual masculinity. Here, he wears a veil of gold spangles hiding the lower part of his face, a swath of gold-green gauze, bare torso, and a conical bra with golden tassels at the nipples (which turn out to be weaponized). Breaking the illusion, he comically quips sotto voce to his partner Artemus Gordon (also played by Kevin Kline) that the brassiere is killing him and the garter belt is "riding up my ass" (*Wild Wild West* 1:22:37–1:22:50). Ebonia dances and flirts with Loveless, not through dialogue but through a pantomime including trilling, barks, and chirps. His purpose is to distract Loveless while his fellow agent Gordon and collaborator Rita Escobar (Salma Hayek) stage the president's escape, which is successful. Smith's scene as Ebonia continues the running competition between West and Gordon as to whose female impersonation is more convincing. Smith gives his best effort in the scene, and it does not quite garner the expected laughs. However, as with many aspects of this film, more is at stake. It raises the issue currently debated about Black male actors and cross-dressing. There is a different line of signification set in motion when Black men dress as women, particularly within the context of Hollywood cultural and ideological practices. Both Kevin Kline and Will Smith cross-dress in *Wild, Wild West*, but there are special meanings that accrue to Smith in drag. He also appears in drag in *Aladdin* which he references in an Instagram post of himself in costume and makeup. He was reminding his fans that *Aladdin* was still playing in theaters. The moment is fleeting, but the reporting about the Instagram photo generated a stream of comments ranging from a critique of his succumbing to the emasculating imperatives of white Hollywood to praise for liberating himself from psychological restraints and exercising his full freedom of expression (Bennett).

There seems to be an unwritten rule in Hollywood that Black actors must cross-dress at some point in their careers to gain exposure and access, to wear the dress for success. If this is true, this requirement of drag could be another form of the containment of the threat of Black masculinity. Ronald Jackson explicates this racial logic: Black male actors from Sidney Poitier both backward and forward in film history have experienced onscreen some form of emasculation or neutering to render them safe for mainstream consumption. According to this line of thinking, the willingness on the part of Black actors to do so assures the corporate powers at some level that they present no threat to white male authority. It may also help to reduce the fear, envy, and anxiety within the white male portion of the audience.

White male actors at the top of the star system, such as Tom Cruise, Brad Pitt, Leonardo DiCaprio, and Ben Affleck have not done drag in films and have not been "required" to do so. Others, such as Tom Hanks, Matt Damon, Johnny Depp, George Clooney, and Ryan Gosling have, so there doesn't seem to be a rule. Still, does George Clooney playing a transvestite in *The Harvest* (1993) have the same effect as Jamie Foxx playing Wanda Wayne on *In Living Color*? Why does the spectacle of a Black man in a dress seem to be such an easy vehicle for a laugh? Black men are often stereotyped as threateningly hypersexual and hypermasculine, so the deflation and contrast provided by the dress perhaps makes the comic point more emphatic. Nonetheless, the image still works in terms of a diminishment of Black male power, making him more acceptable by means of a joke. White actors do not contend with these stereotypes nor with the systematic impediments to opportunity that would make them vulnerable to compromise when the main chance, sometimes in the guise of a dress, does arrive. Some might counter this point about a conspiracy involving coercive white male studio power with the fact that in some cases Black actors have written themselves into drag. These actors have producing and creative control and still create cross-dressing characters to portray. Following the logic of the conspiracy argument, they are doing the work of emasculation themselves.

The list of major Black male actors who have cross-dressed in film and television is considerable: Tyler Perry, Eddie Murphy, Martin Lawrence, Wesley Snipes, Jamie Foxx, Marlon and Shawn Wayans, Ving Rhames, Kevin Hart, and Cuba Gooding, Jr., to name a few. One might add Flip Wilson, Redd Foxx, and Richard Pryor from earlier years. The list of Black actors who have not done drag is equally notable: Denzel Washington, Samuel L. Jackson, Morgan Freeman, Danny Glover, Laurence Fishburne, Forrest Whitaker, Don Cheadle, Morris Chestnut, and Lou Gossett. The difference is that the actors in the latter list are mostly dramatic actors, not comic actors or comedians. Another difference is that the actors who have done drag interestingly have achieved the highest levels of success in terms of seven-figure paydays and record-breaking box office. Actors like Denzel Washington and Forrest Whitaker are consummate actors and have earned well deserved accolades and awards. Perry, Murphy, Lawrence, and Smith are or have been associated with large scale commercial success, which would tend to lend some credence to a correlation between wearing the dress and star status.

During an interview with Oprah Winfrey, Post-Black comedian Dave Chappelle brought the issue of Black male cross-dressing to the fore as he narrated an incident on the set of *Blue Streak*, a film he was making with Martin Lawrence. He discovered that for an escape scene, he was asked to put on a dress and fake being a prostitute. He was confused at first because this bit of drag was not in the script; the writers and producers thought it would be hilarious if he were to wear a dress for the scene. He refused: "'I'm not doing that,' he said. 'I don't feel comfortable with it.' The filmmaker persisted, 'But all the great ones have done it'" ("Dave Chappelle Doesn't"). Notice how the white film's director makes a connection between wearing the dress and "all the great ones," as if cross-dressing were a prerequisite for success. Chappelle reflecting on this moment with Oprah said, " 'Every Black actor at some point in their career is asked to put on a dress…. I don't need to wear a dress to be funny. I'm funnier than a dress'" ("Dave Chappelle Will Not Wear a Dress"). The powers of the studio were all brought in to convince him to do the scene, and he was reminded of the time and money the delay was costing. He was steadfast in his refusal. The screenwriters were brought in to rewrite the scene without the cross-dressing. It was just as effective, which proved Chappelle's point.

This incident generated much debate from perspectives that both corroborate and refute the idea of a conspiracy against Black actors, positions summarized and explored by Guy Braxton in *The Los Angeles Times*. One view is that cross-dressing is comic staple, like the pratfall, the spit-take, or the pie in the face. Also, this form of comedy is not limited to race. The great comic actors of the past, such as Keaton, Chaplin, and Milton Berle have resorted to this. Again, white actors at the top of the profession have performed in women's clothing. One can point to Robin Williams in Mrs. Doubtfire or Dustin Hoffman in *Tootsie* or Jack Lemmon and Tony Curtis in *Some Like It Hot*, or William Hurt's Oscar-winning performance in *Kiss of the Spider Woman*. On the other hand, so few Black actors have risen to the highest echelon that the ones who do and have performed in drag and have enjoyed outsize success may seem more numerous than is the reality. Some argue that cross-dressing for a role is a sign of dedication to the art of acting and an opportunity to flex and stretch thespian skills. Others argue that it is a matter of paying dues for greater opportunity and career advancement. Jamie Foxx concurs on this, stating that playing Wanda, the ugliest woman in the world, on *In Living Color* paved the way for his Oscar (Best Actor in 2004 for *Ray*). He reaped the benefits of Hollywood stardom, moving on to a sitcom and film superstardom, but "first, he had to play the buffoon" (McFarland). This accurately describes the arc of his career and that of some others. The conspiracy theory about racist studio executives emasculating and humiliating Black men by maneuvering them into a dress may seem a stretch, but when the phenomenon is pointed out, many are surprised and can see the plausibility of such a pattern.

The short-lived 2017 Showtime comedy *White Famous* took this issue as its controlling theme in its opening episode. It starred *Saturday Night Live* comedian Jay Pharoah (who does a preternatural imitation of Will Smith[3]) as Nick Mooney a young comic new to Hollywood. His goal is "to become 'white famous'—i.e., so famous that his celebrity 'transcends race,' according to his agent Malcolm (Utkarsh Ambudkar)—while holding onto his artistic integrity and not allowing himself to be, in his words, 'emasculated,' as a Black man or as a man, period" (Seitz). He wants to follow in the footsteps of "Will Smith, Eddie Murphy, and … Jamie Foxx [who] are 'white famous,' in that they had reached a level of fame that allowed them to find continued success in a mostly white industry" (Travers).

He has the possibility of a big break when he is called in for an interview with his role model, Jamie Foxx. He is offered a role in a film, but the stumbling block is that he is required to play a woman and wear a dress. He is faced with a dilemma as was Chappelle whose experiences inspired the show. He is uncomfortable with the role and the dress and feels that to do so would compromise his integrity. This is one thing he has promised his father that he would not do. In dialogue from the show, Floyd says: "It's just that thing. Every time there's a funny Black brother in Hollywood, they try to emasculate him. I know this might sound corny, but I don't want to sell out" (Deggans). He also feels as though he is not able to refuse this opportunity. This situation captures the ethical bind so many Black actors face: do they maintain their sense of who they are, or do they sell out to advance their careers. The dress/drag issue becomes emblematic of a larger issue.

When Nick enters Jamie Foxx's trailer for their meeting, Foxx is wearing a red, kilted skirt signaling that he has worn "the dress" and has reaped the benefits. Even more disconcerting is that Foxx while sitting is flashing his penis. Even more telling is the fantasy sequence later in the scene wherein Floyd imagines that he has donned the dress. When he lifts the skirt to inspect himself, he discovers a blank space between his legs. The penis beneath (or not beneath) the skirt is an apt image to capture the racial and gender dynamics behind this issue.

Scholars Jennifer Renee Page and Mia Mask address the subject of Black male actors in drag. Page argues that from the subjective perspective of the actors, Black male cross-dressing is essentially liberating. She analyzes the cross-dressing strategies and outcomes of four Black male stars (Eddie Murphy, Martin Lawrence, Flip Wilson, and Tyler Perry) and contends that cross-dressing allows these actors to tap into their feminine sides and to communicate messages that they cannot as Black men. Instead of emasculation, she sees their transvestitism as subversive and deconstructive of conventional notions of manhood. She references Stephen Greenblatt's concepts of "self-fashioning" and "self-cancellation" to bolster her point. These actors dismantle their male selves (forged by history and trauma) and construct female identities in radical acts of healing, empowerment, and rebirth (6). Their gender transformation is revolutionary because it resists societal stereotypes of Black men as threatening, animalistic, and overly sexual. For Page, Black actors putting on a dress and assuming a female character explodes those ideas and images.

Page offers positive interpretations of the female personas created by these actors. She scores critical points with her analysis of Flip Wilson's Geraldine who promotes personal expression, self-worth, and freedom. He turns what might seem alienating about her and invalidates that first impression: "Wilson seems to empower his audience with the same freedom he found from masquerading? as a female himself" (67). She claims that Eddie Murphy's Rasputia shows the desirability of obese women. Martin Lawrence's Sheneneh is a role model for being a self-sufficient woman even though she is working class and uneducated. Tyler Perry's Madea gives voice to the value of the Black family and "moves the matriarchal figure to the foreground of the community and emphasizes the importance of strong family values" (73). Page's strongest support for her view of this group of actors is the parallel she finds in African tribal culture wherein men dress as women to teach morality and ethics, elevate women, and resolve conflict (35–36). These are objectives achieved by all the actors in question.

By way of counterargument, one might ask what are these Black actors not allowed to say within the context of Hollywood films? In their own identities, can they not say that family is important, faith is crucial, and self-love is essential? Black men's voices may be constrained, but more so than those of women? Are not women also silenced and subject to oppression in ways that are uniquely intersectional? Does a Black man need to put on a dress to be heard? One might even ask if these actors beneath their masks are not still speaking as men. One might also raise the question as to whether these characters are representations of women or caricatures and whether they are truly mouthpieces for women's wisdom or vehicles for easy laughs. Page also asserts that these actors have done what they need to do to survive in the entertainment industry. This again is the point. They are doing what the powers that be demand, and they receive the rewards of the profession. Fortune, influence, and mainstream acceptance is predicated on their denial of a male screen persona and the necessity of their male power being contained.

Mia Mask approaches the issue of Black male actors cross-dressing from the perspective of the discourse surrounding obesity, but still includes commentary on the various implications of those screen impersonations for the actors in question as well as for the culture in general. Mask, unlike Page, does not see the spectacle of Black male actors in drag as empowering for obese Black women and takes a more critical position on the subject: "Occasionally, movies like *Big Momma's House*, *Diary of a Mad Black Woman* and *Norbit* call attention to the social ostracism of heavy people, but they primarily reproduce sexist and misogynistic fat-slapstick humor by positioning the older Black female body as the site of grotesque excess and abjection" (158). She notes the popularity of these films among African American audiences and how they provide opportunity for Black filmmakers. She also worries about the "social price tag" that has been paid for such popularity (159). She laments that cross-dressing comedies dominate the market and delimit the production of other types of films that might offer Black audiences more artistic choices. She goes on to conclude that these films "employ identity categories, deploy dominant ideology and utilize narrative strategies to produce entertainment for African Americans that is ultimately overtly hostile toward the very audience it purports to amuse" (171).

Mask further describes the abjection of the female characters portrayed by Black male actors. She claims: "The characters are literally abject because they are not male or female, neither alive nor fully human but rather latex-laden transgender incarnations of women impersonated by men. The characters are neither subject nor object, but rather something in between: the fictional, transgendered creations of the film's narration and their impersonating actors" (160). Notice the different take on the liminal status of these characters. Page asserts that their state of in-between-ness allows for liberating language for Black women (64). Mask, on the other hand, sees these characters as constructions of these Black male actors for their own purposes. At the same time, both Page and Mask agree that these characters are effectively disruptive of the status quo, as Mask articulates: " Because they are comedic caricatures of women, Momma, Madea, and Rasputia can function as female subjects who—like Kathleen Rowe's 'unruly women'—disobey the dominant patriarchal social order with sassy efficacy because they literally and figuratively exist outside of this matrix as liminal figures" (160).

Ultimately, Mask sees the female personae of these actors as potentially representing a form of feminism:

As politically regressive and sexist as they often are, fat-suit movies also ventriloquize a feminist sensibility. The fat-suited comedian manipulates the tenor of his voice to sound female and to project a woman's worldview. They also deploy the criticality or radicality of unruly, full-figured female subjects who critique the center from the margin; who menace the dominant discourse; who have an alternative sensibility [162].

This statement also supports Page's argument that Wilson, Murphy, Lawrence, and Perry use their female alter-egos to say what they cannot say as Black male characters and actors. Mask would counter this claim by pointing to the problematic nature of their messages and how they are used. Her condemnation of the Black cross-dressing comedy is unambiguous:

Although they rely on the saucy radicality of unruly womanhood, contemporary "fat-suit" movies appropriate the various corporeal signifiers and behavioral markers associated with marginal womanhood … for their own ideological projects. They displace the feminist sensibility implicit in unruly womanhood, replacing that sensibility with the simple sight gags of a man impersonating an unruly woman. In doing so, these films usually excise or displace any existing feminist cultural critique, making a contemptuous spectacle of full-figured Black womanhood [163].

Page sees a wealth of meaningful and uplifting messages in the representations of unruly and/or obese women in these characters created and performed by Black men. The female personas stand for self-worth, self-sufficiency, resilience, folk wisdom, faith, social responsibility, and communal support. Mask offers a sharp critique of the Black male actor cross-dressing enterprise based on its effects on the African American filmgoer as well as its seeming failure to communicate serious progressive ideas in relation to race, gender, body image, and community.

Timothy Lyle goes even further than Mask in his critical assessment of Tyler Perry's drag performances. He questions how well Perry serves his African American female audiences. Lyle examines "the degree to which Perry appropriates drag in a politically liberating or constraining manner" (944). He identifies in Perry "a conflicted dialectic between his activist aspirations and oppressive tendencies [that] emerges quite problematically, particularly in regard to questions of safe feminist spaces, motherhood, female self-sacrificing, female self-definition, and domestic violence" (944). These are the issues that Page deems as beyond the authority of the male voice unless that voice speaks as a woman. Lyle wishes to determine the degree to which Perry, even in his drag persona, carries out a masculinist and patriarchal agenda. He argues that in Perry's universe Black women need to be rescued from untenable situations through the help and advisement of another Black woman (impersonated by a man), or they need to be guided from an unacceptable male partner to one who is acceptable (i.e., not mendacious or abusive), again by a wise older woman (played by a man). The message is that a man of some kind (even if dressed in matriarchal drag) is the answer to Black women's dilemmas. The message of these narratives is to return Black women to the place of oppression from which they started (945). Lyle makes the point that though Perry's films create a safe space for women's concerns to be heard and not silenced, the loudest voice is that of Perry's Madea who commands the mise-en-scène and the other female characters in an act of male domination. Madea's wisdom involves "strategies that promote obedience and dependency rather than independence and female self-sufficiency" (952). This puts into a different light the claim that Black male actors cross-dress in order to say what they cannot say as men because they are still saying what they have always said—that women need to subordinate themselves to men and know their place. Speaking through a female persona is just a more palatable way of enforcing patriarchal control.

Lyle invokes Judith Butler in an interrogation of the efficacy of drag as social and political commentary, which, for Page, is its value. Sometimes drag does not convey irony. According to Butler, "parody by itself is not subversive, and there must be a way to understand what makes certain kinds of parodic repetitions effectively disruptive, truly troubling, and which repetitions become domesticated and re-circulated as instruments of cultural hegemony'" (Butler 184). Lyle argues that Perry's drag performances fail to rise to the level of subversion, which would allow them to be considered feminist in ways that empower women. Instead, they "domesticate" drag and render it a "tool to re-circulate conservative, normative logics and to sustain and even to perpetuate culturally sanctioned ideas about gender and its oppressive consequences for females" (946). Lyle also references Black feminist critics such as Patricia Hill Collins to articulate the failure of Black male actor drag to do the cultural work that has been claimed for it and to rise above the comic reduction of Black women. Collins has bluntly written: "Black male comedians dress up as African American women in order to make fun of them" (Collins 125). Putting on a dress and impersonating an unruly, fat Black woman produces easy laughs and not political subversion or challenge. This conclusion is not just applicable to Perry, but can be distributed over the other Black male actors and their drag personae. The problem goes beyond the matter of how cross-dressing emasculates Black men, but how it has an impact on Black women.

These are the issues that are summoned up and the debates that are set in motion when Will Smith appears as a female belly dancer named Ebonia in a scene in *Wild, Wild West*. His drag performance has a place within the politics, history, and tradition of such performances by Black male actors. What is the significance of such a scene? Does Smith as Ebonia say something that he could not say as a Black man? The scene generates no meanings beyond its motivation within the logic of the film's plot. It says nothing about women, Black women, or their marginal perspective or position in the world. It doesn't empower women in any perceivable way. The scene says nothing about gender issues but asks for a response to Smith's character successfully carrying off his disguise as a woman and the way he uses it to his advantage in his conflict with Loveless. It works for Smith in the same way that the drag strategy works for the other Black actors—it gets the laugh. The scene also summons up the issue of cross-dressing as a practice that when required by the studio powers is interpreted as the emasculation of Black men. In this case, Smith validates that notion. Jon Peters, the film's producer, insisted on this scene. According to Sonnenfeld, "'Jon always wanted a scene with Will Smith in drag'" (Weiss). If there is indeed a requirement of wearing the dress for the sake of advancement, Smith checked that box and kept going, right to the top of the Hollywood firmament.

Men in Shorts

Like the suit, men's underwear is also a fraught fashion subject. Bruce Weber's photographs of Brazilian pole vaulter Tom Hintnaus for Calvin Klein's fall 1982 underwear ad campaign initiated the era of sexual objectification of the male body in popular culture. The substitution of a Black male model in such a visualization changes the meaning, upping the quotient of sexualization. An example is the 2017 Calvin Klein ad campaign featuring Trevante Rhodes from the Oscar winning film *Moonlight*.[4] The spectacle of the Black male body, the perpetual object of the "American ocular imagination" continues to lend itself to interpretation (Alexander 160).

In *Enemy of the State* (1998), directed by Tony Scott, there is a sequence in which Smith's character, lawyer Robert Clayton Dean, gets caught up in a conspiracy plot and is forced to escape his pursuers by climbing out of a hotel window in his boxer shorts. Smith ends up running for his life through Washington traffic in his underwear and a robe (fig.3.4). He has been the victim of surveillance and violation of privacy. His lack of attire underscores his peril and vulnerability, as it would for any unracialized protagonist in an action thriller. Yet, Black male actors in a state of underdress usually carry a different message, one of danger, threat, and sexual power. Even more, the threat carried by their bodies must be diminished if not destroyed.

Compare Smith's benignancy to Tony King's threat in 1975's *Report to the Commissioner*. His character, Thomas "Stick" Henderson, a suspected drug dealer and Black radical, evades the police in a wild chase through mid-town Manhattan, over

Fig. 3.4. Robert Dean (Will Smith) running for his life against Washington, D.C., traffic in *Enemy of the State* (1998). Directed by Tony Scott (Touchstone/Photofest).

rooftops and finally on streets, naked except for a pair of hastily donned boxers (fig. 3.5). The city is immobilized as long as he is running loose. The inexperienced policeman, Bo, played by a young Michael Moriarity, pursues Stick into an elevator in Saks Fifth Avenue where they are trapped in a twenty-four-hour standoff, ending in an ambush by the police force during which Stick is killed in a barrage of bullets. With this denouement, the threat of the uncontrolled Black male and his violence and sex is contained.

In 1991's *Ricochet* Denzel Washington plays Nick Styles, a police officer who rises to political office only to lose everything because of a revenge plot carried out by a psychopath, Earl Blake (John Lithgow) whom Styles had put in jail. At the beginning of the film, there is an extraordinary scene in which Styles convinces Blake, who is holding a woman hostage, that he is unarmed and unthreatening by stripping off his police uniform down to his underwear. Styles says to Blake: "'I'll be your hostage … the only weapon I got left is useless unless you're a pretty girl'" (*Ricochet* 0:12:46). Notice how he equates his penis with a weapon. The next second, he pulls out a gun that was hidden in his shorts and with utmost precision shoots Blake (fig. 3.6). There was indeed a weapon in his shorts. Here the threat posed by the Black man's body and the fear of it was justified. He must pay a price for his desirability and his power, and thus the rest of the film is designed to ruin him.

Fig. 3.5. Stick (Tony King) escapes the police in a chase on New York City streets in *Report to the Commissioner* (1978). Directed by Milton Katselas (United Artists/Photofest).

Ricochet is noteworthy for the way it renders Styles (and Denzel Washington) the receptor of a floating erotic gaze. His image is caught by multiple cameras. His striptease is filmed by a videocam of a bystander and then broadcast over the media. The capturing of his image on video is constant throughout the film, thus reinforcing its theme about the surveillance, containment, and consumption of the Black male body. As Elizabeth Alexander notes, "*Ricochet* is a movie whose camera work asserts that we all want to look at Black men, whether we are gay or straight, Black or white, male or female" (161). Just as Styles is fetishized and glorified, the film's narrative at least his adversary Blake does everything to bring him down: kidnapping him, binding him, shooting him up with drugs, filming him having involuntary sexual intercourse with a prostitute, thus ruining his career as a detective and prosperous bourgeois family life that his success has afforded him. The nadir of Styles's misfortunes comes when Blake convinces him (again through a faked videotape) that his daughters are danger at a children's charity event. Delusional and desperate to save them, he runs through his neighborhood wielding a gun and wearing only boxer shorts and a pink bathrobe. When he arrives at the scene, he attacks what he thinks is the perpetrator who turns out to be the clown hired for the event. He is humiliated by seeming to have had a mental breakdown, by being wrapped in the absurd, feminizing pink robe and by appearing in public in boxer shorts, which were the focal point of his act of heroism in the film's early scene. While the film has constructed Styles as a Black man who lives the American Dream, rising through the system by stint of his hard work and ingenuity, it then feels the need to strip him of his achievement and dignity and, before his climatic redemption, to strip him down to his shorts. Styles's success is experienced as a threat by his white male enemy, reflecting the ambivalence, anxiety, and hostility white men feel about Black male power. Even though Styles does everything right and moves into the mainstream, unlike the drug dealer Stick, they share the same fate; they both fall victim to the forces of society that come together to negate them.

Fig. 3.6. Denzel Washington as Nick Styles strips to his boxer shorts and yields a lethal weapon in *Ricochet* (1991). Directed by Russell Mulcahy (Photo 12/Alamy).

Will Smith's iteration of the Black man in shorts carries fundamentally different messages. Instead of a threat, he becomes a Black male protagonist who happens to be in jeopardy and whose safety is of concern to the viewing audience. As for the Black male body in boxers, it elicits vicarious embarrassment rather than desire. Smith's ability to negotiate complex and contradictory racial significations renders him exceptional—in the history of African American representation, in the annals of Hollywood, and in global film markets. His star persona lends itself to multiple interpretations and can even serve as an indicator of a change in how race, at a certain register, is represented. By briefly tracing the history of this filmic trope of the Black man in boxers, as well as other figurations of fashion and the body discussed earlier, one can see the complex and contradictory relationship between Smith's image and prevailing notions about Black manhood. One can also discern the possibility of a diminishment of the negative associations with the Black male body and a tendency toward its normalization in the post-racial, Post-Black stardom of Will Smith.

FOUR

Hottentot Adonis

Will Smith's function as an icon is to represent Black experience. As a deconstructed text, he conveys contradictory racial messages. As an agent of deconstruction, he interrogates and rewrites existing notions of Black masculinity. This last function deserves closer examination. During the '90s there arose a discourse concerning the visual representation of Black men. This discourse found its crystallization in the controversial 1993 show at the Whitney Museum of Art titled "Black Male." In this show of traditional, conceptual, and avant-garde art, seventy-five Black artists, mostly male, posed questions about the ways Black men are perceived in our society. The most powerful images of the show centered around the two most complicated themes through which the Black male body has been most often represented in modern art: lynching and pornography. Smith's ascendancy is coincident with the rise of this discourse about the Black male body, and his image invites a reading through this lens.

Fear of the Big Black Penis

Although the cool pose masculinity that Smith can inhabit pushes back against white patriarchal hegemony, it is still effectively contained by the overarching narratives of his films. He is still not entirely free of association with the cultural stereotypes and myths about Black men regarding excesses of masculinity: namely, hyper-sexuality, a propensity toward rape (of white women), prodigious sexual performance, and exceptional penis size. The cultural anxiety about the Black male penis and its representation has generated much commentary and debate over the years from many quarters and perspectives. All of which has bearing upon Smith's stardom and his ability to negotiate the pitfall of the perceived threat of Black manhood, synecdochally in the form of the penis.

Stuart Hall cites a prime example of this peculiar cultural obsession and its stereotyping of Black men. In a discussion about how images can be read and their meanings fixed by the discourses of the written word and photography, he asserts that the representation of minorities often incorporates binary oppositional meanings that the subject must carry simultaneously. His test case is a photograph of Linford Christie, the Black British track star, taking his victory lap after breaking the world record for the 100 meters and winning the Gold Medal at the Barcelona

Olympics in 1992. His arms are outstretched, and draped over his left forearm is the Union Jack. The photograph conveys multiple messages about his personal pride, his representation of Black heroism, and the glory he brought to his country. At the same time, it communicates a recognition of his difference: he achieves this greatness despite his Blackness. He becomes a contradiction—he is both Black and British. His triumph is noteworthy because it is not customary to couple Blackness with Britishness which connotes whiteness. Another binary exists within the picture that posits a negative in conjunction with the positive. Instead of highlighting Christie's achievement, certain newspapers focused on a different meaning within the photography—the significance of the bulge of his genitals in his Lycra running shorts. These accounts crystalized a popular preoccupation with Christie's penis, its size and shape. This fixation is founded upon a derogatory construction of Black masculinity that Christie himself acknowledges and rejects:

> "'I felt humiliated…. My first instinct was that it was racist. There we are, stereotyping a Black man. I can take a good joke. But it happened the day after I won the greatest accolade an athlete can win…. I don't want to go through life being known for what I've got in my shorts'" [Hall, "Spectacle" 220].

More recently in a 2016 essay, *New York Times* film critic Wesley Morris contemplated the obverse of the wish to see Black men in terms of their genitals, which is the fear of what might be seen. This translates into a reluctance of films to confront that fear and to show the Black male penis on screen. Morris notes that in contemporary films, male frontal nudity is in vogue, but only for white actors. Hollywood hesitates and resists equal treatment for Black men out of an ongoing cultural ambivalence and guilt about race and sex. This has not always been the case. Hollywood films of the late '60s and '70s were replete with male nudity of all kinds. Morris's claim may not be entirely true. There is a history of Black male frontal nudity in films ranging from shower scenes featuring Mike Warren in *Drive, He Said* (1971) to Thaddeus Rahming embodying Owen Wilson's deepest Black phallic nightmare in the Farrelly Brothers' *Hall Pass* (2011). On HBO's series *The Deuce*, about the denizens of Forty-Second Street during the '70s, the penis both Black and white is on constant, almost casual, display but with special attention paid to Gbenga Akkinnagbe as a pimp turned porn star. Morris goes on to relate his personal favorite among these recent examples of Black male nudity. He writes: "A Black penis, even the idea of one, is still too disturbingly bound up in how America sees—or refuses to see—itself. I enjoyed HBO's summer crime thriller, 'The Night Of,' but it offered some odd food for thought: The most lovingly photographed Black penis I've ever seen on TV belonged to a corpse in the show's morgue" (Morris, "Taboo").

Black male nudity has come up for comment in another HBO show, *Westworld*. Kathryn VanArendonk notes the momentary display of a big Black penis in an episode in which a robot host is being repaired, his unclothed anatomy being examined by a female scientist who makes a joke about his "talent." Some commentators have criticized VanArendonk for reading the scene out of context. There is no dehumanization here because the body in question is that of an android. The point of the scene, some claim, in the larger scheme of the series, is to critique and subvert the system of oppression under which the entertainment fantasy domain of Westworld operates. These considerations still do not explain away the problematic nature of the scene. The robot Bart has been constructed as a sex machine to service the paying clients whose desires are animated by racial and sexual stereotypes. The scene rests upon an assumption of sexual racism. It could have been conceived and written in a manner that would have signaled more unambiguously a critical or ironic intent, but instead it turns on a joke that is given its point by a racist preconception about Black men.

Furthermore, this scene also conveys a resistance to the spectacle of and meaning behind the Black phallus: "Bart has been built as an inert, controllable sex toy, appealing for his size and the resulting implication of power and sexual prowess. And at the same time, he's rendered safe because he's restrained" (VanArendonk). The Black penis has to be contained and rendered unthreatening. In this case, the racialized penis is not that of a dimensional character or a human being, but that of a human facsimile that is supine and deactivated. Notice that Morris's example from *The Night Before* is the member of a dead man in a morgue. It is telling that the Black penis is given such importance in the cultural imaginary, but when it is shown, it is attached to a joke, a robot, or a corpse.

To return to the essay by Wesley Morris, what he affirms is the persistence of the myth of the Black phallus and the need for its containment. He traces this idea from slavery through Abolitionist fantasy fiction to Sidney Poitier and the films of Quentin Tarantino. He also includes examinations of the music videos of Cameo, the recent O.J. Simpson documentary by Ezra Edelman, and Barry Jenkins's film *Moonlight*. The myth may be self-consciously mocked or subtly subverted, but always ultimately reaffirmed. Morris refers to the thoughts of conceptual artist Glenn Ligon: "In the end, what he asserts is that a Black penis is mysterious only to those who don't have one. He's right: Black male sexuality is of interest in American popular culture only when the people experiencing it are white" ("Taboo"). Morris concludes: "For white artists concerned with Black life, the myth matters, and it should: It's a white invention. But attempts to dispel that myth tend to reinforce it" ("Taboo").

David Friedman in his history of the penis details the fascination and dread with which the white Western world regards the Black male penis. From ancient Greece to the Roman Empire to Christian medieval Europe to the European discovery of Africa from the fifteenth through the seventeenth centuries, the size of the Black phallus has been imbued with mythic and malevolent power. According to Frantz Fanon, it is unimportant whether the Black penis is larger. He contends: "What is a fact is that many people, white and Black, believe it is larger. What is also true, and probably more important, is that many of those white people believe that 'larger' Black penis has a major—read: 'dangerous'—cultural meaning" (qtd. in D. Friedman 125). The most important response is fear and a concomitant need to control or destroy it. The control came in the arguments for racial inferiority based on the premise that large genital endowment placed the Black race closer to animality. The destruction came in the form of castration, whether for the purpose of gathering specimens for scientific study in the seventeenth and eighteenth centuries or, later historically, as part of the violent ritual of lynching.

Of course, the fear of the Black penis reaches its apogee in American history. Friedman writes: "According to Frank Shay, author of *Judge Lynch, His First Hundred Years*, more than four thousand Negroes were lynched in the United States between 1882 and 1937. (Shay was not suggesting that the practice of lynching ended in that second year; it most certainly did not.) At many of those illegal executions, death by hanging was the final act of something even more grotesque—a ritual castration. To really kill a Black man, you first had to kill his penis" (128). Friedman continues:

> No such choice was given a Black man accused of raping a white, however. But death was merely the final act in a long and perverse drama. Only by stripping the "beast" of his primal power could that force be transferred to the white man, where it belonged . Eyewitnesses tell us that many lynchers took time to examine the penis of the Black men they were about to kill . Professor Calvin C. Hernton found a weirdly religious aspect to that grim ceremony. "It is a disguised form of worship, a primitive pornographic divination rite," he wrote in *Sex and Racism in America*. " In taking the Black man's genitals, the hooded men in white are amputating that portion of themselves which they secretly consider vile, filthy, and most of all, inadequate.... Through castration, white men hope to acquire the grotesque powers they have assigned to the Black phallus, which they symbolically extol by the act of destroying it" [129].

The apotheosis of the American fear of the Black penis is D.W. Griffith's 1915 film *The Birth of a Nation*. Friedman thus characterizes the movie that established the standard for film technique: "a racist screed that portrayed Blacks as drooling sex fiends obsessed with deflowering white virgins, a threat stopped by horse—riding knights in white hoods, their swords ready to castrate any Black man who dared to insult white womanhood by even thinking about penetrating her with his huge bestial member" (130). One of the highlights of the original version of the film is the rape of a young white woman by a Black man (played by a white actor in Black face) who is subsequently captured by the Klan and whose body is deposited on the porch of the bereaved family, dead and castrated. Friedman observes: "There the castration of Gus showed the white man's power—Griffith would say his obligation—to stop the Black penis" (131). Friedman goes on to narrate how such moments as the Clarence Thomas hearings in 1991 and the Robert Mapplethorpe obscenity trial in 1990 added to the national anxiety over the fear of the Black penis and its need for the cultural containment and emasculation of Black men.

It is against this history that moments from Will Smith's films resonate. Certain scenes, such as the water tower scene in *Wild, Wild West* or the shower scene in *I, Robot* or the *Men in Black* initiation sequence, demonstrate either Smith's agility in circumventing these racial and sexual fears or his inability to overcome the obdurate cultural realities that work against his celebrated transcendence of race. At this juncture it might be useful to take a second look at the initiation scene in *Men in Black* discussed in the previous chapter. Earlier it was suggested that Smith's star text might be read against the discourses about the Black male body that were circulating during the '90s, specifically the 1993 *Black Male* show at the Whitney Museum in New York. The most controversial photographs in this controversial show were those of Robert Mapplethorpe whose obsession with the Black male body elevated that subject, for fifteen minutes, to a privileged position not unlike that held historically by the white female form. His work has subsequently generated a large body of criticism from a multitude of positions. Although his vision is not entirely pornographic, it is thoroughly racist. As such, it provides a useful lens through which to view Smith's negotiation of race and masculinity.

Mapplethorpe's most famous and most commented upon photograph is *Man in Polyester Suit*. Toward the end of *Mapplethorpe*, Ondi Timoner's 2018 biopic, the famous photographer (Matt Smith) sights on a lower Manhattan street a young Black man (McKinley Belcher III) wearing a tight three-piece suit. Mapplethorpe invites him home to take photographs and, in the process, creates his masterwork. According to the historical record, Patricia Morrisroe's 1996 biography, the work was the result of Mapplethorpe's obsession with the Black male penis and his search the perfect specimen. His quest was motivated by aesthetic vision, desire, and racism. The result was more than a photograph; it manages to capture a historical and cultural anxiety about the power of the Black phallus. The subject of the photograph is a Black man wearing a poorly tailored suit of inexpensive fabrication. The frame cuts off his head and his lower legs. What remains are his arms suspended with his hands slightly curled inward, the jacket open, and emerging from the open fly of the trousers is an enormous Black veined, semi-erect, uncircumcised penis. Friedman observes: "Unlike the men in Mapplethorpe's photos of the gay S & M world, the Man in the Polyester Suit isn't doing anything. He is just being. His massive Black penis is simultaneously fascinating and frightening, suggestive of a primitive, even bestial, sexuality that no garment, polyester or cashmere, could possibly contain" (141). The subject does nothing in the photograph, just stand, and even in stillness, he is transfixed in a powerful erotic gaze. Gilligan asserts the following: "the man's sex becomes the sum both of his Blackness and his maleness. Devoid of social, historical, or political context the men in Mapplethorpe's images are constructed as sexual even when they are not 'doing' anything" (181). In Mapplethorpe's vision, the Black man becomes his penis, thus fulfilling the fear of the potency of Black manhood.

Kobena Mercer continues this line of interpretation:

> The use of framing and scale emphasizes the sheer size of the big Black penis revealed through the unzipped trouser fly. As Fanon said, when diagnosing the terrifying figure of 'the Negro' in the fantasies of his white psychiatric patients, 'One is no longer aware of the Negro, but only of a penis: the Negro is eclipsed. He is turned into a penis. He *is* a penis.' By virtue of the purely formal device of scale, Mapplethorpe summons up one of the deepest mythological fears in the supremacist imagination: namely, the belief that all Black men have monstrously large willies. In the phantasmic space of the white male imaginary, the big Black phallus is perceived as a threat not only to hegemonic white masculinity but to Western civilization itself ["Skin" 177].

Again, Friedman offers a cogent summation: "Three hundred years of American phobias and fantasies, a history marked by lynchings, castrations, and paranoid fears of Black phallic superiority, had become a disturbing, unforgettable , and political work of art" (141). Despite the outrage and criticism the photograph has generated from many quarters, it still makes a brilliant subversive statement. It makes literal the fantasies and phobias that circulate in the minds of American society. It is just such an image entertained by white men in power that prevents Black men from opportunity and advantage. Mapplethorpe's photograph makes literal these racist notions and forces society to confront them and themselves. It should be no surprise that his work was condemned as obscene by members of Congress and put on trial.

On the other hand, the most eloquent and impassioned rebuke of Mapplethorpe comes from Black gay men themselves. Essex Hemphill argues that "Mapplethorpe's eye pays special attention to the penis at the expense of showing us the subject's face, and thus, a whole person. The penis becomes the identity of the Black male, which is the classic racist stereotype recreated and presented as Art in the context of a gay vision" (38). Kobena Mercer has written often about Mapplethorpe as well. He refutes the idea of an inherent critique of the objectivization of the Black male: "Mapplethorpe's carefully constructed images are interesting, then, because, by reiterating the terms of colonial fantasy, the pictures service the expectations of white desire…" (Mercer and Julian 194). The power of the dominant racial ideology is so great that it cannot be overcome even by ironic reinscription.

The *Men in Black* scene under discussion resonates by juxtaposition to Mapplethorpe's photograph, recognizing the anxiety surrounding Black male sexuality. At the end of the assimilation process, Smith Agent J is given his official gun, an extremely small one in comparison to that of his mentor Agent K (fig. 4.1), Smith humorously with expert comic timing and facial expression defuses a Black male stereotype by registering his disbelief. Here is Victor Wong's interpretation:

Fig. 4.1. Agents J (Will Smith) and K (Tommy Lee Jones) in comic conflict over the size of their guns in *Men in Black* (1997). Directed by Barry Sonnenfeld (Columbia Pictures/Photofest).

Long held as an obvious phallic symbol, the guns in *Men in Black* signify the negation of Black sexual threat posed by J. Following [Kobena] Mercer's claim that the big Black penis threatens the whole of civilization itself, the tiny phallus that J is given, in the shape of the "Noisy Cricket" [gun], reassures the audience that he is harmless. The white male reserves for himself an enormous, shiny gun, whilst giving his underwhelmed Black partner a weapon barely large enough to hold. The scene consolidates the power of the white patriarch, whilst emasculating the Black male and thereby relieving the threat posed to the "white male imaginary." … Once again, the danger suggested by the character's (and by extension, Smith's) Blackness is contained and made safe.

And yet, to offer a different reading, the humor in this scene has a special richness because of the racist subtext, and one of Smith's abilities as an icon is to mitigate these prevailing images of Black masculinity. This effect is only momentary and superficial. That he has been made safe also indicates that there is something about him, some threat or wildness, that still needs to be contained. The scene anatomizes how Smith both circumvents this Black male stereotype, but still in the end manages to affirm the oppressive structures and powers that support it.

As Morrisroe's biography states and the film *Mapplethorpe* vividly dramatizes, Milton Moore, the Man in a Polyester Suit, was outraged when he eventually realized the full meaning and implication of his status as Mapplethorpe's muse, or rather, as the object of his racist obsession. He walked out, rejecting Mapplethorpe: "Though he was no student of history, Moore sensed the larger meaning of what had happened to him, maybe better than his educated tutor, Robert Mapplethorpe, ever did. Posing for a series of photographs, rather than live on stage, Moore had become the male version of Saartjie Baartmann—the 'Hottentot Adonis'" (D. Friedman 146). The same could be said of Will Smith, but on a different level and in a different context. Still, the terms remain the same. Even though he is a star of the first magnitude, he is an international spectacle of masculinity that redeems the image of the Black male for heroism, but one that never completely escapes the same reductive gaze trained on his objectified Black body.

At the beginning of *Wild Wild West*, Smith as Captain James West is seen atop a water tower taking a romantic bath with a saloon girl named Belle (Garcelle Gervais). It is 1869, post–Civil war Louisiana, and West, as a secret agent and on his own behalf, is in pursuit of the ex–Confederate General McGrath who is allegedly responsible for the massacre of the African American town of New Liberty, Illinois, during which West's parents perished. The government is after McGrath as well and enlists West in the effort to bring him to justice. In this scene, West has tracked McGrath and his band of ex–Rebels to this town. He spies the henchmen from the tower. As they prepare to depart in their horse-drawn wagon loaded with mysterious boxes, one of the wheels catches on to a leg of the water tower which breaks causing the tower to begin to collapse. West falls out and slides to the ground in a sluice of water only to confront three of the surprised ex–Rebels and a few of the warehouse guards. He is totally naked as he tries to deflate the moment's awkwardness and tension with humor. He calls out to Belle still up in what remains of the tower to throw down his clothes. She tosses his hat, which he takes to cover his private parts. At this point, he engages in fisticuffs with his adversaries. He eventually retrieves all his clothes, defeats the crew of white men, and escapes on the runaway wagon with the contraband boxes. There are two split second moments in this scene that are relevant to the issue of the representation of Black masculinity and Will Smith. As he tumbles from the tower, for a brief subliminal second there is a shot of him from below as he falls, legs apart, revealing his pubes and genitalia. It is a shot that reveals, but in its brevity does not allow for a look. This conforms to the Hollywood practice of evading complete visual disclosure of the phallus, thus preserving its mystery and mythic power. Peter Lehman provides an explicit description: "The penis in our culture either is hidden from sight, or its representation is carefully regulated for specific ideological [reasons].... Silence about and invisibility of the penis contribute to a phallic mystique" (494). That the penis is Black in this case adds to the necessity of this practice, but with additional motivation: both to perpetuate the myth of the Black penis and simultaneously to take back that power through the quickness of the shot.

There is another moment in the scene that registers an anxiety over the spectacle of the Black penis. As Smith rises from the ground where he has landed, there is a shot of him from behind upward through his legs. There is a brief glimpse of his buttocks, but also of the pendulous genitals between his legs. Then, more significantly, during his fight with the ex-Rebels, he engages with one of them, punching with one fist while holding his hat over his crotch with his other hand. During the fight, Smith loses his grasp on the hat which falls to the ground. His adversary looks down at Smith's penis and is momentarily shocked into inaction, which allows Smith to knock him out. Of course, Smith's member is not shown during the fight, and it doesn't need to be. The white man is shown to be incapacitated by the mere sight of this awesome instrument. The moment is played for humor, and the joke registers. Yet, did not this man see Smith's naked form when he first falls from the tower? Why does he gape in awe when Smith drops his hat? In order to make this joke about the big, Black penis the filmmakers had to compromise even the narrative logic of the scene. The intention is clear: to create a humorous moment during the fight scene with the laugh resting upon a cultural preconception about the sexual endowment of Black men. The scene shows no evidence of ironic self-consciousness or subversion of this notion, and Smith, for all his global appeal and transcendence of race, remains fixed within a stereotype.

The fear of Black male sexuality often results in the need to contain or eliminate it in the form of representations of emasculation which become quite literal in the case of Smith's 2004 film *I, Robot*. In his appearances on American talk shows as part of the publicity for the film's opening, Smith regaled the show hosts with one story about the film's production. He jokes about the shower scene that begins the film and how he originally was supposed to appear frontally nude (fig. 4.2). However, for various reasons, his penis had to be digitally erased from the American version of the film. European audiences would see the scene uncensored. Smith explains in an interview: "The scene in this movie was full frontal nudity, but they had to digitally remove it. It was the most expensive CGI shot in the movie. I hope the nude scene appears in other countries" ("Will Smith Censored"). Here he makes a joke about the cost and effort made to remove his penis from the scene, himself making light of the cultural assumption about the size of Black male genital endowment.[1]

Fig. 4.2. Will Smith as Del Spooner in the shower scene originally conceived with a full frontal shot in *I, Robot* (2004). Directed by Alex Proyas (https://cdni.fancaps.net/file/fancaps-movie-images/2536010.jpg.).

The scene itself lends itself to several interrogations. Smith claims that the scene is essential to the establishment of Del Spooner, his character in the film:

> The scene sees Smith's character, Del Spooner, taking a shower, which begins the paranoia. "The shower door [is] open," he said. "[There's] no shower curtain, with the gun hanging over the thing, and they said he would never be able to wash his hair, because he wouldn't close his eyes in the shower. So it's, you know, those kinds of things. But you probably have to have a degree in psychology to take all of that out of it. But it gives it a certain level of reality when … you know that that much thought went into it, and even if you don't, it's just kind of a cool naked guy [laughs]" ["Will Smith Talks"].

The nudity supports Spooner's sense of vulnerability which he has developed because of a past trauma involving survivor's guilt. The revelation of the totality of Spooner's naked body would enhance his frailty and paranoia.

Lorrie Palmer sees another narrative at play in the scene: a conversation between Smith's body and that of Paul Robeson. Palmer discovers the identicality in the poses of Smith in the shower and nude photographs taken of Robeson by Nickolas Murray in 1926. Both are seen from the side with the left leg positioned forward, buttocks exposed but genitals cleverly hidden. She reads Robeson's body as an example of the traditional representation of the male body as a classical ideal form and not as an object of an erotic gaze. This visual status is realized at a cost: the erasure of Robeson's face and genitals from the photograph because of the configuration of his pose. The image renders him, according to Richard Dyer, "heroic and noble; his stillness and 'passive beauty' dispelled any hint of eroticism" (Dyer qtd. In Palmer 32). His facelessness dehumanizes him while the pose desexualizes him, rendering his nude Black male body "safe." Palmer continues: "The discourse that Dyer reports focuses on the racially motivated, desexualizing project of a society that just wanted Robeson to stand still, to be simultaneously visible and invisible" (32). On the other hand, she reads Smith body as having multiple meanings because he is seen in action. Palmer thus characterizes the range of responses to Smith's body: "The reception of Will

Smith's body in the critical and popular discourse indicates a spectrum of responses from (raced and gendered) discomfort to emulation to sexual appreciation" (Palmer 32). This incorporates the ambivalence of adult heterosexual white male critics and audiences over the spectacle of Black male nudity, the adolescent male worship of the ideal body of an action hero superstar, and the sexual appreciation of heterosexual Black female viewers (Palmer 32). According to Palmer, many viewers of the film have commented on the transformation of Smith's body for *I, Robot* into a remarkable specimen of muscular development and articulation. One message that it sends focuses on the hard work and effort that were expended to achieve these physical effects. This attention deflects the erotic gaze. The hard body masculinity of stars such as Arnold Schwarzenegger, whose career arc in genre films Smith himself takes as an inspiration, resists the passivity necessary for sexual objectification, the overdeveloped muscularity forming a defensive carapace of flesh. This resistance to erotic objection is at work in the star of image of Bruce Lee, star of Hong Kong kung fu action films, whose masculine beauty is never still long enough for aesthetic much less erotic contemplation. Another reason for the failure of his sexual appeal to register is the inability of mainstream audiences to see Asian men as objects of desire. The stereotypes that abound do not include the possibility of leading man status or the attribution of a compelling sexuality.

While Smith may display the defensive musculature of the action hero, his Blackness does not allow him to escape the erotic gaze. The stereotypes about Black male sexuality are too deep and powerful for him completely to evade it. He is reduced "to a stereotyped image of Blackness in which (to borrow from Mercer) 'the penis is the forbidden totem of colonial fantasy'" (Mercer qtd. in Gilligan 181). Gilligan's description of this scene makes clear the inevitable objectifying impact of this scene:

> Daylight pours in through the window, creating white highlights on Smith's Black flesh as he lifts his weights and then stands in the shower. The water cascades over his head and body, the droplets glistening as they run down his torso. The spectator is encouraged to survey the hyper-muscular body as the camera fragments Smith's body and the light glistens off his flesh as he is offered up for the voyeuristic gaze, as an idealized image of (black) male beauty [Gilligan 179].

The responses to his shower scene, white male unease and Black female admiration, are both predicated upon ideas about Black male sexuality. The former response, however, is the one that is determinant within the filmmaking hierarchy which shapes its product toward the sensibilities of the male audience. In other words, the spectacle of Smith's penis is too threatening to white male power and must be contained and even erased.

There is yet one detail in the scene that further complicates its interpretation. As the camera tracks in on Smith standing in the shower, it also catches within the frame Spooner's gun in its holster hanging from the shower rod. While Smith's penis may have been digitally removed, the phallic symbol of the gun remains. Gilligan offers the following analysis:

> …in *I, Robot* when he showers the sexuality and potential vulnerability of the naked male body is disavowed through the phallic presence of his gun in its holster, his penis remaining out of

sight. The dichotomy of strategies of showing/not showing Smith's fragmented body is central to both maximizing his crossover appeal and rendering his representation "safe" for audiences through maintaining the myth of the potent (black) phallus [180].

The (symbolic) presence of the penis is necessary for Smith's DGI emasculation to have full meaning. The scene has it both ways. It renders the threat of the Black penis both invisible and visible at the same time. This seeming contradiction is paradigmatic of Smith's star text, his ability to signify multiple discourses simultaneously and reap the benefit of the gaps and ambivalences.

Another scene in *I, Robot* contributes to the pattern of the containment of Black male sexuality in Smith's performances. At one point, Spooner is visited in his apartment by Dr. Susan Colvin (played by Bridget Moynahan), the scientist with whom he is investigating the death of the founder of USR (United States Robots). While he is dressing, shirtless, his torso marked with surgical scars, she notices his body and realizes that he is part cyborg. She asks to inspect his body, identifying the cybernetic parts—hand, wrist, humerus, shoulder, left arm, two ribs, a lung. As she kneels before him and the camera shoots from a high angle capturing his pants loosely hanging around his hips, exposing his briefs and as well the hair trailing from his navel downward. One might expect there to be a joking comment about the bionic status of another part of his body, but the film does not pursue this suggestion. Still, the moment registers, and Smith's body is effectively sexualized.

Supporting this reading of the scene is the characters' alacrity in exiting his bedroom, both feeling some tension about the situation. There is a sexual frisson between them that never fully materializes. Throughout the film the logic of the generic narrative requires a romantic coupling, but it doesn't happen, not because of the characters' reluctance, but because of the calculation of the filmmakers who were reluctant to take a risk with an interracial romance. Too much was at stake in terms of the probability of large box office returns. An interracial romance might offend certain audiences and thus suppress the film's ability to reach the largest and widest markets. Smith is explicit about this in an interview:

> "There was never a pass on the script. We talked about it, but in science fiction, it's like 'ugh!' Science fiction fans don't kind of take to that, and then there's the issue of the black guy and the white girl, in American movies, and it just seemed like it could have taken all of the focus, kind of like how the nude scenes just kind of take over (laughs). We were trying not to have something that would take away that focus" [Gilchrist].

The focus may be on the integrity of the science fiction narrative, but romantic plots are not generally detrimental to science fiction films, nor are nude scenes. What is prohibitive here is race, not only in the prospect of Black male nudity but of an interracial relationship. The question remains: for whom are these representations problematic, for audiences or for the film industry? In any case, the result onscreen is the erasure of Smith's penis and the suppression of the romance plot, which are part of a larger emasculation of Black men in film as often they are depicted in mainstream theatrical features as having no sex lives or intimate partnerships. Smith's Del Spooner is constituted as an asexual action hero. If an actor such as Ben Affleck had been cast, the romance would have been central.

Palmer lays the blame on these representational practices on the Hollywood power structure and on Smith himself. She poses the following question: "Was it corporate conservatism that propelled the predominately white and male Fox execs to make the decision, apparently based on fears of audience sensitivity (or of getting slapped with a profit-inhibiting R rating), to spend a large sum of money to erase the most visual signifier of Smith's sexuality?" (34). She even goes on to implicate Smith: "In the case of Will Smith's star text, the elision of frank sexuality may be a function of the actor's more mainstream ambitions and his desired audience demographic" (35).

Whatever the motivation of the removal of Smith's penis from the film, the erasure still carries significant meaning in terms of Smith's star identity. As has been stated before, on one level this digital concealment preserves the patriarchal mystery of the phallus. However, such an operation on the image of a Black man has different implications. It serves to perpetuate cultural stereotypes about Black male sexual endowment while it also acts as a control upon its feared power. With his penis removed from the scene, Smith is rendered "safe" for mainstream consumption. What ultimately compounds the problematic nature of this ideological imperative is Smith's relationship to it. In his commentary about this aspect of the film, he reduces to a joke his participation in a fulfillment of a racial repression and an affirmation of a stereotype. His complicity is evident in his role as one of the authorities behind the film; his company, Overlook Films, is listed as one of the film's producers. In other words, he gives his assent to this excision and participates in his own castration.

Well Hung

The reference to castration necessitates a consideration of lynching as another form of control of Black male sexuality, and there are significant moments within Smith's body of work that directly or indirectly engage lynching as a plot point or a theme.[2] The most commented upon example is the comic lynching scene in *Wild, Wild West* which begs for analysis and context. It has been asserted earlier that the imagery of lynching provides one of the ways through which the Black male body is visualized in art and popular culture. Here again Robert Mapplethorpe's work offers an example. In the same encounter that produced *Man in Polyester Suit*, Milton Moore was reluctant to pose nude for Mapplethorpe. He asked if it were possible for his face not to appear within the same shots as his genitals. Mapplethorpe obliged by placing a bag over his head. The result is *Hooded Man* which immortalizes Moore's beautifully proportioned physique as well as his macrophallus:

> His hands are clenched in front of his chest, his elbows extend equidistant from his solar plexus, his large penis hangs at the bottom center of the frame, his head is enclosed in a hood. The photo is an aesthetic triumph. It is also probably the second-most controversial image in *Black Book*, making a teasing reference to one of the ugliest periods in American history. Hoods, after all, conjure the unmistakable image of the Ku Klux Klan, the very group that institutionalized lynchings of black men and the ritual castrations that often went along with them [D. Friedman 145].

The irony is that the hood is worn by a representative of its victims and that in this staging Mapplethorpe signals that his erotic quest for the possession of the perfect Black penis is in fact a reiteration of lynching and its attendant rituals.

The case of Claude Neal is often cited as one of the most horrific and emblematic lynchings involving castration on record. After being arrested for the rape and murder of a young white woman in Brewton, Alabama, in 1932, he was seized from the jail by a group of white men who realized they could not hand him over to the uncontrollable mob of thousands who massed seeking retribution and white justice:

> So they killed him themselves, in the woods. Around one A.M., Neal's naked body, attached to a car and dragged along a dirt road, was brought to the Cannidy farm. Lola's father shot three bullets into Neal's head, after which children pushed sharpened sticks into the corpse, and several adults drove cars over it. Others hacked off ears and fingers for souvenirs. At sunrise, what was left of Claude Neal was hanging from a tree in front of the courthouse. An entrepreneur recorded the scene with his camera; he later sold picture postcards for fifty cents each.... Ten days after Neal's death, a white investigator for the NAACP interviewed several of the committee's leaders, who recounted their actions with pride. The last hours of Claude Neal's life, the report said, began like this: They cut off his penis. He was made to eat it. Then they cut off his testicles and made him eat them, too, and say that he liked it [D. Friedman 135].

Two details here are notable. The photographer who documents the atrocity is integral to the killing: "such images document the truth of lynching as trauma and gala" (Marriott 5). Photography validates the acts of violence. The white witnesses want to be seen as present at the moment or at the occasion of the victim's death. They also want the act memorialized. The lynching photographs circulated as illustrations for newspaper accounts and were also meant to be souvenirs. The photographs also served a higher purpose: "as evidence of white supremacy, and as part of a shared communal experience of that identity" (C. Jackson 77).

The other mementos of the Black male victims of lynching were their body parts: ears, fingers, and, most importantly, their penises. It is as if taking possession of the penis as a talisman is a restoration of the white man's virility which has been threatened by the big Black penis. This lethal logic is derived from and given sanction by a specific narrative, one that "features the African American male in the role of mythically endowed rapist, with the white woman as the flower of civilization he intends to violently pluck, and the white male as the heroic interceptor who restores order by thwarting this Black phallic insurgence" (Wiegman 453–454). Wiegman goes on to offer a detailed psychosexual analysis of the white male's need for the castration of the Black man:

> In this regard, the white male creates the image he must castrate, and it is precisely through the mythology of the Black male as rapist that he effectively does this. In the process, the creation of a narrative of Black male sexual excess simultaneously exposes and redirects the fear of castration from the white male to the black male body. And it is in the lynch scene that this transfer moves from the realm of the psychosexual to the material. [Trudier] Harris's descriptive account of the sexual undercurrent of lynching and castration is telling in this regard: "For the white males … there is a symbolic transfer of sexual power at the point of the executions. The black man is stripped of his prowess, but the very act of stripping brings symbolic power to the white man. His actions suggest that, subconsciously, he craves the very thing he is forced to destroy. Yet he destroys it as an indication of the political (sexual) power he has" (47). In

this destruction of the phallic Black beast, the white male reclaims the hypermasculinity that his own mythology of Black sexual excess has denied him, finding in sexual violence the sexual pleasure necessary to uphold both his tenuous masculine and white racial identities [Harris 47; Wiegman 464].

Marriott formulates a more succinct explanation for the white man's projections and anxieties about the threat of Black men and their violent method for resolving them, and he does so by invoking Frantz Fanon: "It is the triumph, and complexity, of Fanon's thinking that he was able to identify the inner life of specular confusion supporting the knot of phobic fantasy. For Fanon, the problem is that white phobic anxiety about Black men takes the form of a fetishistic investment in their sexuality: crudely, being well hung, the Black man must be hung well" (12). He offers a summarizing statement about the meaning of lynching and castration and its impact on representations of Black men and on Black men themselves: "the act of lynching is part of a racial imaginary, a primal scene of racist culture in the southern states of America, in which black men bear the brunt of a hatred which seems, at times, to know no bounds. Burdened by history, black men lived, and perhaps continue to live, in that climate, one permeated by racist fantasy—and the violence to which it so often gives rise" (10).

If this is the gruesome and tragic reality, then how does one understand the lynching scene in Smith's film *Wild Wild West*? This film is one of his least critically successful, but one that is rich for interpreting his star persona in terms of race and masculinity and how these aspects of his screen identity are compromised for the sake of industrial and commercial interests. In the science-fiction Western film, special agents Captain James West (Smith) and U.S. Marshall Gordon Artemus (Kevin Kline) are charged by President Ulysses Grant with stopping a plot to break up the newly formed Union masterminded by ex–Confederate General McGrath (Ted Levine) and mad scientist Dr. Arliss Loveless (Kenneth Branagh).

The two agents break into a masquerade party given by Loveless in his mansion in order to gather intelligence about the plot. During the evening, West mistakes a woman for Gordon in drag (one of his previous disguises). Thinking the Southern Belle is Gordon dressed as a woman, West continues their earlier argument as to whose fake breasts are more realistic. He proceeds to pat her breasts to prove their inferiority. The woman slaps him. This creates a situation in which a Black man has touched a white woman inappropriately. Gordon, in another disguise as a trapper, to get even with West, yells out to the crowd to "Hang him!" Gordon them throws out a rope to the room of outraged racist Southerners. West is captured and taken to a courtyard where the rope is tied to a lamppost. A guest dressed as George Washington prepares West for hanging. At this point, West tries to joke his way out of the situation with the noose placed next to his head (fig. 4.3). He jokes about how drumming is just a part of his African culture and that he was just trying to communicate. He jokes about referring to the crowd as rednecks, which he disavows by claiming that he did not mean to use the term in a negative way. He proposes that "red" has positive meanings: passion, for example. He is at a loss for a positive explanation for the "neck" part of the term. In the original script, he was to claim that some of his best friends are rednecks (Wilson et al. 67). As for slavery, he offers the following positive

Fig. 4.3. Capt. James West (Will Smith) attempts to joke himself out of a lynching in *Wild, Wild West* (1999). Directed by Barry Sonnenfeld (https://cdni.fancaps.net/file/fancaps-movie-images/3793945.jpg).

spin: "That slavery thing, I don't see what the big deal was. Hell, who wouldn't want somebody to run around for them doing chores. Are you going to get your big, fat, lazy ass out of bed every morning and pick your own damn cotton? I don't think so" (*Wild Wild West* 0:40:14–0:40:27). He ends with a marriage proposal as a way of compensating for the physical affront. Given the taboo and illegality of interracial marriage at the time, the crowd is appalled, and the woman faints. Before the noose is put on his neck, Gordon rides onto the scene in a carriage. The wagon on which West has been standing moves. He catches the rope which stretches (another of Gordon's tricks) allowing him to slide to the ground, only to be then catapulted into the carriage with Gordon, and they ride away in safety.

The success of the scene hypothetically rests upon several dubious assumptions: that Will Smith's post-racial body is so removed from historical reality that within the gap between hipness and history is created the space for lynching humor and that his hybrid Blackness and extra-diegetic celebrity transcends racialized victimization. However, within the viewing experience the joke falls flat. This mock lynching scene was mentioned by most of the film's reviewers, and the responses ranged from mild amusement to outrage. Janet Maslin in *The New York Times* barely registers the incongruity of the jokes about slavery and lynching: "'Wild Wild West' trades especially heavily on Smith's considerable appeal. Many barbed references to slavery have been worked into the dialogue, and he delivers them with winning acerbity." For her, Smith's charm overcomes the trivialization of the subject matter. After acknowledging how the film ridiculously filters 1869 through the distorting perspective of the contemporary Hollywood box office juggernaut, Stephanie Zacharek concurs: "Even though the scene is indefensibly silly, Smith has the right cool, stylized mannerisms to make it funny" ("Wild"). Andrew Gumbel of *The Independent* takes exception to the lynching scene and West's joke that slavery wasn't such a big deal: "The sequence doesn't work—first because it isn't funny, but also because it only draws attention to its own tastelessness." Thomas Doherty sharply enumerates the scene's and the film's transgressions:

> Of course, the casting of Will Smith as a secret service agent circa 1869 is certainly audacious but inevitably problematic. Given the spectre of American racism, even a film as proudly dim-witted as W3 can't sidestep the incongruity of a Black man playing a role forbidden him by historical reality. Maybe director Barry Sonnenfeld should have just pretended everyone was color blind. Smith is called on not once but twice to do a bit of Sambo soft shoe. The sequence to really wince at showcases that perennial wellspring of comedic material, the Deep South lynching of a Black man who has touched a white woman. Smith does a mock standup routine before the mob (talk about a tough crowd!) before Artie rescues him from the noose [50].

The problems with the film consist of the irreverent concept and tone of the lynching scene, the offensive casual use of racial insult in the dialogue (West's character being referred to as "half a man," "a monkey's uncle," "boy," or indirectly as a "coon") and the historical inaccuracy of West's character, a Black man as a secret service agent during Reconstruction. The disparity between hipness and historical horror gives the lie to the former. Even the star power of Will Smith cannot redeem this lapse of artistic and ethical responsibility and make this strain of humor work.

Compounding the inaccuracy of the existence of the West character is the fact that there is no historical precedent for a Black man talking and joking his way out of a lynching. Amy Louise Woods in her book *Lynching and Spectacle* describes the various kinds of hangings that were enacted, ranging from the savagely violent lynchings to the equally spectacular public hangings. Often Black men found guilty of serious crimes were hung in public before crowds of thousands just like the victims of vigilante justice. These executions were special events, some staged in public spaces, with refreshments and sideshow entertainments. Many brought picnic baskets. The condemned men were often given new suits to wear to the gallows and even cigars. They were afforded the opportunity to address the crowd, one of the rare occasions when Black men were able to speak to a racially integrated public. Some gave sermons and sang hymns. Despite these privileges, it did not change their situation or alter the reason for these events. The hangings went forward. There is one case of a condemned man performing a comedy routine on the platform—to no avail: "In one execution in Georgetown, Texas, in 1896, the condemned began telling jokes to the crowd, 'caus[ing] the people to laugh'" and the news report of the hanging offered the headline "Hanging of a Humorist" (Woods 36).

The irresponsibility of the lynching scene in *Wild, Wild West* cannot be explained or excused by appeals to post-racialism or Post-Blackness. In recent years, the ironic perspective that Post-Black artists have taken to the Black past and slavery has come under great scrutiny. For instance, Baz Dreisinger muses on this subject in a *New York Times* review of James McBride's novel, *The Good Lord Bird*, about the adventures a fictional cross-dressing mulatto boy experiences with the abolitionist John Brown. He speculates that this approach is "a new way of talking—indeed, joking—about race in America today: it is officially O.K. to be boldly irreverent about not just the sacrosanct but also the catastrophic. Does this mark the triumph of irony, to the point where it has dulled our emotional response to history? Or does it denote progress: we've come so far from historical horrors that we freely jest about them? Either way, it's a risky endeavor; maladroit jokes about slavery aren't just bad, they're hazardous."

This is what happened in the production of *Wild, Wild West*. The filmmakers took a risk with the subject matter in the hope of garnering laughs from the audience but failed to reach the right note to carry it off. Beyond this, the director and star might be questioned as to their intentions with this problematic representation of race and slavery. Smith, cast in a role originated by a white actor, Robert Conrad, on the television show, suggested that race be incorporated into the script in order to acknowledge his Blackness (as if it would not be apparent to the film's audiences). Barry Sonnenfeld, the film's director, decided to go for risky racial dialogue and situations. He felt that "'it's fun for me to be politically incorrect…. I had to do it because life in America is so boring we have to do something to spice it up a bit'" (Bonin). His motivations were not serious ones and lacked a certain degree of sensitivity. His decision to go forward betrays an almost cynical calculation to provoke audiences into nervous laughter. It also reveals that such decisions get made within a creative environment where racist dialogue and situations are not conceived within the framework of critique or subversion but are embraced as provocative or pushing the envelope. Thus, the lynching scene took shape, but Sonnenfeld realized that it was possible to go too far. Therefore, in the lynching scene the noose is positioned near Smith's head but not around his neck. He realized that lynching essentially is not a joking matter: "'There were lynchings, and it's not funny. You're always walking this fine line between comedy and one too many racist jokes. But Will makes it all somehow accessible and okay'" (Bonin). Note that the director relies upon his star's ability to negotiate the pitfalls of difficult racial subject matter with his charm and the indulgence of his multiple constituent audiences. Smith himself takes no position on the issue; he is willing to let audiences decide for themselves as to the appropriateness or offensiveness of jokes about slavery and lynching.[3]

Smith's distancing from the ethical issue involved in the subject matter of *Wild, Wild West* illuminates a larger dimension of his star identity. Just as Smith's image engages and circumvents discourse about the Black male body and its hypersexualization and emasculation in other contexts, his ability to elude the consequences of racialization has implications for his film representation of the Black male body in history. Critics of *Wild, Wild West* note the historical repercussion of Smith's colorblind casting as Captain James West. Gumbel wonders "how on earth a Black man managed to land the job of US marshal in 1869, four years after the end of the Civil War." Doherty concurs: "Given the spectre of American racism, even a film as proudly dimwitted as W3 can't sidestep the incongruity of a Black man playing a role forbidden him by historical reality." The character of Jim West would not exist in history. That Smith inhabits this role and in the kind of narrative framed in *Wild, Wild West* highlights the essential ahistorical nature of his star persona.

This does not mean that there are no attempts to historicize and racialize the Jim West character. The racially barbed exchanges with Dr. Loveless, for instance, serve this purpose; they make him the recipient of racist name calling as reminders that he is Black. There does seem to be a need for this reminder because he is being portrayed by Smith whose racially transcendent image usually deflects such language. There is also an effort to give West a racialized back story. His parents were among the victims of the massacre of New Liberty, Illinois, a free slave town, an atrocity thought to have been perpetrated by General "Bloodbath" McGrath but in reality was committed by the mad scientist Dr. Loveless. West reveals this information about his personal stake in the apprehension of the evildoer during an interview with President Grant early in the film. This detail works only as a plot point and as a convenient explanation for West's motivation in wanting to bring Loveless to justice. It doesn't contribute convincingly to a sense of his identity as a Black man in the middle of the American nineteenth century. It provides a singular narrative link to a Black historical reality, but not a full context. West is not seen with other Black characters other than Belle, the saloon girl, in the early water tower scene, which means that he functions not within a Black community but wholly within the white world of the film's diegesis. This is one of the results of colorblind casting; it raises questions about the existential status of the character, particularly when they are Black, as they are placed into narrative worlds which were not created for them.

Portraying characters who are Black but isolated within their fictional film worlds has been Smith's stock in trade, and this has been a way for him not to directly address issues of race in his films. Smith's screen persona exists in timeframes that are not only free of the past, but escape history by being set in the future, thus his significant work in the genre of science fiction. The mise-en-scène in a Will Smith film is often a fantasy or an alternate world where race does not have an impact or is displaced, symbolically figured, or non-existent. This storytelling strategy is not to insist upon race as an issue in order to avoid alienating the broadest swath of the American audience. Without the specific American racial referent, the strategy also allows his films to reach more international, universal audiences.

Will Smith's ahistoricism is thrown into greater relief by a comparison to Denzel Washington whose star status rivals that of Smith. Washington has had a distinguished career as an actor with two Academy Awards (Best Supporting Actor in 1990 for *Glory* and Best Actor in 2002 for *Training Day*) and a permanent position on Hollywood power lists. Yet, his global reach does not rival Smith's. His overall worldwide box-office draw is $4.2 billion while Smith's is $9.5 billion.[4] The difference in their global box office totals is indicative of the difference in their screen personae. What is distinctive about Washington as a star text is the centrality of race to that identity; for Smith, this is not the case. If Smith's image can signify or not signify race at will, Washington, on the other hand, always carries the racial sign. Whenever he appears on screen, he carries Black history, culture, and heritage on his back in a way that Smith does not, which allows Smith to attain a higher and broader global position. Cynthia Baron offers a succinct description of Washington's representation of race: "Washington's portrayals have highlighted the personhood of his characters, who implicitly draw their talent, strength, and problem-solving strategies from African-American cultural traditions" ("Notes" 168). Elsewhere she writes: "After becoming a crossover star in the 1990s, he retained the approval of African-American audiences 'as a screen persona that reflected ethnic authenticity to that particular ethnic community [and] an offscreen personality who reflected a combination of racial pride and individual integrity'" (*Denzel* 29). Washington's star persona and his public image reflect each other, and both are unambiguously Black.

Washington's emblematic Blackness becomes literal in his performance as Silas Trip in Edward Zwick's 1989 film *Glory*, about the 54th Massachusetts Infantry Regiment, the Union Army's second African American regiment in the American Civil War, commanded by Colonel Robert Gould Shaw. The scene that goes down in film history is the whipping Trip receives for leaving the regiment without permission (fig. 4.4). Washington, as Trip, gazes directly into the camera, defiantly, as he receives multiple lashes. He refuses to cry, but one tear rolls down his cheek. His pride and force of character are manifest—and he does not speak a word. It is a heroic moment for the character and the actor. This performance made Washington an Oscar-winning star and a major signifier of race on screen. One fan offers the following assessment of this scene:

> After another disobeyed order, Broderick orders Washington's character to be flogged either oblivious or uncaring of what that particular punishment would mean. After the punishment was ordered, Washington doesn't say a word, he stands in place without restraint and takes his lashes on his already-scarred back all the while locking eyes with the captain in a silent gaze during which Denzel says more with just his face, than most actors could in a career of acting. The scene ends with one tear escaping from his stoic face, and that one tear turned Washington from a rising star, to one of the most sought after actors for decades to come. It's an unforgettable performance in a movie too few have seen ["My Favorite Scene"].

Fig. 4.4. Denzel Washington as Trip reveals the tree of whipping scars on his back in *Glory* (1990). Directed by Edward Zwick (TriStar/Kobal/Shutterstock).

Chris Nickson adds to the praise of Washington's performance: "'Denzel connected the dots through history, illuminating the fury of the Black race ... [and giving] insight not only into the character, but also a culture'" (qtd. in Baron 34–35). Smith's performances rarely, if ever, have been described in this kind of racially and socially referent language.

In terms of a comparison between Smith and Washington the difference between their star personae becomes clear when they take on roles set in the Civil War. Washington's performance (of an admittedly fictional character) is realized within the context of historical events in which race is a defining factor. Smith's Civil War exists within a purely fictional construct, a fantasy shaped from a once popular television series with him portraying a character originated by a white actor. The world of *Wild Wild West* is one in which Smith's character is essentially an imaginary negro and in which race exists as a joke. Yet, this lack of tethering to the real world, to history, and to Black suffering and struggle is the basis for Smith's stardom. His ahistorical and post-racial star identity sets him apart from Denzel Washington and other Black actors who are his contemporaries (and even his predecessors and successors, for that matter). This quality allows him alone to break through the glass ceiling barrier of global appeal and profitability that has impeded the progress of so many Black actors and actresses. Smith's ability to overcome this barrier by means of his unique negotiation of history and race form the essence of his winning "difference."

If the scene in *Wild, Wild West* focuses on a literal lynching, Smith's 2007 film *Seven Pounds* evokes lynching in subtle and unsettling symbolic terms. The film, written by Grant Nieporte and directed by Gabriele Muccino, the Italian director who worked with Smith on 2006's *The Pursuit of Happyness*, is not one of Smith's most critically successful efforts, but it did make money, approximately $169.7 million globally with a budget of $55 million, so it was profitable ("Seven Pounds—Box Office Mojo"). *Seven Pounds* was released on December 19, 2008, a little more than a month after Barack Obama's election to the presidency. This was a period when Smith was feeling optimistic about America in contrast to the film's dark themes.

The title *Seven Pounds* comes from Shakespeare's *The Merchant of Venice* in which Shylock exacts a literal pound of flesh in payment for a debt. In the film, the protagonist, Ben Thomas (Will Smith) gives the equivalent of a pound of flesh to each of the seven people he has chosen to help. The film begins with a 911 call in which Ben announces his own suicide. The rest of the film reveals the mystery behind his actions. Throughout, his behavior is erratic. He is an IRS agent who interacts with several unrelated people: the manager of a nursing home, a blind man who works as a phone customer service representative, a young woman who has a serious heart disease, and his concerned brother. He is a man on a mission, which becomes clear in the film's denouement. Years earlier, he was involved in a multiple car accident that killed his wife and six other people. He was distracted by his phone for seven seconds. Although he is not legally or criminally held responsible, he lives with an overwhelming sense of guilt. He conceives a plan to atone for the wrong he has committed. He will save the lives of seven worthy people by sacrificing his own. He gives his beach house to an immigrant Hispanic woman to escape a life of domestic abuse. Earlier, he had given his brother a lung transplant. He has also given part of his liver to a woman who works in child services. Upon Ben's suicide, a generous hockey coach receives his kidney while a boy receives bone marrow. Finally, the blind man receives his eyes, and the young woman with whom he developed a relationship receives his heart. The film deals with themes guilt and redemption and has deep religious resonances and the potential power to elicit strong emotional responses from its audiences.

Smith received good notices for his performance, with critics most often citing how the film allowed him to show his acting skill: "Will Smith displays a rather impressive range of emotional speeds here. He can be a tough, merciless IRS man.... He is angry with people sometimes, but he seems angriest of all at himself. It's quite a performance" (Ebert, "Taxman"). The film itself did not fare well with the critics for many reasons. Todd McCarthy in *Variety* provides a fairly representative assessment: "'Seven Pounds' is an endlessly sentimental fable about sacrifice and redemption that aims only at the heart at the expense of the head. Intricately constructed so as to infuriate anyone predominantly guided by rationality and intellect, this reteaming of star Will Smith and director Gabriele Muccino after their surprisingly effective 'The Pursuit of Happyness' is off-putting for its manifest manipulations, as well as its pretentiousness and self-importance." The problems with the film include its inability to rise to the level of the ponderous themes it has taken on, its unsuccessful intellectual ambitions, its unearned emotionalism, and its general unbelievability.

Another result of the film's superficial realism and tenuous hold on its thematic implications is that they invite darker subtextual interpretations. For instance, C.S. King reads the film in terms of a messianic trend in Smith's films as he moves from literally saving the world in science fictions to saving individuals through self-sacrifice. *I Am Legend* also repeats this narrative structure. King cites both Wesley Morris and A.O. Scott in support of this line of interpretation ("Car Crashes" 36n4). She argues that Ben's condition is best described as trauma: the destruction of male identity, a growth through suffering and self-sacrifice, and a restoration of male subjectivity (C. King, "Car Crashes" 13). She concludes that *Seven Pounds* ultimately reinforces male hegemonic privilege by metonymically linking ... suffering with atonement" (13). In her discussion King includes considerations of Ben's exceptionalism, professional success, affluence, and confident male identity, but does not factor race into the equation. From a racial perspective, the plot disturbingly approximates nothing less than a reenactment of a historical lynching scenario involving the dismantling of a Black man's body. Colorblind casting forces this reading. In what other contexts are a Black man's body parts a central focus? With a white actor in this role, this connection to lynching could not be made. With a Black actor, the harvesting of body parts summons up that history. There is nothing emphatically Black about the character of Ben Thomas that the narrative recognizes or dramatizes. Ben Thomas certainly could have been played by a white actor and was conceived for such casting. Although the lead role was not written as Black for a Black actor, Smith was the first actor approached for the project on the strength of the box-office and critical record of his previous film, 2006's *The Pursuit of Happyness* directed by Gabriele Muccino who was also approached and hired to direct *Seven Pounds* (Longwell). The inspiration for the screenplay was a chance conversation Pieporte had with a (presumably white) man he encountered at a country club cocktail party who confessed to an abiding sense of guilt for past actions (S. Nelson). Yet, it is Smith's colorblind casting that, despite the absence of racial markers in the script, causes racial meanings to erupt.

A.O. Scott reviewing *Seven Pounds* in *The New York Times* tends to affirm this racial reading of the film. Through his descriptive language, he suggests that Ben's actions constitute a lynching in reverse. He writes: "the movie is basically an inverted, twisted tale of revenge. Ben Thomas, Mr. Smith's character, is in essence a benevolent vigilante, harassing, stalking, and spying on unsuspecting citizens for their own good, and also to punish himself." Notice how Ben's actions are those of a "vigilante," evoking the mob justice of lynching ritual. The "unsuspecting citizens" are analogous to "unsuspecting" victims. His actions are intended to help his "victims," but instead of their deaths, he is the one who is punished, who dies for them. The result of even this reversed lynching scenario is the dead body of a Black man. Here the Black male body is fragmented, dissected, and dispersed for the greater good, not unlike the disposition of lynching victims in the past. In Smith's film, however, the Black man is not the victim of mob violence; instead, he does it to himself.

At the surface level, *Seven Pounds* is about moral culpability and the possibilities of atonement. Here is an account of the director's explanation of the thematic concerns of the film. He sees the import of the film in general and larger philosophical terms:

> Muccino compares the emotional honesty of "Seven Pounds" to American filmmaking of the '70s, which itself was inspired by the European cinema of prior decades. Everything, he says, boils down to human relationships. "No matter if the hero flies on a spaceship or lives in ancient Egypt or San Francisco, the thing is how this man behaves and carries on with his life, with his own obstacles ... and how he manages to make dreams move forward and look ahead to his own future," he says. "Those elements are universal" [S. Nelson].

The film takes on different meanings from a racial perspective. Why does Ben feel such guilt for an accident? What does it mean for a Black man to harbor such feelings of guilt? In the larger scheme of things, he is more likely to be wronged by the powers that be than the other way around. What does it mean for him to take on the guilt of the world and to sacrifice himself for it? What really does he have to make up for? What offense has he perpetrated against the world? Ben's guilt becomes larger than individual culpability; his guilt becomes metaphorical and distributed over Black men as a group. The assumption of guilt for a Black man has different implications because he is always held guilty, almost categorically, and often for things for which he is not responsible. The assumption of guilt, justified or not, is the motivating factor in racial violence and the punishment for it is death and, in many incidents of lynching, dismemberment.

As described earlier, before a public hanging, Black men would be given the opportunity to address the crowd, and they would confess their guilt and express remorse for what they had done to make peace with their maker and to ask for forgiveness. These sentiments and utterances are echoed in Ben's actions in the film. His motivation for his elaborate plot to is atone for his crime of accidentally taking seven lives. The metaphorical dimension of his task is in the fact that he does nothing to offer reparation to the families and survivors of the accident; instead, he chooses seven people unrelated to the incident. To whom is he offering restitution? It seems that his need for sacrifice is to satisfy himself and his outsized sense of guilt and responsibility (fig. 4.5). There is an excess of guilt here that must be compensation for something entirely else.

Vadim Rizov makes the following observation about the character of Ben Thomas: "he embodies self-loathing and discomfort.... Without smashing too many chairs or screaming too loud, he presents a plausible, nuanced portrait of guilt and self-hatred" (72). Another layer of racial meaning concerns Ben's self-hatred. He blames himself for the accident and feels he has committed an unforgivable crime. However, as a character motivator for a Black man, this self-hatred might seem to have another source, a trauma that goes much deeper. There are many reasons for Black self-hatred, ranging from internalized racism to colorism. In "Why I Hate Being a Black Man," his startling and controversial 2013 article published in *The Guardian*, Orville Lloyd Douglas confesses to his loathing of his looks, his failure to live up to the expectations of correct Black manhood, and his humiliation over being so scorned and disrespected. He describes a persistent sense of self-recrimination: "There is nothing special about being a black male—it is a life of misery and shame" (Douglas). Perhaps this sense of shame and guilt also informs Ben's anguish. The accumulated pressure of living in a white world opens fissures of vulnerability in Black self-esteem and racial identity which allow for self-abnegation and the assent to the power of white supremacy. It can be construed that he has reached a place

Fig. 4.5. Will Smith as Ben Thomas who offers the ultimate atonement for an excess of guilt in *Seven Pounds* (2008). Directed by Gabriele Muccino (Columbia Pictures/Photofest).

where his overwhelming guilt and shame over taking those six (white) lives compels him to feel worthlessness. (His feelings about the death of his Black fiancée are not examined.) As Fanon has written: "'The oppressed will always think the worst of themselves'" (qtd. in Pinkney). In his situation, Ben feels he owes a debt to those white people. His excess of guilt and the overestimation of the value of those white lives ultimately mean a devaluation of his own.

Fanon also describes the phenomenon of "collective guilt" which also may be the burden carried by the character Ben Thomas: "Collective guilt is borne by what is conventionally called the scapegoat. Now the scapegoat for white society—which is based on myths of progress, civilization, liberalism, education, enlightenment, refinement—will be precisely the force that opposes the expansion and the triumph of these myths. This brutal opposing force is supplied by the Negro" (Fanon 170). Ben could be a societal scapegoat for the sacrifice he makes in his attempt to rectify the injustices of the world around him. Again, because the character is performed by a Black actor, his Christ-like attributes are countered by problematic racial implications. The use of the word "sacrifice" to describe the nature of Ben's altruistic actions summons up a trope of Black representation, the Black "heroic death," whereby the Black character in fiction and film (particularly in the action and horror film genres) sacrifices his life for the greater good; in most cases this means the other white characters. Robin Means Coleman provides an apt description: "Black characters saw imagistic recuperation only if they became the symbol of a unilateral, cross-racial devotion. While there was no exchange of kindness coming their way from the Whites they sought to help, Blacks' reward was that they went to their deaths facilitating the continuation of Whiteness" (*Horror* 167). She continues in an account of Blacks in horror films: "a Black character's constancy to Whites was frequently evidenced by a willingness not only to pitch in, but often to die a horrific death on Whites' behalf" (*Horror* 151). These descriptions capture how Ben Thomas functions as "a character who dies in the course of saving Whiteness" (151). Usually this figure is peripheral to the story in observance of generic expectations and is brought in only to diversify the world of the film and to block accusations of racism by functioning as a person of color who is an exemplar of morality and virtue. However, *Seven Pounds* is oddly innovative in making this expendable stereotypical figure the protagonist of the film.

Smith, for the most part, is one of the few Black actors who successfully embody characters who have not been originally conceived as Black. Smith's own brand of Blackness usually disarms the possible negative associations with race. He neutralizes these forces with his charm, likeability, and "safeness." His characters occupy spaces that advance Black male representation and his own absolute stardom. In *Wild Wild West,* his character puts a Black man in a time and space not often occupied by Black men in films—namely, the Western genre. In *Seven Pounds* his character is a young professional Black man who is the heroic moral center of that film's universe. Despite his Blackness, his films still work in the terms originally intended and go on to spectacular success around the world. Yet, his Blackness cannot be totally discounted. It is instructive to see how Smith's stardom and screen persona benefit from juxtaposition against the discourse within visual culture about the Black male body in relation to themes such as art, pornography, and racial violence. Just beneath the surface of his portrayals, there are suggestions and nuances that pull against his touted transcendence of race, and his characters are affected by the social and cultural forces, the racial and racist scripts, and the Black male stereotypes of both the present and the past.

FIVE

A Postlude to a Kiss[1]

This chapter contributes to an examination of the Smith phenomenon by taking another look at his first major film performance in Fred Schepisi's 1993 film *Six Degrees of Separation*. Smith's casting as the hustler who impersonates the son of Sidney Poitier has a rightness; Smith is indeed the inheritor of Poitier's legacy in terms of breaking new ground for Blacks in film.[2] Poitier won visibility and dignity for Black representation in Hollywood film; Smith extends and complicates this legacy as his performances engage racial representation as it intersects with class, gender and sexuality. This complex of issues contained within Smith's screen persona sustains his iconicity, and these valances of significance find their source in his seminal performance as Paul Poitier in *Six Degrees of Separation*.

Based on a series of actual incidents reported in *The New York Times* in 1983, the story of the film and the play details the encounter of a New York power couple with a young Black man who cons and charms his way into their lives for an evening by impersonating the fictional son of Sidney Poitier. Flan and Ouisa Kittredge (Donald Sutherland and Stockard Channing) are a private art dealer and his wife who are entertaining a possible investor in a crucial sale. They are burst in upon by the doorman and a young Black man (Will Smith) who is bleeding from a knife wound to his side. It turns out that the intruder is a Harvard classmate of their children. They administer first aid, and he begins to talk. He persuades them to stay in, and he will prepare a meal. This he does and, in the process, dazzles them with his conversation. He discourses on *The Catcher in the Rye* and the death of the imagination. On top of this, it turns out that his name is "Paul," and he is the son of Sidney Poitier. It is a magical evening, and the deal is sealed. Subsequently, they discover that Paul Poitier is not who he claims to be and that several of their friends have had similar experiences with him. The path of their investigation into the real identity of this strange young man leads them to a friend of their children named Trent (Anthony Michael Hall), a student at M.I.T. He admits to befriending this Paul and sharing his knowledge of their lives with him. This seems to be the answer, but it does not begin to explain what has happened to them and how their lives have been profoundly affected.

Paul also seems to have had an effect on Smith as there are distinct parallels between their narratives. In his ascendant trajectory Smith replicates Paul Poitier's project of attaining celebrity and social status. Indeed, it could be said that Smith learns valuable lessons about how to succeed in the mainstream from the character he portrays, and then surpasses him. Paul insinuates himself into the white and privileged world of the Kittredges through canny and deliberate strategies to overcome the two salient aspects of his identity that might otherwise prove to be barriers: his race and his sexuality. He does so through a process of minimizing his race and sexuality while at the same time subverting conventional notions of those identities. Similarly, Smith's broad-based stardom is predicated on his choice of film characters whose racial identities are non-threatening and whose sexuality is muted or erased, especially given the hyper-sexualized stereotype of Black men in film.

"Mrs. Louisa Kittredge, I am Black"

The film adaptation of John Guare's *Six Degrees of Separation*, particularly in the construction and significance of the character Paul Poitier and as performed by Will Smith, constitutes an important meditation on race in America. Beneath its self-presentation as a satiric comedy of manners lie cogent interrogations of notions about race and class, the history of Blacks in America, the limits of assimilation, the representations of Black gay men, the nature of African American and Hollywood homophobia, and the fluidity of racial identity. Smith performs, resists, and usurps this character in order to effect certain cultural interventions and to further the cause of his public star identity. His performance, in fact, is a part of a larger pattern within the film in which Paul Poitier is marginalized, patronized, and distorted.

One critic, Scott Poulson-Bryant, has observed that *Six Degrees of Separation* is the history of America in two hours (96), and he is right. It is an allegory of the history of Blacks in America. Certain scenes involving Paul and his interactions and confrontations with the white characters in the film register several historical, social and racial points. It is ironic that Paul whose ambivalence about a racial identity should carry so much Black signification. Three scenes are essential to this reading.

After Trent picks up Paul and brings him back to his apartment near M.I.T., there ensues a charged exchange. Paul picks up Trent's address book and is curious about the people in it. His trickster's master plan is not yet fully formulated. Trent, on the other hand, has another agenda: seduction. They come to an agreement. For each piece of information Trent gives Paul, Paul will remove an article of clothing. This bartering of clothes reinscribes the plot of the children's story of Little Black Sambo in which an Indian boy, who is threatened by four voracious tigers, barters his clothes in exchange for his life. Paul exchanges his clothes for the possibility of entrée to a better life. This exchange also constitutes a reenactment of the economic transaction of slavery. A privileged white male bids for the possession of the body of a Black man. One crucial difference, of course, is that the Black man here is actually an agent in the negotiation and stands to gain, in this case the knowledge that will allow him the social mobility he desires. Paul enjoys a certain empowerment in this moment: he acquires the intellectual capital by which to take control of his fate, and he also wields an erotic control over Trent. However, this kind of power can only be virtual. Regardless of the amount of leverage Paul attains, he will always function in a society that has not been constructed for him; he must always play by someone else's rules. It cannot be forgotten that Trent, though sexually marginalized himself, nonetheless still operates from the advantaged position because of his race, gender and class. In truth, Trent's education of Paul, apprising him of the fact that the best gift to give the wealthy is jam in little pots, is essentially an imperialist project. By teaching Paul the details of the lives of his parents and their circle, he is teaching him the codes and values of a supposedly superior civilization. Trent is indoctrinating Paul, annexing or colonizing his mind. Guare makes a joke about this process when he has the South African millionaire joke about the sums of money his government is putting into the education of Blacks in his country. He says, "And we'll know we've succeeded when they kill us" (10). Revolution is the furthest thing from Paul's mind; the end of his education is something perhaps more disturbing: he wants to become his oppressor.[3]

Paul's profoundly culturally conservative desire is not merely to transcend race, but to appropriate whiteness. His agenda confirms Fanon's assertion that one of the results of colonialism is that "the Black man wants to be white" (Fanon 9). The basic motivator of Paul's social agenda throughout is a denial of Blackness, which is also the operating mode of Smith's subsequent post-racial film persona. Notice how in his fictional identity as celebrity son "Paul" characterizes his racial identity:

> "I never knew I was Black in that racist way till I was sixteen and came back here…. Very protected. White servants. After the divorce we moved to Switzerland, my mother, brother and I. I don't feel American. I don't even feel Black. I suppose that's very lucky for me even though Freud says there's no such thing as luck. Just what you make" [*Six* 0:21:57–0:22:18].

Here he expresses his wish for a Black identity not informed with the wounds of history and racial oppression. His desire is for an autonomous identity which in American society is synonymous with whiteness.

Paul's will to whiteness, which is also the measure of his own sense of marginalization, is reflected in his choices of lovers. The three young men with whom he chooses to have sexual encounters are all white, and certainly the choice of object cathexis, on some level, reflects identity. In his preference for young white men, he is expressing a desire to become one with them, or even to become them. At least, he seeks validation from them. It must be taken into account that none of these relationships involves love, but instead some variety or degree of exploitation. This idea of import/export strengthens the point about identity. These men may use Paul for sex, money, or information, but he also uses them in his own way. They support him in his quest—to acquire and affirm his simulation of a white identity. Paul's associations with Rick and the hustler are bound up with his highest sense of self, the peak moments of his self-realization. After the evening's triumph with Geoffrey and the Kittredges, Paul's happiness demands that he celebrate his accomplishment with sex. The sex with the hustler thus validates his successfully performed identity. In the second half of the film during the evening with Rick at the Rainbow Room and in the hansom cab, again Paul's powers of imagination and transformation are given free rein, and it is this young white man from Utah who provides the moment and the audience for Paul's assumption of his complete and essential self.

Sexuality is only one means of social and identity mobility. Another is through family connections. One can gain entry to privilege by sleeping with it, or one may simply be born into it. Paul makes use of both methods. Paul's project with Flan and

Ouisa is to seduce them, not as lovers, but as parents. He sets out to rewrite history and biology to become their son, thus to claim their status, wealth, and cultural legacy. It is significant that he devises the fiction of a famous Black parent to gain access to the desired white parents.[4] This goal is efficiently achieved, if only for an evening. The acquisition of the pink shirt (emblematic of class), the possession of the Kittredge's real son, becomes Paul's inheritance and investiture.

There are many textual references to Paul's assumed status as the Kittredge son. Late in the story the Kittredge's doorman, believing Paul's claims, spits at Flan for having abandoned his "Negro" son (*Six* 1:11:10–1:11:34). Certainly, there is a family resemblance between Flan and Paul in terms of their gifts for the con. Flan's entire profession is based upon dissembling, if not the actual defraudment of his clients. On a different level, Paul does the same. As for Paul's relationship with Ouisa, her maternal feeling for him informs the long telephone conversation she has with him during which she promises an enduring relationship on the condition that Paul surrender to the authorities. It is during this scene that Paul usurps the position of the actual Kittredge children, signally in the moment when Ouisa disconnects her daughter on the other line in order to concentrate on Paul.

Yet, it is Ouisa, for all her sympathy and solicitousness, who also acknowledges the failure of Paul's identity project. At the final dinner party during which she comprehends and defends the true meaning of her encounter with Paul, she pronounces the following truth about Paul's dream: "He wanted to be us. Everything we are in the world, this paltry thing—our life—he wanted it. He stabbed himself to get in here. He envied us. We're not enough to be envied" (*Six* 1:43:33–1:43:37). This speech echoes a passage in James Baldwin's *The Fire Next Time*:

> White Americans find it as difficult as white people elsewhere to divest themselves of the notion that they are in possession of some intrinsic value that Black people need, or want.... Alas, this value can scarcely be corroborated ... there is certainly little enough in the white man's public or private life that one should desire to imitate. White men, at the bottom of their hearts know this [94–5].

The measure of Ouisa's transformation is that she can acknowledge this lack of value. In the end, what Paul aspires to is not worth his effort and imagination. His goal of social and racial transcendence, though genuinely and passionately pursued, remains nothing more than a dream.

The second significant sequence in the film that carries racial and historical signification is that in which "Paul" intrudes upon the Kittredges and subsequently charms the company during that evening (fig. 5.1). The Kittredge's Fifth Avenue apartment carries with it a certain value. What is this overstuffed red apartment but a metaphor for a materialistic, capitalist American society?[5] This is one of the stated intentions of the film's set designer, to capture an '80s moment of New York history in an apartment that serves as a kind of epicenter of American society and culture.[6] Paul's quest for passage through these portals is an enactment of the project of assimilation. The goal of his journey is to gain admittance to this American Dream; he wants to see for himself what it is he has been educated to covet. It is significant that in order to gain entry Paul has to wound himself, the wound being a metaphor for

Fig. 5.1. "Paul Poitier" enchants and disarms the Kittredges, the Upper East Side society couple he cons in *Six Degrees of Separation* (1993). Directed by Fred Schepisi. From left: Stockard Channing, Ian McKellen, Will Smith, and Donald Sutherland (MGM/Photofest).

the psychic violence required for social acceptance.[7] He has to discard his own identity, whatever that may have been given his essential ambiguity, and then assume another identity that he has learned, appropriated, and constructed. His new fictionalized identity, one that has been shaped for this specific audience, is one that decentralizes or deracializes Blackness. In a previously quoted speech, Paul characterizes his non-racist Blackness as luck and then claims that luck is what one creates. Clearly, he has constructed this fictional identity to seize the opportunity that he orchestrates.

In his next speech, Paul discusses how his father, Sidney Poitier, has no real identity because he is an actor: "he has no life—he has no memory—only the scripts producers send him in the mail through his agents. That's his past" (Guare 31). Critic David Roman makes the observation that this concept of role-playing as identity is the essence of the Black American experience, identity as a fulfillment of those social roles that have been conceptualized and authorized by the white power structure (203). Certainly during the course of the evening described in the film, Paul functions in a number of these prescribed social roles that historically have been designated for Black people: he cooks the meal, cleans up afterward, and serves as the entertainment.[8] Even more emblematic of "Paul's" representation of Black progress is the fact that he does get to sit at the table, but (ironically, at his own insistence) he doesn't get to eat.[9]

The third key scene is the one that transpires on the Sunday morning after the art deal is completed. Ouisa's discovery of Paul and the hustler in flagrante is a moment of truth in more ways than one. Of course, a side of Paul is revealed, his secret sexuality. Guare has said in interviews at the time of the original release of the film that he insisted this scene remain in the film because he wanted the Kittredges to face the Other, to have it brought right into their home for a direct confrontation (Milvy). In this way Guare allows not only Paul to be exposed, but also the seemingly blameless couple. Their actions disclose the inauthenticity of limousine liberalism. Notice how this couple will embrace this young Black man only when they find out he is the son of a celebrity. In the act of admitting Paul they are committing a subtle act of racism. He is admitted to their home because his embodiment of a benign intersection of race and class, or its subsidiary, celebrity, confers upon him the status of an honorary white person. How appropriate that their guest that night is from South Africa whose presence underscores this racial dynamic. Notice also that they evict Paul in a veritable act of disenfranchisement not because he is Black, which seems to be acceptable by itself. What they cannot abide is his association with a transgressive sexuality. It is almost as if this doubleness or confluence of difference is too much for them to bear. Their action also interestingly suggests that their homophobia resides in a place much deeper in their liberal hearts than racism.

Autobiographies of Ex-Colored Men

Still, it is race that is the primary barrier Paul must overcome. Paul achieves his goal of assimilation into the mainstream symbolized by his penetration of the Kittredge home through a manipulation of how he is perceived. He circumvents possible resistances to his race by denying it and at the same time transcending it. During his early interactions with Flan and Ouisa, Paul makes a conscious effort to downplay his racial difference. Claiming to be the son of Sidney Poitier, he fabricates stories about his past that serve three functions: to render his fictional identity plausible, to mitigate possible negative responses to his Blackness, and to affirm the couple's self-congratulatory non-racist liberalism. In the stories Paul tells and in his performance for the Kittredges and their guest, there is a reference to a deeper past than his personal one; he actually reproduces African American history in such a way that further ingratiates him to his audience. In cooking the meal and providing the entertainment through his soliloquy about Salinger and the death of the imagination, he references the history of slavery as well as the servant and entertainment roles Black actors occupied in American film history. He intentionally invokes the racist stereotypes of the past. These subservient images of Black people cater to white audiences who may feel comforted and safe with these conventional stereotypes in that they reaffirm their sense of a social hierarchy as well as their own positions of privilege and superiority within it.

Paul's choice of Sidney Poitier as his father also makes a specific appeal to the liberal consciences of his hosts and their guest. Poitier is a symbol of the Civil Rights Movement, and his film career broke racial barriers not only in Hollywood but in the world. By selecting Poitier, Paul moves his image from associations with slavery in the nineteenth century to the great social transformations of the twentieth century. By accepting the son of this iconic actor who embodies racial good will, the Kittredges can feel good about themselves and their sense of their decency and fairness. In describing his fictional childhood as the child of an international celebrity, Paul moves his image from slavery to the civil rights movement and finally into a post-racial position, one which transcends the historical experiences of Black people with racism and oppression. When he says that growing up in Switzerland he never felt Black, he reassures the couple that he will not make an issue of race or confront them about their racial attitudes. Thus, they are free to embrace him.

Paul creates this fictional identity not only for the benefit of his white hosts, but also for himself. He has seduced himself with the idea of being the son of a famous international movie star. (Notice it is the celebrity dimensions of Poitier's fame that attracts Paul as opposed to what Poitier stands for in terms of the advancement of Black people.) That this Paul inhabits a Blackness that is free of history and the experience of racism is meaningful to him and must express a deep wish to be delivered out of his marginality and alterity. This is one of the messages conveyed in Paul's famous death of the imagination speech that is the centerpiece of the evening at the Kittredges. Paul explains to his mesmerized audience: "The imagination has moved out of the realm of being our link, our most personal link, with our inner lives and the world outside that world.... I believe that the imagination is the passport we create to take us into the real world. I believe the imagination is another phrase for what is most uniquely us" (*Six* 0:29:22–0:29:51). Paul believes that essentially we are what we imagine ourselves to be. This speech is his justification for his impersonation; this act expresses his truest self. That invented self is one that is free of all contingency, including the burden of race.

His desire is like that expressed at moments by Du Bois in *Souls of Black Folk* when he discovers his racial difference and wishes to live above the veil of race "in a region of blue sky and wandering shadows" (Du Bois 4). In both Paul and Du Bois, this desire for a free, raceless identity is really a wish for the fully realized self that would be recognized and accepted if society were truly just.

Like Paul Poitier, Will Smith deftly negotiates race to achieve his agenda. Victor Wong in *Alternate Take* offers an analysis of how the terms of Smith's stardom are constituted:

> Smith's Blackness is one that has been made safe for consumption by Hollywood audiences in several ways, including a lessening of conspicuously Black characteristics, and by imposing some level of white authority upon him. There should not, incidentally, be any doubt that it is the creation of Will Smith's image as safe which has directly enabled him to assume his status in the upper echelons of Hollywood's A-list.

Wong isolates one of the primary maneuvers Smith utilizes to mask and contain his Blackness: to choose roles originally intended for white actors. The role of Agent J in *Men in Black* was originally offered to Chris O'Donnell. The role of Robert Dean in *Enemy of the State* was offered to Mel Gibson and Tom Cruise. The original Agent Jim West in the television series *The Wild, Wild West* was played by Robert Conrad. Smith is a beneficiary of colorblind casting, and he pulls off these roles with considerable ease. Film audiences accept him in leading heroic roles usually filled by white actors. It is also remarkable how little racial baggage he carries into these roles. Usually colorblind casting of Black actors in white roles creates repercussions in the film's narrative because of unexpected racial implications and interpretations. The casting of Denzel Washington as Gray Grantham opposite Julia Roberts in 1987's *The Pelican Brief*, a character conceived as white by the author John Grisham, created problems in terms of the depiction of the central love relationship that develops. The anticipated interracial kiss was not included in the film, which resulted in a noticeable narrative gap for the film's audiences. The logic of the plot leads to this moment, and its absence raised more questions perhaps than the actual kiss might have. Interestingly, like Smith's resistance to the male kisses in *Six Degrees of Separation,* Washington himself refused to do the kiss with Roberts. He claimed he did so out of respect to his Black female audience (Ojumu 27).

Billy Dee Williams's performance as Lando Calrissian in *Star Wars: The Empire Strikes Back* is another problematic example of colorblind casting because his racial presence raises questions about his personal life and his relationship with a racial community which the film does not begin to answer. He is the only Black man in the universe of the film. These are issues that would not be so salient were a white actor to play this role.[10] In most of his films, Smith plays a character who, quite often having been conceived as white, inhabits an all-white world. Smith's persona fits easily into these film environments, and his Blackness does not signify. In fact, Smith, more than any other major Black actor, can mask the racial sign. His screen persona can signify race or not signify it at will, depending on the narrative and the situation; this perhaps is his genius. For the most part Smith chooses not to carry the racial sign, and this allows him to not only to function in white screen environments as characters originally conceived for white actors, but also to be accepted by mainstream film audiences. Wong concludes, quoting Paul Harris in *The Observer*: "'Race just did not seem to matter to the parts offered to Smith.' This would almost suggest that Will Smith does not even belong amongst Hollywood representations of Blackness, being outside of them—certainly he himself would seem to encourage such a view."

For the Kittredges and their guest, Paul displays his best self beyond the categories of class, sexuality, and, above all, race. The problem is that this essential Paul, beyond his past and background, beyond his Blackness and gayness, unsettles those easy definitions and offers a glimpse of the possibilities of freedom and wholeness. The figure he strikes becomes a transgressive threat that his audience cannot bear and thus resists. Frank Rich invokes Ralph Ellison on the subject of the self-invented American protagonist: "As one modern master of the theme, Ralph Ellison put it, America's capacity for the protean reflects the country's 'rich diversity and its almost magical fluidity and freedom' and yet also 'illusion which must be challenged, as Menelaus did in seizing Proteus'" (Rich 98). If Paul is such a Proteus, then he must be put in his place. Flan ejects him from the American Dream, and Guare relegates him to the criminal justice system.

Smith shares Paul's desire for racial transcendence. The momentum of his career has been driven by his desire to be the best without considerations of race. His ambition from the start has been to be the biggest star in the world, not the biggest Black star. He has said: "My goal is to be the most famous actor on the face of the earth" (Fleming, "Mr. Smith" 36). Another example of Smith's racial attitude is a statement he made upon the election of Barack Obama as president of the United States which has been discussed at length earlier. He said:

> "when Barack Obama won, it validated a piece of me that I wasn't allowed to say out loud—that America is not a racist nation…. I love that all our excuses have been removed. African-American excuses have been removed. There's no white man trying to keep you down…. I'm African American, and I was able to climb to a certain point in Hollywood. On that journey, I realized people weren't trying to stop me…." [W. Smith].

In other words, he believes that Black people have not been able to succeed because they have been held back by their own sense of racial impediment. Race can no longer obstruct Black progress. Black people should be judged on their achievement, and race should not be a factor. This is how he wants to be assessed. Like Paul, he wants to be taken for his best self, free of contingency and identity politics. Unlike Paul, who realizes this ideal for only a moment, Smith has actually achieved it, and he has been validated in this racial transcendence by Hollywood and audiences around the world. *Newsweek* in an article titled "The $4 Billion Man," quotes a studio executive about Smith: "'He can do anything.' His appeal is so universal that it transcends race" (S. Smith). Mike Sager in *Vibe* magazine supports this idea: "Women and children love him; men identify with him; nobody envies or feels insecure around him. A reflection of a model hero in a colorblind, idealized America" (134). Smith occupies in the real world the post-racial space that for Paul exists only in his imagination.

"Don't be kissing no man"

The post-racial identity that Paul Poitier and Will Smith inhabit is complicated by their performances of sexuality. The intersection of Blackness and homosexuality is located in a space at the center of *Six Degrees of Separation* that is resisted on several levels: those the film's critics, the film's writer, and the filmmakers.

Some critics of the film (and play) have found the introduction of Paul's sexuality to be extraneous, arguing that his Blackness is enough to make the point. This addition of homosexuality compromises his believability as a character, as if the nexus of race and sexuality is a mere theatrical stunt, as if Black gay men do not exist, or should not. Again, this component is integral to Guare's conception of this character and certainly it is consistent with Paul's historical referent. What remains is the resistance to Paul's gay identity, an identity which contributes so much to his complexity and significance.

Though Guare provides his own best defense on this point, he, too, participates in this denial of Paul's sexuality. It is as though Ouisa's recoil is inscribed over his own resistance. When Ouisa encounters this same-sex primal scene with Paul and the hustler, notice it is the body of the hustler that serves as the eruption of chaos. Given the logic of the narrative, Ouisa is transformed by her confrontation with Paul. Her leap of imagination is to see him in his human wholeness, and what better way to dramatize this than for her to encounter his nakedness. Curiously, Guare displaces the exposure onto the naked body of the white male, as if to imply that the revelation of Blackness is too much to be imagined. To support this charge is the way Guare handles the three men who engage Paul sexually: the nameless hustler, the amorous college boy Trent Conway, and Rick, the innocent from Utah. In the second half of the film, Rick is seduced and robbed by Paul in an action that tragically parallels Ouisa's experience. All three are silenced by their intimacy with Paul. (Rick is quite permanently silenced by suicide.) They disappear from the film, as if the experience were a devastation. Guare seems unable to place white men who have sexually encountered the Black male. As David Roman points out in his commentary on John Clum's analysis of Guare in *Acting Gay*, "Black gay sexuality is constructed as duplicitous, aggressive and uncontainable, rendering white men passive, penetrable, and as Clum suggests, 'unmanned'" (201–2). The film ultimately contributes, through reticence and avoidance, to the regressive effect of fetishizing, demonizing and mythologizing the Black gay male and his perceived dangerous sexuality.

The filmmakers also participate in the resistance to Paul in their failure to visualize his sexuality fully and coherently. As Stephen Farber has noted, the internal evidence of the film seems to indicate that Schepisi shied away from the homosexual nature of the screenplay's content and did not insist upon certain fidelities to the letter of Guare's conception because he simply was not sufficiently emotionally invested in that aspect of the story (33). Paul is therefore resisted, and his sexuality is marginalized, even denied, at the directorial level.

This resistance is also compounded at the level of the interpretive artist. During the months following the film's release, there was a minor controversy after it was reported that Smith, the then untried actor cast as Paul, when on set, refused or claimed inability to perform the role as written. This was surprising behavior as he had actively campaigned for the role, seeing it as an opportunity to prove his legitimacy as an actor. In effect, he would not engage in any of the dramatized homosexual activity required. The intersection of race and sexuality that Paul Poitier constitutes created a crisis of masculinity in Smith who chose a public performance of heterosexuality over the queer performance required by the role. Much has been written about Smith's failure to negotiate this aspect of the film, and the repercussions have followed him as it remains an issue that is raised in television interviews and magazine profiles even today. After the release of the film, Smith proclaimed, and still does, his wrong-headedness in dealing with this matter and that now he would have no problem performing the role as written. This stance is disingenuous as now he has nothing to risk with the film released, reviewed and a part of cinematic history, a touchstone film of the '90s. At the time, however, there was much comment concerning Smith's homophobic behavior. Following an article on Smith in *Premiere*, the Letters to the Editor section featured some outraged reactions. The most cogent critique raised the question of what position would Smith, as a Black actor, take if a white actress were to refuse to kiss him? (Yarborough 16)

What has not been often remarked upon is the thoroughness and completeness of Smith's resistance to the necessary representations of Paul's sexuality. The problem is not that he was unable to kiss the actor Anthony Michael Hall on that particular day of shooting; the problem is that from the beginning he had no intention of doing so. The compromised scene is the one in which Paul extorts information from Trent about the people in his address book in exchange for a discarded article of clothing. At one point, instead of continuing with the game, Paul breaks the rules, approaches Trent, and kisses him fully on the mouth. It is neither a romantic nor an erotic kiss, but an act of aggression whereby Paul seals his pact with Trent and asserts his power over him. When performed on stage, it is a powerful dramatic moment. Both James McDaniel and Courtney Vance, who portrayed Paul on stage in New York, did not hesitate in this depiction and gave full value to the scene. In the film the illusion of the kiss is created by an extreme close-up of the back of Smith's head, compensatory editing, and sound effects. The result is a dramatic moment whose power and point are diminished.

Also missing is the other crucial kiss in the second part of the film, one that mirrors the first. During the midnight hansom cab ride, Paul kisses Rick (Eric Thal) in a spontaneous romantic gesture. In the film Smith makes only a vague embracing movement toward Thal. This important scene thus loses its concluding punctuation, and an interesting layer of the story is obscured. Again, as reported by Richard David Story in *New York*, Smith claimed the inability to perform what was required on the day of shooting (43). The third compromised scene is the discovery of Paul and the hustler in bed. Onstage, this scene, in order for it to achieve its full shock and surprise, is performed by the actors in the nude. Even this detail is sabotaged by Smith who in an interview boasts of having avoided this additional requirement of the role (Morrison 4). As can be seen, Smith's approach to the sexual dimension of Paul's character constitutes more of a systematic resistance as opposed to a momentary lack of nerve. An essential part of Paul is not merely marginalized here; it is sabotaged.

In defense of his position, Smith at the time made the argument that as a Black actor whose position is paradigmatic and iconic, he could not afford to risk any damage to his public image because his constituent audience would be unable to make a distinction between him and any role he might inhabit (Story 43). Unlike a white actor, who can play any character without personal ramifications, a Black actor, Smith reasons, is more completely identified with any role he might play, and therefore has a responsibility not to do any social or personal damage. The underlying premise here is that to portray a gay character and to do so with artistic commitment is inherently compromising. Furthermore, in support of his decision as to his interpretation of the role, he has cited the advice of fellow actor Denzel Washington: "'You can act all you want, but don't do any physical scenes.' In other words ... 'don't be kissing no man'" (Chambers 76). Whatever the merit of his argument, the result in the film are moments of technical awkwardness, needless ambiguity and a character who seems even more opaque than perhaps necessary. Here is a case of a fledgling actor who overrode the power and artistic visions of both John Guare and Fred Schepisi and was able to get away with it because he had the backing of the producer and a base of power in a celebrity which needs to be interrogated.

Queer Willie Style

Both Paul, within the film, and Smith, in his performance of Paul, react to the assumption of a heterosexist norm. For all his gayness, which is revealed halfway through the film, Paul covers his sexual identity by adhering to the requirements of the white upper class into which he attempts to assimilate. His language, his manners, and his dress conform to the WASP social code, and his performance of class is seamlessly effective. He follows the regimen required for assimilation as Stuart Hall outlines: "Blacks could gain entry to the mainstream—but only at the cost of ... assimilating white norms of style, looks, and behavior" (*Representations* 279). When he enters the Kittredge apartment after simulating an attack by muggers in Central Park, he is wearing the prep school/Ivy league uniform of khakis and blue blazer. His conversational gambit is to flatter Flan and Ouisa by reporting that their children do not criticize them at school. In addition to these blandishments, he makes the white couple comfortable with his presence by making them feel that he is not what he so obviously is: a young Black man. Such a categorization carries with it certain assumed characteristics, the most relevant here being the cultural sexualization of Black masculinity. Historically, Black men are associated with stereotyped sexual attributes relating to genital size, sexual performance, and a predisposition toward rape. All of these can pose a threat which results in the stigmatization of Black men by mainstream society. Paul's markers of class neutralize his sexualized racial identity, and he is read as acceptable, the Black equivalent of their privileged and wholesomely heterosexual children.

In his stories about his acquaintanceship with their children, Paul does not hint at any special friendship with the Kittredge daughter. Aside from the fact of his homosexuality, which would exclude such an interest, he knows very well the white anxiety over interracial relationships and furthers his assimilationist goal by distancing himself from such a problematic sexual perception. Successful Black men continually negotiate this charged issue, and Will Smith does the same. In fact, Paul Poitier and Will Smith share an identity in their performances of the non-threatening, desexualized Black male. While Paul gains entry into Fifth Avenue apartments, Smith ascends to the Hollywood A-List of the most marketable and highest-paid male stars. The construction of Smith's screen personae is predicated upon a resistance to a sexualized profile as well as an avoidance of interracial heterosexuality. Most often Smith is teamed with another actor in his films: Martin Lawrence (*Bad Boys* and *Bad Boys II*, 1995 and 2003), Jeff Goldblum (*Independence Day*, 1996), Tommy Lee Jones (*Men in Black* and *Men in Black II*, 2002 and 2002), Gene Hackman (*Enemy of the State*, 1998), Kevin Kline (*Wild Wild West*, 1998), and Matt Damon (*The Legend of Bagger Vance*, 2000). In some films he is linked briefly with a Black actress: Marcelle Beauvais (*Wild, Wild West*), Thandie Newton (*The Pursuit of Happyness*, 2006), Salli Richardson (*I Am Legend*, 2007), and Sophie Okonedo (*After Earth*, 2013). In all these cases, these Black women's characters disappear from the film. In two films he is engaged or married to Black women (Vivica A. Fox in *Independence Day* and Regina King in *Enemy of the State*), but these relationships are not sexually visualized.[11] Gugu Mbatha-Raw in *Concussion* (2015) is given more screen time that most, as is Naomie

Harris in *Collateral Beauty* (2016). In *Enemy of the State*, Smith's protagonist has an affair with a character played by Lisa Bonet, but this sexual relationship occurs prior to film's plot.

In other films Smith is paired with women of Latino or of other ethnic backgrounds: Eva Mendes (*Hitch*, 2005), Alice Braga (*I Am Legend*, 2007), and Rosario Dawson (*Men in Black II* and *Seven Pounds*, 2008). *Seven Pounds* is the only case of Smith engaging in a sustained sexual scene in his career. When he is opposite white actresses, the relationship is either chaste or adversarial: Linda Fiorentino (*Men in Black*), Bridget Moynahan (*I, Robot*, 2004), Charlize Theron (*Hancock*, 2008). The latter film does feature Smith's only interracial heterosexual kiss though in the most extreme and vexed and not romantic or sexual circumstances.[12] Smith's character engages in a sexual relationship with Margot Robbie's character in *Focus* (2015), a development that is taken up in a later chapter. The record of Smith's performances of a contained Black male sexuality attests to how carefully he has shaped his career in order to avoid the difficulties of racial and sexual politics, and he has been rewarded by a remarkable mainstream success.

Paul Poitier's performance of a classed heterosexual normativity mitigates the threat of a stereotyped Black male sexuality, and it also completely masks his homosexuality. The success of Paul's impersonation of class and a normative sexuality is measured by the degree of shock registered by the Kittredges when he is discovered in bed with the male hustler. It is a shock that resonates as well with Guare and the makers of the film, as has been discussed. Paul's sexuality is the source of demonstrable unease at multiple levels of the film and text. What does Paul mean to these different interests, and why is he in all his Blackness and gayness so consistently resisted? Perhaps an answer can be found in Paul's relationship with Flan. Paul affects him in various ways. Paul affords Flan the opportunity to test his liberal convictions when he shows up on his doorstep. His magnanimity toward the young man affirms his sense of his best self. Even when Paul is exposed and is in trouble with the law, Flan, though reluctantly, assumes a fatherly role. He is forced into postures of tough parenting that he has never exerted with his own children. He is shamed by the doorman of his building for neglecting his Negro son and begrudgingly puts forth an effort. Flan is symbolic of the great American patriarchy whose social responsibility, which it continually fails to meet, is to care for all its children. Paul is a nagging reminder of his stake in racial equality and social justice and also of what he has not done to secure them.

Paul's sexuality is more problematic. At one point Ouisa confesses her attraction to Paul and urges Flan to admit to similar feelings. He replies: "Cut me out of that particular pathology" (*Six Degrees* 1:44:10). His use of the word "pathology" to describe same sex attraction registers his need to distance such a possibility from himself. Homosexuality for him is disordered and perverse. (It is interesting that Guare within the logic of the narrative equates homosexuality and Blackness with chaos.) Yet he would not need to assert that sense of distance if those feelings were truly alien to him. Paul makes him question his identity as a privileged, white heterosexual male and confront aspects of his identity and sexuality that he cannot accept. Gillan quotes Diana Fuss to explain Flan's situation: "Flan repositions Paul as the 'outsider' who enacts the process by which 'heterosexuality secures its self-identity and shores up its ontological boundaries by protecting itself from what it sees as the continual predatory encroachments of its contaminated other, homosexuality'" (51). Consequently, Flan must denounce Paul and expel him from his home and life.[13]

By resisting and rejecting Paul, Flan is simultaneously acknowledging and denying a formative trope in American literary representation: the homoerotic bond that motivates a thematic strand in American literature and film. The cultural wish for a rapprochement between the races is most often expressed in the American imaginary through the interracial male bond. For instance, writing about the buddy action film genre, Donaldson observes that "feature films function as a keeper of America's collective conscience—the repository for fears, guilt, and hopes—the interracial buddy film creates a world where that conscience can find a peaceful balance, that is to say where conflicts can find resolutions" (11).

Leslie Fielder also describes this homoerotic bond famously in the essay "Come Back to the Raft, Huck Honey" which focuses on the relationship between the slave Jim and Huckleberry Finn: "The mythic love of white male and Black [is] buried at a level of acceptance which does not touch reason, so desperately repressed from overt recognition, so contrary to what is usually thought of as our ultimate level of taboo—the sense of that love can survive only in the obliquity of a symbol, persistent, archetypal, in short, as a myth" (Fiedler qtd. in Phelan 522).

Christopher Looby notes that Fiedler's argument about the interracial homosexual subtexts of American literary history contradicts itself because of Fiedler's uneasiness with the real implications of homosexuality (529). This uneasiness is embodied in Paul whose Blackness and gayness doubly destabilizes patriarchy. His presence makes the film's other characters and the filmmakers confront the centrality of race in American society and history as well as the homoerotic desire that haunts the American mythos. The intersection of these two forces that Paul represents is a powerful threat as if the nexus is unthinkable. Certainly, it was too much for Will Smith. As with Flan, Smith has no other choice but to reject the reality and implications of Paul's sexuality. Flan is invested in preserving his life and his identity while Smith seeks to protect his career. In interviews published around the time of the film's release, Smith commented on his motivations for refusing to perform the physical manifestations of Paul's sexuality. He claimed that the film came at a pivotal point in his career as he was making a transition from television to the big screen, and he didn't know how those scenes would be received by audiences. He ran the risk of alienating his fan base and of losing face within the rap music community and its constructions of manhood which incorporates "the historic tropes of Black heterosexual, masculine (hyper)sexuality, insensitivity, detachment and cold-bloodedness" (Gray 178).

This is a masculinity that is also noted for its misogyny and homophobia.[14] Yet, despite the assumed homophobia of rap, Smith later revealed that doing the part ironically gained respect for him because within these notions of Black masculinity facing and overcoming the most difficult challenges, even playing gay in a film, is a test of manhood. When asked about the reaction of his peers in rap, he has said, "Everyone applauds me for having the heart to take the role. Rap is about macho, being hard. In a weird way, it turned out that it was a macho and hard thing for me to have had the balls to do" (Gordon 54). He gained credibility for doing the film and facing its challenges, even though technically he did not fulfill all the requirements of the role.

Perhaps it was not so much his rap music peers about whom he needed to be concerned as the Hollywood establishment itself. In making the decision to limit his investment in portraying the gay aspects of Paul's character, it could be argued that he made the right choice for a young actor attempting to establish himself in a film career. Smith in his off-screen persona, despite the usual gay rumors that accrue to any actor who attains celebrity status, is exemplarily heterosexual. This still does not mean that taking on the role in *Six Degrees of Separation* was not without real risks.[15] Although Hollywood is considered to be a site of liberalism, in terms of its film representations of homosexuality and in terms of its treatment of homosexual actors, it is not as progressive as it appears. Certainly, the visibility of gay Black male representation is minimal.[16]

Mainstream film production is relatively conservative compared to television or theater. The stakes of film stardom are much higher than in other entertainment forms because mainstream films are so expensive to make. Thus, bets are hedged. Elements that might compromise profit are not embraced because they may not attract large audiences who wish to have the film experience affirm their deepest beliefs. Film powerfully reproduces traditional American social ideology, which still does not fully embrace homosexuality. There are many exceptions. Tom Hanks won the Oscar for *Philadelphia* in 1993. Sean Penn won the 2008 Academy Award for Best Actor in *Milk*. Yet, *Brokeback Mountain* did not win the Oscar for Best Picture in 2005 after winning every other major best picture accolade around the globe. It was as if Hollywood resisted having this film represent its best and highest achievement because of its subject matter. There are very few out gay male actors, and the ones who are have limited careers. Rupert Everett, for example, now publicly regrets his decision to be an out gay actor because of the roles over the years he has been unable to secure ("Coming out"). Richard Chamberlain has also stated the following in an interview with *The Advocate*: "Personally, I wouldn't advise a gay leading man-type actor to come out" (Voss 3).

Even young straight actors think twice about taking on a gay role for fear of being stigmatized or marginalized. Brendan Fraser was in a position quite like Will Smith's when he took on the role of Clayton Boone in Bill Condon's 1998 film *Gods and Monsters*. In the film, Boone becomes the object of desire of the aging, legendary film director (patterned after James Whale of *Frankenstein* fame) for whom he poses for sketches. The logic of the narrative requires that Boone finally accede to the wishes of the older man and pose for him in the nude. The scene asks for full-frontal shots, but Fraser refused, claiming that the nudity would detract from the scene's emotional impact (Condon). The scene was filmed utilizing alternative staging and camera angles, and the result perhaps is not as fully effective as it might have been. Fraser has gone on to a respectable and high-profile career as has Smith. The wisdom of caution in the face of homophobia is borne out. Smith ascended to stardom to a certain degree because he resisted Paul.

Another reason that Paul's sexuality is such a resisted force in the film is the possibility of freedom that it offers. The revelation of Paul's other side, like the other side of the two-sided Kandinsky that is displayed in the Kittredge living room, is an eruption of chaos, as intended by Guare. It is also the manifestation of a joyous unruly spirit at the core of Paul's identity. His sexuality is integral to his sense of self, and he is unselfconscious and unapologetic about it. At one point, Ouisa asks him why he brings the hustler into their home. Paul replies that the evening was so magical and that the experience made him so happy that he wanted to add sex to it. When he inquires of her if she does not do the same, she is speechless. The idea of sex as an enhancement of joy has never occurred to her, and he opens for her a new world of erotic possibility. Paul has this effect on several characters in the film: Trent, the MIT student who schools him in the ways of the upper classes; and Rick, the aspiring actor from Utah whom Paul dazzles with a magical evening at the Rainbow Room. Despite the devastation he wreaks and the unease he instills, Paul, through his sexuality, has the ability to be a transformative figure for the people he deceives.[17]

There are also two sides to Will Smith's relation to Paul's sexuality. Smith is as double-sided and contradictory as Paul. His capacity for containing opposing messages is key to his broad-based appeal. He functions as a universal signifier. He is an open figure onto whom audiences can project their needs. He can mask the implications of a Black identity for white audiences while simultaneously riffing in vernacular for his Black viewers. He can play a homosexual character to earn the praise of the film industry at the same time he manages not to invest fully in that character in order to maintain the respect of his rap and neighborhood peers. In an extension of this duality, Smith denies Paul's sexuality through aspects of his performance, but at the same time he accesses Paul's queer spirit in his career as it has developed. The criticism that Smith received for *Six Degrees of Separation* is in some ways refuted by the body of his work. One pronounced irony contained within Smith's refusal to play gay in this instance is how often he performs queerness in his films. In "Unintentional Camp and the Image of Will Smith," Seth Nesenholtz argues that Smith's persona is informed with a camp sensibility as defined by Susan Sontag in her seminal essay "Notes on Camp" and claims that "there are numerous instances in his filmography where homosexual camp is reinforced."

Within several of his films there are outbreaks of camp or queer desire similar to the revelation of Paul's gayness in *Six Degrees*. In *Made in America*, there is a scene in which Smith as the best friend of Whoopi Goldberg's daughter, to make a comic point, ends their conversation by suddenly taking on a stereotyped female persona and walking away with exaggerated swinging hip movements. In *Independence Day*, there is a scene early in the film script when Smith as pilot Captain Steve Hiller reports to his military base. In the locker room, as he begins to change his clothing, he discusses his disappointment over a rejection letter from NASA. Harry Connick, Jr., as his best friend, Captain Jimmy Wilder, asks, "What else do they want you to learn?" Steve answers, "How to kiss ass" (Devlin and Emmerich 42). Connick, kneeling behind Smith then says, "Sometimes you just have to pucker up and..." (Devlin and Emmerich 42). As performed in the film, Connick says, "I'm sorry, man. You know what you need to do. You need to like kiss some serious booty to get ahead in this world, man. That's what I'm trying to tell you. See, I like the one knee approach because it puts the booty like right in front of the lips" (*Independence* 0:35:08–0:35:20). As he says this, still kneeling, he makes a motion forward as if to plant a kiss on Smith's backside. The scene is played for comedy, but it registers the homoerotic dimensions of their friendship and summons up the same sex emotional dynamics of Hollywood war films going back to *Wings* in 1927.

In *Wild Wild West*, as government agent Captain James West, Smith engages in a comic rivalry with U.S. Marshall Artemus Gordon played by Kevin Kline. In one scene on a gadget embellished train, the two masters of disguise argue as to whose female impersonation is more convincing, particularly their costuming and their false padded bosoms. Each claims that his artificial breasts are more lifelike. The unsuspecting conductor overhears them and has his suspicions about their relationship confirmed. He exclaims, "I knew it!"(*Wild Wild West* 0:27:00). Even more explicit is a scene later in the film when the two men find themselves stuck to each other by magnetic metal collars. The positions they find themselves in simulate sex acts when Smith's face is pressed against Kline's crotch as his collar becomes attached to Kline's belt buckle.

In *Hitch*, Smith plays a relationship expert who attempts to teach a hapless client (Kevin James) how to win the unattainable woman of his dreams. Smith offers to instruct him in the art of the goodnight kiss. Smith stands in for the date so that James can practice his technique. The two end up accidently kissing to great comic effect. The payoff of this moment is that Smith is nonplussed by the kiss and takes it in stride. His own masculinity is so assured that a male kiss cannot faze him. This scene clearly is a reference to the kissing scenes in *Six Degrees of Separation*. It is as though Smith is doing penance for his lack of nerve earlier in his career. He rewrites the past and seems to get the scene right this time.

There is one more significant scene in a Will Smith film in which there is an errant homoerotic subtext. *Enemy of the State* dramatizes the plight of an everyman attorney who finds himself the target of a government conspiracy. At one point he is aided by an older man played by Gene Hackman, who is a surveillance expert. When they meet in a hotel hallway, where Smith has momentarily escaped, Hackman, who knows that microphones and tracking devices have been planted on Smith's person, orders him to take off his clothes. This moment has a deep resonance. The situation of an older white man telling a young Black man to strip replicates a pivotal moment in the Frederick Douglass's narrative when the slave-breaker Covey commands Douglass to remove his clothing and follow him into the woods. Presumably Covey intends to whip him, but the situation is open for alternate interpretations. Covey perhaps has a sexual motive in uncovering the young man's nakedness and securing the seclusion and privacy of the forest. Their intimacy is staged for either a beating or for sex, the two perhaps being synonymous.[18]

There is a similar scene in *Six Degrees of Separation* when the wounded Paul is attended by Flan after he has removed his shirt. As Gillan notes, "One can find … traces of a sexualized racial anxiety in the moment when Flan cleans and bandages Paul's bleeding wound…. The moment is also interesting because Paul is naked to the waist, posed on the edge of the Jacuzzi like a lounging Greek statue … emphasizing the erotic nature of the position in which he and Flan find themselves" (60). The sexual dynamics between Covey and Douglass are reproduced in Flan and Paul as well as the characters Hackman and Smith portray. The reoccurrence of this charged moment indicates once again the presence of a strong homoerotic interracial component in American mythology and its reproduction in Hollywood film.

These moments in Will Smith's films reveal a contradiction at the center of his film persona, and his ability to contain oppositions is central to the construction of his stardom. Despite his resistance to a homosexual character in his first major role in a major Hollywood film, and despite his exemplary heterosexual public identity, his performances enter into queer spaces, and as such he destabilizes stereotypes about Black masculinity and does significant work in deconstructing and reconstructing images of young Black men in American popular culture.

A Good Will to All

As a result of the jump start that *Six Degrees of Separation* gave to his career, Will Smith has gone on to major stardom. His astronomical box-office successes have earned him a high ranking on Hollywood's A-list of bankable stars, a position shared by no other Black male actor and which constitutes assimilation on the highest level.[19] What is even more remarkable about his success is its symbolic power. Will Smith now can be read as a cultural sign of the state of American racial relations, or rather a cultural wish for racial transcendence. In film after film Smith is cast as heroes who literally save the world or is the last man on earth, and given the public response to the films, America seems to be quite comfortable with the idea of this particular Black man being the repository of traditional societal and cultural values. Of course, the cost of this image is the masking of the real racial problems that persist and a de-emphasis on Blackness. Certainly, the key to Smith's success is an image and persona that deracializes Blackness,

Fig. 5.2. "Paul Poitier" (Will Smith) makes one last phone call before his arrest in *Six Degrees of Separation* (1993). Directed by Fred Schepisi (MGM/Photofest).

that voids Blackness of its historical and cultural content. If this is so, then it is entirely appropriate that Smith's rise should begin with Paul Poitier and his post-racial dream.

At the end of Paul's part of the story, he is defeated. He is driven off in police custody, an image of irony in that he has arrived at the exact fate his identity has been constructed to contradict. In this ending, his identity is not in any way validated by external reality, which in a just world it would be. Here he is just another statistic, a young Black man in trouble with the law (fig. 5.2). What is even more poignant about this Paul's case is that he cannot even maintain authority over his own identity, fictional though it may be, but still expressive of his truest and best self. Simply, he is usurped by the actor who enacts him. Paul's sexual identity may be betrayed by his audiences, his creators and his interpreter; however, his project of race and class transcendence, whatever its inherent worth, which he ultimately fails to realize himself, is finally fulfilled by the actor who embodies him, and on a scale and to a degree that exceeds even his own wildest dreams.

Six

Science Fictions and Racial Facts

Will Smith has been able to prevail in Hollywood because of his adroit navigation of his screen persona through the potential pitfalls of the two intersecting and determining aspects of his identity: race and masculinity. He shapes a viable image of Black manhood that circumvents and transcends the stereotypes about Black men that would be impediments to reaching the widest range of international audiences. The vehicle for reaching these global markets are those films that appeal across national borders, cultural differences, and language barriers. The films that accomplish these tasks are genre films, and this has been the case since the rise of the Hollywood blockbuster in the 1970s. These films include action thrillers, science fiction spectacles and animated features. Genre films and their reliance on narrative formula have their justification in profit. The other significant aspect of genre films is their relationship to ideology and the way they reinforce conservative American values and ideals. Smith creates a space for Black representation within this ideological construct. This is the intervention he performs on genre films. His is a delicate negotiation of the imperatives of the various movie genres in the films that constitute the body of his work. The outcomes are several, and some are contradictory. Smith resolves those contradictions as a function of the nature of his hybridized, semiotically indeterminate stardom. Still, the power of his persona can bend and even overwhelm genre. His persona effects subversions of genre, but it can also fulfill generic expectations. He can mock or parody the stereotypes inherent in those genres, but he can also be put into positions that reaffirm the problematic images of the past and the stereotypes that his persona has been shaped by the industry and himself to transcend. What follows are examinations of how this tension between progressive and regressive tendencies in his star identity plays out in his individual genre films.

Will Smith has a special relationship to the science fiction film genre, and that connection is predicated upon his global appeal, his position within the Hollywood film industry, and his shaping and maintenance of his screen persona. Adilifu Nama in *Black Space* identifies Smith's unique contribution to the science fiction film:

> In the same way that Sidney Poitier and Eddie Murphy were pivotal figures who secured a cinematic space for Blackness during the 1960s and 1980s, respectively, Will Smith is a seminal figure in American SF cinema … he opened the door for Black characters to become at least central figures, if not headliners, in a small but growing canon of SF films. In fact, Will Smith's cool-guy persona enabled him to explore strange new worlds and to go places few Black actors

have ever gone before, such as being the headline star of a major SF motion picture—*I, Robot* (2004) [39].

Palmer confirms this account of Smith's generic accomplishment:

> Through science-fiction cinema, a genre not traditionally associated with either Black actors or Black audiences, Will Smith has forged a sea change in Hollywood's expression of heroic masculinity by deliberately integrating his star persona into its narrative and representational spaces. His presence there opens up multiple levels of dialogue around race, visibility, and identity in the popular media imaginary [29].

Smith's intervention is making Blackness visible in science fiction worlds. He confronts the conventional whiteness of the genre by demonstrating that race and racism are not just historical phenomena and that Black people can exist in representations of space and the future.

Smith is well suited to bear this representational burden, and he is fully aware of this. He brings to the table his image as a "cool leading man/action hero and his shrewd understanding of the global market (especially in terms of genre cinema)" (Palmer 30). Hollywood capitalizes on Smith's savvy by framing "Smith as its global representative" and then using "science-fiction cinema as the means of that framing" (Palmer 30). The studios are heavily invested in "putting Smith into these alien worlds and then sending him out into the global marketplace," where he performs miracles at the box office (Palmer 36). A Black actor with ambition and a colorblind, post-racial disposition and with the goal of global stardom would do well to concentrate on the genre of science fiction which is reticent and resistant to direct engagement with race. The problem is that race cannot be suppressed and manifests in ways that inevitably reflect social reality.

Smith's success in the genre also means that he has had an impact on the representation of race in science fiction. Nama writes of the surprise registered when he divulged that the topic of his research was Blacks in science fiction films as there was very little Black representation in the genre at the time. This is what makes Smith's achievement so remarkable. In general, Nama locates a Black presence in the genre, even in its absence. This presence takes many forms: Blackness as symbolic absence, Blackness as symbol or allegory, Blackness as token, Blackness as hegemonic inferiority, Blackness as deformity or monstrosity, Blackness symbolized as alien other, Blackness displaced as other by alien presence, Blackness erased in the face of alien threat, Blackness as contamination, Blackness erased through post-apocalyptic interracial procreation. These themes and narrative strategies weave their way throughout Smith's body of work within the genre.

What makes Smith a fitting actor to assume heroic science fiction roles (some originally conceived for white actors) is his ability to mitigate the problematic aspects of race. Stephanie Larrieux observes:

> Smith's performances thus enable both white and Black audiences to temporarily forget the material conditions many Blacks face, for example, decreased economic and educational opportunities, health disparities, and increasing incarceration rates among the male population. In this regard, Smith serves as an example of how Black racial difference has been incorporated into dominant society, but in a way that renders it neutral. His tremendous commercial success is proof that racial difference has been made palatable. Being a "racialized

Other" is now acceptable, acknowledged, embraceable, and even celebratory but consequently also potentially depoliticizing [210–211].

C.S. King also offers a description of this ability: "Smith's persona makes him an ideal candidate for delicately negotiating tensions with American public culture around the subject of race: a popular and entertaining actor, not known for speaking out politically, Smith can appeal to both Black and white audiences without forcing too blunt a confrontation with racial politics" ("Legendary" 259). In Smith, mainstream audiences can have it both ways; they can embrace difference, his Blackness, but it is Blackness without the baggage.

There is also a historical dimension to Smith's emergence in science fiction films during the '90s which coincided with a crest of post-racial identity politics, particularly in Hollywood. An emphasis on post-racial representations (which did not insist upon race and racism) allowed the white status quo to remain in place unchallenged. O'Brien gives this account of the preservation of Hollywood hegemony: "For the most part, commercial cinema remained interested only in Black characters and issues intelligible and agreeable to white sensibilities, embodied by a marketable and therefore exceptional Black actor; the results refracted a society in an ongoing state of racial denial, unable or unwilling to deal openly with its inequalities and conflicts" (181). Smith's ascendency in science fiction film was a matter of the right actor at the right time, and was dependent upon his ability to assuage racial anxiety.

Justin Phillip Reed asks a crucial, critical question about Smith's post-racial stardom: "Smith has placed Black protagonists into uncharted regions of space, time, and technology, but to whose benefit?"

One might also ask, "At what price?" Is Smith's intervention a matter of progress on all levels? Reed sets forth a provocative interpretation of the significance of Smith's reign in science fiction films:

> It matters that Smith's roles in sci-fi films largely consist of state agents: Civil War hero, detective, military virologist, celebrated general, ex-NYPD turned alien surveillance operative. And here's one reason why: these films are received messages of potential progress for the large movie-watching population of a society that allowed itself to believe it was "post-racial." Smith's characters act as witnesses for the rehabilitated offender, the white supremacist nation-state [J. Reed].

Smith's roles even as unprecedented heroes still reduce him to functioning as a servant in service to a higher authority, namely the interests of a white hegemony.

The science fiction hero does not evade the retrograde Black representations of the past, nor does he iterate or embody coherent messages that link to historical Black struggle. Black people do not benefit significantly from Smith's genre intervention, and the price Smith pays for global stardom is his silence. Reed sees Smith's role in science fiction as contradictory; it is both progressive and regressive at the same time. Philippa Gates offers the following perception which is applicable to Smith's relationship to science fiction: "Although the presence of African Americans on the screen can be regarded as a positive step, these images are offered only when they can be contained and regulated by specific cinematic codes of representation.

In Hollywood film, the black male body is offered as heroic only when it is contained by a lack of sexuality or action, isolation from black community, or class" (21). Smith may have made incursions into the genre, but he doesn't escape the counter pull of the historical and cinematic past. To what extent do his films offer an advance for the race or a benign accommodation of the racial repressions and evasions of the mainstream?

Independence Day: *Will Smith's Defense of His (Human) Race*

Independence Day (1996), directed by Roland Emmerich, cast Smith in a prominent role in a science-fiction film, his first, and established his box-office clout. This would be the start of his reputation as the King of the Fourth of July Weekend. For years he "owned" that weekend in the calendar of release dates for Hollywood summer films because his films consistently opened at number one and broke box-office records. This would be the first of a succession of ten science fiction related films to open at number one, and this instituted him as a force in the genre. The film earned $817 million worldwide, making it the top grossing film of 1996 ("Independence Day [1996]").[1]

In the film Smith plays Captain Steve Hiller, a Marine pilot, who is called to action to combat a hostile alien invasion. With the help of scientist David Levinson (Jeff Goldblum) and under the command of the president of the United States (Bill Pullman), he prevents the annihilation of Earth. For the first time in science fiction film history, a Black hero saves the world. Smith's genre intervention here enjoins several issues: the nature of the characterization of Hiller, the displacement of otherness from Blackness onto the alien, and the film's final reassertion of white patriarchy despite the spectacle of Black heroism.

If *Independence Day* offers a post-racial, multicultural vision of America, then Smith as Captain Hiller potentially is the perfect embodiment of that idea. For instance, here Hiller is seen with a Black wife and stepson. As Reed observes, the audience in a post-racial frame of mind wishes for both the Black family and the family of the white president to survive the alien attack. Within this plot configuration, Blackness and whiteness are subsumed under a universal humanity while the aliens occupy the position of the Other usually held by Black people. According to Nama, the science fiction film often uses "an alien enemy to make racial strife obsolete" (*Black* 7). At this point in his career, Smith had not become "Will Smith," meaning that the edges of his Blackness had not yet been effaced as evidenced by his identification with a Black family. This film marks his transition into a star for a post-racial age. After this in subsequent films he is not paired with a Black wife (or one who survives through to the film's conclusion), following the Hollywood wisdom that a Black male star opposite a Black actress equals a "Black" film, which equals suppressed box office returns. After *Independence Day*, Smith would be paired (chastely) with white or racially ambiguous actresses to augment and sustain a rising stardom that rests upon his non-threatening and palatable brand of Blackness.

Yet, despite his elevation to the status of hero beyond the confines of race, Smith's characterization of Hiller does at times regress to racial essentialism. He is seen in terms of body (shirtless, muscled) rather than mind (his opposition to Jeff Goldblum's David Levinson), furthering the body/mind and Black/white binaries. His conventional Blackness is also accented through his brash, cool, wise-cracking personality. His Blackness is paramount, but there is a subtle qualification; it is a conciliated Blackness that appeals to white film viewers. Taubin claims that Will Smith "is probably the only African American actor in Hollywood guaranteed to be non-threatening to a white middle-class audience" (8). His racial presence is acceptable if "it is not thematized in terms of difference" (Kakoudaki 136). His Blackness is more than just non-threatening; it is desirable for purposes of imitation and appropriation. If Smith is hip and cool, then he offers a dimension of Blackness that is attractive to (white, male) mainstream viewers. It is acceptable to be like Will. His race is "forgiven" because he teaches white men how to be Black, that is, hip and cool.[2] This cultural and racial transaction is illustrated in the film in Hiller's relationship with his best friend, Jimmy (Harry Connick, Jr.) who riffs and signifies in Black cool style (Kakoudaki 128–129). Smith's ability to render Blackness across racial lines is key to his star persona and to the success of his films, including *Independence Day*.

The film is peopled with characters of a range of ethnic and racial differences, but these differences are subsumed within a universal humanity that is defined against the alien Other. Their differences disappear as they join forces against a common enemy. The scene that signals this shift of otherness from the raced human character to the alien is Hiller's encounter with the invader from space. After parachuting into the desert following an airborne clash, he comes across the downed alien spacecraft. When he approaches, the creature raises its head out of the wreckage. Smith punches it out, quipping, "Welcome to Earth…. That's what I call a close encounter" (*Independence Day* 1:02:17–1:02:31). This moment garners one of the biggest laughs in the film. The scene has become iconic, and it is probably the one scene that made Will Smith an international star (fig. 6.1). This is also the moment when the Black character moves from the margin to the center: "Acceptance of Smith as the hero signals and affirms that traditional cinematic representations of black subjectivity in the genre of science fiction film that were previously relegated to the margins through structured absence and token presence have now migrated from the margins to the mainstream" (Larrieux 212). He becomes the science fiction film hero, and his alterity is displaced upon the alien. Kakoudaki poses the following question: "What happens when the African American body is finally there in the narrative of national survival, as savior or a valuable ally, and participates in the myths of nationhood and 'America'?" (127). What happens is the elision of the hero's Blackness and his incorporation within a larger power structure.

Kac-Vergne reads the film's ending as a reassertion of white male power despite the film's objective of bringing together the heroic Black pilot and the genius Jewish scientist who have saved the world. In the final scene, the two men walk together and are joined by the white figure of authority, the president and his military advisors, who validate the men's courage and include them in the sphere of white patriarchal

Fig. 6.1. A swaggering Capt. Steven Hiller (Will Smith) savors his knockout victory over an invading alien in *Independence Day* (1996). Directed by Roland Emmerich (20th Century–Fox/ Photofest).

power (138). She concludes: "In the end, the victory of humanity in *Independence Day* is the result of American ethnic cooperation under the leadership of white patriarchy" (138–39). Brayton also sees *Independence Day* as affirming white hegemony even though it may offer a vision of racial equality and harmony. In the end, this vision functions "without asking characters or viewers to account for white privilege" (Rogin 46; Brayton, "Racial" 73). He goes on to assert that in films like *Independence Day* "Black courage and masculine leadership are tailored to the needs of the dominant (white) culture" (73). The Black hero serves the purposes of nation and society unquestioningly and without an assertion of a minority perspective.[3] There is a slippage between star and role in that Smith and Hiller function similarly. Just as Hiller serves his country with colorblind devotion, Smith bears the banner of Hollywood and its attendant idealistic American ideology while representing a diversity that does not insist upon itself.

Men in Black: *Aliens Are the New Black*

Men in Black (1997) solidified Smith's reputation as box-office champion of the July Fourth weekend, grossing $589 million worldwide ("Men in Black [1997]"). It was his second big budget hit in a row and based on a comic book series. The title

Men in Black refers to a government agency that controls the presence and activities of aliens who are surreptitiously living on Earth. The film narrates the recruitment, training, and initiation of a recruit to the film, Darrell Edwards (Smith), who is transformed into Agent J by the older Agent K (Tommy Lee Jones). The comic action plot dramatizes their efforts to locate and contain a dangerous alien who changes form as it victimizes humans who are its desired food source.

Smith's intervenes in the science fiction genre by claiming a central space for Blackness in those narratives through his conciliatory negotiation of race, namely by inserting his non-threatening, post-racial persona. This operation works in different ways. *Men in Black* repeats the narrative strategy of displacing Otherness from the film's Black character onto a proliferation of aliens (fig. 6.2). In the final fight scene, Agent J or Jay struggles with a giant cockroach alien and gets the better of it when he offends it by killing smaller terrestrial cockroaches. As he smashes the insects underfoot, Jay taunts his adversary. He says, "Uh-oh, I'm sorry. Was that your auntie? Oh, then that must mean that that's your uncle then, huh? You know y'all look alike" (*Men in Black* 1:25:06–1:25:20). Here Smith takes the place of the (white) hero, eliding his Blackness, and the alien cockroach becomes the racialized other, associated with African Americans through the racist assumption that all Black people are indistinguishable to white people.

The evasion of Smith's Blackness by means of racial displacement, putting him

Fig. 6.2. Agent J (Will Smith) encounters the alien "other" in *Men in Black* (1997). Directed by Barry Sonnenfeld (Columbia Pictures/Photofest).

into a white position, does not work consistently because the characterization of Agent J does not bear any less burden of racialization. Aliens may take the position of the racialized Other, but the Black man will always be Black. Originally, the role of Agent J was to be played by Chris O'Donnell. The casting of Smith generates racial meanings and implications that could not have been fully anticipated. In an early scene, Darrell/Agent J is seen in pursuit of an alien in "a stunning performance of pure athleticism" (Hicks 122). Hyper athleticism is a conventionally stereotypical attribute associated with the Black male body, and Agent J is to be read through this stereotype. What complicates matters is the film's subtextual discourse about immigration and an equation of aliens, aliens from outer space, with Latinos. There is a need for the state to exercise control over these populations in the same way that the film needs to contain its Black male co-star. All forms of difference at every level within the film must be subjugated to the prevailing structure of authority. The film may be symbolic of immigration, but more tellingly it is about the racial and gender construction of Agent J's character.

Jay's characterization runs the gamut of ways Hollywood narrative reduces the Black male: direct control, deracialization, castration, and desexualization. Jay is controlled in numerous ways, such as Kay's use on Jay of the neuralyzer instrument which erases the minds of its subjects. When used on Jay, he exhibits a "disturbing docility" (Hicks 126). He is rendered passive and powerless, the way whites in certain historical contexts preferred Black people. In *Men in Black 2*, Jay is utterly anesthetized without personality—his Blackness is also erased. In the time-traveling *Men in Black 3*, Kay uses the neuralyzer on Jay so that he will not be traumatized by his father's death. Here is a case of "the white man deciding what is best for the Black boy who will become his colleague. Knowledge control is thus re-established as the responsibility and privilege of white patriarchy" (O'Brien 185). Jay is also de-raced by the films' failure to show him with Black friends or any connection to a Black community. Jay is castrated in the famous scene wherein Kay gives him the tiny Cricket gun, thus refuting the myth of Black male phallic superiority. Furthermore, the claim of cool style is finally undercut. Jay's racial difference is ultimately subsumed under the power of the Men in Black organization: "Far from a man in Black, then, he becomes a man effaced by generic whiteness" (Hicks 129). In *Men in Black 2* a desexualized Jay procures girlfriends and dates for his white co-workers but does not have female companionship for himself. O'Brien observes: "It seems that Black men promoted to jobs previously held by white men cannot expect or are not entitled to have a sex life" (185). This condition parallels Smith taking on roles previously cast or intended for white actors and these characters then not having full sex lives as a way of diminishing the threat of Black male phallicism. This is borne out by a scene in *Men in Black 3* in which Kay visits Jay in his apartment. Jay is found alone in a spare, minimally decorated space in seemingly lonely isolation. The scene is striking as it unintentionally registers the price Jay pays and what any Black person pays for white acceptance. Jay while functioning as an effective and successful neophyte agent is nonetheless constructed out of the old, familiar tropes of Black representation: containment, diminishment, and the reaffirmation of the white power structure.

I, Robot: *Allegories of Revolution*

In *I, Robot* (2004) the time is 2035, and the place is Chicago which is populated by humans and a servant robot class. Smith stars as detective Del Spooner who harbors a bad case of robophobia. He is called in on a case involving the murder of Dr. Alfred Lanning (James Cromwell), the creator of a new fleet of robots that is about to be distributed. Spooner teams up with Dr. Susan Calvin (Bridget Moynahan), a robot psychologist, to pursue the investigation. The prime suspect is Sonny, a special creation of Dr. Lanning, equipped with independent thought and human feeling. His difference from the other, older robots is that he does not adhere to the three cardinal principles of robots: (1) not to harm or allow harm to human beings; (2) to obey all human beings; and (3) to protect itself as long as it doesn't interfere with the first two laws. Through contact with Sonny, Spooner begins to overcome his prejudices and enlists Sonny's help not only in hunting down the real perpetrator, but to quell a violent uprising by the new generation of robots who have been reprogrammed by the V.I.K.I., the main computer, who has developed an independent consciousness as well as a mission to save humans from themselves.

Smith's revision of the science fiction genre here is to thematize race allegorically by portraying a character who is racist. What does it mean for a Black actor to inhabit the skin of a character type usually portrayed as white? Theoretically, the inner workings of racism should be highlighted by this race reversal. For instance, racial profiling takes on a different meaning when a Black cop unfairly profiles a shining white robot. Armond White pinpoints the problem here: "Instead of illuminating the social problem of police bias, the film minimizes it. Smith's presence itself soothes real-life anxiety about hostile cops and racist authority because in this fantasy, the only cop with a problem is himself Black" ("I, Robot"). To justify making the cop Black, the film needs to make a serious comment about or critique of police mistreatment of minorities. The film does neither. The film fails to follow through with its conception and ends up conveying messages that are contradictory and confused. This failure also puts Smith as a Black actor in an untenable position.

One problem is that Smith's persona is too likeable for the allegory to work successfully. The viewer needs to see and feel how he is a representation of hate in order to understand and see through the dynamics of racism. Instead, the audience is asked to identify with him, which is to excuse his antagonistic attitudes toward the racialized other. Even more problematic is if Smith is a proxy for whiteness in this scheme of racial reversal, then his actual Blackness cannot be too pronounced. Del Spooner must be Black according to the film's racial logic, but safely contained, which is Smith's stock in trade. Brayton asserts: "for Del Spooner's character to function in this white liberal film, , he must be Black but not too Black.... Smith's accommodating brand of Blackness is essential to *I, Robot*" ("Post-White" 80–81). As has been seen before, even when the insertion of a Black actor into a science fiction film constitutes a putative step forward, in its execution his Blackness must be kept in check.

The process of Black containment is set in motion with the premise of Spooner's guilt over the death of a white girl. The origin of Spooner's hatred for robots is a car accident which finds Spooner and a little girl trapped in their vehicles at the bottom of a river. The rescue robot makes the decision to save Spooner because logically he has a greater probability of surviving. He hates the robot because it saved his life! He would have preferred to have sacrificed his life for that of the little white girl. (This attitude taps into yet another racist trope: the Black character who gives up his life to save a white person.) Kac-Vergne argues that Spooner's guilt over the girl's death in the film's flashbacks indicates a depth to his character. She claims: "Smith's 'safe' brand of Blackness can be criticized as being sanitized for white viewers, but it also offers an emotional model of masculinity" (148). She sees Spooner as an example of a redeemed masculinity and puts into evidence the sensitivity revealed in his choice of mellow R&B music as well as the vulnerability demonstrated in the much commented upon nude shower scene. What may appear as a figure of a reconceived heroic manhood can also be seen as an Uncle Tom. In this case, the comparison is almost literal. The scene of Spooner saved from a drowning death evokes an incident in *Uncle Tom's Cabin* by Harriet Beecher Stowe. Tom and Little Eva are swept off the steamship that is carrying them southward into the depths of slave territory. Tom saves Little Eva in dramatic fashion, which sets up the dynamic of their subsequent quasi-romantic relationship.

The underwater scene in *I, Robot* is a perfect example of a phenomenon in Hollywood film: the Little White Girl Syndrome. Here the adult male protagonist is attached to a prepubescent white girl as her protector. This is a trope that appears in the films of major Black male stars. This connection is one way of containing the perceived threat in the Black male image. Even Denzel Washington, for all his status as an exemplar of Black male dignity and pride, in contradistinction to Smith's more accommodationist and hybridized Blackness, participates in this interracial, intergenerational narrative. In *Virtuosity* (1995) his character redeems himself by saving a young white girl from death in an explosion. In Tony Scott's *Man on Fire* (2004), he plays a former government agent employed as a bodyguard to protect a precocious pre-teen (Dakota Fanning) from kidnappers in Mexico City. In both cases, the Black male hero goes to significant and even the ultimate lengths to save the life of the white girl. In *I, Robot* Smith's character's guilt over not having saved the girl's life at the cost of his own invokes this syndrome as well, thus reducing the post-racial Smith to the original Black male stereotype.

Spooner and Smith's Blackness does not function as a social reality but as a high concept. Smith is so distanced from conventional Blackness that the film needs self-conscious and deliberate references to Black culture as reminders of his Blackness. One example is the R&B music with which Spooner is associated. Kac-Vergne interprets this music as humanizing Spooner and his environment, but it is also music that is so appropriated by the mainstream that it renders him "safe." The other example is his grandmother's sweet potato pies, which serve to situate Spooner within a Black identity, but it is anachronistic as if Black life would be unreconciled to the future. The presence of Spooner's grandmother highlights his social isolation. This is a well-known trope of Blacks in mainstream films as articulated by Guerrero:

Another all-too-common industry strategy for containing the range and potentialities of Black filmic talent is that of giving a Black star top billing in a film in which he or she is completely isolated from other Blacks or any referent to the Black world. In this situation, what there is of Black culture is embodied in an individual Black star surrounded and appropriated by a White context and narrative for the pleasure of a dominant, consumer audience [237].

Smith's presence represents Blackness in *I, Robot*, and Spooner may have a grand-mother, but he doesn't have a community.

Smith's Spooner is self-consciously "Black," but he functions as white author-ity. Smith admits in interviews that he was directed to conceptualize and perform Spooner as a racist white sheriff, the Rod Steiger role in *In the Heat of the Night*. O'Brien observes: " Spooner's reaction to robots evokes the archetypal nervous white response to Black presence: a robot at the door is startling; a robot running down the street is automatically suspect. White racism transmutes into Black robopho-bia" (186). If this is true, then the implications of this race reversal must be followed through to its logical conclusion. Brayton reads the film taking its racial coding liter-ally with Spooner as Black and the preternaturally white robots representing a white minority. He sees the film as "a complex racial allegory" ("Post-White" 73) and "a par-able of white antiracism" ("Post-White" 72). He goes on to argue: "Smith's leading role in a 'white' sf film is not to be easily dismissed. He is not simply saving the white world from aliens or teaching white men Black style; instead, he is partially responsi-ble, through the emancipation of the white robot, for the emergence of the reformed white subject" ("Post-White" 81–82). The Black hero puts down their rebellion and then leads the robots who symbolize disenchanted and alienated whites out of their ideological position into an enlightened state of anti-racism and redeemed whiteness. The robots become the stand-ins for "the white male victim of the conservative right" ("Post-White" 77). The problem with Brayton's interpretation is that it discounts his-tory and foregrounds whiteness in a plot about a revolution of the Black oppressed.

That *I, Robot* is about a slave revolt is clear. It is evident that if Spooner, played by a Black actor, assumes a white power position, then the robots, despite their gleaming whiteness, are stand-ins for Blacks in slavery. The textual cues are many. The Three Laws of Robotics, which institutionalize servility to the humans who can be read as whites, are eerily like the Black Codes enforced during slavery. Heather Hicks argues for this interpretation: "Will Smith again plays a character whose primary dramatic function is to contain and control a threatening group of 'others,' yet here those oth-ers are more identified with African Americans than immigrants (the robots are 'slaves' who are kept in a storage facility that resembles a slave quarter and who par-ticipate in a rebellion of sorts against their human owners)" (135). The robot rebel-lion in the film parallels the revolts of Nat Turner and Denmark Vesey. V.I.K.I. wants the robots to rebel and take over the city from the flawed and corrupt humans who parallel the dominant, slave-owning class. Following historic precedent, such a revolt must be put down in order to save the humans/whites and to restore the rightful social order. This destruction of the other is like the idea of the Black Frankenstein whereby the creator feels compelled to kill his own creation before that revengeful creation has a chance to kill him. Racialized, this refers to the fear the white power structure harbors against a Black threat whose rage it has created.[4]

One complication in the plot is that Spooner, who operates as a state agent, is part cyborg himself. After his accident, various parts of his body have been replaced bionically. This means that if he is part cyborg, this is not unlike being of mixed race. Spooner becomes a futuristic version of a mulatto male character in turn of the century African American fiction, one who struggles against the Black (or, here, the robotic) part of himself. His hatred of robots is motivated by his own self-hatred.[5] Through his interactions with Sonny, Spooner reaches greater comfort with his identity. This still does not prevent him from mounting a vigorous campaign to put an end to the robot rebellion and to destroy V.I.K.I. (fig. 6.3). Despite his ambivalences, his goal is to reestablish the status quo wherein humans (read whites) maintain control.

At the end of the film, the conquered rebel robots are decommissioned, but their raised consciousnesses are still fomenting. They seem to be looking for something or someone to guide them. They look to Spooner who passes the responsibility onto Sonny whose figure is seen in the distance on a hillside. The image is biblical like Jesus on the Mount. If he is to be the new leader of a new (non-violent) resistance, it is because of Spooner's mentorship. Spooner thus becomes a white savior to a new movement of the oppressed. This invokes another trope, that of the white figure who teaches Blacks how to fight for their freedom. Spooner acts like a white abolitionist in this race-reversed narrative.

The problem with Sonny becoming the new messiah is that throughout the film he has participated in the effort to suppress his own kind. In the process, he continuously betrays them. Sonny is not unlike the young slave boy in Nate Parker's ill-fated *The Birth of a Nation* (2016) who informs on Nat Turner's ravaging insurrectional band leading to their capture and deaths. At the end of the film, the boy, now grown up and politically matured, is seen in uniform fighting against the Confederacy.

Fig. 6.3. Will Smith as Del Spooner confronts a phalanx of rebellious robots in *I, Robot* (2004). Directed by Alex Proyas (AF Archive/Alamy Stock Photo).

A greater problem is the confused message at the end of the film. The ideologically conservative ending asserts that the slave revolt is unacceptable and must be crushed. Then the film seems to offer a radical ending as well as it seems to say that resistance is acceptable if it is non-violent and does not seriously threaten the existing hierarchy of power. The film implies that there must be another slave uprising. If this is one justified, then the previously unsuccessful one could not be wrong. Mark Fisher writes in *Film Quarterly*: "What's interesting, here, is that the robot hubris is not opposed on the grounds V.I.K.I. is mistaken; the artificial intelligence has neither malfunctioned nor gone power-crazed. The film is haunted by the possibility that the eventual defeat of V.I.K.I. was misconceived and effectively amounted to the destruction of collective intelligence." If this is true, then Spooner is on the wrong side of justice. The robots were always right. In suppressing the slave uprising, Spooner reestablishes the power of the state over dissenting, marginalized, revolutionary forces. The film demands that the robots are stopped, but it also affirms the acceptability of the revolution to come. The film wants to have it both ways. What is unambiguous is that on some level between the literal and the symbolic, Spooner's heroics in defeating the robots turns him into a traitor to his race.

Bright: *Reversal of Race*

Another example of a Will Smith film based on race reversal is *Bright* (2017), one of his more recent forays into the science fiction genre. The film is more accurately described as a hybrid of fantasy, sci-fi, and the buddy film. Its director is David Ayer who specializes in interracial police dramas such as *Training Day* (2001) with Denzel Washington (whose performance won a Best Actor Oscar) and *End of Watch* (2012). He also helmed *Suicide Squad* (2016), Smith's second attempt at a superhero film. Although *Bright* was one of the most watched films on Netflix and the streaming service's most expensive productions, it was not critically well received. In fact, the film has generated much negative commentary about its treatment of race. For instance, Hansel Rodriguez asserts that "*Bright*'s treatment of race feels exploitative and opportunistic" (128). He goes on to cite the film's trading in racial stereotypes despite its fictional social structuring involving fantasy species. Even more troublesome are Smith's function as a race-reversed white savior and the casting of white actors to play the oppressed "other" in a variation of "blackface" (H. Rodriguez 128). David Ehrlich in *IndieWire* is even more condemnatory, describing the film's racial dynamics as "flimsy" and questioning "how black people fit into a story that problematically recodes them as a violent breed of orc who are responsible for their own subjugation." Both critics speculate that the compromised racial themes in the film are the result of corporate strategizing and not genuine social conviction and creative thought.

One problem with *Bright* is that it is an amalgam of film genres that are not always concordant with each other and forecloses the possibility of coherent messaging. Even more, Smith gets lost within the genres rather than making significant interventions. The film takes place in a futuristic Los Angeles populated by humans of various ethnic backgrounds who form a middle class. The elites are elves, and orcs are the oppressed underclass. Smith plays Daryl Ward, an African American veteran cop who is uneasily partnered with an orc, Nick Jakoby (Joel Edgerton). The species breakdown is telling in that it illustrates one of the ways science fiction films conventionally deals with race. The human contingent of this futuristic society functions as the middle class. They are also the center of racial/species animosity. They are biased against the other species "rather than each other" (Rose, "Bright Review"). What this means is that whatever racial differences humans may find contentious are subsumed under general discrimination against other species. In other words, race does not matter in this futuristic world. Racial difference is elided under a more universal notion of humanity. This is the same strategy for avoiding racial issues used in many other Smith films such as *Independence Day* and *I, Robot*. Blackness becomes an integral part of the social fabric while otherness is displaced from Blackness onto aliens or other species. Race can be discussed only in these abstract and allegorical terms.

Even more complicated for racial representation is that Smith as the Black hero does not represent Blackness but becomes a proxy for prevailing power structures (fig. 6.4). He is not Black, but human with all those human vulnerabilities and predilections toward prejudice. He represents the police in *Bright*. In *I, Robot* he also functions as a racist cop who is antagonistic to robots. In these cases, Smith is portraying the typical white cop role in a reverse allegory of race. The purpose of such inversion of racial meaning is theoretically to critique or illuminate the workings of racism, but here instead it only serves to affirm the dominant attitudes toward race,

Fig. 6.4 Will Smith stars as Daryl Ward, a jaded cop in a fantasy vision of a future Los Angeles in *Bright* (2017). Directed by David Ayer (Netflix/Photofest).

and it is given further validation by the fact that these attitudes are displayed by the "Black" hero. Smith has his own perspective on the utility and import of the film's race reversal:

> "Flipping that social dynamic was informative," explains Smith about playing a blatant racist for the first time in his career. "One of the ideas that came through was that all of the isms—racism, sexism, nationalism—are a result of our craving for comparative superiority. I could see and I could feel how racism comes from fear and from insecurity, and from ignorance. I never saw it from that perspective before" [Sen].

Smith's epiphany about racism is that it comes from a sense of superiority, a truism of which remarkably he had not been aware.

Rose points to the implications of the film's social and species hierarchy. He writes: "In *Bright*'s scenario, elves are now the moneyed elite, humans are in the middle of society and orcs are the underclass—distrusted, mocked, discriminated against, persecuted and socially deprived. Many orcs are gang members, who hang out in sportswear and chunky jewellery and finger-gun the cops driving by" (Rose, "Bright Review"). This is a clear case of racial reversal where the orcs are stand-ins for the Black minority and humans and elves stand in for the mainstream and the upper class. Elves are at the top of the social order, with the top 1 percent being classified as Brights (or whites). This allegory does reflect real social hierarchies, but what does the film do with them? Rose comes to the following conclusion: "Racial allegories such as this are a staple of sci-fi and fantasy, and are often assumed to shine a light on modern-day society. But if *Bright* shines a light on anything, it's how problematic these kind[s] of movies are. There's a thin line between racial allegory and straight-up racist" (Rose, "Will Smith's Bright"). The representation of the orcs is racist because they are presented as metaphors for Blackness and then depicted as inferior, lawless, and not intelligent (unable to discern irony) without doing the necessary work of subverting these depictions. The film doesn't take a point of view that would salvage its racial allegory so that it makes its point with clarity. On the other hand, "defenders pointed out that *Bright* made interesting points about power structures, intolerance and prejudice. And the fact that racism between humans no longer exists in *Bright*'s world is a positive, right?" (Rose, "Will Smith's Bright"). To posit a future in which racism does not exist is positive only if it is framed in a responsible way. To wish racism away in a high concept sci-fi narrative also denies the reality of race as lived by minorities in the present, and this erasure also ignores the hard work that must be done to achieve a racism-free society.

I Am Legend *and* After Earth: *Alpha Males and Omega Men*

I Am Legend (2007), directed by Francis Lawrence (*The Hunger Games* films) and based on the novel by Richard Matheson, is a post-apocalyptic science fiction/horror drama that stars Will Smith as Robert Neville, a military virologist who finds himself the last man on Earth after a pandemic caused by a man-made virus has decimated the world's population. Throughout the film, he lives in an empty, quarantined New York City and defends himself against other survivors who have degenerated into a violent zombie life form. His primary objective is to find a cure for the virus using himself for his experimentation because of his immunity to the disease. The film did extraordinarily well, earning $585 million worldwide, setting a box-office record for a December opening and achieving a third-place ranking among Smith's all-time moneymakers (Bean).

I Am Legend is the third film version of Matheson's novel. The first was *The Last Man on Earth* (1964) starring Vincent Price, and the second was *The Omega Man* (1971) starring Charlton Heston in another iteration of his hero persona. Casting Smith in the same role sets in motion specific resonances both racial and political. The film is also inspired by *The World, the Flesh, and the Devil* (1959) starring Harry Belafonte who preceded Smith in playing the last (Black) man on Earth. The racial interpretations of this story formulation are inevitable. *I Am Legend* can be read as another post-racial science fiction vision; as a narrative about a redeemed, vulnerable Black masculinity; and as a showcase for the trope of the sacrificial Black hero.

In her examination of Black identity in *I Am Legend*, Subramanian further supports the idea that the film advances a post-racial ideology by envisioning "a patriotically multicultural future in which Blackness can be divorced from its historical associations with violent injustice. *I Am Legend* exemplifies the 'colourless' American nationalism'" (37). If the film posits a post-apocalyptic, dystopian America where race no longer matters, it is in part because of the casting of Will Smith. In the 1971 version, Neville was played by Charlton Heston. The 2007 remake was conceived as a vehicle for Arnold Schwarzenegger (Beale). When Smith comes to the role, despite his brand of "'mild' Blackness" that is reconciled to white liberalism and a concomitant post-racial ideology, he destabilizes racial meanings (Brayton, "Racial" 67). In *I, Robot*, for instance, within a framework of race reversal symbolism, his Black character can be read as functioning as white in relation to the hyperwhite robots who stand it as an oppressed slave class. In *I Am Legend*, his character is supposed to function as white, but the symbolic structure sometimes fails, rendering him fully Black in contrast to the ghostly white mutants called darkseekers who also inhabit an abandoned New York City. This gives certain moments a racial charge such as the scene in which Neville gets caught in a mutant's trap and is suspended upside down at their mercy. The scene evokes the imagery of lynching. If this scene were played with a white actor being hung in a trap by the darkseekers, it would be an ironic commentary on lynching, with the races reversed. With a Black actor, even a post-racial one, what is visualized is just another Black man about to be lynched.

The meaning of the mutants is also unstable. Although they look white, they are nonetheless associated with Blackness themselves. Brayton reads the film as a commentary on the victims of Hurricane Katrina in 2005. He writes: "In the context of disaster, however, the 'darkseekers' may also be a proxy for a predominately Black underclass stranded in New Orleans" (72). Neville's climatic understanding of the nature of the darkseekers further adds to a reading of them as Black: "Not only has he misapprehended the nature of his enemy, preferring to see them as 'all the same' and thus being unprepared for the strategic trap laid for him by the Alpha Male who has defied his presumptions both in terms of intelligence … and social capacities" (Ransom 171). Neville's view of the darkseekers is identical to racist perceptions about Black people: indistinguishable from one another, unintelligent, and uncivilized. If this view is accepted, Smith is positioned once more as the (white) hero who must defend against the Black Other. Within this interpretive scheme, the original ending in which Neville sees the humanity of the darkseekers and establishes a détente with them could be seen as a reversal of colonial power. As is, with the released film's ending, Neville's annihilation of both himself and the darkseekers conveys two messages: that the best way to deal with the alien Other is to eliminate them and that the white-positioned Black protagonist ennobles himself by making the ultimate sacrifice and reinforcing the terms of mainstream heroism.

The reading of Smith's Neville as a conquering hero furthers a post-racial vision in the usual way. As in his other science fiction films, otherness is displaced from the Black man onto the mutant-zombie-vampire darkseekers. This leaves Smith Black but without the stigma or its full cultural and historical significance. His Blackness does not matter, and he becomes a representation of humanity. Once again, Smith's screen persona transcends race.[6] The edges of his "safe" Blackness are smoothed, and other characteristics, such as his masculinity, are thrown into greater relief. With a world devoid of sentient human beings, Neville finds himself isolated, traumatized, and experiencing a crisis of masculinity. C.S. King describes his condition: "Doubly displaced from his former life, Neville has both his public position of authority as a military scientist and his private position of authority as the patriarch of a nuclear family.… In the absence of a public sphere in which to act and a private sphere in which to lead, Neville seems uncertain about how to be a man" ("Legendary" 251). Neville's traumatized vulnerability furthers the emasculation of the Black male. In addition, Neville is effectively desexualized and rendered celibate. Ransom, however, describes a symbolic moment of sexual consummation when Neville injects the darkseeker woman with his blood. She elaborates: "If we note that the legendary large penis of the black man is substituted with a needle—a metaphor for a small penis—in IAL07 [*I Am Legend* 07], we see that he remains 'safely' deflated" (169). He may be the last man on Earth, an unexpected position for a Black man at the center of a science fiction film, but in the end he is powerless if not impotent.

Yet, throughout the film Neville manifests all the outward appearances of a dominant masculinity. In the flashbacks he is depicted as an exemplary husband and father, reflecting Smith's own star persona in a slippage between actor and role. The confluence is more marked as Smith's own daughter plays Neville's daughter in the film. Another example of his masculinity is through his class position. Neville is presented as an affluent member of an upper middle class as visualized through the trappings of his life even in a post-apocalyptic Manhattan: the townhouse on Washington Park, the vintage Mustang he races through the empty city streets, the artwork he protects within his home, and the designer survival outfits he wears throughout (fig. 6.5). As Kac-Vergne observes, even the geographical parameters of Neville's New York City wasteland are classed. The destinations of his roaming through the city include Wall Street and the Metropolitan Museum of Art, but he never wanders into Harlem (150). Subramanian makes the following claim about the impact of race and

Fig. 6.5. John Neville (Will Smith), the last human man on Earth, is ever vigilant within the confines of his Manhattan townhouse in *I Am Legend* (2007). Directed by Francis Lawrence (Barry Wetcher/Warner Bros/Kobal/Shutterstock).

class on Neville's identity: "Neville's Washington Park townhouse and his former prestigious position as a government scientist associate him with an upper-middle class urbanity that … set[s] him even further apart from … any kind of historical connection to the Black community" (50). He lives in an upper-class world where race is irrelevant and in a film that doesn't mention race. He transcends race through upward social mobility. His is a masculinity that is based on capitalism and consumerism: "While the image of Will Smith/Robert Neville reclaiming and owning the city streets might seem radical in terms of the history of African American representation, in reality his one-man stance merely reflects the film's neo-liberal context" (Subramanian 50). As Ransom notes, "the message about Smith's Neville to a majority white, middle-class audience is 'yes, he's black, but he's like us'" (157). This characterization affirms a colorblind liberal ideology that success comes to those who have done everything right according to the rules of meritocracy and respectability.

The apotheosis of patriarchal masculinity established in *I Am Legend* is found in 2015's *After Earth*. It extends this mode of classed masculinity: "His films offer a positive image of Black masculinity through the trappings of the middle or even upper class, so that they tend in the end to reinscribe it in the hegemonic capitalistic patriarchal mold, as evidenced most blatantly in *After Earth*" (Kac-Vergne 143). Directed by M. Night Shyamalan, *After Earth* was not one of Smith's most successful films; it was the first Will Smith summer science fiction film in twenty years not to open at number one (Masters). Critics faulted it for being incompetent and predictable (Berardinelli). The film is nonetheless interesting for underscoring tendencies in Smith's films, his inhabitation of heroes who can be hardened and stoic and who are positioned within a bourgeois mainstream. This film also reiterates the father/son theme in contemporary science fiction films (*War of the Worlds, Interstellar, Ad Astra*). It also takes on an extra-diegetical dimension with the debated casting of Smith's son Jaden as his son.

Smith plays Cypher Raige, a military commander 1000 years in future. After a war, humans have abandoned an unlivable Earth and removed to the planet Nova Prime where they live in conflict with the native species Ursa. Cypher goes on one last mission, and after colliding with an asteroid, his spaceship crash lands on Earth. The only survivors are Cypher and his son Kitai, a cadet in training (played by Jaden Smith). To survive, Kitai must retrieve the rescue beacon against challenging odds, including a hostile environment, mutant wildlife, and a vicious Ursa that was being transported on the spaceship.

The narrative emphasizes the father's initiation of his son into manhood. After the crash of their spaceship on Earth, the son must complete a series of mental and physical tasks in order to save his father's life. The greatest lesson Cypher can teach his son is not to show emotions. When Kitai is reunited with his father and saves his life, Cypher's sign of acknowledgment is a formal salute. This gesture accomplishes two things. First, it affirms a hegemonic model of manhood that discounts feeling and insists on discipline and duty. Secondly, it establishes a form of Black manhood that refutes the notion of irresponsible Black fatherhood through Cypher's exemplary care and instruction of his son. Kac-Vergne derives a generalization from the example of this film: "In effect, the science fiction films starring Will Smith turn a *subordinated* masculinity into a *hegemonic* masculinity by conforming to the mainstream dominant model, that of middle-class *pater familias* who adheres to the structures of power…. The Black man is welcomed into the fold by becoming an upper-class patriarchal capitalist. Only, in that way, it seems, can the Black male become Man, humanity's last hope and its best representative" (154). The result is that Smith's characters reap the benefits of a capitalistic society, and they are admitted into the fold of a manhood shaped by white hegemonic norms. Subramanian asserts that Smith reflects his characters: "Smith's Hollywood career has a similar neo-liberal emphasis on individual effort and monetary gain" (51).

The final aspect of Neville's masculinity is established through his relationship or non-relationship to women. Brayton writes: "The promotion of Neville's 'manliness' relies on an active displacement of women through most of the film, a maneuver that does obvious hegemonic work" ("Racial" 73). In *I Am Legend*, the women are either villainized or killed off. Neville's wife and daughter perish in a tragic helicopter accident at the beginning of the film as they are being evacuated from the city. The darkseeker female is captured and experimented on by Neville and is ultimately killed by Neville in his successful quest to find a curative serum. Dr. Alice Krippin is the film's villain as it is her cancer cure that has infected and decimated the world's population. The marginalization of women in *I Am Legend* is symptomatic of Smith's films in general. It has been commented upon elsewhere how Black women are not paired with Smith in his biggest projects partly because of a studio calculus that assumes that two

Black leads would suppress box-office. Another reason for the effacement women in Smith's films is to define and enhance his masculinity.

The ending of the film resolves these interconnected thematic threads concerning race and masculinity. At one point in the film, Neville is joined by two other immune survivors: Anna (Alice Braga) and a young boy Ethan (Charlie Tahan). They have made it to New York en route to a survivors' settlement in Vermont. At the film's climax, Neville has successfully formulated a serum against the virus which he gives to Anna before he saves her and the boy from an attack by blowing up the darkseekers along with himself. Anna and Ethan make it to the colony which is populated with a multiracial and multiethnic mix of survivors. Kac-Vergne claims that "it is the hero's Black blood that will enable the human race to regenerate" (147). This is not precisely true. Neville passes along the blood of the cured darkseeker female he has been experimenting upon to Anna for her to make it possible to save what remains of the human world. C.S. King confirms this: "Having just discovered that his serum is curing a captive Darkseeker, Neville realizes that her blood may now transmit immunity to others. He draws her blood and passes on the vial to Anna and Ethan to dispense after his death" ("Legendary" 255). He, as a Black man, is denied the role of reconstituting the world; that function is reserved for the zombie white woman.

This interpretation rests, of course, upon the assumption of the failure of the symbolic race reversal framework. Because of this, the film ends on a note of white affirmation. King concludes: "Despite the film's overt discussion of racism, its translations of race and place maintain the privilege of both U.S. national identity and whiteness" ("Legendary" 258). King extends her argument: "Refusing to offer up Neville's blood as a source of new life, *I Am Legend* maintains fantasies about the purity and naturalness of whiteness such that not one drop of Black blood will be used to restore humanity" ("Legendary" 262). Unlike the ending of *The Omega Man* in which Charlton Heston saves the world with the purity of his white blood, this is a gesture that is denied to the same character played by a Black, even a post-racial Black, actor. Through this intertextual linkage, King finally states that the combined narrative of the films based on *I Am Legend* "asserts that the greatest authority lies in bodies that are both male <u>and</u> white" ("Legendary" 262). O'Brien goes one step further in supporting this sense of the ending's meaning: "Anna passes the cure to a white male military officer … suggesting the fate of the human race is linked to, perhaps dependent on, a recognition and restoration of white hegemony" (189). Even though Smith as Neville performs his final act courageously and honorably, he does it for the greater good, but as always, one must ask who or what is the ultimate beneficiary. Neville's "heroism" at the end of the film permits him to save Anna and Ethan while he chooses to thwart the violently threatening darkseekers by detonating an explosive that annihilates both them and himself. Anna and Ethan reach the colony, but the Black man does not make it to the promised land. Instead, falling into yet another staple of Black representation, the Black savior, he sacrifices himself for the sake of "humanity."

In the original ending of Matheson's novel and the film's alternate ending, Neville realizes the error of his violent treatment of the darkseekers. He understands that they constitute their own legitimate society with claims to the city and to a basic humanity. They are not the monsters; he is the monster who has been preying on them for his experiments in search of a cure for the virus. He returns the darkseeker woman to her husband, the Alpha Male. Carrying the successful serum, Neville, along with Anna and Ethan, seek entry to the survivors' colony with the promise of a multicultural future (King, "Legendary" 256). It is telling that the audiences and studio executives preferred the ending in which Neville blows himself up in a heroic act of self-sacrifice. When Charlton Heston does this in *The Omega Man*, it registers as indicative of the demands of the genre. When Will Smith commits this act, perhaps other conventional expectations are fulfilled. His heroic death is something the audience is also conditioned to expect, but for a different reason—because he is Black.

As we have seen, Smith does achieve breakthroughs in the genre of science fiction by extending the range and scope of Black representation and by tending to elevate the image of the Black male in the popular imagination. It is also true that Smith's screen persona in these films succumb to the social and racial conventions that mark the genre. As Black men, his hero protagonists are contained in terms of their race and masculinity in numerous ways. These characters have their power checked or invalidated by the narrative logics of the diegeses of their films. They often exist as tokens in social and cultural isolation, a Black figure living in a white world of the future. They exist under a prohibition against miscegenation. Thus, they are often rendered as eunuchs in terms of basic human needs such as intimacy and sexuality. Even when their identities appear to be progressive, their characterizations devolve into stereotype wherein Blackness is equated to body and not mind. They must operate within the confines of an interdiction against an excess of Blackness. Their Blackness can be effaced by class wherein a post-racial Black masculinity is shaped by a white, capitalist, patriarchal model, one that distances them from the realities of Black racism and struggle. They do not always stand up for Blackness but function as white in narratives based on symbolic racial reversal. Ultimately, they serve as agents of the status quo. Tani Danica Sanchez refers to Smith's film characters as "'males working within a white systemic order. They correct problems within the system but not the system itself'" (qtd. in Kac-Vergne 150). Smith interrupts and disrupts and mounts interventions into the genre, but he does not dismantle it for Blackness. He may be heroic, and he may transcend race, but, in the end, it is impossible for him to transcend whiteness.

SEVEN

Dynamic Duos
and Magical Negroes

The key to Will Smith's iconicity is a post-racial masculinity that nonetheless is not unaffected by the images and racial scripts of the past. If his ability to proffer a vision of race that transcends the usual associations is the basis of his international appeal, then his subtle yet evident evocations of Black male stereotypes, on the other hand, may offer reassurance to certain constituents within the domestic audience. This negotiation of race plays out in Smith's films as they engage and subvert the conventions of genre. We have explored the repercussions of his contributions to the genre of science fiction. These contradictions and conundrums continue in his ventures into the interracial buddy film and the Magical Negro narrative.

The Dynamics of Duos

One of Hollywood's preferred ways of dealing with race is through the genre of the interracial buddy film. The genre has its roots in the formation of the Hollywood system wherein was established an ideological practice of contrasting white male heroes with men of color in order to valorize the virtues of the former. African American men increasingly were cast in the role of serving as foil to and supporter of the white male protagonist "even to the point of denying their own interests and welfare" (Donalson 9). *The Defiant Ones* (1959), starring Tony Curtis and Sidney Poitier as escaped convicts who grow toward mutual respect, is a defining example of the genre as it developed mid-twentieth century. The significance of the interracial buddy film is that it purportedly moves beyond an antagonistic configuration of power. In the '80s, Black crossover stars were paired with white actors, and this coupling proved economically advantageous and further established the genre. In the '90s the genre burgeoned with the rise of multiculturalism. It became evident that "the buddy formula is able to attract demographically the broadest possible audience" (Guerrero 240). The reaction at the box office between 1987 and 2002 bears this out: "the average gross of black-and-white buddy movies is $101,939,175, while the average gross for all buddy movies is $67,081,163" (Malanowski 1). The genre clearly strikes a chord in audiences and affirms a deep cultural wish for racial harmony if not equality.

Donalson defines four constitutive elements of the interracial buddy formula. First, the interracial relationship between the two male protagonists is central to the narrative. Second, the lives of the two men are connected at all levels both professional and private, which allows for a transcendence of racial difference. Third, the two males are heterosexual to affirm cultural norms of masculinity and heroism and to assure the purity of their developing intimacy across the racial divide. Fourth, the central relationship goes beyond the bounds of mere friendship and thus can incorporate trust, sacrifice, and confession (10).

Donalson goes on to define the ideological ramifications of the interracial buddy film pattern. These films hold out the hope that conflicts, even racial ones, can be overcome; that racial rapprochement on screen can be achieved in lived experience; that "the American capitalistic system nurtures humanity and tolerance"; and that all men share in patriarchal power (11). Donalson admits that the problem with the desired effects of the genre is that they make audiences think the work of achieving social equality and progress has been accomplished. Even more problematic is Donalson's conclusion: "for men of color, the messages provided state that acceptance into the dominant male culture depends upon maintaining and replicating the demeanor and attitudes of the dominant group that has oppressed them" (11). Guerrero extends this conclusion asserting that containment of Blackness is central to the interracial buddy film as it established itself in the '80s: "Hollywood has put what is left of the Black presence on the screen in the protective custody, so to speak, of a White lead or co-star, and therefore in conformity with the dominant, White sensibilities and expectations of what Blacks should be like" (239). This containment takes the form of a casting protocol that requires the pairing of a white actor opposite a Black actor who has risen to the level of above-the-title status as a complement or as a check. This was Smith's route to stardom. He has most often been paired with white actors (not actresses Black or white) even in films in other genres during his rise to stardom in the '90s.

Smith as a post-racial Black male star intervenes in the logics of the genre primarily because of his hybridized Blackness. He embodies a kind of cool that is a style of Blackness appealing to a broad demographic of filmgoers. His persona conveys a societal wish to transcend race. He extends to audiences the assurance that in his films race will not be an issue, thus enhancing their entertainment value. O'Brien observes: "For the most part, commercial cinema remained interested only in Black characters and issues intelligible and agreeable to white sensibilities, embodied by a marketable and therefore exceptional Black actor; the results refracted a society in an ongoing state of racial denial, unable or unwilling to deal openly with its inequalities and conflicts" (181). The emergence of Smith at that historical moment of the '90s was a fortunate convergence of the Zeitgeist and Hollywood's interests.

If the buddy film's message of racial harmony is dependent upon a clear opposition of white and Black positions and identities, what happens when the Black partner introduces a different, non-essentialist variation of Blackness? The intended racial points become confused allowing for the emergence of other meanings, for instance the eruption of homoerotic currents that for the most part are otherwise suppressed and denied in the genre almost by definition. Fuchs goes so far as to argue that the homosocial-homosexual dynamic is the driving force beneath the interracial cop-buddy bond to the extent that this powerful force becomes displaced upon racial difference ("Buddy" 194–195). Furthermore, when the Blackness of the Black partner does not fully conflict with or oppose the force of the white partner, the result is a final affirmation of white hegemonic power. Smith's racial transcendence in his star image and screen persona may inflect the dynamics and messaging of the buddy film genre, but even his racial dexterity cannot always overcome the insistence of Hollywood upon its ideology.

Man to Man

Although an assertive heterosexuality is the norm in the genre, the interpersonal workings of the interracial buddy team still incorporate homosocial and homoerotic elements. Fuchs even claims that the racial and homoerotic/homosocial/homosexual dimensions of the buddy team's relationship vary inversely. The more firmly the same sex feeling is suppressed, the greater is the racial tension and conflict between the two. When the racial pressure is lessened (here with Smith's hybridized, assimilationist Black identity in contrast to the Blackness of Richard Pryor and Eddie Murphy in their interracial buddy films), the homoerotic anxiety manifests itself as can be seen consistently in Smith's body of work.

Jennifer Gillan reads Smith's first major film, Fred Schepisi's *Six Degrees of Separation* (1993), as a variation of the interracial buddy film. Smith's con artist impersonating the fictional son of Sidney Poitier is paired with Flan Kittredge (Donald Sutherland), the art dealer whom "Paul" dupes into entertaining him in his Fifth Avenue apartment for the night. Gillan argues that the film fulfills the expectations of the genre while at the same time subverting and exploding them.[1] She elaborates on the homoerotic dimension of the film, specifically Flan's fraught and resistant attraction to Paul. Same sex desire does not just exist beneath the surface but emerges at key moments, such as the scene in which Flan tends to Paul's knife wound. Paul is shirtless and suggestively seated on the edge of the tub as Flan administers first aid. A charged look passes between them, the meaning of which Flan denies for the rest of the film.

There are several moments in *Bad Boys* (1995) that queer the self-conscious, obligatory heterosexuality of the two buddies, Mike Lowery (Smith) and Marcus Burnett (Martin Lawrence). During the early action, the two switch identities in order not to confuse Julie Mott (Tea Leoni), a witness to a drug related murder. Marcus and Julie retreat to Lowery's condo which Marcus pretends to be his. Julie is confused as to why there are so many photographs of a handsome man in the apartment. (They are Mike's photographs of himself.) She asks Marcus if the man in the pictures is his lover, and she confesses she was wondering if he were gay. She assures him that she is fine with homosexuality. Offended and incredulous, Marcus goes into an elaborate comic denial that contributes to an air of homosexual panic and homophobia that informs the film. Extradiegetic homophobia appears in the stories about the offscreen strife during the filming of the last scene. The script has Lowery say to Marcus, "I love you, man." Such a line is de rigueur in the buddy film genre, designating a bridge between the two races. In this case, with both partners being Black, the homoerotic dimensions of the buddy relationship become inflected. Perhaps this is what Smith sensed when he at first refused to deliver the lines on set, a repetition of his refusal to kiss Michael Anthony Hall in *Six Degrees of Separation*. In the end, he acceded to the wishes of the director Michael Bay and delivered the line as written (Iannucci 42).

Near the beginning of *Independence Day* (1996), Smith's character, marine pilot Captain Steve Hiller, is called to action when the Earth is attacked by alien space-ships. In the locker room at the military base, Hiller opens a rejection letter from the space program in response to his application to be an astronaut. His best friend, Captain Wilder (Harry Connick, Jr.), Smith's first buddy partner in the film (to be succeeded by Jeff Goldblum's Dr. David Levinson), advises him that in order to get ahead he as to kiss "booty." At this point, Wilder kneels behind Hiller and attempts to kiss his posterior. Wilder also happens to be holding the engagement ring Hiller intends to give to his girlfriend, Jasmine. Another pilot enters the space and reads the interaction as a gay proposal. He backs away, and the scene elicits a laugh from the film's audiences. Further establishing the romantic, homoerotic male bonding of the two is the scene when they are given their commands, and Wilder effeminately feigns fear and rests his head on Hiller's shoulder (fig. 7.1). Again, because the racial opposition between Smith and Connick's characters is not emphasized, other forces such as same sex desire can emerge in such a moment. Notable as well is what happens during the attack on the alien ship. The marine pilots are forced to flee. Wilder's jet

Fig. 7.1. Capt. Steve Hiller (Will Smith) and Capt. Jimmy Wilder (Harry Connick, Jr.) share a comic close moment during a mission briefing in *Independence Day* (1996). Directed by Roland Emmerich (20th Century–Fox/Photofest).

explodes, but Hiller escapes. This is a reversal of the usual plot formula whereby the Black sidekick sacrifices his life or dies first. Here, the white buddy dies to allow the Black partner, Smith as character and star, in an historic act of genre intervention, to move to the center of the narrative and to assume his position as hero.

The homoerotic subtext is not pronounced in *Men in Black* because the racial (and generational) difference between Smith's Agent J and Tommy Lee Jones's Agent K is highlighted. The power dynamic between the two is stressed and sustained. Agent K is the mentor while Agent J is his subordinate. This racially imbalanced dynamic is in keeping with the genre which advances racial resolution while it implicitly insists upon the containment of the Black male body. Nowhere is this more evident than at the end of the sequence in which Jay is initiated into the Men in Black organization. After he receives his corporate Black suit, Jay also receives from Kay an official gun, the Noisy Cricket, in contrast to Kay's larger weapon, the J2. The joke references the stereotype about Black male genital endowment size. Soon after, the two shoot their guns in unison, a metaphorical mutual ejaculation that discloses a submerged homoerotic bond (Hicks 124; Fuchs 199).

In *Wild Wild West* (1998), Captain James West (Smith) and U.S. Marshall Artemus Gordon (Kevin Kline) are established as heterosexual through their shared interest in and rivalry over Rita (Selma Hayek) who has joined them on their mission. Despite this, their relationship has its queer aspects. Beyond their joking competition about their respective drag disguises, there are specific moments that put them into physical and sexual contact, such as the comic sequence wherein the magnetic collars they wear cause them to become entangled, ending with West's face before Gordon's crotch, comically implying fellatio. At the end of the film, Rita, on whom both West and Gordon have had romantic designs, reveals that the man she was in search of all along is not her father but her husband. She kisses them both off with the line, "At least you still have each other" (*Wild, Wild West* 1:39:33–1:39:35).

In *Enemy of the State*, Smith plays Robert Dean, a lawyer who gets unwittingly embroiled in a conspiracy with the government to assassinate a senator. When Dean, who has incriminating evidence, is targeted by the covert group, he relies upon a retired veteran agent, Brill (Gene Hackman), to maneuver through the attempts on his life. Donalson admits that in this film there is not a fully achieved buddy partnership, but there is a frisson of homoeroticism. In order to protect Dean from imminent danger involving surveillance and hidden microphones, Brill commands Dean in the hallway of a hotel to take off his clothes and go into the hotel room. There is no implied sexual intent, but the situation in its momentary imbalance of power and male vulnerability moves it, as occurs so often in Smith's films, into a suggestive, ambiguous space.

Avoiding Race

For the interracial buddy film, racial difference is the attraction, but only to the extent that it is overcome. The genre presents a post-racial vision of America. O'Brien notes, "If there is no legally recognized racial difference or distinction, there is no racial discrimination and therefore no need for corrective measures" (180). The ability to circumvent and mitigate the realities of Blackness is what Smith's stardom is predicated upon, and his buddy films showcase race without directly engaging or confronting it.

In *Six Degrees of Separation*, Paul, the impersonator of Sidney Poitier's (fictional) son, utters a direct disavowal of race and racism when he explains his background to the Fifth Avenue couple who has given him shelter. He says, "I never knew I was Black in that racist way till I was sixteen and came back here. Very protected. White servants. After the divorce we moved to Switzerland, my mother, brother and I. I don't feel American. I don't even feel Black" (*Six Degrees of Separation* 0:21:57–0:22:11). His denial of race gives comfort to his hosts and parallels Smith's own strategy for prevailing in Hollywood. Although jokes are made in the film about apartheid in South Africa, race hovers over the proceedings but operates as an amusing detail within an anecdote told by the story's central white privileged couple.

Although produced during the O.J. Simpson trial and racial upheavals in Los Angeles and other locations, *Independence Day* offers an anodyne view of race in America, one that conveys "a fantasy resolution of the racially tinged rupture" that pervaded America in the '90s (O'Brien 182). In the film, a multicultural group of men with different skills and areas of military and scientific expertise join forces to defeat the threat of an invasion by hostile aliens. Through collective effort, they achieve their goal of winning the safety and survival of the human race, an effort that results in the effacement of individual racial and ethnic identities. Smith's character here, Captain Steve Hiller, is specifically coded as Black, with an African American fiancée, a future stepson, and a cool and hip attitude that almost borders on stereotype. He has a brief encounter with racism in the rejection letter he receives in response to his application for the space program. He even marries a Black woman in an act of affirmation of the Black family. These narrative details are unusual for a Smith role, but it comes before he became "Will Smith." The film's historic success catapulted him to stardom and an attendant alteration of his screen persona to one that is more benign and racially reticent. Even in this film the racial markers are subsumed under group effort and the universal good. While racial difference may be superficially recognized, then elided, it is not contemplated, nor are racial issues confronted. Smith as Hiller may be an exemplary, but his Blackness is less important than his heroism.

Donalson notes that whenever there are racial references in *Men in Black*, they are made by Agent J in ways that are jocular and hip: "Early in the movie during a chase sequence, Edwards/Jay jumps onto a moving tour bus from a bridge, proclaiming: 'It just be raining Black people in New York'" (135). These references serve to underscore his Blackness and to put him in opposition to Agent K. The racial quips and observations function as added entertainment value and not as windows into any Black reality even as reflected within a science fiction narrative. *Men in Black 2* avoids race by having Agent J operating with his entire identity erased as a result of his total assimilation into the Men in Black corporate order and having his memory wiped by the top-secret weapon, the neuralyzer. The erasure of self also effects an erasure of his Blackness and thus frees the film from having to deal with race.

Men in Black 3 is predicated on a focus on race as its action travels in time to points in the recent past, namely 1969, that were racially charged. However, as Josh Nelson notes:

> MiB3 avoids any substantive reference to civil rights protests or the treatment of African Americans in the 1960s. Instead, the film reduces these conflicts to a single-scene gag in which J is pulled over by two overzealous white police officers who suspect him of driving a stolen motor vehicle. That J has in fact stolen the car allows the film to indulge racial stereotypes of African Americans under the guise of a contemporary racial awareness, without questioning the basis of those racist assumptions.

Smith's Agent J handles this situation with his usual quick wit and cool, but there is no contextualization for his being targeted as a Black man or what that means or how it affects him. It is just another opportunity for a comic line. Brody observes that Smith's character here is a "superseded racial cliché" or "the Hollywood stereotype of the Cool Black Dude" (Brody). Agent J is the creation of a screenwriter's imagination stuck in a '90s Hollywood concept of the past and not the past ostensibly depicted in the film. Brody surmises that Smith is ultimately constrained by the film in terms of racial representation as his character conforms to "cloistered industry norms and expectations" (Brody). One of its more persistent norms is to play with race rather than to plumb it.

In *Wild Wild West* Smith plays Captain James West who is an anachronistic Black government agent four years after the Civil War. The film makes special efforts to define West as Black, ranging from the utterances of racial epithets and insults "framed by humor and sarcasm" to a backstory that invokes historical racial violence to a comic lynching scene that "trivializes the horror of lynching, as well as the destructiveness of slavery" (Donalson 149). Again, West's Blackness is accentuated for humor based on historical dislocations, but curiously his Blackness, while present and emphasized, does not play a part in his antagonism with his white partner, the intellectual inventor Artemus Gordon. There is no racial divide they must cross to arrive at mutual respect; the only things they overcome are their personal idiosyncrasies and quirks (fig. 7.2). Theirs is an interracial buddy partnership basically without the race.

This absence of race is accentuated by one scene in the film that can be profitably compared to a similar scene in *The Defiant Ones*. The 1958 film, starring Sidney Poitier and Tony Curtis and directed by Stanley Kramer, follows the genre master narrative wherein the two men overcome their racial conflicts to reach a place of mutual understanding and respect. In the film the two prisoners, Cullen (Poitier) and Joker Jackson (Curtis) are thrown from a train that is transporting them to a penitentiary. The two are chained together as they struggle to escape. They must break through the racial, psychological, and cultural barriers that separate them to secure their freedom. The nuances of struggle can be seen in the sequence during which they have difficulties getting themselves out of a clay pit. One makes it halfway up the slippery embankment and then slides back down. Then the other tries to no avail. Only through concerted effort and mutual support do they succeed, and the metaphorical message is clear. In *Wild Wild West*, Smith and Kline fall into a mire of quicksand, and the ending of the scene is punctuated with Smith sneezing into Kline's deadpan face.

Fig. 7.2. Capt. James West (Will Smith) and Artemus Gordon (Kevin Kline) comically clash in the steampunk action/comedy *Wild, Wild West* (1999). Directed by Barry Sonnenfeld (Warner Bros./Photofest).

The laugh is achieved, but nothing remotely resembling racial reconciliation is registered.

Enemy of the State would appear to be a narrative about the ability of government intelligence and its powerful, ubiquitous technological resources of surveillance to destroy the life of an upstanding, affluent Black man. It is true that the film would have a different impact if Smith's character were to be played by a white actor (as originally conceived), but ultimately it doesn't make a difference because of the "safe" Blackness Smith brings to the role. Dean's Blackness is ornamental in that the film seems to score points for social consciousness by having a Black protagonist but does not dramatize or explore the meaning or conditions of that Blackness. Though marked as Black through dialogic details including racial insults (which seem incongruous give Smith's deflective brand of Blackness), Smith's character functions in the film as any leading man whose jeopardy elicits the concern and emotional investment of the audience.

Smith's two science fiction buddy films, *I, Robot* and *Bright*, would seem to be anomalies, but they find their own ways of avoiding race in keeping with the norm of the genre. In these two films race is addressed in reverse allegory form wherein Smith plays the white cop while his partner is the Other: a robot and an orc, respectively. The racial reversal throws into relief the attitudes and processes of racism. It is then possible for racial difference to be reconciled through mutual understanding. The conservative, racist cop (played by Smith) in both films overcomes his prejudices in order to appreciate and accept his counterpart. The larger problem with the race reversal ploy is that it is only a cosmetic and not fundamental alteration of the buddy formula because the narrative dynamics and outcome remain the same. These futuristic science fiction buddy action films argue that difference can be overcome, that racial differences between humans are obsolete, that racism is a matter for individual and not systemic remedy, and that grievances of the oppressed must be elided in the interest of the greater good. Once again race is prominently featured as a controlling issue in the films, only to conclude with confused, contradictory, or nullifying racial messages.

Another problematic aspect of the racial reversal is that the objective is never realized. In *I, Robot,* the allegory itself becomes hard to read. If Smith represents the human (white) majority against the robot (Black) insurgent minority, then how is the robot rebellion to be interpreted? The film argues that the rebellion must be stopped to restore order, which also means that minority assertion must be contained and the rebellious robots (Blacks) must be put back into their place. Similarly, in *Bright* the equation of fantasy creatures with human minorities is done without the necessary careful and thoughtful development. The result is the reinforcement of racist representation, which could not be what the film intends to purvey. Additionally, since the audience is sympathetic to the orc character Jakoby (Joel Edgerton) who faces discrimination, the Black character played by Smith is moved to the ideological center. The result is that the issues of race and racism are borne by the fantasy species, and the struggles of people of color are effaced. Karen Han is explicit about this: "I almost couldn't help but wonder if working fantasy species into this story wasn't just an excuse to not have to deal with any 'real' politics and try to come off as progressive or edgy as a result, or a sort of cover-up to disguise the fact that this is a movie about racial discrimination and struggle written by a privileged white man (the son of John Landis) lacking any grasp of race relations." The film wants to thematize race but without dealing directly with Black people.

Racial reversal wants to illuminate racism, but it requires viewers to take an interpretive leap—to see the workings of power from the other side, from the perspective of the oppressor who undergoes a change. In *I, Robot,* as Spooner overcomes his aversion to robots (the Other), so does the viewer. This is expedited by the viewer being asked to identify with the eminently sympathetic Will Smith. The viewers relate to Smith and not to the revolutionary robots. Spooner's "change" is effected by a truce he forges with Sonny who is not in league with what should be the sympathetic robot force and who can be read as a race traitor aligned with (white) humanity. This is like Charlton Heston's situation in *The Planet of the Apes* (1969) who, as the lone white survivor on a planet controlled by apes, is treated like a slave.[2] The idea of race reversal here is that audiences will understand the outrages of Black slavery through empathy with Heston's plight. The truth is that mainstream viewers would probably identify more with his besieged whiteness and read the apes as out of control Blacks in power. The problem with racial reversal is that it asks for a suspension of white privilege and a leap of empathy and imagination that audiences are not capable of making.[3]

Smith's innovation within the genre with the film *Bad Boys* is for him not to be paired with a white partner but with another Black actor (fig. 7.3). This case is unlike

Fig. 7.3. Will Smith (Mike Lowery) and Martin Lawrence (Marcus Burnett) star in an all-Black variation of the police buddy film in *Bad Boys* (1995). Directed by Michael Bay (Columbia Pictures/Photofest).

the choices made by Eddie Murphy whose box office success in the '80s depended upon his starring in interracial cop buddy films which established a contemporary iteration of the genre. These films include *48 Hours* (1982), and *Beverly Hills Cop I* (1984) and *II* (1987), the latter two being the top grossing films of their years (Guerrero 243). Smith seemingly has avoided the stereotypical racial narratives that Murphy so often perpetuates. Murphy performs a certain expected kind of Blackness. These "films are driven by the disruptive effects of Murphy's irreverent and cocky interpretations of Blackness on the dominant White social order" (243). Murphy effects subversions of white society, but this is a staple of the interracial buddy formula. There is finally a limit to his racial interruptions. Guerrero sees "Murphy's Blackness challenging White exclusion, but not domination or privilege" (243). Murphy may be disruptive, but ultimately, he, too, is contained by whiteness.

Smith's partnering with Martin Lawrence seemingly does offer something new. The film is notable to its supporters because "it defies expectations and shifts the paradigms of race and cinematic genres" (Rex). Both Smith and Lawrence were coming to films from popular television shows, *The Fresh Prince of Bel-Air* and *Martin*, respectively. The studio was taking a risk in toplining them in a major release. The other factor in the film's breaking of norms is the director Michael Bay who forges his signature style incorporating chaotic action sequences and irreverent, profane humor. Even though both leads are Black men who inhabit Black worlds, race is never engaged except through a liberal use of racial epithets and improvised comic riffs that border on buffoonery. The fact that two Black male actors star in a major Hollywood release does not have the same cultural significance as, say, a pairing of Sidney Poitier and Bill Cosby in the '70s. *Bad Boys* does not do important cultural work nor refract the challenges or concerns of the Black community.

Even in terms of genre, the *Bad Boys* films are not as subversive for teaming two Black actors as they appear because the interpersonal dynamic between the two replicates the formula. The white member is the straight man while the other is more antic. (In other films, both actors have occupied the comic relief role.) Here, Smith inhabits the position usually taken by the white actor. That he does so is indicative of the post-racial Blackness that he represents, his "difference" within Blackness. This difference is borne out by the revelation that his character, Mike Lowery, is playing at being a policeman, that, in fact, he comes from the upper class and is supported by a trust fund. This does much to extend the parameters of the representation of Black men (and this is emblematic of the Smith persona and career), but it doesn't further a conversation about race.

Affirming Whiteness

Beyond the matter of the interracial pairing being a subordination of the Black partner, there is also a hierarchical relegation of racial characteristics whereby white equals mind and Black equals body. This is often true in Smith's films: Jeff Goldblum's brainy scientist vs. Smith's bold fighter pilot *in Independence Day*; Tommy Lee Jones's stoic and rational Agent K vs. Smith's intuitive and athletic Agent J in *Men in Black*; and Kevin Kline's mercurial and brilliant Artemus Gordon vs. Smith's fast talking and hard fighting James West in *Wild, Wild West*. In each case, the balance tilts toward white superiority. Hicks deems the "interracial buddy film to be a medium through which Hollywood reasserts the power of white men" (125). This privileging is especially apparent in the endings of Smith's buddy movies as will be delineated below.

In the denouement of *Six Degrees of Separation*, Paul is arrested and disappears into the criminal justice system. His Blackness is just an interruption in the lives of the couple who disappear back into their elitism and whiteness. Although the wife Ouisa claims to have been inspired by her encounter with Paul and walks away from Flan, her husband, it is not clear that world she inhabits has undergone a similar transformation.

At the end of *Independence Day* when the hostile alien forces have been defeated through the collaborative heroic efforts of Hiller (Smith) and Levinson (Goldblum), they are greeted on land by the president (Bill Pullman) and his support team. Hiller, Levinson and the president are equally reunited with their wives and children. The president offers thanks and acknowledgments first to Hiller and then more attentively to Levinson. O'Brien reads this conclusion as an apotheosis of racial equality, describing it as "a microcosmic refraction of global racial/ethnic reconciliation, solidarity and collective action" (183). Though Hiller is apparently afforded equality, the editing of the scene privileges Smith. The president's daughter wishes her father a Happy Fourth of July. Immediately thereafter Hiller, holding his stepson in his arms, says, "Didn't I promise you fireworks?" (*Independence Day* 2:15:40). The film ends with streams of light falling to earth, the remnants of the exploded alien mothership. In an earlier sequence, the alien spacecrafts have landed in locales around the world. As a result, O'Brien concludes that the world has not been saved just for white people. The world may have been saved by Hiller, but on whose behalf? In the end Hiller has been acting as an agent of the United States which in its encompassing global power has taken on the mission. Ultimately, Hiller must salute the president and call him, "Sir." This is an action not repeated by Levinson who is not military. Hiller's gesture of respect on another level establishes his subordinance to a white man and the institutional structures he represents.

The elevation of the white partner in interracial buddy films is effected by the emasculation of the Black partner. In the *Lethal Weapon* films, Danny Glover is domesticated whereas the Mel Gibson character is an alpha male loose cannon. In *Men in Black*, Agent J is feminized. He becomes associated with feminine feelings when "he urges K to interact more compassionately with humans who have seen aliens" (Hicks 125). More important, however, are the endings of the *Men in Black* films which find Agent J seemingly on equal footing with K but inevitably absorbed into a white organization whose power remains unquestioned and undiminished. Hicks elaborates on how Agent J is assimilated into the corporate culture and in the process how he separates himself from his Blackness ironically by donning the Black suit. She concludes: "Far from a man in Black, then, he becomes a man effaced by generic whiteness" (129).

Like *Independence Day*, *Wild, Wild West* advances the idea that evil adversaries can be overcome when race is set aside for larger cooperative effort. Here, West (Smith) and Gordon (Kevin Kline), despite their personal conflicts which are not necessarily race based (the film refusing to insist upon this), are still able to confront, outwit, and defeat the villain Loveless (Kenneth Branagh). As O'Brien describes, "For the showdown, West and Gordon stand shoulder to shoulder in matching brown suits, this complementary attire refracting an interracial unity of purpose and resolve" (192). The racial rapprochement remains uneasy at the conclusion. West continues to be annoyed by Gordon's habit of questioning. The two have been inducted into the newly formed Secret Service by President Grant as Agents One and Two. Although the president says it doesn't matter which one of them takes precedence, the blocking of the scene favors Gordon to whom the president gives the first badge. Again, the president offers thanks and commendations to the two (although it is West who does finally kill Loveless), accentuating that their efforts have been on behalf of the government. This pronouncement effectively contains West's heroics within a manageable frame of racial dynamics.

Enemy of the State in which Smith is paired with Gene Hackman is founded upon the basic tenets of the interracial buddy film: the transcendence of race and the superintendence of the Black partner. Smith's Robert Dean is a Washington, D.C., labor lawyer who stumbles upon evidence of an NSA plot to execute and cover up the murder of a Congressman who backs crucial anti-terrorist legislation. Rogue agents are out to eliminate Dean and recover the evidence stored, without his knowledge, on a disc in his possession. He is aided and protected by a veteran intelligence expert

(Hackman) throughout his ordeal. The 1998 film uncannily predicts the issues concerning intelligence and privacy that circulate today twenty years later. The film also illustrates certain dynamics of the buddy genre. The Black-white team here is differentiated by a generational divide, the white member being older than the Black man. This set up resembles that of Agents K and J, Tommy Lee Jones and Smith in the *Men in Black* films, or even the Nick Nolte and Eddie Murphy pairing in *Beverly Hills Cop*. This is also consistent with the casting of Danny Glover and Mel Gibson in the *Lethal Weapon* series but with the races reversed.

Usually the younger Black partner brings hip irreverence, unorthodox methodology, and shrewd intuition to the working relationship while the older man contributes logic and experience. This is not particularly true in *Enemy of the State* because the relationship seems imbalanced toward the older partner. The Gene Hackman character functions as a mentor or savior for Dean, getting him out of multiple dangerous situations. Brill is in control of the younger Black man. There is no back and forth camaraderie based on racial tension. Instead, the racial tension is minimized, which is the forte of Smith's star persona and his disruption of the genre. It might be added that the role of Robert Dean was written for a white actor and other actors such as Arnold Schwarzenegger were originally considered for the role. Will Smith was cast, and though there are racial character markers in the film, he inhabits a conceptually white character so well, as he is wont to do, that his Blackness doesn't matter. Instead of the partners overcoming racial difference, what remains is a Black star who transcends race and thus disrupts the expectations of the genre.

The casting of two Black actors as the buddy cop team in the *Bad Boys* films would seem to upend the ideological position of the genre. Although these films are otherwise true to formula (car chases, explosions, shootouts with stock villains) and they do reach closure with the restoration of order, there is no explicit representation of a white presence that presides over and benefits from the film's resolution. In *Bad Boys*, Burnett (Lawrence) and Lowery (Smith) kill Fouchet (Tcheky Karyo), the drug lord responsible for the theft of a cache of heroin worth $100 million from police custody. The two Black detectives are deployed by Internal Affairs and are supervised and harangued by their captain played by Joe Pantoliano. At the end of the film, having completed their job, the two briefly recover from their injuries incurred during the climatic gun battle. The only white characters present are the medics whose help Burnett refuses and a white cop who does not have the keys to free Lowery from the handcuffs he shares with Julie. Burnett has just conjoined them. All three characters are surrounded by a circle of police cars as a reminder of a larger authority to whom they are responsible. Burnett returns to his wife and home while Smith is left handcuffed to Julie, the white woman who has been assisting in the case. The rejection of a controlling white patriarchal power would have been much better registered with both men walking away free and unconstrained. The symbolism of Smith bonded to a white woman begs interpretation, and it does connect Smith to whiteness as so often occurs in his films.

The science fiction hybrids of the Will Smith buddy film, *I, Robot* and *Bright*, are true to formula in terms of the settlement of interpersonal racial conflict and the final affirmation of whiteness. In *I, Robot*, Smith's character, Del Spooner, an African

American cop of the future, where robots constitute a servant class, is paired with Sonny, a robot who has been accused of murder, to solve that crime and to suppress a robot rebellion. Because of his now fraught history with robots as well as his own part-cyborg physical status, Spooner is antagonistic to Sonny and all robots. His animus thus is motivated by self-hatred. His bias against robots also has a complex racial dimension. In a racial reversal, Smith occupies the role of the white cop with a minority (robot) junior partner. Over the course of the film as they make progress in their mission, Spooner overcomes his prejudice and learns to respect Sonny. Again, this is a race reversal as Smith's Spooner is Black and Sonny is a cyborg of unnatural gleaming whiteness. Their racial accord which conforms to genre is highlighted in the film when the two shake hands in close-up. This is one of the film's key images.

The film's racial ideology at its closure is relatively clear cut. The revolt of the robots has been put down, and V.I.K.I., the central computer intelligence that controls the robots and masterminds the insurrection, has been destroyed. At this juncture, it seems that Sonny's consciousness has been raised by his experience with Spooner. A figure appears on a hill who draws the robots to him; implied is a new uprising with Sonny, not Spooner, as its leader. If the race reversal is read correctly and consistently, Spooner functions as the white mentor to Sonny's messianic role. Not only has he restored order and made the world safe for humankind (and here humans can be read as the white majority), he has also empowered the robot (slave/Black) minority. In the end, the film affirms whiteness on two levels—in saving the world for the status quo and in Smith's character, in relation to Sonny and the robot population, functioning, though Black, as a white savior.

Bright continues the racial reversal narrative stratagem into a futuristic Los Angeles inhabited by humans, fairies, elves, and orcs. Smith plays Daryl Ward, a seasoned and cynical police officer who mistrusts and dislikes his orc partner, Jakoby, played by Joel Edgerton. Smith takes the position of what is usually the bigoted white cop while Edgerton portrays the reviled first minority member on the force. Together they reconstitute the interracial buddy duo but this time across species lines (fig. 7.4). During the film through ambushes, shootouts, kidnappings, and escapes, in true genre fashion, Ward comes to trust and respect Jakoby. He even makes it possible for Jakoby to rejoin his orc clan from which his assimilation into human society had estranged him. In doing so, "Ward even assumes the role of white savior except he's Black" (Bowen). Ward and Jakoby have been engaged to protect a young elf woman in possession of one of three magic wands with legendary powers. The wands can be handled without fatal consequences only by special beings known as Brights. In the racial hierarchy of this world, orcs are the underclass with multi-ethnic humans occupying the middle class, and elves being the equivalent of a privileged One Percent. Brights are special beings from this upper class. The social class divisions stem from wars fought thousands of years ago. Astonishingly, near the end of the film when the cop team locates the wand, it is Ward who can seize and handle it without dying, thus revealing his identity as a Bright. According to magic lore, Brights are elves. Reading the racial allegory correctly, Brights are also the equivalent of whites. What does it mean then for Smith's Ward to be a Bright?

Fig. 7.4. Will Smith as Daryl Ward and Joel Edgerton as Nick Jacoby star in a science fiction fantasy version of the interracial buddy film in *Bright* (2017). Directed by David Ayer (Netflix/Photofest).

One might invoke the racial categories of apartheid and see Ward as a Bright or an honorary white. The character's racially reversed symbolic whiteness becomes something more literal as the revelation of his magical power keeps the resurgence of the Dark Lord at bay and reinforces the existing social structure. Even within a complex, confusing, and incoherent science fiction fantasy narrative, the status quo and a fantasy form of whiteness are reaffirmed.

Will Smith's star persona that negotiates race so adroitly argues for alterations and transformations of the buddy films in which he stars. His presence should enact interventions in the genre. There of intimations of this when his postraciality destabilizes the racial opposition between the Black and white male couple and allows for homoerotic subtexts to emerge from the depths of a heterosexual dynamic. The racial harmony that is achieved by the Black and white partners, a symbolic, liberal cultural wish, is done so in these films only through the suppression of any direct or responsible representation of the real challenges and struggles of the Black community. Though these films foreground race, they simultaneously elide it. The buddy genre also seeks to establish the equality of the races despite difference and to elevate the status of the Black partner. Yet, at the end of these films, for the most part, the narrative resolves itself so that the Black man is contained not only by the authority of the white partner but by a large structural whiteness as well. Given his reputation for racial transcendence and its potential for disrupting and reshaping the genre, it is remarkable that Will Smith's buddy film vehicles persist in adhering to form.

A Magical African American Friend

In her description of the interracial buddy film, Jennifer Gillan refers to Black film historian Donald Bogle's characterization of aspects of the genre:

> Donald Bogle describes interracial buddy films as wish-fulfillment vehicles in which the Black character is often a supporting player or "background material" in the story of the white man's spiritualization or maturation. Bogle characterizes the Black buddy as a cross between an Uncle Tom and a Mammy: "all giving, all-knowing, all-sacrificing nurturer." Such a character often imparts spiritual insight, heightens the white buddy's heroism, and sometimes helps him achieve maturity. He often shows a willingness for self-sacrifice and frequently gives his life for the "white massa/friend." The ideal Black buddy is also cleansed of too strong a racial identity and shows no sign of cultural gaps or distinctions that would have to be bridged in order to form a relationship with the white character [Bogle 276 qtd. in Gillan 48].

This account of the Black partner in the interracial buddy duo also specifies some salient attributes of another stereotype, the Magical Negro. The appearances of this figure in films, particularly in the '90s, virtually constitute a subgenre. The term was coined and put into popular circulation by Spike Lee in 2001 during a series of public lectures at college campuses. The Magical Negro is the Black character in fiction and film who has a magical power or spiritual wisdom that is used to solve the problems of a white protagonist or to give moral advice leading to personal redemption. This character has no purpose but to serve the needs of the main, usually white male, character or the interests of white people in general and is willing to sacrifice his or her life for them. This figure has no history or connection to family or community. The Magical Negro appears and, when his or her redemptive or restorative task is accomplished, mysteriously disappears.

The Magical Negro stock character has come under serious sociological study. Glenn and Cunningham arrive at a definition of the figure through a systematic examination of eight films within the category:

> Based on previous research and this analysis, the magical Negro is defined as the only Black lead character in a film with a predominantly White cast endowed with folk wisdom as well as spiritual and/or magical gifts and abilities. Magical Negros utilize their gifts externally for the benefit of the White characters in the film. The magical Negro has limited depth—any other facets of the character are secondary to wisdom and magic, and he or she does not have significant contact with or ties to anyone other than the White lead characters. The magical Negro usually exhibits a blatant disregard for self, never using his or her abilities to improve personal situations. Although on the surface these characters appear to be harmless and even an improvement from the roles Blacks played in early-20th-century entertainment, some magical Negroes still resemble old, debasing racial stereotypes [147].

The study continues to demonstrate how these films seem to portray racial reconciliation, but upon closer scrutiny only serve to perpetuate racist stereotypes and problematic cultural assumptions about Black people.

Hughey refines the definition of Magical Negro in more sophisticated theoretical terms, coining the term "cinethetic racism" to describe how the trope conjoins various dimensions of racial stereotypes within the context of the film medium. The following is the conclusion of his investigation of twenty-six films within the genre:

> The films in this sample can be understood as a bold refusal to settle for the kind of invisibility and "shucking and jiving" that had once been so routine (and which still exists) in much of Hollywood films. However, just as challenges to patriarchy are "articulated in the context of masculinist ideologies" (Gamman 1989:18), the challenges posed to white supremacy by these films draw from, and are situated within, a popular culture permeated by white normative ideologies and the pervasive, strategic rhetoric supporting it. These films can reaffirm the status quo in a subversive, mystified way that makes them all the more dangerous and insidious. In this sense, the racial ideologies of cinethetic racism are always produced and rearticulated in relation to material circumstances. Although these films can be incredibly entertaining, these media products do important ideological work and are, "meaning in the service of power" (Bonilla-Silva 2003:25–26) that rationalize systems of inequality and relations of domination [Hughey 569].

He indicates how difficult it is for a film to evade the pull of prevailing ideology, especially a film foregrounding Black representation within a white dominated art form and industry, and risk affirming the forces of oppression with adverse effects upon the very people being represented.

This numinous figure has appeared in narratives across time, history, and cultures, from ancient Chinese literature to Spanish Renaissance drama. It is a continuing presence even today, for instance in American politics. President Obama has been referred to as a Magical Negro in a proliferation of articles and commentary. It is argued that his persona fits the stereotype in order to offset other stereotypes about Black men. Ehrenstein, writing about Obama a year before the 2008 election, asserts that Obama was "running for an equally important unelected office, in the province of the popular imagination the 'Magic Negro'" (Ehrenstein). He goes on to contend: "He's there to assuage white 'guilt' (i.e., the minimal discomfort they feel) over the role of slavery and racial segregation in American history, while replacing stereotypes of a dangerous, highly sexualized black man with a benign figure" (Ehrenstein). He concludes: "Like a comic-book superhero, Obama is there to help, out of the sheer goodness of a heart we need not know or understand. For as with all Magic Negroes, the less real he seems, the more desirable he becomes. If he were real, white America couldn't project all its fantasies of curative black benevolence on him" (Ehrenstein). Had Obama not appeared and risen to the highest office in the nation in order to save the republic and to heal its divisions, the culture would have had to invent him.

In terms of film history, the Magical Negro can be traced to the beginning of film in America. Roland Leander Williams, Jr., cites actor Sam Lucas in the 1914 version *Uncle Tom's Cabin* as the originating cinematic shaman ("Introduction" 140). In the '60s Sidney Poitier came to prominence as "the ebony saint figure" in such films as *The Defiant Ones* (which is more closely aligned with the buddy tradition), *Lilies of the Field, To Sir, With Love, and Guess Who's Coming to Dinner?* In subsequent decades there were "the badass Superspade images of the 70s to the cool hip images of the 80s, the 'utopian reversal' images of Black bourgeois success and then the neo-minstrelsy era of the 90s" (Hughey 545–546). The appearance of the Magical Negro trope coincides with the rise of the new racism during the late '80s and '90s:

> The new racism supports the social order while seemingly challenging the racial inequality constitutive of that order. I point out that new racism reinforces the meaning of white people as moral and pure characters while also delineating how powerful, divine, and/or

magic-wielding Black characters may interact with whites and the mainstream. In so doing, these on-screen interactions afford white people centrality, while marginalizing those seemingly progressive Black characters…. [W]hile the explicit readings of these visual texts may be progressive and emancipatory, they may implicitly function to reify dominant racial discourses and narratives concerning white identity [Hughey 544–45].

The new racism presents itself as benign and colorblind, but effectively enforces discrimination and inequality in innovative, insinuating ways.

The '90s were a period of increased racial segregation, division, and conflict. The public figures that personified the era were Anita Hill, Clarence Thomas, Rodney King, O.J. Simpson, and Louis Farrakhan. Accordingly, films reflected a social and cultural wish for the bridging of the racial gulf through films that depicted friendships and alliances between Black and white, whether through the film genre of the interracial buddy film or through the not often commented upon Magical Negro film. This remained a wish or an artificial cinematic construction that did not reflect a social reality. In addition, the racial rapprochement depicted in these films depended upon the ultimate containment of the Black character to affirm the centrality of the white character's concerns and thus to maintain the white hegemonic status quo. This is the social context for the emergence of the Magical Negro film phenomenon as well as the rise to stardom of actors such as Denzel Washington in roles that were not racialized (although he carries more of a racial sign than other actors) and Will Smith whose appeal transcended race. Hollywood was sensitive to its racist past and was eager to put forward "positive" images of Blacks, i.e., Magical Negroes.

The '90s and early 2000s were years that saw a multiplication of performances within the genre. Morgan Freeman carved out a major career out of Magical Negro roles: *Driving Miss Daisy* (1989); *The Shawshank Redemption* (1994); *Bruce Almighty* (2003); *Evan Almighty* (2007); and *Million Dollar Baby* (2004) for which he won a Best Supporting Actor Academy Award. Other actors distinguishing themselves in Magic Negro films included Mykelti Williamson in *Forrest Gump* (1994), Eddie Murphy in *Holy Man* (1998), Cuba Gooding, Jr., in *What Dreams May Come* (1998), Michael Clarke Duncan in *The Green Mile* (1999), Don Cheadle in *The Family Man* (2000), and Will Smith in *The Legend of Bagger Vance* (2000). In contrast to these films and performers is Danny Glover as Harry in Charles Burnett's *To Sleep with Anger* (1990). Here Glover plays a Magical Negro who shows up in a Los Angeles neighborhood only to unnerve its Black inhabitants. Audrey Colombe makes the point that Harry is a real Black character operating within a real Black community: "He's complex, as are the community's reactions. We can read this character against the later magical characters and even take Burnett's vision as satirical and therefore interrupting." The focus on Black culture from a Black perspective makes this film an exception that proves the rule.

The Magical Negro film has garnered criticism from many cultural commentators, performers, filmmakers, movie reviewers, and literary critics. The reviewer in *Time Magazine* writes the following about the phenomenon of The Magical African American Friend: "MAAFs exist because most Hollywood screenwriters don't know much about Black people…. So instead of getting life histories or love interests, Black characters get magical powers" (Farley 14). Todd Lothery seconds this sentiment:

"Roles such as these give African Americans opportunities to appear in big-budget, high-profile films and thus make a mark on the movies. But how they make that mark is still largely defined by whites. And that won't change until the Hollywood powers that be—the gatekeepers—welcome more Blacks into the fold. No race is a monolithic group, of course, But when the white man tells the Black man's story, regardless of his intentions, he usually gets it wrong." Even such comedians as Dave Chappelle, Chris Rock, Keegan-Michael Key, and Jordan Peele in their television sketches have lampooned the Magical Negro figure.

The most vociferous complaint against the genre has been lodged by director Spike Lee. In an interview in *Cineaste* during the release of his film *Bamboozled* (2000) he registers his contempt for this negative stereotype:

> What really bothers me is this new phenomenon … that you see in films, such as *The Green Mile*, *The Family Man*, *The Legend of Bagger Vance*, and *What Dreams May Come*. These films all have these magical, mystical Negroes who show up as some sort of spirit or angel but only to benefit the white characters. I mean, Michael Clarke Duncan gave a good performance in *The Green Mile*, but when I saw that movie I knew he was going to get an Academy Award nomination. The Academy just loves roles like that because it makes them feel so liberal. But if this character has such magical powers that he can touch Tom Hanks and cure him of his urinary tract infection, why can't he use those gifts to walk out of prison? [Crowdus and Georgakas 5]

Lee points out the illogic of these magical narratives and characters and underscores the inauthenticity and artificiality of their creation.

Feminist film critic Tania Modleski also offers a critique of the genre and of *The Green Mile*. She takes *The New York Times* film critic Janet Maslin to task for noting the racism within Coffey, the character played by Michael Clarke Duncan, and then not following through with a full confrontation with the stereotype. She goes on to anatomize the film's unbelievable repetition of Magical Negro tropes. Coffey, a huge, mentally challenged Black man, is falsely accused of killing two innocent white girls, convicted of the crimes, and given the death sentence. In prison he discovers his magical powers. He cures his executioner (Tom Hanks) of a urogenital disorder with a single touch of his genitals. About this moment, Modleski writes: "not only does the Black man take into his own body the ills of the white man, but the white man also gets to absorb the sexual potency that white people have long projected onto Black men" (B9). Coffey also cures a white woman, the warden's wife, of cancer by kissing her on the mouth and sucking the disease out of her (!). This act both defuses and invokes the threat posed to white womanhood by Black male sexuality. For his efforts, he is offered a chance to escape, but refuses, preferring to go to the electric chair to atone for a crime he did not commit (!). His sacrifice serves as edification for the Tom Hanks character, which fulfills an American racial fantasy and the dictates of the genre.

Surpassing *The Green Mile* in its exemplification of the Magical Negro film is *The Legend of Bagger Vance* (2000), directed by Robert Redford and starring Will Smith.[4] Set in Savannah, Georgia, during the Depression, the film centers on Rannulph Junuh (Matt Damon), a former golf prodigy who has been traumatized by his experiences in the Great War. In order to save the failing golf resort inherited from her father, Adele Invergordon (Charlize Theron), Junuh's former romantic interest, plans a charity tournament featuring legends Bobby Jones and Walter Hagen. To add to the spirit of the event, the community demands that a local golfer be included. Junuh has lost his genius for golf and is dubious about participation until a tall, mysterious young Black man appears to him out of a darkened field. His name is Bagger Vance (Smith), and he is blessed with folk wisdom and a miraculous knowledge of golf. He educates, supports, and advises Junuh in order to restore him to his game and to grasp some larger truths about existence. His advice includes such lines as follows: "'You can't make that ball go anywhere, you got to let it' ... 'You got to find your one true authentic swing' ... 'Don't think about it, feel it'" (qtd. in Fuchs, "Don't Think"). He is telling Junuh that in order to gain control, he must give it up. He is referring not just to the sport but to one's inner spiritual harmony. He advocates a reliance on intuition and not the brain. Consequently Junuh wins the tournament as well as the love and hand of Adele. As Junuh is restored to his original heroic state, Bagger disappears having accomplished his mission of ensuring Junuh's redemption.

The film has the distinction of filling virtually every requisite of the Magical Negro trope.[5] Bagger Vance appears out of nowhere and immediately establishes how he can be helpful to the white male protagonist. In addition, he only appears in scenes with Junuh and only to impart his otherworldly wisdom. His role is that of a servant; he functions as a caddy and coach and astonishingly refuses compensation for his services. Bagger offers his advice based on intuition, not knowledge, and feeling, not thinking. He preserves the hierarchy wherein the white man's logic is firmly established at the top. He has no history nor memory of a personal past. Interestingly, Colombe observes that "the magical status of the Black male figure apparently requires even less contextualization than the typical 'buddy-formula' Black male." His special powers are for the white man's benefit, not for his own. When he has served his purpose, he disappears from the film. Bagger's indeterminant existential status is another indication of his magical dimension. No one else really sees him, which reflects not just his otherworldliness, but the general invisibility of Blackness to white people. The culture creates a Bagger Vance in order to nominally recognize Blackness and yet to deny assumptions of superiority. He may serve a particular white man, but he also serves the racial needs of white people. According to Colombe, "he becomes a floating sign of desire." For white audiences he assuages their racial guilt without having to confront any kind of Black reality.

Amy Alexander notes that the film critics who are usually clueless about race got it right about *The Legend of Bagger Vance* and panned it for the right reasons ("Reading"). Nick Davis's review hits the mark: "This claptrap is so busy sanctifying its genteel nostalgia and congratulating itself for featuring a Black actor in a prominent role that no one ever realizes that the nostalgia is for a place and an era that never existed, or that the claps on the back are for a character who revives extravagant racist stereotypes rather than surpassing them." Kam Williams dismisses Bagger as "the stereotype of the grateful Uncle Tom delighted with poverty and not challenging his second-class status." Perhaps the most scathing excoriation of the film is provided by Spike Lee:

> And what about The Legend of Bagger Vance? No disrespect to Will Smith because I really put this more on Robert Redford, the director, but this is a film set in early 1930s, Depression-era Georgia. Georgia has always been one of the roughest states for Black people, a lot of Negroes were castrated, lynched and whatnot in Georgia. So this is sick—they didn't even have Black caddies! And if this magical Black caddy has all these powers, why isn't he using them to try and stop some of the other brothers from being lynched and castrated? Why is he fucking around with Matt Damon and trying to teach him a golf swing? I don't understand this! That is insane. What world was that?! Please tell me [Crowdus and Georgakas 5].

Lee gives voice to a Black perspective on the film, one that sees through the illogicalities of the plot and the shortcomings of a character who is the figment of a racist imagination.

There are different ways that Black actors can approach stereotypes when and if they choose to perform them. For instance, Samuel L. Jackson takes the Uncle Tom stereotype, goes so deeply inside it with irony and parody, turns it inside out, and finally explodes it in Quentin Tarantino's 2012 *Django Unchained*. Smith in *The Legend of Bagger Vance* does something different with the stereotype of the Magical Negro. He inhabits the role so completely that his performance defines the stereotype. The film was not one of Smith's successes, one of the few box office failures in his career. As for Smith's performance, there was a mixture of praise and puzzlement. Some reviewers were generous to him, and took him at face value. Before her strong critique of the film, Fuchs does acknowledge Smith's performance, praising "the magic Smith works—and he is a tremendously charming and increasingly skilled performer" ("Don't Think"). Similarly, another reviewer concludes that "the character of Bagger is interesting, and he's given depth and soul" by Will Smith (Mapes). Yet another offers profuse praise for Smith's use of language:

> The Bagger Vance character is not a new archetype for Hollywood, but Smith's delivery of Vance's Black Southern dialect manages to convey an element often missed in such film portrayals. Where other stereotyped victims of segregation appear merely ignorant or uneducated, we find a wit and, more importantly, a will in Bagger's voice. It's a subversion of language intrinsic to African American culture, born of wisdom and cunning in the face of adversity. Will Smith's ability to carry this to the surface lends wondrously to our imagination of his character, and forges a heightened standard for future actors. Something in Smith's delivery is so conducive to the suspension of disbelief as to render all things permissible [Strohmeyer].

Other commentators do not find even his charm and locution enough for such suspension. Stephanie Zacharek offers a diplomatic critique:

> Although Smith may be more of an appealing personality than a solid actor (sometimes it's a suitable substitute), his role here doesn't give him latitude to do much more than flash his smile and dispense valuable advice. He plays the character as a gentle cartoon, not a broad one; it's almost as if he's trying to single-handedly maintain a masterly control over the movie's weird racial tone (or, more accurately, its lack thereof), a task that would be close to impossible for any actor to pull off ["Legend"].

She astutely notices the strain in Smith's performance to control the racial messaging, which in his other films he accomplishes effortlessly. Some critics found other aspects of his performance for scrutiny: "Smith is popular when he plays the superhero roles that made him famous. He is not ready to be taken seriously is a straight dramatic role yet…. But if they had put all the race problems in the film, then there would not have been a movie with Smith" (Goodman). Two implications stand out here. This critic acknowledges how the avoidance of race is central to the Magical Negro formula. He also demonstrates his understanding of a basic truth about Smith's persona and career: that a film that directly engages the subject of race is not a film Smith would make.

Given how the critical reputation of the film and attitudes toward the Magical Negro have developed, what does Smith think about the film, his performance, and its effect upon his career? The most pressing question is: why did he choose to make this film? Spike Lee reveals that Smith had a choice between *The Legend of Bagger Vance* and his own *Bamboozled*. In fact, he reveals that Smith and his wife, Jada Pinckett-Smith, read the scripts side by side in bed, and she decided on *Bamboozled*. Smith turned down Lee's film to play Bagger Vance. Lee goes on record saying: "I don't know if Will understood the material as well as Damon [Wayans], because if you understood what *Bamboozled* is about, you don't do *The Legend of Bagger Vance*" (Crowdus and Georgakas 8). There was no compelling reason to make that decision. Lee is scathing in his assessment of actors who are not discerning in their choice of roles and who fail to exercise a raised racial consciousness in the decision-making process. He cites the older generations of actors and actresses who played maids and buffoons on screen and how he appreciates their situations. He elaborates:

> At the same time it's made me much more critical of the roles African American entertainers or athletes choose to play today. If we don't take a demeaning role, we're not reduced to cleaning up somebody's house. I'm not saying there's a wealth of opportunities available to Black performers today, but no one is going to the poor house if they turn down some of this stuff. Otherwise, I think we betray those performers who came before and who played those roles so we wouldn't have to do them now in the twenty-first century [Crowdus and Georgakas 6].

If this is true, then it makes Smith's decision even more dubious. Colombe notes that "Will Smith is often the butt of comments about Black actors willing to play to White stereotypes." Robin Means Coleman directly denounces Smith as a sell-out ("Elmo" 60).

Smith has given a few reasons for starring in *The Legend of Bagger Vance*. For him it was a chance to stretch his acting skills. In an interview he admits, "'I'm not always comfortable with subtlety…. I like it loud and clear, but for that reason it was good to play a character who isn't big and funny and is a lot more subdued … to explore other aspects of myself and to emote in a way that's different from any of my past work'" ("Will Smith Stars"). He acknowledges the way he utilizes his star power in his acting, which he couldn't rely upon in *Bagger Vance*. In another interview, he relates: "Where I create, it's a persona that overshadows all of that. So this was really the first time in my career where I knowingly just turned it off" (Washington). Here, he admits that in his work he relies heavily on his personality. Another attraction for him was that the role constituted a Black character who "holds all the cards" (Lothery). In fact, he would be playing God. A few years later, Morgan Freeman would play God in *Bruce Almighty*, one of the major roles within the Magical Negro pantheon.

Interestingly, Smith confesses he was aware of the stereotype associated with the role and was uncomfortable with the subservient deference to the white characters.

He also wanted to avoid any associations with Step'n Fetchit. In this he was not successful, as one observant critic notes: "And of Smith, whose idea of a concluding grace note is a Stepin Fetchit–style two-step on a beach, we can only wonder what he was thinking when he took this part" (Davis). The question remains: What was he thinking? He was thinking that this role would be an invaluable experience and an opportunity to work with director Robert Redford (fig. 7.5). He has said that "'When Robert Redford calls you, you'll do anything'" ("Will Smith Stars"). He has confessed that he just closed his eyes, took the plunge, and trusted the director. He has also said, "I just completely gave myself as a tool to Robert Redford to create the film he wanted to create" (Longsdorf). In their discussions about the film, they agreed that it should not focus so much on Black images and race, but on "life" and the message that destiny is a choice (Washington). In the film, however, Bagger Vance has neither choice nor destiny, unlike Smith who has the wherewithal to do anything he wants. Yet, following the example of the character he portrays, he chooses to put his stardom and his prodigious powers of box-office magic at the service of a white man's vision.

Fig. 7.5. Will Smith signed to star in *The Legend of Bagger Vance* (2000) for the experience of working with Robert Redford. Shown: Will Smith and Robert Redford (DreamWorks/ Photofest).

EIGHT

Genre, Interrupted

As Will Smith's career has developed, his choices of roles have varied over a range of films. Although his major successes have been in the genres of science fiction and the interracial buddy film, he has also starred in superhero films, a romantic comedy, and several biopics. Upon these genres he has made his mark or has brought to them the issues of race and masculinity that inhere in his unique brand of postmodern, post-racial global stardom.

Black and Super

The Magical Negro with his special powers could be a form of the Black superhero. They both reflect the racial and political issues of their times. Focusing on Black male superheroes within the Marvel and DC Comic universes, Nama in *Super Black* traces the development of the Black superhero figure in comics and films from Black Lantern in the '60s and '70s to the Black Panther, Luke Cage, Falcon, and Black Lightning. His approach is to go beyond racial stereotypes "to draw deeper connections across significant cultural dynamics, social trends, and historical events" (5). His characterization of the attributes of the Black superhero resembles aspects of Smith's star identity. For instance, he believes that "these Black figures frequently challenged conventional and preconceived notions concerning Black racial identity by offering a futuristic and fantastic vision of Blackness that transcended and potentially shattered calcified notions of Blackness as a racial category and source of cultural meaning" (5–6). As has been articulated before, Smith's singular contribution to racial representation is his refutation of conventional Blackness through a transcendence of race. If Black superheroes effect "fantastic (re)imaginings of Black identity" (4), this is also what Smith accomplishes in the cultural work done by his stardom. Nama describes how Black superheroes constitute societal hopes for racial reconciliation, which is the cultural desire that sustains Smith's success. On the other hand, Black superheroes symbolize social and political ideals and racial realities in ways that Smith does not attempt. If Black superheroes represent historical moments and movements such as the Black Power movement and the Blaxploitation era, Smith does not fulfill this function, and this puts him in a position theoretically to subvert the dictates of the genre.

Will Smith's intervention here is 2008's *Hancock*.[1] John Hancock is a failed superhero (amnesiac, unkempt, homeless, alcoholic) who lives on the streets of Los Angeles. Not only is he not a role model, as is the norm for superheroes, he is not in control of his superpowers. In addition, the community, the city, and the world would all be better off without his efforts. For instance, when he prevents a train from colliding with a stalled car, he inadvertently smashes up the rest of the train. His fortunes change after this when the rescued man, Ray Embrey (Jason Bateman), out of gratitude, offers Hancock his services as a public relations expert to remake his image. First, Hancock is advised to volunteer to go to prison to atone for his disruptions of society. Upon release, he uses his superpowers truly to benefit the city. At this juncture, the film shifts gears to explore Hancock's origins which involve Ray's wife, Mary (Charlize Theron), who also turns out to be an immortal who was once married to Hancock. They lose their superpowers when in proximity to each other. Their union was a troubled one reflecting the racial conflicts of the historical periods they lived through as an interracial couple in their human forms. The film ends with a resolution of the awkward triangular romantic conundrum between Hancock, Mary, and Ray. Hancock steps aside, blessing the marriage of Ray and Mary, removing himself to the moon and moving to New York where he assumes his new position as a superhero.

The film was a top box office hit for the year, earning $624.4 million globally ("Hancock–Box Office Mojo"). Smith's international popularity in this film was notable, especially in the U.K. and Germany. *Variety* claimed, "Foreign audiences once again fell hard for Smith, who has officially replaced Tom Cruise as the world's biggest star" (McClintock). The critical response was mixed, focusing on the film's problems with its conception, story logic, and tone. There was, however, appreciation for Smith's work in the film. Several critics claim that Smith makes the film work. *The New Yorker's* reviewer notes, "For the first time in his life, Will Smith doesn't flirt with the audience" (Denby). Ebert describes Smith's approach to the character as "serious, thoughtful" ("A Superhero"). *The Hollywood Reporter* offers the following account: "The true star is Smith, who again demonstrates acting chops as well as effortless charisma in a vehicle that's only occasionally worthy of his superhuman skills" (Farber, "Hancock"). It is a testament to Smith's performing intelligence that he enacts a potential genre intervention within a film that itself is a self-conscious parody.

Hancock as a film nonetheless has problems as Nama enumerates in his critique of the film: "What began as a gritty satire of the superhero genre … became a jumbled mix of special effects, poor comic timing, and a saccharine conclusion" (*Super* 148). Yet, he still finds greater significance in the film. Here is the case of "an imaginary Black superhero embodying real racial anxieties" (*Super* 149). He sees Hancock's rise and redemption as symbolic of various Black men who attain superstar status in the sports and entertainment fields. Nama cites the examples of Kobe Bryant, Tiger Woods, and Michael Vick, who sought atonement for their falls from grace via public apologies, just as Hancock does in the film (fig. 8.1). It might be interesting to note that Smith himself has never needed to ask for such forgiveness. He exists above and beyond such fallibility. It is only in this performance that he and his persona are associated with falling from grace and with "contemporary male urban Blackness" (*Super* 148). In a sense, Hancock is Smith's "Blackest" role, and the difference between it and

Fig. 8.1. Will Smith as Hancock, a reprobate superhero, atones for his transgressions at a press conference in *Hancock* (2008). Directed by Peter Berg (Sony Pictures/Photofest).

Smith is marked. As one commentator observes: "The on-screen violence and rancor contrasts with Smith's squeaky-clean rap recordings" (White, "Crappyness"). Some critics remarked on the disjuncture between star and role and how at certain levels Smith can't close the distance: "'Hancock' makes a valiant attempt to reexamine comic-book-hero conventions by fraying their edges a little bit. It's the sort of role Smith ought to be able to pull off easily. But even his superpowers apparently have their limits" (Zacharek, "Hancock"). In this film, even when he plays a racial stereotype, it does not adhere to him. His star aura allows him to transcend and transform. Another reviewer notes that "the scuzziness essential to the role of John Hancock, everyman superhero, simply slides straight off Smith's wipe-clean persona" ("Will the Real"). As the film tries to subvert the genre, Smith is engaged in an intervention upon himself: to free his image from the irreproachable post-racial iconicity that has defined him to embrace a role that comes to ground and touches a recognizable Black reality.

Smith's persistent and superhuman exceptionality aligns him with Barack Obama who during his campaign for the presidency was often likened to a Black superhero. Nama and Edward Bacal cite the Obama "Hope" poster as evidence. The image shows Obama's face and chest against a red, white, and blue background with the word "HOPE" beneath. Nama also points to the DC Comic image of Obama tearing open his suitcoat and shirt, showing an "O" similar to Superman's "S." Nama goes on to conclude: "With his square jawline, a captivating origin story, elegant oratory, lightning quick intelligence, and sleek athletic profile, Barack Obama fulfilled the needs of a nation yearning for a superhero persona to confront the multiple challenges facing America" (*Super* 152). Of course, only when the country is in extremis, about to fall off an economic cliff, as a last resort and hope, does it elevate a Black (super) man to the presidency in order to save itself.

Bacal makes even larger claims about the connection between Smith and Obama. He goes so far as to assert that the release of *Hancock* in the summer before the 2008 election served as an implicit and subliminal campaign strategy to prepare America for a Black man occupying a position—superhero president—always held by white men. Bacal considers the similarity between the Obama poster and the publicity poster for Smith's film *Seven Pounds* released in 2008 after the election, finding that "its representational purpose, I'd argue, is to further institute the image of Obama—as president—into the cultural consciousness" (Bacal). Smith here captures and projects the essence of "Obamacity," as Bacal terms it, following Barthes.[2]

Another characteristic shared by Obama and Smith is their ability to shift the racial signification of their images:

> The function of these images reinscribes them with a uniform, purportedly "authentic" … concept of race that functions merely as visual code rather than something culturally relative, leaving racial identity as something to be overcome or overlooked, and allowing difference to be disavowed and Blackness to be pacified in order to ultimately create figures suitable for identification by white audiences [Bacal].

This description is especially true of Smith's star persona and crossover appeal. He is a Black star whose Blackness is nominal and does not carry social. cultural, and historical weight. His Blackness is indeed a "visual code" while his image is distances from racial reality. This allows his screen presence to mitigate or deflect the perceived negative aspects of Blackness and render him acceptable to mainstream and global audiences.

The amelioration of potentially problematic Blackness that both Obama and Smith effect in the end is limited, resulting in the reassertion of racial essentialism—even upon these celebrated exceptions—and hierarchy: "Hence, shuffling instituted character types goes only so far when those roles played with ultimately return to their initial place within a structure that posits them as immutable figures. This is to say, rather than present new alternatives for representing the superhero, those atypical differentiating factors are disavowed in order to reinstate traditional type-role relationships" (Bacal). For Smith, this means that for all the interruptions he may effect upon generic conventions of racialized characterizations, as in superhero narratives, the films revert to the prevailing racial formulas and reassert the imperatives of genre. In *Hancock*, the mitigation of Smith's character's Blackness functions finally to reinscribe the white superhero paradigm. Christina Amadou comes to the same conclusion: "The question that is implicitly posed here is whether he becomes 'whiter' or 'more American' at the end of the film" ("Evolving Portrayals"). In general, the latitude given Smith's racially deracinated characters is taken back to reconfirm the existing system of values and power.

Not only does *Hancock*, despite its effort to lend irony to the genre, reinforce convention, it eventually replicates many of the by now familiar Will Smith film tropes, and this despite his effort to test his image. For instance, Hancock is rendered a "safe" Black male character when he volunteers (!) to go to prison (much like the Magical Negro character, Coffey, in *The Green Mile*). He is also emasculated when he steps aside to facilitate the union of the white woman who is his immortal wife and the white man who has rehabilitated him. Although Hancock is angry and home-less, as inhabited by Smith he is removed from the realities of race-based economic and social inequality. This is noted in *The New York Times* review: "Mr. Smith may be playing a provocative role in a city famous for its troubled race relations, but he's also a megastar and largely shielded from everyday stings, which, as it happens, is also true of his character. Hancock kicks back in a couple of derelict trailers (the Shack of Solitude) instead of a mansion, but his pain is existential, not material" (Dargis). Being removed from common Black experience, even as an anti-heroic superhero, causes Hancock and the film not to give due diligence to race. One Black critic reg-isters: "The imputation of America's racist history (evoking the scars of slavery and involving Hancock's past brutalization by racist Southerners) is recalled with bewil-dering nonchalance" (White, "Crappyness"). This attitude to the racist past is like the joking lynching scene in *Wild, Wild West*. *Hancock* deals in another Will Smith trope, the avoidance of race, here by evoking slavery without its effects.

The most significant repetition of a Will Smith plot formula is the process whereby the Black heroic protagonist is contained. This is the real meaning of Han-cock's transformation: "Hancock submits to Ray's image makeover, a matter-of-fact acquiescence to media manipulation—Smith's stock in trade" (White, "Crappyness"). Ray's makeover of Hancock is a reinforcement of conventional generic racial dynam-ics. It is an imposition of white male power over the Black male body. White sug-gests something even more in his observation about Ray's redemption of Hancock, that Smith's stardom has also been reshaped and constructed by media and celebrity culture. This is true of most actors, but this has a special applicability to Smith who has been a willing and brilliant participant in the creation of "Will Smith." The dis-tance between character and star collapses here; they virtually share an identity. Like Hancock, Smith is also a superhero, but one who performs supernatural feats at the box office for Hollywood (Morris, "Landing"). Perhaps this constitutes another Will Smith trope, the way his films are sometimes reiterations of his own personal story. Notice the transformation of Darrell Edwards into Agent J in *Men in Black*, from a hip street cop into a cool corporate agent. One critic observes: "What we're getting in Hancock is a metaphor for the making of Will Smith" ("Will the Real"). Hancock is reshaped from an angry, unruly Black superhero into a genuine American hero, and Smith has been transfigured from a Black middle-class rapper into a peerless inter-national superstar.

Taboo

Hancock is also significant in Smith's oeuvre and the development of his screen persona in terms of The White Woman Problem. There is an imperative in Holly-wood filmmaking practice to avoid interracial relationships in films featuring Black male stars. The history of this racial anxiety reaches back to D.W. Griffith's *The Birth of a Nation* (1915) where it was dramatized in the rape of Flora by the sexually ravening mulatto Gus (played by a white actor in Blackface) and in the marital designs of the mulatto carpetbagger politician Silas Lynch (played by white actor George Siegmann) upon the virtuous Elsie Stoneman (Lillian Gish). This racial anxiety persisted through Sidney Poitier at the height of his career when he engaged in necessarily chaste encounters with white women (nuns in *Lilies of the Field*, the blind woman played by Elizabeth Hartman in *A Patch of Blue*, the teenage Judy Geeson in *To Sir, With Love*). In the milestone film *Guess Who's Coming to Dinner* (1967), he is engaged to Katharine Houghton and meets her well intentioned liberal parents played by Spencer Tracy and Katharine Hepburn. It is an interracial relationship that proves a point, but there is no intimacy depicted between them.

The trend continues with Denzel Washington and Julia Roberts in *The Pelican Brief* (1993). In the film he portrays a newspaper reporter and she a law student who are endangered as they investigate the deaths of two Supreme Court Justices. They uncover a plot involving conflicting agendas between environmental interests and the oil industry. As the film develops, the two grow closer, but what does not happen is a romance between the two as happens in John Grisham's original novel. Washington's character in the book is white. Casting Washington as a Black male actor necessitated the alteration of the story to avoid an interracial romance which the filmmakers feared would alienate viewers. Washington himself was reluctant to pursue this development in the characters' relationship. Instead, the reticence of the couple only drew attention to itself. Audiences would have been willing to extend its good will to the cinematic coupling of these two highly regarded, attractive, and charismatic stars. Over the years, it has become the prime example of Hollywood's retreat from representations of romantic racial boundary crossings and its reinforcement of old fears and prejudices.

The same is true of Morgan Freeman and the crime thriller films he made with Ashley Judd: *Kiss the Girls* (1997) and *High Crimes* (2002). Although the disparity between their ages is notable, the chemistry between them was noticeable, to the point that it also becomes obvious that Hollywood took extra effort to avoid any suggestion of an interracial romantic relationship. The Freeman/Judd films became almost a subgenre in itself: the Black man/young white woman buddy film. In these films, the potential sexual/romantic dynamic is submerged and turned into a mentorship relationship over the course of their collaborative crime solving. Philippa Gates observes that in these films when the Black male hero takes the place usually occupied by the white male star, he assumes a position of the cerebral "mind" of the partnership while the woman becomes "the body" or the agent of action. The woman becomes the sexualized spectacle rather than the Black male whose threatening sexuality is contained. Despite this alteration of roles, there is still no sexual connection dramatized or implied (Gates 24). Another example of this ploy is another film starring Denzel Washington, *The Bone Collector* (1999) in which he is partnered with Angelina Jolie as the cop who does the legwork of the investigation while he is incapacitated. Not only is his character stripped of physical heroism, there is no possibility of an interracial romance because he is paralyzed (Gates 24–25).

Will Smith enters this discussion with *Hancock* and the kiss he shares with Charlize Theron, the first interracial kiss in his career. There is a mysterious tension between Hancock and Mary, the wife of the public relations agent who has been remaking the superhero's damaged reputation. The backstory is that Hancock and Mary have been married in previous lives. They are supernatural immortals who cannot be together. They lose their powers and become mortal when in close physical proximity. (One wonders how it is possible for them to have been a couple or married or have consummated their marriage.) The other conundrum about their marriage is how to deal with the inevitable societal resistance to their interracial marriage over the centuries. Racism is implied but never addressed. They were the victims of racist attacks in 1858 and then in 1931, the latter being the incident that drove them apart. These incidents remain expository plot points without framing or context: "The premise that Hancock and Mary cannot be together for cosmic, preternatural reasons is clearly stated in the film, but implicitly, sociopolitical forces have also wreaked havoc upon their lives over the centuries, and these are very real outside the fictive world of Hancock. But the forces of <u>racism</u> and violence while alluded to, are never made explicit in the movie's universe" (Killian). The racial dynamics and consequences of their relationship are presented as givens and without interrogation. The result is that the film does not offer a critique of the rejection of their union and tacitly affirms the condemnation it receives from the film's narrative. Killian concludes:

> In sum, the film's implicit messaging about the mortal dangers inherent in interracial coupling, and on-screen solution of a self-imposed racial segregation to the extreme (Hancock at one point flies to the moon, which is far, far away from Mary), feels like familiar territory, and reasserts the old Hollywood logic about interracial couples. So, film depictions of interracial couples continue to provide particular (usually negative) ways of thinking about interracial relationships, and frequently serve to both reassert/reinscribe the principle of homogamy and to reproduce racial borders [Killian].

The film interrupts the line of its story midway and goes in a different direction seemingly to entertain the possibility of interraciality, only to invent a preposterous plot twist to keep a Black man and a white woman apart. While the kiss seems to break new ground for Smith, it ends up negating this gesture toward racial and sexual liberation. Will Smith finally gets to kiss a white woman but does not get to enjoy it.

Another repercussion of the Will Smith/Charlize Theron kiss is the reaction of Black women. One Black female critic asks, "Why is it that once an actor like Smith reaches A-list status, Hollywood never seems to pair him with a Black actress in a potential blockbuster?" (Watson). She mentions several Black actresses who could easily star opposite Smith. She also points to the damage done in general to Black women's self-esteem from not seeing themselves and their reality on screen. She also longs for Black actresses to be cast opposite white actors in films that do not problematize the central interracial relationship. Interestingly, in *Hancock* the Black male/white female coupling is not a point of contention. Race is not mentioned, and the tension between them is a matter instead of their supernatural identities. This is how interraciality is handled in a Will Smith film. Although some might point to the Smith/Theron kiss as a step toward lifting a cinematic taboo, perhaps the truly revolutionary milestone would be to see Smith in a fully realized relationship with an unambiguously Black actress. Even more telling would be if such a Black coupling could break box office records. This would be the true test of Smith's transcendent stardom.

The White Woman Problem leads to Smith's incursion into another genre, the romantic comedy. In 2005's *Hitch*, he plays another kind of hero, the romantic leading man. Here his character is Alexander Hitchens, a charming and charismatic love advice expert specializing in teaching unprepossessing men how to win the women of their dreams. The story focuses on Hitch's attempt to elevate the courting skills of Albert Brennaman (Kevin James), a portly and awkward accountant who has fallen in love from a distance with a beautiful heiress, Allegra Cole (Amber Valletta). During his training regime with Albert, Hitch meets and falls in love with Sara Melas, a popular gossip columnist played by Eva Mendes. He discovers that his own advice and expertise ironically do not work for himself. After plot twists, complications, and misunderstandings, both couples are finally united.

Despite a lukewarm critical reception, the film was a huge success with the biggest weekend opening ever for a romantic comedy. It has gone on to be the third highest-grossing romantic comedy in film history (A. Rodriguez). In addition, *Hitch* is one of the two top ten romantic comedies with minority leads (the other being *Crazy Rich Asians* from 2018) (Lawrence). This outsized box-office performance proves the almost infallible power of Smith's stardom even as it extends into a genre with which he is not usually associated. Despite its box-office, the film was not well reviewed. Its critics faulted it for being predictable, labored, and overlength. Still, there was praise for the performances, with citations of Smith's effortless charm, Kevin James's physical comedy, and the comic chemistry between the two. Often referenced is the male kiss between Smith and James. This was an opportunity for Smith to reprise and redeem the past: his infamous failure to kiss actor Anthony Michael Hall in *Six Degrees of Separation*. The attempt at redemption fails as the scene, utilizing the Cyrano de Bergerac stratagem (under the guise of romantic instruction, one man pretending to be the female love object of the other for a lesson in sealing the first-date kiss), devolves into jokey homophobia.

Critics have identified another problem with the film: the second story line involving Hitch and Sara, which seems superfluous. It is a narrative invention to avoid the perceived negative implications of race or an interracial theme in a mainstream entertainment. Hitch's love interest at least does give the Black male a personal life to reverse the usual emasculation of Black men in mainstream films by denying them private lives, sexuality, and love. He also does not function solely to educate a white male. Still, it must be admitted that Hitch does possess certain Magical Negro qualities as he serves to educate and improve white men. As for his own love life, despite his infatuation with Sara, his relationship with her is another form of avoidance and containment. According to the logic of the romantic comedy genre, Hitch in mentoring Albert would fall in love with Allegra who would reciprocate his feelings. Albert would become the odd man out. This is the role that Ralph Bellamy perfected in the classic Hollywood romantic comedies of the '30s and '40s. On the contrary, one could argue that the film's conceptual innovation is to redeem the Ralph Bellamy character by allowing him, finally, to get the girl. As is, this plot constitutes

Smith's failure to enact an intervention on the genre; he fulfills Hollywood's racial evasion. Because of the male romantic lead being Black, the film is altered in a negative way and becomes a romantic comedy without the conventional main romance. Tom Carson comments on the fraught relationship between Black male actors and the romantic comedy genre: "Whatever else African American actors bring to the party, Hollywood usually asks them to leave their sexual magnetism at home" (119). The film should end with Hitch and Allegra walking down the aisle. There is no reason for this not to happen. Will Smith's transcendent stardom should give him leave to appear in a film in an interracial coupling without the resistance and backlash of white audiences. Carson offers the following explanation: "Will Smith may be the biggest African American box-office draw in history, but he knows he'd get a studio to green-light that combo [Hitch and Allegra] when pigs fly, and his shrewdness about exactly what he can and can't get away with is a major reason he's successful" (120). The reason this does not happen is a matter of hedging bets, of playing it absolutely safe.

Instead, a subplot is created to match the African American male protagonist with his own love interest (fig. 8.2). Even this is problematic because of the casting of Eva Mendes, an actress who is Cuban American and reads as racially ambiguous. This casting practice is a trend with films starring Black male actors. Denzel Washington is often paired with actresses whose looks are racially and ethnically indeterminant, or to be more correct, neither white nor Black. Examples are Paula Patton in *Déjà vu* (2006) and Sarita Choudhury in *Mississippi Masala* (1991). The reason,

Fig. 8.2. Will Smith as Alex Hitchens is paired with Eva Mendes as Sara Melas in the romantic comedy *Hitch* (2005). Directed by Andy Tennant (Barry Wetcher/Columbia/Kobal/Shutterstock).

once again, for this practice is to avoid pairing these men with Black actresses, which would make the film appear to be a "Black film," and thus financially risky. Maryann Erigha terms this practice "Hollywood Jim Crow" (141). Although Mendes received favorable critical notices for her feisty, comic performance, this does not allay the cynicism of her casting. It has been commented upon how she has made a career out of serving as a racial compromise to avoid difficult racial dynamics in mainstream Hollywood films. Carson terms her a "decoy" and her being hired for various projects as exercising "the Latina Option" (120). She is a proxy for white female leads opposite African American actors and a substitute for exotic Black women with white A-list actors (Carson 120).

Angela Onwuachi-Willig examines Mendes's position and this race-based hiring trend from a legal standpoint. She writes that Mendes "recognizes the limits placed on her career by many filmmakers' perceptions about audience receptiveness to on-screen interracial relationships" (331). To consider audience racial preferences in the casting of entertainment is troublesome because the law "does not allow—at least openly—such discriminatory influences in other workplaces under current antidiscrimination law" (325). Mendes could file a lawsuit for the way she is variously cast in movies opposite Black and white actors depending on how that pairing might or might not affect the racial sensibilities and prejudices of potential audiences.

Since *Hitch*, Smith's career and his image in relation to interraciality has evolved. Ten years later in 2015's *Focus*, the crime caper thriller, for the first time he has a white leading lady, Australian actress Margot Robbie, as his partner in con and crime (fig. 8.3). The result has not garnered the backlash and resistance that has always been predicted by the Hollywood establishment. On the contrary, the film did respectably well, finishing in first place at the domestic box-office during its opening weekend. Eventually, it would gross $159.1 million worldwide in 31 markets, doing especially well in the U.K., Mexico, and Russia ("Focus–Box Office Mojo"). This would indicate that an interracial relationship at the center of a major motion picture is not an impediment to its reception. *Focus* did as well as any non-blockbuster Will Smith film. Audiences would have accepted Smith in an interracial coupling long before this. He was always the beneficiary of the good faith and will of global audiences. If there was a hesitation, it was a matter of his own calculated reluctance to take the risk. He has expressed this explicitly: "'We spend $50 something million making this movie and the studio would think that was tough on their investment. So the idea of a Black actor and a white actress comes up—that'll work around the world, but it's a problem in the U.S." (Ifeanyi). Here Smith pinpoints the key to his global appeal: his representation of a post-racial ideal. He acknowledges that the world has no problem with a film starring a Black male and a white female because it is consistent with how the rest of the world views race. Implicit in his comments is the belief that the United States needs to catch up. For instance, the Academy Award winning Best Film of 2018, Peter Farrelly's *Green Book*, which was excoriated by conscious Black and white critics for its regressive racial attitudes, was a huge hit in China. The film depicts the journey through the American segregated South in 1962 made by the patrician African American pianist Don Shirley (Mahershala Ali, who won the Oscar for Best Supporting Actor) and his working-class Italian chauffeur Tony Vallelonga (Viggo

Fig. 8.3. An interracial relationship between Nicky (Will Smith) and Jess (Margot Robbie) is at the center of the crime caper *Focus* (2015). Directed by Glenn Ficarra and John Requa (Warner Bros./Photofest).

Mortensen). The film was valued for its depiction of the respect and friendship between the two men: "'The journey connects people of different skin colors, classes, and cultural backgrounds together. They had stereotypes, but they made peace at last. We chose to believe a story of this kind because we hope people can achieve kindness, understanding, and equality'" (Huang). Chinese audiences may not have been aware of the history of racism in America, but instead viewed the film through an optimistic cultural lens about race and wished to affirm a preference for the spectacle of differences being overcome.

This view of race is like the idea of a post-racial society, an ideology that has animated Smith's entire career. Certainly, it is operative in *Focus*. There is no evasion about the relationship between the Smith and Robbie characters: "But it's the full-on affair (sex scenes included) that deserves a closer look, most notably for the fact that race isn't mentioned once in the movie—Nicky and Jess's romance is colorblind" (Ifeanyi). This is something of an achievement and constitutes Smith's intervention if not into a genre then into racial representation. Smith contributes to "normalizing interracial couplings in mainstream movies…. *Focus*'s fully realized interracial, colorblind coupling sets a new standard in Hollywood" (Ifeanyi). It also sets a new standard for Smith.[3] *Focus* marks a turning point in his career. In his delineation of the stages of stardom, Marshall defines a later stage as a point at which the star transgresses against his or her star persona to attain a higher level of freedom. *Focus* may be Smith's moment when he transcends the racial restrictions that have been exacted by the industry and by his own professional caution and is liberated from the limitations of his stardom.

The Real Thing

Another mode of transgression is the acting code. Marshall theorizes that the screen star must separate him or herself from their public personality and star persona to achieve an "autonomous subjectivity" (106). One way this is accomplished is by a resort to the acting code: "screen stars, in order to demonstrate that they have abilities that go beyond the limited construction of their screen personalities, work to establish their abilities as actors by playing roles that transgress their previous sign constructions" (Marshall 107). For all the good performances Will Smith has crafted, they have not released him from his star persona. He became aware of this problem as early as *The Legend of Bagger Vance* when he realized that "the persona I created had become too big for the stories I wanted to tell. I had started to overshadow the characters I play. People see me on screen and go, 'Oh, look, it's Will Smith'" (Longsdorf). Another challenge for Smith is overcoming the tendency to fall back on his charm and wit. The biggest lesson he has learned over his career is to let go of the desire to be liked. Smith is also aware of not only the pitfall of celebrity for an actor but also the lack of training. When he started his acting career on television in *The Fresh Prince of Bel-Air*, he was so new to the craft that he could be seen mouthing the lines of the other actors. As for his own assessment of his acting, he has confessed the following: "'I don't consider myself particularly talented—I consider myself slightly above average in talent—but nobody's going to outwork me. I'll take a slight talent and then add the skill to it and can make it look magnificent'" (Feinberg). Despite his own critiques of his work, Smith's achievement as actor, not as star, has not been given its full due. Indeed, he has given some remarkable performances and interestingly these have come in films in which he plays real people: *Six Degrees of Separation* (1993), *Ali* (2001), *The Pursuit of Happyness* (2006), and *Concussion* (2015). The biopic affords Smith rich opportunities not necessarily for interventions of genre but for negotiations of his stardom.

Although Fred Schepisi's *Six Degrees of Separation* is fiction, it does tell the story of David Hampton, the con artist who in 1983 impersonated the fictional son of Sidney Poitier to gain entry into Studio 54 and the Upper East Side homes of New York's elite. He was the essential grifter. The art of the grift is defined as "'an opportunity for plying criminal talents,' suggesting not so much the pursuit of illicit profit as general delight in the act of deceit.... Grifters are small-time lawbreakers, not the kind of epic liars who leave the wreckage of lives and nations in their wake. They're not even bad people, per se: They stand outside morality, defying the social binary of good and evil. They tend to pilfer enough to disrupt but not devastate" (Mishan). The devastation often comes back to them. Hampton came to a bad end: prison and a solitary death from AIDS complications. The announcement of his death appeared in the July 19, 2003, issue of *The New York Times*, ironically on the same page as reportage of accusations of rape against basketball legend Kobe Bryant. Here were cases of two young Black men, one aspiring to elevation above and beyond the stereo-types of young Black men and the other having attained true fortune and celebrity, both brought down to earth. Yet not all Hampton's victims rebuke him. One of his dates "had this to say about his night with the notorious David Hampton, seeker of the fabulous. 'Honestly?' he said. 'It was one of the best dates that I ever went on'" (Barry). He was capable of magic, and this is what Smith captures in the film. From the *Catcher in the Rye* monologue to the speech about the death of the imagination, Smith is charming, witty, seductive, optimistic, and inspiring, all at the same time. Smith brings off this feat, which involves complex leaps of logic, modulations of tone, and linguistic shifts, skills that go beyond mere charisma. The film was made before his ascendency, so he did not have his public image to fall back upon. This excep-tional acting coup is achieved because Smith at this point is not a star. Some have commented that Smith has had his career in reverse: "Smith's most interesting film role, as the schizoid gay sociopath in *Six Degrees of Separation* (1992), came at the wrong end of his career—it was before movie audiences had a stake in his persona and before Smith became so protective of his image" (White, "Crappyness"). This is one of his better performances, and this is his first serious role. Despite his failure to perform certain aspects of the role, such as the infamous male kiss, Smith in other ways rises to the task and does justice to David Hampton.

It is not entirely true that Smith's star persona and films do not engage racial and political realities. When he portrays real people, he has no recourse but to enter their historical moments and singular conditions. This is the case with 2015's *Concus-sion*. When the media reported that Will Smith was signed to a film about the phe-nomenon of brain injuries suffered by ex-professional football players, it was easy to imagine Smith giving a moving, Oscar worthy performance as a former NFL star who suffers mental lapses and who has lost everything and is driven to sudden acts of violence and to the brink of suicide. It would have been a showcase for a display of a range of emotion and a deep dive into a specific kind of Black male despair. This is not the role Smith inhabits here, which should come as no surprise. This is not a Will Smith role. Instead, he portrays Dr. Bennet Omalu, a forensic pathologist from Nige-ria engaged in the study of the brain and nerve damage sustained by boxers and pro-fessional football players by repeated blows to the head. The film traces his efforts for the recognition of his discoveries about CTE (Chronic Traumatic Encephalopathy) and the resistance he encounters from the National Football League (fig. 8.4). Smith's performance is not obvious, nor does it draw attention to itself. It goes deeper and into unexpected directions for Smith to the essence of a Black identity.[4] Interestingly, this appreciation comes from Armond White, the contrarian Black film critic who has coruscated Smith in the past for his many shortcomings: being a sell-out, pander-ing to his audiences, failing to exercise a developed racial consciousness, and adher-ing to political correctness and trendy colorblind post-raciality.

White credits the film for not compromising its depiction of Omalu's intimida-tions and humiliations at the hands of the football establishment: "It skips over the familiar Black man's struggle against glass-ceiling professionalism to dramatize the seldom-told story of how a Black professional faces the oppression brought on by being too smart, of being more capable than his peers will tolerate" ("Concussion").

Fig. 8.4. Will Smith as Dr. Bennet Omalu, who confronted the NFL over its treatment of players with brain trauma, expresses the pain of insults to his intellectual pride in *Concussion* (2015). Directed by Peter Landesman (Columbia Pictures/Photofest).

White offers this full explanation of what he believes Smith achieves in his performance: "the ignominy Omalu endures becomes the focus. It goes from examining physical pressure on the Black body … to Omalu's internalized stress. When he is publicly humiliated, Omalu exclaims: 'It's offensive. I am offended.' No Black actor has ever before had the chance to perform such a scene on screen … this is singular: the screen's first dramatization of Black intellectual pride" ("Concussion"). White concludes: "Although Smith is far from a Paul Robeson–style 'race man' … he has finally found access to his most serious on-screen moment" ("Concussion"). Although there are questions about the film's historical and scientific accuracy, as well as its predictability, *Concussion* nonetheless circumvents the pieties of the biopic genre and allows Smith an intervention, to make this film portrait of this very real man not only essentially factual but emotionally true.

The stakes were much higher when Smith took on the responsibility of starring in Michael Mann's *Ali* (2001). Smith approached the project with trepidation and had to be convinced to take on the role. He recalls how Mann came to his house and promised that he would "'create the curriculum that will render you Ali.' 'That was the most amazing director's meeting I ever had,' Smith says" (Johnson 60). Smith continues: "'I was like, *Wow!* The only thing I was struggling with was my confidence. I knew I had the discipline and the talent, but I didn't know how I could pull it off'" (Roy 60). The word "discipline" is key. If there is any one consistent component to a Smith performance, it is the hard work that he puts into the creation of a character. His work ethic is well known within the industry, and this is one reason so many filmmakers want to work with him. In his meeting with Mann it was as if he had met his match in perfectionism. Smith's dedication to embodying Ali first required him to transform his body: "Smith's transformation—physically and psychologically—from 185-pound actor to 220-pound athlete went well beyond normal preparation for a movie role" (Howard 38). Smith's training regimen lasted approximately a year and included "five-day-a-week, six-hour-day" workouts. He did distance running in the high altitudes of Colorado. He undertook heavy weight training. He also had to learn to box under the tutelage of Ali's own legendary trainer, Angelo Dundee. He had to acquire both the physical instincts and mental rhythms of a boxer. All of which he completed with a heightened sense of accomplishment. In an interview he confessed: "'More than anything it took me to my limit…. I know what kind of person I am after this film'" (Johnson 60).

The result is a performance that won critical acclaim for Smith and an Academy Award nomination for Best Actor. Brian Raferty commends Smith for ultimately making the film work and director Mann for keeping in check Smith's tendency to play to the audience. Mann's deft handling of Smith is responsible for "the most even-keeled, dialed-in performance of his decades-long career." Mann is especially appreciative of Smith's command of the nuances of Ali's speech patterns: "Ali rotated among different regional accents, and sometimes in the same rap he would switch perspective. He would have a narrator voice, an Uncle Remus voice, and innocent voice and then come back right around again…. Will was determined to nail the nuance in the speech patterns and he did" (Fleming, "Michael"). Even more impressive is what Smith communicates non-verbally. Raferty expresses his appreciation of this aspect of Smith's acting:

> Still, the biggest surprises are Smith's (relatively) quieter moments, like the scene in which Ali—having been conscripted to the military—refuses to step forward and accept his assignment, instead quietly shifting his head and cocking his stance, secure in his own righteousness.
>
> Or the sequence before his fight with Foreman in Zaire, when Ali goes jogging with a bunch of children, stumbles upon a mural of himself standing in victory over an opponent and simply … stares, internalizing the magnitude of something that Ali, for once, can't explain with a poem or a few quips. There's no way the Smith who made *Independence Day* or *Enemy of the State* would have let these [*sic*] kind of potentially big-reveal moments slip away with such ambiguity, nor would he have been able to resist throwing in some sort of scenebuttoning send-off. Smith's smoothness with a one-liner helped made him famous, but in *Ali*, he's at his finest when he's quiet.

The acquisition of this quiet assurance was a mark of his growing maturity as an actor.

Behind this quietude is another layer of insecurity that Smith felt in approaching this role. He had to undergo an educational process in coming to terms with the social, political, and historical contexts of Muhammad Ali's reality. Smith has said, "'It's very difficult to relate to the tone of the era if you weren't there'" (Johnson 60). According to Kegan Doyle, there were obstacles for Smith that went beyond the matter of tone:

> Although he, like Ali, has a somewhat megalomaniacal sense of himself…. Smith was reluctant to take on the role because he felt he could not legitimately identify with the hardship of Ali's

life: "I'm a child of rap music…. We've got Bentleys. We can't relate to not being able to sit in somebody's lunch counter. I'll buy the counter and throw you out" [388].

Smith was born during the peak years of Ali's fame, so there might have been a generational gap impeding Smith's ability to identify with Ali's situation.[5] Ali was a crusader for Civil Rights, the anti–Vietnam movement, and religious freedom and paid the price for his convictions. Smith was a post-racial superstar of rap, television, and the movies. His casting was the coming together of two global icons from seemingly different life experiences and ideological positions. It is a testament to Smith's hard work and artistic commitment that he was able to make the physical and imaginative journey to become Muhammad Ali (fig. 8.5). It is one of the few times in his career that he sufficiently submerges his star identity to become someone else.

American Dreams, Italian Style

Smith's second Oscar nomination came in 2007 for *The Pursuit of Happyness*, based on the memoir of Chris Gardner which recalls his rise from homelessness to an internship at a brokerage firm and ultimately to his own multi-million-dollar investment company. The film details his struggles making ends meet selling bone

Fig. 8.5. Will Smith received his first Best Actor Oscar nomination for his dedicated work in *Ali* (2001). Directed by Michael Mann (Columbia Pictures/Photofest).

scanners and caring for his five-year-old son. They sleep in the men's room at a sub-way station. They stay at a homeless shelter operated by a local church. All the while, he impresses his sponsors at the brokerage firm as he competes for and ultimately wins a permanent position as a stockbroker. The film was another box-office suc-cess for Smith, earning $307 million worldwide ("The Pursuit of Happyness—Box Office Mojo"). It was also Smith's sixth consecutive film to open at number one, and one of his ten consecutive films that have earned above $100 million. The film received mostly favorable reviews although some critics noted its sentimentality and its politically conservative take on poverty, the American Dream, and high finance. Smith himself was praised for his emotional expressiveness which reached depths of authenticity that audiences and commentators found moving. This is arguably his best screen performance.

One aspect of *The Pursuit of Happyness* that has not been enough acknowledged is the unique contributions of Italian director Gabriele Muccino (*The Last Kiss*, 2001). This collaboration brings to light significant connections between Will Smith, Afri-can American actors, Italian cinema, and global stardom. A 2007 *New York Times* article about African American actors and global film markets acknowledged the existence of a new glass ceiling in Hollywood. Actors and actresses of color are being held to a particular standard: they are cast on the basis of their ability to generate box office outside the United States. Given the economic realities of the film busi-ness, American films find more than 50 percent of their revenue from foreign sources (Cieply). The other reality is that African American actors and films do not trans-late and do not generate the profitable kinds of business that are fiscally viable. This situation has changed over the last decades with a few breakthrough films such as the musical *Dreamgirls* and studio investment in a number of stars such as Denzel Washington. What has remained a constant through this period is the success of Will Smith whose international appeal is beyond the reach of his compeers. Of the twelve most internationally bankable male stars, Smith is the only Black actor.

The way Smith's appeal operates for American audiences is clear. Key is the remarkable ability of his image to signify or not-signify race. As has been discussed in an earlier chapter, he is able to carry or mask a racial "sign" at will. He conveys opposing messages, racial presence and absence, simultaneously in a kind of post-modern double consciousness. Perhaps his popularity varies directly with his abil-ity to suppress the racial sign. Perhaps his oppositions cancel each other out, thus freeing his image to be consumed by his diverse audiences. It is not clear if this del-icate racial balancing is truly the basis for his international appeal. Is an absence of race important to filmgoers in Europe, Asia, Africa, South America? It very well may be possible that it is his Blackness that compels these audiences who might see something of themselves in him. Smith's global reach is probably dependent on larger film industrial and economic forces. Throughout the last three decades the prevailing goal in Hollywood, which has been taken over by multinational media conglomerates, is the production of the event film or the blockbuster whose audi-ence is young and international. This practice privileges genres such as action, fan-tasy, science fiction and horror films whose appeal transcends languages as well as national and cultural boundaries. These audiences seemed "to want films featuring well-known performers (including TV and pop music stars) in simple stories displaying humor, physical action, and awesome special effects. There should also be … an aura of flippant cool" (Thompson and Bordwell 684). All these characteristics describe Will Smith. His ability to transcend national and racial identity is a phenomenon that is not a matter of chance. He has figured out this formula for success and has deliberately pursued it. From the beginning of his career his ambition has been to be the biggest actor in the world and he has calculatedly shaped his work in mainstream genre films (most successfully in science fiction) as well as his star persona (the regular guy next door).

A recent permutation of his quest is his entry into another area of global film in another artistic register. This experiment is marked by his decision to hire Italian director Gabriele Muccino for two of his recent films: *The Pursuit of Happyness* (2006) and *Seven Pounds* (2008). The latter film has been examined earlier in another context, so the former here is the focus. *The Pursuit of Happyness* was well received when it was released in 2006, and Smith turned in one of his most nuanced and

Fig. 8.6. Gabriele Muccino and Will Smith on the set of *The Pursuit of Happyness* (2006). Directed by Gabriele Muccino (Sony Pictures/Photofest).

deeply felt performances (fig. 8.6). In fact, Smith chose Muccino for his unusual facility for eliciting remarkable performances, as evidenced by his work with the ensemble of actors in *Last Kiss* (2001). The other reason Smith hired the Italian director was Muccino's take on the film's narrative of the American Dream. Muccino told Smith that "'an American shouldn't direct 'Pursuit of Happyness' because Americans don't understand the American dream" (Abramowitz).

Into the bargain Smith gained in Muccino a director steeped in Italian film history and tradition. For instance, in *The Last Kiss*, which is about the romantic and career angst of a group of twenty-something men, he sets up intertextual references to Fellini's great early film *I Vitelloni* (1953). For *The Pursuit of Happyness*, Muccino draws upon the rhetoric and film practices of the school of neorealism and creates resonances and dissonances between African American representation and international film modernism.

Before offering a brief account of *The Pursuit of Happyness* and its thematic and stylistic parallels to De Sica's *The Bicycle Thief*, one might note a few other connections between African American film and Italian neorealism. This style of filmmaking, which flourished in post-war Italy from 1945 to 1955, sought to reflect the renewal of liberal idealism as well as national social problems such as inflation and poverty. These films, *The Bicycle Thief* being a defining example along with Roberto Rossellini's *Open City* and *Paisan* and Luchino Visconti's *La Terra Trema*, offer a devastating picture of insuperable social forces operating against the common man and the failure of social institutions (Church, police, state, organized labor) to provide help or solutions. The aesthetics of the movement, formulated against studio artifice and Fascist propaganda, required of film a "greater realism and an emphasis on contemporary subjects and the life of the working class" (Thompson and Bordwell 362). This greater realism was effected through the deployment of certain film techniques: location shooting, the use of non-actors, musical scores of great emotive power, documentary grade film stock, paratactical dedramatization, and plots following chance encounters rather than linear narrative logic. Other cinematic practices included "open endings, and microactions; and extreme mixtures of tone—all these strategies would be adopted and developed by filmmakers around the world over the next four decades" (Thompson and Bordwell 366).

One cinema that benefited from the legacy of neorealism was the movement of Black American independent filmmakers in the '70s and '80s, particularly the group termed the L.A. School. These directors included Charles Burnett, Haile Gerima, and Julie Dash. Their project was to forge a new Black cinema in opposition to the escapist blaxploitation phenomenon promoted by Hollywood. They wanted to capture real Black life through a different lens: "these filmmakers attempted to renegotiate the Black image on screen and ground it firmly in issues of realism" (Norton). They looked to neorealism as a model and shared with it basic concerns: hope, futility, and struggle in the face of oppressive social forces.

The masterpieces of Black neorealism are Charles Burnett's *Killer of Sheep* (1977) and Michael Roemer's *Nothing but a Man* (1964). Although Roemer is white, his work is important in defining this school of filmmaking. In both films there are strong connections to the earlier Italian films:

Killer of Sheep finds its main character, Stan, trying to cope with his limited existence. All he has are his family and his nightmarish job in a slaughterhouse. Despite this, he perseveres in the hope of a better life bringing to mind the many terrible existences of characters in the Italian neo-realist films and their struggle to survive. *Nothing But a Man* finds it main character, Duff, struggling against a racist social climate, repeatedly coming up against the walls white America constructs around him. This too brings to mind Italian neo-realism's concern with the inability of the individual to change, escape or circumvent the social strictures that bind him into place [Norton].

Despite these shared narratives and themes, Black neorealism diverges from its predecessor in one significant way. It assumes a final positivism in the face of a futility that neorealism cannot overcome. Both *Killer of Sheep* and *Nothing but a Man*, while recognizing the futility inherent in the neorealist vision, work through to a position of affirmation and hope. Both protagonists refuse despair and find value in perseverance. The emphasis on struggle is different from Italian neorealism and has a specific African American meaning: "the 'struggle' which produces hope is directly tied to Black identity" (Norton). Furthermore,

[these Black films] are also concerned with portraying reality. However, these films are also engaged in a mission that was on-going. The "'struggle" for a rightful place in society is a defining element of Black identity in this country. Toni Cade Bambara has said that the L.A. School filmmakers "recognized cinema as a site of struggle" [Norton].

This new Black cinema announces a new Black identity—"a renegotiation of the representation of the Black figure on the screen. This new figure has agency and refuses to give in to white subjugation despite his repeated failures in the face of racism" (Norton).

African American independent filmmakers have looked to Italian neorealism as a frame for shaping racial struggle, for forging new empowered identities, and, through the deployment of its themes and techniques, for allowing "the film viewer into the reality of life for the inner city Black family" (Norton). One such view into this reality is offered by the 2009 film *Precious* directed by Lee Daniels, which references Italian neorealism in a self-conscious, postmodern way. Based on the novel by Sapphire, this film details the struggle of an adolescent Black teenager with her obesity, her lack of education and opportunity, and an abusive, sociopathic monster of a mother. Her reality is the obverse of the American Dream. There is an extraordinary moment in the film when Precious turns her attention away from the obscene verbal harassment of her mother to the television which happens to be playing De Sica's 1960 late neorealist masterpiece *Two Women*. Daniels chose this reference because he felt at that moment in this difficult scene not only for Precious but also for the audience, she needed an escape. It is a harsh commentary about one's condition if Italian neorealism is considered an escape. In this film Sophia Loren (who an Oscar for her performance) and her daughter are caught in the ravages of post-war Italy, victims of social and economic forces. Their situation is similar to the trap of poverty and desperation in which Precious and her mother are forced to exist. At one juncture in the scene, which is a brilliant conceit, Precious and her mother are transported into the film. Daniels had the set of *Two Women* recreated for this scene, and the characters speak in Italian with

English subtitles. One irony here is the relative privilege of the two sets of women. Even within their poverty, Precious and her mother have access to basic necessities. What this scene does is to make concrete the confluences between African American representation and the aesthetic and ideology of Italian neorealism. It operates as a conflation of time, place, race, and culture. The women are bound by shared realities, and the films touch a point of universalism.

The universalist dimension of neorealism is also operative in *The Pursuit of Happyness*. Muccino taps into this aspect of neorealism, and this may one of the reasons the film did so well at the box office, which is a substantial accomplishment for a non-genre Will Smith film. Critics also noted the film's debt to the neorealists. Omer Mozaffar observes: "This American film by this Italian Director is somehow a mixture of Vittorio De Sica and Frank Capra. Somehow, we are handed an Italian Neorealist film in the body of a Jimmy Stewart classic." Frank Burke writes: "I believe *Bicycle Thieves* is a cornerstone of the 2006 Will Smith vehicle *The Pursuit of Happyness*.... Muccino's American debut captures the psychology of deprivation that we see in *Bicycle Thieves*, with the added factor of race, in a way that I don't believe either American critics or Smith realized." The film traces Chris Gardner's struggles as a salesman of medical bone scanning machines. His wife leaves him, and he is left as the caregiver of his five-year-old son (fig. 8.7). His fortunes decline to the point of his becoming homeless. In this depiction of a reduction of status and an assault on personal dignity, the film parallels De Sica's *Umberto D* (1952), which is about an aging college professor who is challenged by poverty and despair. The parallels to DeSica's 1948 *The Bicycle Thief* are more pronounced (fig. 8.8). In this film, the protagonist Ricci is unemployed and thus unable to provide for his family until he gets a job putting up ads on billboards. This job requires a bicycle, and when it is stolen, his life is in crisis. He spends the duration of the film in search of this bicycle which is the source of his livelihood as well as his identity. In the theft scene, the bicycle has just been stolen, and he and his small son, Bruno, pursue the thief through the streets of Rome. For *The Pursuit of Happyness*, Muccino approximates this scene. Chris runs after the homeless man who earlier has stolen one of his scanning machines. The difference is that Chris retrieves his stolen property. Ricci never finds his bicycle. These two outcomes represent the difference between neorealism and its descendants.

The note of redemption that *Happyness* strikes is revelatory of Smith and Muccino's cooption of neorealism and how the film revises the relationship between African American experience and neorealistic modes of visualization. The film's appropriation is transacted through its narrativizing of two themes: universalism and hope. Neorealism's universality is accessed through its emotional appeal. The spectacle of the conflict between futility and hope is emotionally charged. The experience of witnessing a character touching bottom and seeing reality through that perspective raises an awareness of social injustice and human suffering. The viewer apprehends these realities through feeling which reaches across cultures and becomes a universal film language. This emotional power clearly contributes to its international success and continuing influence. The late film critic Pauline Kael once wrote about a De Sica film: "For if people cannot feel *Shoeshine*, what

Fig. 8.7. Jaden Smith as Christopher Jr. with his father Chris Gardner (Will Smith) face difficult economic challenges in *The Pursuit of Happyness* (2006). Directed by Gabriele Muccino
(Sony Pictures/Photofest).

can they feel?" (qtd. in Brantley 29). *The Pursuit of Happyness* does not quite reach
that level, but, despite its lapses into sentimentality, it is affecting. Smith's performance contributes to this emotional effect, and this is a calculated career move
on his part. As an actor and as a star, he benefits from being situated within this
particular emotional field. The emotional environment of the narrative and the
filmic associations enhance the effectiveness of his performance. The universality of neorealism's appeal also deepens and extends his reach as a star on an international stage.

Finally, *The Pursuit of Happyness* offers a variation in its conceptualization of

Fig. 8.8. Bruno (Enzo Staiola) consoles his father Antonio (Lamberto Maggiorani) after the loss of his bicycle and his job in the neorealist classic *The Bicycle Thief* (1948). Directed by Vittorio De Sica (Arthur Mayer & Joseph Burstyn, Inc./Photofest).

hope. In the Italian films hope is defeated. In the Black independent films, hope had to be dramatized because it was essential to the political struggle for equality and against racism. The extraordinary thing about *Happyness* with its Black protagonist is how little that Blackness is recognized. Chris suffers from the forces of society that converge upon him, but curiously the one force that is not manifest is racism. Some reviewers of the film noticed this. His hope is a different hope. The film frames his project as a wish to prevail as an individual over specific personal challenges in order to achieve self-actualization, which means becoming a multi-millionaire. The hope here is "the redemptive power of capitalism" (Stables). It is almost as if Muccino has kept the effects but freed neorealism of its Marxist and populist ideology, just as Smith elevates the Black identity of the film Chris Gardner. The film describes a process, not of racial liberation, but one that can be replicated by everyone. Again, the appeal is universal. Race has been transcended in the film in order to universalize the message about the possibilities of success and to reach a larger audience.

The collaboration of Smith and Muccino showcases the connection between African American representation and Italian neorealism, which, as discussed, has a history as well as contemporary examples. This collaboration has other uses as well. In the film Smith portrays Chris Gardner who suffers in a neorealistic fashion, but in Hollywood fashion still rises to fulfill his ambitions. Gardner's success is eclipsed by that of his interpreter. Smith's foray into the style of the international art film, and his reshaping of it, finally serves to advance his ambition, his own American Dream, which evidently he has achieved—which is to become the biggest movie star in the world.

Conclusion

The Biggest Movie Star in the World

At this point it might be appropriate to repose the original question of this study: How has Will Smith become the most successful global African American film star? How did he make the climb to the top of the Hollywood racial mountain? He has accomplished this in the face of daunting obstacles, such as the Hollywood glass ceiling for Black actors.[1] The answer is that he made it happen. He had an outsized goal and figured out a way to attain it. One acerbic observer has described Smith as "a manipulative film actor who has never offered more to the public than he can consciously calculate as being personally beneficial" (White, "Crappyness"). His objective was to become the biggest movie star in the world. There is the often-reported story of how he researched the top grossing films of all time and with his business partner, James Lassiter, devised his masterplan:

> "I said to JL, 'I want to be the biggest movie star in the world.' And he said, 'Okay. Well, let's figure out what that means.' And he went and got the top 10 movies of all time, the list of the top 10 movies of all time at the box office—top 10 box office successes—and we also looked at them, adjusted for inflation and views versus dollar value. Also, we looked at all the different variations. What we found is at the center, there were always special effects. So it was always special effects, there was always creatures, there was always a love story. So we started looking for movies that had special effects, creatures, and a love story" [Feinberg].

He set out with a plan that was executed with great logic, efficiency, concentration, and systematic application: "Smith's career has been driven by arguably the most formulaic and battle-tested strategy ever deployed in modern Hollywood" (Katz).

Overbrook Entertainment, Smith's independent production company formed with high school friend James Lassiter in association with Universal and then Columbia Pictures, has been the instrument for his success. The company has instituted a practice of cross-over synergy between the multiple entertainment platforms that Smith surveys. The height of this strategy was reached with *Men in Black* whose financial coup was effected through a combination of film grosses, record sales of his single for the film, and the wide broadcast of the "Men in Black" video (G. King 63). This pattern was repeated in 1999 with *Wild Wild West*. Smith's revenues generated power and sustained Columbia: "in the first decade of the twenty-first century Columbia's annual performance at the domestic box came to rest on Smith's summer movies" (McDonald, "Business" 171). Indeed, the key to Smith's global dominance is his ability to command three mediums: music, television, and film. This is a profile virtually unmatched by any other Black male star. In the '50s and '60s there was Harry Belafonte who also performed impressively over all three entertainment platforms as evidenced most recently by the 2020 documentary, *The Sit-In: Harry Belafonte Hosts the Tonight Show*. In the '80s there was Eddie Murphy whose accomplishments incorporated film and television with music coming later. One would have to go back to someone like Bing Crosby or Elvis Presley for comparison.[2] The closest contemporary equivalent to Smith, but on a smaller scale, would be Justin Timberlake. When compared to other top echelon male stars such as Tom Hanks, Tom Cruise, Robert Downey, Jr., Keanu Reeves, George Clooney, and Brad Pitt, Smith in his global reach within three areas has achieved something none of them can match.[3] Yet, according to African American wisdom, one might conclude that Smith has had to be three times as good to be counted among their company.

Overbrook has also masterminded Smith's ascendency into global markets. The truth is that Smith always had an international fan base from the beginning. His early rap music immediately made inroads in Europe, and his television show *The Fresh Prince of Bel-Air* was also a hit abroad. He had moved his music into the suburbs, to the mainstream, and then to markets beyond national borders. The same principle of elevation was used later in films, seeking international collaborations and financing to circumvent racially exclusionary Hollywood business practices. Overbrook was one of the first production companies to see internationalism as the wave of the future before anyone else, and Smith has always had an eye to the international potentialities of his projects. He is explicit about this: "It's been said, 'Why sell something to 10 people when you can sell it to 10 million people?' … You have to have a global perspective" (Holson). McDonald claims that "Smith is not simply an effect or product of the system but a smart and knowing manipulator of the system" ("Business" 176). He is known for his "aggressive international publicity campaigns" (Quinn 203), laying siege to the audiences and potential revenues from the usual markets in Europe as well as Brazil, Mexico, and Central and Eastern Europe (McDonald, "Business" 173). His special targets have been Russia, China, India, and the Middle East. He goes to these countries in a media blitz when his films premiere, even learning phrases of the languages for the round of interviews and appearances. Smith's efforts have paid off considering that his films have been more popular and profitable abroad than they are at home.

Overall, Smith has certainly realized his stated goal. In 2008 *The New York Times* reported that "Will Smith is now the world's No. 1 movie star" (Barnes). As of 2020, he has made twenty-eight films which have earned a total of $6.5 billion worldwide ("Will Smith the Numbers"). He has eight consecutive films to open at number one, eight consecutive films to earn over $100 million domestically, and eleven films with international grosses of over $150 million (Feinberg). His remuneration (salary and box office percentage) for *Men in Black III* of $100 million was the biggest payday ever for an actor (Clark). What Smith has achieved is unparalleled, and, as one reviewer quips, he has done it all while being Black (Morscheck).

The purpose of this study has been to examine the meaning of this achieved stardom, its larger social and cultural implications as well as the representational accommodations on various levels that have been contributory. Smith has been able to overcome the impediments to Hollywood acceptance presented by perceptions of Black male race and sexuality through deft deployments of humor and charisma. His work involves a necessary mitigation of race as an issue and subject and a neutralization of sexual stereotype. He has mastered the ability to signify and not signify race onscreen and thus to move Black representation forward while simultaneously recognizing regressive racial attitudes that persist. While the messages of his films often capitulate to mainstream ideology, there is always a counterforce at some register of affirmation and empowerment, an essential positivity that make him a post-racial Prometheus whose project of uplift and rescue remains noble but elusive.

Smith has successfully created his own myth about himself: the hero of American cinema, a star persona composed of charm and affability, and a family man above reproach. Indeed, after more than thirty years of fame, his reputation has remained free of scandal.[4] Yet, there has been a cost in terms of Black representation for his personal victories won by his accommodation of the demands of the marketplace. In enumerating the rules of Smithian success, a commentator for *The Root* points to this edict: "Do not—EVER—make a movie whose subject matter treats or concerns the facts of Black life in America in an accurate or illuminated way, this even when said facts are somehow encoded or embedded in the conventions of genre" (Dauphin). Quinn puts this critique in more theoretical terms: "While some scholars persuasively suggest that veiled racial critiques circulate in particular Smith films ... there is a general, and generally convincing, view that Smith's star image of professionalism under duress, transcendence and sacrifice, and acculturated Black charisma, by and large, serve to disavow continuing, entrenched racial injustice in America" (Quinn 206). Wright is more direct: "Smith does not challenge racial stereotypes, nor does he truly engage with racial hierarchies in Hollywood" (144). Smith has had his eye on the prizes of fortune and renown and has not admitted that there are other kinds of victories.

After reaching middle age, and after experiencing several professional disappointments, Smith reached an impasse. He reflected in an interview: "'I had so much success that I started to taste global blood and my focus shifted from my artistry to winning.... I wanted to win and be the biggest movie star, and what happened was there was a lag—around Wild, Wild West time—I found myself promoting something because I wanted to win versus promoting something because I believed in it'" (Miller). He was increasingly not able to sustain the kind of success that he had previously achieved. There was even at one point a four-year hiatus. Articles began to appear with titles such as "Everyone Is Saying That Will Smith Is Over" and "Make Will Smith Great Again." The authors argue that Smith's dilemma points to a larger issue: the death of the movie star in the age of new media and the franchise (Duca). Even Smith has observed that it is impossible to make new movie stars today in the way he or Tom Cruise created themselves (Feinberg). Some have observed that Smith is the last movie star (Adam White). Others argue that in the era of Trump, the country needs someone like Smith "who can heal the divisions, who can talk to everyone, who can embody a semblance of an American Dream that is not based on bigotry or bitterness" (Rose, "Make Will Smith"). Smith seems to be aware of the political contributions he could make in his films and in his life. He says: "'And, you know as I look at the political landscape, I think that there might be a future out there for me. They might need me out there. This is the first year that I've been incensed to a level I can't sleep, you know? So I'm feeling that at some point, in the near future, I will have to lend my voice to the conversation in a somewhat different way'" (Feinberg). It may be interesting, for instance, to hear what he would have to say about the lives and unjust deaths of George Floyd and so many Black men and women in America.[5] Smith has taken steps toward more political engagement as evidenced by his Netflix series, *Amend* (2021), which he co-produced and hosted, focusing on the Fourteenth Amendment. Smith also made a major statement in April 2021 by pulling his film *Emancipation* from production in Georgia to protest the state's passing of restrictive and discriminatory new voting laws (Sperling). The film itself is a departure for Smith in that it directly addresses historical reality, albeit in action thriller mode, as he portrays a runaway slave who successfully makes his way to freedom.

In response to his perceived current stasis, Smith must reinvent himself or cede his position at the top to a successor. There are many ways he can leave a legacy or make way for an inheritor. Marshall claims that a true star cannot be imitated or replaced: "If the type is replicable by other performers, then the inherent value of the emerging screen star is limited" (99). What Smith has achieved has not been approximated by younger actors who have appeared in recent years. Some are accomplished actors who have given memorable performances (Michael B. Jordan, Stephan James, Chadwick Boseman, Trevante Rhodes, Daniel Kaluuya, John Boyega). Of special note is Corey Hawkins who starred as Paul in the 2017 Broadway revival of *Six Degrees of Separation*. He also starred as Dr. Dre in the 2015 film *Straight Outta Compton*, in an impressive demonstration of range. Some have enjoyed near Smith level box office success such as Kevin Hart. None, however, have risen to the standard set by Smith.

Yet, there are glimpses of another Smith that sometimes appear. In an episode of *CSI: Miami*, "At Risk," from 2012, a young Black tennis pro is interrogated about a child abuse case. The actor's resemblance to Smith is unsettling. The actor is London-born West Indian actor Aml Ameen. What is disconcerting is the image or quasi-persona of Smith in an unaccustomed context, a crime suspect rather than an agent of the law. Ameen's association with Smith continues with his starring role in Anthony Onah's 2017 film *The Price*, which replicates the world of *Six Degrees of Separation*. Ameen plays Seyi Ogunde, a young Nigerian American man working on Wall Street who gets involved in an insider trading scheme. He goes against his family beliefs and expectations to pursue his ambition as well as a relationship with an upper-class white woman. Things fall apart for him. He tries to make amends before the authorities descend upon him. The film, though minor, is relatively well made and negotiates its themes and ideas with sensitivity and intelligence. One unusual achievement is the portrayal of Liz (Lucy Griffith) not as a shallow liberal elite, but as a woman of substance and integrity, well worth Seyi's esteem. On the other hand, he, in a stroke of three-dimensional characterization, may not be worthy of hers. Again,

Ameen takes on a Smith-like role, but morally ambivalent and miscegenetic, and one that Smith himself would never have played.

The one figure with the most legitimate claim as inheritor is Smith's son, Jaden, who has established his distinct public persona with a highly eccentric and sometimes controversial presence on social media. His introduction to the entertainment field has been facilitated by his father. He has appeared in two films with him: *The Pursuit of Happyness* (2006) and *After Earth* (2013). He also acted in the 2008 remake of *The Day the Earth Stood Still*. Of more interest is his starring role in he 2010 remake of *The Karate Kid*, produced by his parents. It was on this project that Smith seemingly tried to fashion his son's stardom in his own image. The agenda to place the film and Jaden on the global stage was clear when it was reported that Smith had arranged for Justin Bieber to appear on the soundtrack (Nashawaty 14). The intention was to appeal to the widest possible audience across musical and cultural boundaries. The film was set and shot in China which provided the opportunity for widening the Smith family global brand. The film allowed for strategic intercultural collaboration such as co-funding by China Film Group (Quinn 202). A major coup was the casting of the legendary Jackie Chan. Jaden promised to repeat his father's box office mastery when *The Karate Kid* garnered an astonishing $55.7 million, which was not anticipated (Nashawaty 14). In contrast, the critical and public response to *After Earth* was a major disappointment, and Jaden retreated from film to concentrate on his music by releasing two albums, thus following his father in operating in multiple media platforms.

Another area in which Jaden has made his mark is fashion. He has his own design label MSFTSrep and has attracted much media attention for his adventurous fashion choices, such as a white Batman suit worn to the wedding of Kim Kardashian and Kanye West. His most transformative fashion statement was to adopt skirts as an anti-bullying gesture and to give expression to genderfluid identities. In an unprecedented fashion move, Jaden signed with Louis Vuitton and became the first male to be featured in the brand's womenswear campaign. Teamed with three female models, he appeared in ads wearing skirts and looks from the 2016 spring-summer collection designed by Nicolas Ghesquière. Jaden wore creations straight from the runway without irony or inflection: "He is a man who happens to be wearing obviously female clothes. And while he doesn't look like a girl in them, he actually looks pretty good" (V. Friedman). He is completely aware of the wider implications of his fashion work. He reflects on his modeling for Vuitton: "It was lit because we all knew that we were going to impact the culture and change the game and make a difference" (Giannini). The message that Jaden in a skirt carries is not about transgender identity; it is more about freedom of choice to express the self through clothing. In an Instagram post he writes: "Went To TopShop To Buy Girl Clothes, I Mean 'Clothes'" (qtd. in V. Friedman). His is a genuinely genderqueer vision, and he has earned his title as a non-binary icon. His father has come around to understand Jaden's questioning of gender norms and praises him for his fearlessness. In a way, Jaden is following the example of his father in terms of breaking boundaries. What Smith has accomplished in negotiating race, Jaden is doing for gender.

Jaden's transcendence of gender continues in his resumption of his acting career in Baz Luhrmann's mini-series for Netflix, *The Get Down* (2016–2017), about the early days of hip hop in New York during the '70s. Jaden portrays Dizzee, a graffiti and comic book artist who forms a close relationship with fellow artist Thor (Noah Le Gros). In episode six of the first season, their attraction reaches the point of a kiss one night at an underground club. The moment has been much discussed for several reasons. The gay plot between Dizzee and Thor and their environment recognizes the often-denied queer components of the formation of hip hop. The kiss itself has undergone much analysis because it is not clear that it actually happens: "Dizzee and Thor are caught up in the moment of revelry and lean in to almost kiss on another on the lips before stopping short and resting their heads together" (J. King). When the two are about to touch lips "we get bombarded with a montage of queer-baiting imagery, including an exposed breast…. Then we're left with the two of them locking … foreheads" (Braithwaite). The ambiguity of the kiss matters because it withholds a victory for queer identities. The narrative may intend to create a space for queerness in the reputedly homophobic world of hip hop but does not go far enough. The reason for this reluctance to fully visualize the kiss is inexplicable as the scene takes place within an entirely queer space, a drag ball at an underground gay club. The point of the scene is that Dizzee here represents a connection between disco and hip hop, and the kiss provides a symbolic link. Perhaps the failure of the kiss is a larger statement about the ultimate distance between the two worlds. Still, the moment seems like a lost opportunity, for instance to rewrite Will Smith's failure to kiss another actor in *Six Degrees of Separation*.

Smith has humorously referred to Vin Diesel of the *Fast and Furious* franchise as his rival (Miller).[6] However, the star whose trajectory comes closest to his own is Dwayne Johnson, otherwise known as "The Rock." Johnson is the former professional wrestling superstar and pop culture icon who has made a phenomenally successful transition to films. Since 2001 he has appeared in forty-three films, as opposed to Smith's thirty-three films over the last twenty-eight years. Johnson has earned a total of $12.2 billion at the box office, compared to Smith's $9.5 billion ("Dwayne Johnson the Numbers"; "Will Smith the Numbers"). His accruement of records already rivals and even surpasses Smith's. He was the number one worldwide movie star for both 2018 and 2019 ("Dwayne Johnson the Numbers"). Most impressive is his being deemed by *Forbes Magazine* in 2019 the highest paid actor in the world (Clark). For the period of June 1, 2018, to June 1, 2019, he personally earned $89.4 million. The previous year he earned $124 million, the most in the history of *Forbes* record keeping (Clark). Johnson has starred in a range of genre films: historical fantasy, action comedy, action, family comedy, fantasy, comedy, action spy comedy, science fiction, disaster, the *Fast and Furious* franchise, and the *Jumanji* series. Of interest here are the films in which he takes on the role assumed by Smith in the past, that of saving the world. The *New York Times* has given a breakdown of all the films in which he has rescued the world from calamity: *The Scorpion King* (2002), *Doom* (2005), *G.I. Joe: Retaliation* (2013), *Fast & Furious 6* (2013), *Hercules* (2014), *San Andreas* (2015), *Central Intelligence* (2016), *The Fate of the Furious* (2017), *Rampage* (2018), *Skyscraper* (2018), and *Fast & Furious: Hobbs & Shaw* (2019). According to the critic, "the foundation, or rock, if you will, of Johnson's film career is the confidence he brings to being humanity's savior on repeat … this action star has made the fate of the world his business" (Murphy).

Johnson draws from the Smith playbook in other areas, rendering himself safe and unthreatening by avoiding sexuality and race in his films. His racial ambiguity (African Canadian and Samoan) gives him wide latitude, even to venture into Black representation. He can play, for instance, Janet Jackson's romantic deus ex machina at the end of Tyler Perry's *Why Did I Get Married Too* (2010). In the HBO series *Ballers* (2015–2019), Johnson as Spencer Strasmore starred as a retired football star turned business manager at the center of the high testosterone and racially volatile world of professional football. Just as has Smith, Johnson has navigated the pitfalls of race and racism throughout his career, but in the world of sports. One commentator asserts: "The seven years he spent as a wrestler prepared him to be Hollywood's biggest action hero by placing in his path just the kind of obstacles and pitfalls he'd face before the cameras" (Dennis). Johnson absorbed the slights, insults, and racist fan criticism and avoided the Black male stereotypes common in the world of WWE. He has been described as "a master of code-switching" (Dennis). He downplays his racial identity in order to advance his film career, to fit into roles written for white actors without the need to change other dimensions of the film. Mainstream audiences accept him in these starring hero roles (as proven by his box-office power), and his race makes no difference. The terms of Johnson's stardom echo, reproduce, and in certain ways seem to supersede those of Smith. Still, Johnson's success is predicated upon the precedent set by Smith.

In the end, the only actor who can replicate Smith is himself. Smith's turn as the Genie in 2019's remake of *Aladdin* has returned him to box office prominence. Earning more than $1 billion worldwide, it is now Smith's highest performing film, eclipsing his first blockbuster, *Independence Day* (Siegel). Even 2020's *Bad Boys for Life*, reteaming him with Martin Lawrence, has proven to be a surprise critical and box office hit. *Entertainment Weekly* reports that *Bad Boys for Life* was the top-grossing movie during the Covid-19 pandemic (Nolfi). This amazing statistic proves Smith's perdurable power and ability to save the world in yet another way. His career has been given new life by mining his cinematic past. Smith's reinvention is narrativized in his recent film *Gemini Man* (2019) in which his character is cloned. Directed by the esteemed auteur Ang Lee, *Gemini Man* stars Smith as Henry Brogan, a former assassin for U.S. intelligence who finds himself a target for elimination by his agency because he has discovered too much about its operations. He is tracked and attacked by another assassin who is as skilled and ruthless in the job as he is and who turns out to be a cloned younger version of himself.[7] The only person who could be successful in killing Brogan is himself. "Junior," as the clone is called, has been created by Brogan's former boss, Clay Varris (Clive Owen), who runs the GEMINI project which produces hit man clones. These engineered assassins are nearly invincible as they feel neither human emotions nor physical pain.

Gemini Man, which opened on October 11, 2019, is one Smith's rare disappointments, not breaking even at the box office. The critical reception was negative. Many critics faulted it for the predictability of it storyline and its failure to engage the larger thematic and even philosophical issues inherent in the material.

Most often cited for the film's poor performance is the failure of the technological risks to yield the intended effects and impacts. Lee filmed utilizing a high frame rate, a 120 frames per second format (as opposed to the traditional 24 fps), in order to make the action sequences feel more immediate. The look of the film is disconcerting, dark, and cut-rate, not unlike the camerawork for television daytime dramas. As for the much-publicized special effect processes invented to de-age Smith to play his younger nemesis, many found the results oddly unconvincing. The film was slated for production for many years until the technology finally caught up with the film's concept. The other problem with the de-aging effects is that Smith, at fifty while the film was shot, has not aged that much, and the visual difference between Brogan and Junior is not dramatically pronounced. Perhaps this is because the image of the young Will Smith is so indelibly imprinted upon the cultural memory.

Like *Wild Wild West*, *Gemini Man* is a disappointment that is nevertheless a rich text for interpretation. In it are to be found the issues that have been explored throughout this study: the price that is paid for universal acclaim by a Black male star, the mitigation of Blackness within the film text, the emasculation of the Black male, the eruption of homoerotic subtexts, the containment of Black agency by white hegemony, and the reproduction of racial stereotypes and narratives. The very name of Smith's character is telling: Henry Grogan. It is consistent with the names of many of his film characters: Mike Lowery, Steven Hiller, Robert Dean, James West, Del Spooner, Alex Hitchens, Robert Neville, John Hancock, Tim Thomas, Nicky Spurgeon, Floyd Lawton, Howard Inlet. These names have a generic, everyman quality to insure mainstream audience identification and to advance an all-American neoliberal ideology. In contrast are the few cases of names that carry some racial signification: Tea Cake Walters, James Darrell Edwards III, Bagger Vance, Bennet Omalu, and Daryl Ward. What the naming of his characters also indicate is that most of these roles were originally written for white actors. For instance, *Gemini Man* in its twenty-two-year life as an unproduced project had at some point virtually every major white male star connected to it. It is a testament to Smith's determination and industry power that the film was made. He inhabits the role seamlessly, and this is achieved through the brand of Blackness that he projects, a hybridized, post-racial Blackness that functions as a "visual code" rather than a statement about a material Black reality. Yet, to acknowledge his race, should anyone forget, there is the insertion of "Blackisms" into the dialogue. This occurs quite often in Will Smith movies. In this film, they take the form of joking, stereotyping references to a fear of water and an inability to swim.

At the beginning of the film, Brogan is seen living a solitary life in rural coastal Georgia. The fact of his Blackness is never mentioned, true to the Smithian formula. He is without wife or child. This state of almost unnatural isolation is a construction of Hollywood narrative logic created for the diminishment of Black masculinity. Along the same lines is his relationship with Dani Zakarewski (Mary Elizabeth Winstead), a fellow operative who works at a nearby boat rental office while she keeps him under surveillance. She shares his encounters with danger from Cartagena to Budapest without a suggestion of romantic interest or chemistry. The age difference between the two (fourteen years) is consistent with male/female starring dynamics in contemporary film and suggests the earlier Morgan Freeman/Ashley Judd pairings.

The interracial dimension of their alliance is never mentioned much less explored or problematized. At the end of the film, Brogan and Dani check up on Junior who is now attending college. They seem to function as surrogate parents, but there is no clarification of the exact nature of their relationship. This curious ambiguity is another form of containment of the perceived threat of Black male sexuality at least to desired film audiences. Smith's pairing with a white actress highlights another pattern in his films, the absence of Black actresses. Winstead's presence overwhelms the racial mise-en-scene; there are no Black women in film, not even seen walking across the street in the background.

As often happens in Smith's films, an inevitable homoerotic current circulates just beneath the surface of the action. This becomes apparent in the implied relationship between Brogan and Varris. The question arises: why does this man clone Brogan and then raise this replicant as his son? His actions must stem from an obsession that the film does not address. Cloning in this instance is a form of possession. This process allows him to "possess" Brogan in every possible way. It is almost as if the two men have mated to produce Junior. Note that this is accomplished without the reproductive participation of a (Black) woman. Even more disturbing is the racial power dynamic at play between Brogan, Varris, and Junior. Who is Junior's father? Brogan biologically is the father, but Varris has raised and trained him. It is a determination that Junior eventually must make. This situation evokes the moments in African American slave novels when a male slave child must decide whose command to answer, that of his slave father or his slave master. The slave dynamic continues in the way Varris functions as Junior's white father who exercises an implacable control. (Smith's character Nicky in *Focus* also turns out to have a white father.) Controlling Junior is a way of controlling Brogan. Once again, the Black male protagonist in a Will Smith film is contained by white male power and, according to Guerrero's phrase, held in a prevailing protective custody.

The very premise of *Gemini Man* has larger implications. The situation of Brogan being pursued by a younger version of himself is parallel to Smith at this juncture of his career (fig. 9.1). He also must come to terms with his younger, overwhelmingly ambitious self who figured how to conquer the world and succeeded.[8] He must contemplate if it is possible for him to match his earlier achievements. He will always have "Will Smith" at his back. One critic observes about the emotional effect of his recent films: "the pathos of the climax stems from seeing Smith symbolically grapple with his past; in his performances it's easy to detect some regret over the persona that made him an action hero for so long, leaving his career muddled as he begins to age out of the genre" (Sims). As he did upon the disappointing reception of *After Earth*, Smith could only become reflective upon the results of *Gemini Man*. He makes the following confession to Trevor Noah on *The Daily Show*:

> "Because I was Will Smith there were things I couldn't say and things I couldn't do in certain projects I couldn't take and I had sort of painted myself into a little bit of a fearful corner and … that sort of marked a moment where I told myself … that's it, I'm gonna do what I want, I'm gonna say what I want, I'm gonna live the way I want without the fear of losing something … precious I've created, and…. I've been more free and more joyous and more peaceful than in my entire adult life" ["Will Smith Talks"].

Fig. 9.1. Will Smith as Henry Brogan confronts a clone of his younger self (Will Smith) in *Gemini Man* (2019). Directed by Ang Lee (Paramount/Kobal/Shutterstock).

Clearly, the failure of this film has been liberating for Smith. It indicates the possibility that he has reached the final transgressive stage of freedom that releases him from the bounds of his star persona. He is now poised to take artistic chances he has never taken before or to continue to do with greater clarity and intentionality what he has always done and what he does best: transcending race and saving the world two hours at a time in the darkness of movie theaters around the world.

Filmography

1992

Where the Day Takes You. Dir. Marc Rocco. Perf. Will Smith (Manny), Dermot Mulroney, Alyssa
Milano, Lara Flynn Boyle, Sean Astin, Balthazar Getty. Writ. Marc Rocco, Kurt Voss, Michael
Hitchcock. Prod. Paul Hertzberg, Philip McKeon. New Line Cinema, 1992.

1993

Made in America. Dir. Richard Benjamin. Perf. Will Smith (Tea Cake Walters), Whoopi Goldberg, Ted Danson, Nia Long, Jennifer Tilly, Paul Rodriguez. Writ. Holly Goldberg Sloan, Mar-
cia Brandwynne, Nadine Schiff. Prod. Michael Douglas, Rick Bieber, Arnon Milchan. Warner
Brothers, 1993.

Six Degrees of Separation. Dir. Fred Schepisi. Perf. Will Smith (Paul), Stockard Channing, Donald Sutherland, Ian McKellen, Heather Graham, Mary Beth Hurt. Writ. John Guare. Prod. Fred
Schepisi, Arnon Milchan. Metro-Goldwyn-Mayer, 1993.

1995

Bad Boys. Dir. Michael Bay. Perf. Will Smith (Mike Lowery), Martin Lawrence, Tea Leoni, Theresa
Randle, Tcheky Karyo. Writ. George Gallo, Michael Barrie, Doug Richardson, Jim Mulholland.
Prod. Jerry Bruckheimer, Don Simpson. Columbia Pictures, 1995.

1996

Independence Day. Dir. Roland Emmerich. Perf. Jeff Goldblum, Will Smith (Captain Steven
Heller), Bill Pullman, Vivica A. Fox, Judd Hirsch, Randy Quaid. Writ. Roland Emmerich, Dean
Devlin. Prod. Dean Devlin. Twentieth Century Fox, 1996.

1997

Men in Black. Dir. Barry Sonnenfeld. Perf. Will Smith (James Darrell Edwards III/ Agent J),
Tommy Lee Jones, Rip Torn, Tony Shalhoub, Vincent D'Onofrio, Linda Fiorentino. Writ. Ed
Solomon. Prod. Laurie MacDonald, Walter Parkes. Columbia Pictures, 1997.

1998

Enemy of the State. Dir. Tony Scott. Perf. Will Smith (Robert Clayton Dean), Gene Hackman, Jon
Voight, Lisa Bonet, Regina King, Jason Lee. Writ. David Marconi. Prod. Jerry Bruckheimer.
Buena Vista Pictures, 1998.

1999

Wild Wild West. Dir. Barry Sonnenfeld. Perf. Will Smith (Captain James West), Salma Hayek, Kevin Kline, Kenneth Branagh, Bai Ling. Writ. S.S. Wilson, Jeffrey Price, Peter S. Seaman, Brent Maddock. Prod. Barry Sonnenfeld, Jon Peters. Warner Brothers, 1999.

2000

The Legend of Bagger Vance. Dir. Robert Redford. Perf. Will Smith (Bagger Vance), Matt Damon, Charlize Theron, Bruce McGill, Joel Gretsch, J. Michael Moncrief. Writ. Jeremy Leven. Prod. Robert Redford, Jake Eberts, Michael Nozik. Twentieth Century Fox, 2000.

2001

Ali. Dir. Michael Mann. Perf. Will Smith (Cassius Clay/Muhammad Ali), Jamie Foxx, Jada Pinkett Smith, Jon Voight, Mario Van Peebles, Ron Silver. Writ. Michael Mann, Christopher Wilkinson, Stephen J. Rivele, Eric Roth. Prod. Michael Mann, James Lassiter, Jon Peters, Paul Ardaji, A. Kitman Ho. Columbia Pictures, 2001.

2002

Men in Black II. Dir. Barry Sonnenfeld. Perf. Will Smith (Agent J), Lara Flynn Boyle, Tommy Lee Jones, Barry Sonnenfeld, Rosario Dawson, Rip Torn. Writ. Barry Fanaro, Robert Gordon. Prod. Laurie MacDonald, Walter Parkes. Columbia Pictures, 2002.

2003

Bad Boys II. Dir. Michael Bay. Perf. Will Smith (Mike Lowery), Martin Lawrence, Michael Bay, Gabrielle Union, Jordi Molla, Peter Stormare. Writ. Ron Shelton, Jerry Stahl. Prod. Jerry Bruckheimer. Columbia Pictures, 2003.

2004

I, Robot. Dir. Alex Proyas. Perf. Will Smith (Del Spooner), Bridget Moynahan, Alan Tudyk, Bruce Greenwood, James Cromwell, Shia LaBeouf. Writ. Jeff Vintar, Akiva Goldsman. Prod. John Davis, Laurence Mark, Wyck Godfrey, Topher Dow, Michel Shane. Twentieth Century Fox, 2004.

Shark Tale. Dir. Rob Letterman, Bibo Bergeron, Vicky Jenson. Perf. Will Smith (Oscar, voice), Angelina Jolie, Robert De Niro, Jack Black, Renee Zellweger, Martin Scorsese. Writ. Rob Letterman, Michael J. Wilson. Prod. Bill Damaschke, Janet Healy, Allison Lyon Segan. DreamWorks Studios, 2004.

2005

Hitch. Dir. Andy Tennant. Perf. Will Smith (Alex Hitchens), Eva Mendes, Kevin James, Amber Valletta, Paula Patton, Julie Ann Emery. Writ. Kevin Bisch. Prod. Will Smith, Teddy Zee, James Lassiter. Columbia Pictures, 2005.

2006

The Pursuit of Happyness. Dir. Gabriele Muccino. Perf. Will Smith (Chris Gardner), Jaden Smith, Thandie Newton, Dan Castellaneta, Brian Howe, James Karen. Writ. Steven Conrad. Prod. Will Smith, James Lassiter, Todd Black, Steve Tisch, Jason Blumenthal. Columbia Pictures/Sony, 2006.

2007

I Am Legend. Dir. Francis Lawrence. Perf. Will Smith (Robert Neville), Alice Braga, Willow Smith, Charlie Tahan, Salli Richardson, Dash Mihok. Writ. Akiva Goldsman, Mark Protosevich, Richard Matheson. Prod. Akiva Goldsman, James Lassiter, David Heyman, Neal H. Moritz. Warner Bros, 2007.

2008

Hancock. Dir. Peter Berg. Perf. Will Smith (John Hancock), Charlize Theron, Jason Bateman, Johnny Galecki, Eddie Marsan, Jae Head. Writ. Vince Gilligan, Vy Vincent Ngo. Prod. Akiva Goldsman, James Lassiter, Michael Mann, Will Smith. Columbia Pictures, 2008.

Seven Pounds. Dir. Gabriele Muccino. Perf. Will Smith (Ben/Tim Thomas), Rosario Dawson, Woody Harrelson, Michael Ealy, Barry Pepper, Elpidia Carrillo. Writ. Grant Nieporte. Prod. Will Smith, James Lassiter, Todd Black, Steve Tisch, Jason Blumenthal. Columbia Pictures, 2008.

2012

Men in Black 3. Dir. Barry Sonnenfeld. Perf. Will Smith (Agent J), Tommy Lee Jones, Josh Brolin, Michael Stuhlbarg, Emma Thompson, Jemaine Clement, Nicole Scherzinger, Alice Eve. Writ. Etan Cohen, Jeff Nathanson, David Koepp, Michael Soccio. Prod. Walter Parkes, Laurie MacDonald. Columbia Pictures, 2012.

2013

After Earth. Dir. M. Night Shyamalan. Perf. Will Smith (Cypher Raige), Jaden Smith, Isabelle Fuhrman, Zoe Kravitz, Sophie Okonedo, Kristofer Hivju, David Denman. Writ. M. Night Shyamalan, Gary Whitta. Prod. Will Smith, M. Night Shyamalan, Jada Pinkett Smith, Caleeb Pinkett, James Lassiter. Columbia Pictures, 2013.

2015

Focus. Dir. Glenn Ficarra, John Requa. Perf. Will Smith (Nicky Spurgeon), Margot Robbie, Rodrigo Santoro, Gerald McRaney, Adrian Martinez, B.D. Wong. Writ. Glenn Ficarra, John Requa. Prod. Stan Wlodkowski, Charlie Gogolak. Columbia Pictures, 2015.

Concussion. Dir. Peter Landesman. Perf. Will Smith (Bennet Omalu), Gugu Mbatha-Raw, Alec Baldwin, Albert Brooks, David Morse, Luke Wilson. Writ. Peter Landesman. Prod. Ridley Scott, Giannina Facio, David Wolthoff, Larry Shuman, Elizabeth Cantillon. Columbia Pictures, 2015.

2016

Suicide Squad. Dir. David Ayer. Perf. Will Smith (Floyd Lawton/Deadshot), Margot Robbie, Jared Leto, Cara Delevingne, Jai Courtney, Joel Kinnaman, Viola Davis. Writ. David Ayer. Prod. Charles Roven, Richard Suckle. Warner Bros. Pictures, 2016.

Collateral Beauty. Dir. David Frankel. Perf. Will Smith (Howard Inlet), Helen Mirren, Keira Knightley, Kate Winslet, Edward Norton, Naomi Harris. Writ. Allan Loeb. Prod. Allan Loeb, Michael Sugar, Anthony Bregman, Bard Dorros, Kevin Scott Frakes. Warner Bros. Pictures, 2016.

2017

Bright. Dir. David Ayer. Perf. Will Smith (Daryl Ward), Joel Edgerton, Noomi Rapace, Lucy Fry, Edgar Ramirez, Nadia Gray. Writ. Max Landis. Prod. David Ayer, Ted Sarandos, Eric Newman, Bryan Unkeless. Netflix, 2017.

2019

Aladdin. Dir. Guy Ritchie. Perf. Will Smith (The Genie), Mena Massoud, Naomi Scott, Marwan Kenzari, Navid Negahban, Nasim Pedrad, Billy Magnussen, Numan Acar. Writ. John August, Guy Ritchie, Vanessa Taylor. Prod. Dan Lin, Jonathan Eirich. Walt Disney, 2019.

Spies in Disguise. Dir. Nick Bruno, Troy Quane. Perf. Will Smith (Lance Sterling, Voice), Tom Holland, Rashida Jones, Karen Gillan, DJ Khaled, Ben Mendelsohn, Masi Oka. Prod. Peter Chernin, Michael J. Travers. Twentieth Century Fox, 2019.

Gemini Man. Dir. Ang Lee. Perf. Will Smith (Henry Brogan), Clive Owen, Mary Elizabeth Winstead, Benedict Wong. Writ. David Benioff, Jonathan Hensleigh, Darren Lemke, Billy Ray, Andrew Nicol, Stephen J. Rivele, Christopher Wilkinson. Prod. Jerry Bruckheimer and David Ellison. Paramount, 2019.

2020

Bad Boys for Life. Dir. Adil El Arbi and Bilall Fallah. Perf. Will Smith (Mike Lowery), Martin Lawrence. Writ. Chris Bremner, Peter Craig, Joe Carnahan. Prod. Jerry Bruckheimer, Will Smith, Doug Belgrad. Sony, 2020.

Selected Videography

"Gettin' Jiggy Wit It." Directed by Hype Williams, 1997, official video, *YouTube*, uploaded by WillSmithVEVO, 2011, www.youtube.com/watch?v=3JcmQONgXJM.

"Just the Two of Us." Directed by Bob Giraldi, 1998, official video, *YouTube*, uploaded by WillSmithVEVO, 11 Dec. 2009, www.youtube.com/watch?v=_WamkRSDeD8.

"Miami." Directed by Wayne Isham, 1998, official video, *YouTube*, uploaded by WillSmithVEVO, 27 Mar. 2011, www.youtube.com/watch?v=IwBS6QGsH_4.

"Parents Just Don't Understand." Directed by Scott Kalvert, 1988, official video, *YouTube*, uploaded by DJJazzyJeffVEVO, 2010, www.youtube.com/watch?v=jW3PFC86UNI.

"Wild Wild West." Directed by Paul Hunter, 1999, official video, *YouTube*, uploaded by WillSmithVEVO, 27 Mar. 2011, www.youtube.com/watch?v=_zXKtfKnfT8.

"Will 2K." Directed by Robert Caruso, 1999, official video, *YouTube*, uploaded by Alex Lenada, 1 May 2018, www.youtube.com/watch?v=EnN4lSLAf6E&t=9s.

Chapter Notes

Introduction

1. For reportage of the kiss and slap incident between Will Smith and Vitalii Sediuk, see Loinaz and Valdy.

Chapter One

1. All box office numbers are from the website *The Numbers*. See "Eddie Murphy The Numbers," "Samuel L. Jackson The Numbers" and "Will Smith The Numbers."

2. Smith's average gross per film is $134.3 million as compared to Eddie Murphy's $100.3 million and Samuel L. Jackson's $59.9 million. All numbers are taken from the website *The Numbers*.

Chapter Two

1. According to *Vulture*, "In 2006, Chris Tucker was the highest paid actor in Hollywood, receiving a $25 million paycheck for *Rush Hour 3*" (Evans).

Chapter Three

1. Will Smith's only notable performance of rage is a cameo in Avika Goldsman's *Winter Tale* (2014) in which as Lucifer he has a startling, uncharacteristic explosion of vitriol.

2. For all his transcendence of racial stereotypes in general, it is interesting to note one exception: Smith's embodiment of the Magical Negro stereotype in *The Legend of Bagger Vance*. Even more ironic is that in this film he is subservient to the character played by Matt Damon previously mentioned as sharing equally with Smith in terms of the American trickster/con man archetype they play in *Six Degrees of Separation* and *The Talented Mr. Ripley*, respectively.

3. For his impressions of Smith and Washington, see Pharoah.

4. For a discussion of the racial implications of the 2017 Calvin Klein ads featuring the Black male cast of the film *Moonlight*, see Stephens.

Chapter Four

1. Smith also sends up the myth about Black male genital endowment in his cameo appearance in *Jersey Girl* (2004). Here he plays himself sharing child-rearing advice with Ben Affleck's paternally challenged character who has been fired as Smith's publicist. Smith jokingly reflects about himself: "But we all know that I'm not famous 'cause of my brains. It's 'cause I'm, like, strikingly handsome, crazy sexy, and I'm, like, hug like it's ridiculous" (*Jersey Girl* 1:24:58–1:25:10). The line operates at a comic level, but it does nothing to refute the stereotype.

2. There are other lynching references in Smith's oeuvre. In *I Am Legend*, there is a scene in which Smith's Neville is lured and tricked by the darkseekers, the human victims of a virus intended to cure cancer but instead destroys the world's population turning them into hyperkinetic zombies with white skin. Kac-Vergne describes the scene as follows: "This move is a trap to capture Neville, who ends up hanging upside down from the road lights, awaiting his lynching by the darkseekers.... The darkseekers can thus be read as figures of white supremacy instilling terror in all those not of their race, creatures of white biotechnology gone awry" (146). Another reference takes place in *Enemy of the State* in which Smith plays a lawyer on the run for his life from agents of a government conspiracy: "Pursued by a gang of white men, Dean is shot at and even set on fire, evoking Ku Klux Klan lynchings" (O'Brien 182). In *After Earth*, after Jaden Smith's character, Kitai, crash lands on a post-apocalyptic Earth, he surveys within a jungle canopy the bodies of human soldiers killed by mutant monsters and impaled on tree limbs like lynching victims. This pattern of lynching imagery is an unexpected manifestation in the films of an actor whose persona has been constructed to transcend both race and history.

3. Smith has apologized for *Wild Wild West* at several points in his career. For the most recent disavowal, see Nadkarni.

4. These worldwide box office records can be found in "Denzel Washington The Numbers" and "Will Smith The Numbers."

Chapter Five

1. A version of this chapter has appeared in *Bright Lights Film Journal* and in *Poitier Revisted: Reconsidering a Black Icon in the Obama Age*, edited by Ian Gregory Strachan and Mia Mask, Bloomsbury Academic U.S., an imprint of Bloomsbury Publishing, Inc., 2015.

2. Smith was voted the top box office star of 2008 by the Quigley Poll, the first Black actor to be so honored since Sidney Poitier in 1968 (Serjeant).

3. It might be noted that David Hampton's motives for his deception of the Fifth Avenue couples is more subversive. He has said, "It serves them correct that they were taken for a ride because they have clustered themselves into this little world and sheltered themselves from the realities of New York City" (Kasindorf 44).

4. It is significant that Paul presents himself in the assumed identity of the son of Sidney Poitier. His fantasy requires the privilege and status that inhere in the reflected glory of a celebrity. Note that it never occurs to Paul to earn fame by his own efforts. Instead, he wants only the association with greatness. He prefers appearance to legitimacy. David Hampton himself explained that he originally chose Sidney Poitier for his scam rather than Harry Belafonte or Sammy Davis, Jr., simply to get into Studio 54 (Kasindorf 42). His ruse was an improvisation of convenience. Paul's ambition, on the other hand, is considerably raised by Guare to the level of self-recreation.

5. The design of this apartment in its symbolism makes a reference to Poe. Interestingly, Tom Wolfe also uses this trope of a red room in his novel *The Bonfire of the Vanities* which is set in the same New York social milieu. He titles chapter 15, which involves an AIDS-stricken celebrity writer at a social function, "The Mask of the Red Death." Also, the decor of the Kittredge apartment in the film may take its chromatic clue from the famous red-on-red decor of fashion designer Oscar de la Renta's apartment which served in the early 80s as a salon representative of a "new professional elite—those who represent current power, current talent and current fame" (Stanfill 25).

6. According to set designer Patricia von Brandenstein, "'There's a certain section of New York that, if you inhabit it long enough and you're insular enough, you think you're the center of the universe. And Fred wanted that feeling'" (Calhoun 9).

7. Paul is like the protagonists of passing narratives in African American literature who "take the risk of identifying differently [from their Blackness] in order to access the privileges of whiteness, and most of them pay a high price" (Rottenberg 443).

8. Paul harkens back to a specific Hollywood Black character type which was established in the 1930s and described by Donald Bogle: The Servant. Bogle writes: "The toms, coons, mulattoes, mammies, and bucks were no longer dressed as old-style jesters. Instead they had become respectable domestics. Hollywood had found a new place for the Negro—in the kitchens … and the pantries…. In almost any film of the period … a Black face was bound to appear. And whether that face was seen for two minutes or three and a half hours, it was invariably there to tidy up the house [or] cook a meal…" (36).

9. The metaphor of America as a great communal dining table at which her Black children are not welcome is the basis of Langston Hughes's poem "I, Too." Paul's experience with the Kittredges recognizes the racial wish to overcome exclusion, to come out of the kitchen, and to take one's rightful place at the "American table" (Fleming 9). Maria Fleming describes how this poem expresses the hope of "the men and women who, when told by the larger society to 'stay in their place' instead chose to pursue another narrative" (9). Thus, it is particularly ironic that Paul sets a limit on this victory by securing a place at the table but, by his own choice, choosing not to partake.

10. For a more positive analysis of Billy Dee Williams's character that reads his tokenism as a comment on 1980s affirmative action experiences, see Nama.

11. The one exception is *Ali* (2001) in which Smith is paired with three Black actresses who portray his wives. However, he is portraying the historical Muhammad Ali and is not acting through his own star persona.

12. The one rare exception is Smith's pairing with Margot Robbie in *Focus* (2015), which is discussed in more detail in a later chapter.

13. For a full reading of the homoerotic dynamics between Paul and Flann, see Gillan.

14. Tricia Rose writes the following about rap's hard masculinity: "The hypervalorization of the hard, invincible young Black male who has no chinks in his armor, who is always ready for battle, grandly refusing most forms of emotional vulnerability, is an asset in today's urban zones; but such intense imperviousness (feigned or realized) has grave liabilities as well. We learn a great deal about ourselves in these spaces publicly and privately after injury. In hardcore rap, these forms of bravery are completely expelled, branded 'soft' and 'weak' and, God forbid, 'feminine.' These rigid identity markers partially fuel the homophobia and anxiety-ridden, hypersexism for which rap has developed a reputation" (155).

15. Smith's stardom is constituted upon a slippage between his public and private personas. His off-screen identity informs his screen performances to a greater degree than most film stars. As Marshall in *Celebrity and Power* asserts, the film star is "configured through a tension between the possibility and impossibility of knowing the authentic individual" (90). To the degree that Smith lacks this tension and that his public image overlaps his authentic self, the mode of his stardom is closer to that generated by television. Marshall writes: "Whereas the film celebrity plays with aura through the construction of distance, the television celebrity is configured around familiarity" (119). He continues: "The

gap between the fictional or mythical and the real life of the celebrity is narrowed" (131). The Will Smith whose private life is defined by his marriage and family life is not that different from his screen personae. For example, the Will Smith who negotiates white Hollywood shares an identity with his screen characters who also exist in white non-racialized spaces. Thus, perhaps there is some risk involved for Smith in the roles he chooses to play. Since in his case there is an elision of the private and public, there might be a problem with roles that fail to affirm them both.

16. The more memorable representations of Black gay men in mainstream American film before the 1990s include Bernard (Reuben Greene) in 1970's *Boys in the Band*, Bernstein (Antonio Fargas) in 1976's *Next Stop, Greenwich Village*, and Lindy (Antonio Fargas, again) in 1976's *Car Wash* (Harper 142–145). Will Smith's Paul Poitier in 1993's *Six Degrees of Separation* is an addition to this lineage. This character and performance constitute one of the most visible representations of the Black gay male in American popular culture.

17. Paul's seductive charm is attributable to David Hampton, his original. For his obituary, *The New York Times* interviewed Hampton's last victim who was duped out of $1000 and obligated for a $423 restaurant bill. Still, despite the deception and humiliation, the young man concluded that "it was one of the best dates that I ever went on" (Barry A1).

18. For more detailed interpretations of the homoerotic implications of the Douglass/Covey encounter, see McFeeley 44, Wallace 92–94, and Hardin 102.

19. Given Smith's ranking at the top of the list of bankable stars, his position goes beyond assimilation to predominance.

Chapter Six

1. *Independence Day* was superseded by *Aladdin* (2019) as Smith's top money maker (Fuster).

2. Note that this role of educating white men in the art of Black cool is the premise of his later film *Hitch*.

3. The title of this section is inspired by the title of a chapter in Pauline Hopkins's 1900 novel, *Contending Forces*. The main character, Will Smith, is a race man modeled on W.E.B. Du Bois. In the chapter "Will Smith's Defense of His Race," he delivers an impassioned speech about the best ways for Black people to achieve equality. The reference to this title is ironic given how Smith's character in *Independence Day* has no specific racial consciousness or motivation.

4. For a full examination of the Black Frankenstein concept, see Young.

5. Denzel Washington's character in *Virtuosity* (1995) also has a cybernetic arm but does not have a problem with it. It does not trigger anxieties about identity or racial allegiance. Connections between Smith and Washington proliferate. It is interesting

that both had major releases in the summer of 2004, Smith's *I, Robot* and Washington's *The Manchurian Candidate*, in which they play Black men who are compromised by technology (and contained by Hollywood). Smith has robotic body parts while Washington's character has a device implanted in his back that controls his behavior.

6. To understand Smith's "difference," one might compare him again to Denzel Washington whose role in 2010's *The Book of Eli* parallels Smith's in *I Am Legend*. They both portray Black male protagonists in post-apocalyptic worlds. Smith's John Neville is supposedly the last man on Earth, with the emphasis on man in general—not Black man. Smith assumes the identity of an Everyman, and he does so with ease. Despite specific racial markers in the film's mise-en-scène, Smith embodies a Blackness that functions beyond race. Washington, on the other hand, even within a fictional diegesis of the future, always carries Black history on his back, in this case literally, as he bears upon his back the kind of scars that resemble the shape of trees. These scars resemble those seen in photographs of ex-slaves, most notably the famous 1863 photograph of the ex-slave Gordon.

Chapter Seven

1. For a full account of the manifestation of the buddy formula in the film version of *Six Degrees of Separation*, see Gillan.

2. For a discussion of the problems with racial allegory in science fiction films, see Rose, "Will Smith's Bright: Racial Allegory or Straight Up Racism?"

3. Another example of a race reversal that does not quite work is Neil La Bute's *Lakeview Terrace* (2008) in which an interracial couple (Patrick Wilson and Kerry Washington) are terrorized not by a white racist neighbor, but by a "racist" Black neighbor, a member of the LAPD, played by Samuel L. Jackson. The film fails to elucidate the dynamics of racism; it only draws attention to the preposterousness of the plot. The film was co-produced by Will Smith.

4. There are four other Will Smith films that might fit into the Magical Negro category: *Six Degrees of Separation* (1993), *Seven Pounds* (2007), *Collateral Beauty* (2015), and *Aladdin* (2019). Although Seven Pounds was discussed in a previous chapter in relation to its subtextual theme of lynching, here it does bear interpretation as a Black savior narrative in which the protagonist sacrifices his body and life for others, most of whom are white. *Collateral Beauty* reverses the stereotype by having three white savior figures come to the spiritual rescue of Smith's character who is suffering from a debilitating depression after the death of his young daughter.

5. *The Legend of Bagger Vance* essentially defines the genre. In his sociological study of Magical Negro films, Hughey sampled twenty-six films across

various genres and then evaluated and coded them according to ten criteria/themes under the general rubrics of Anti-Black Stereotypes and White Normativity and Superiority. *The Legend of Bagger Vance* emerged with the highest average score of 353, indicating frequency and number of Magical Negro tropes, and a percentage of 9 percent. Its closest rival was *Holy Man* (1998) starring Eddie Murphy with a score of 278 and a percentage of 7 percent (Hughey 552; table 2).

Chapter Eight

1. Smith's other foray into the superhero field is *Suicide Squad* (2016), directed by David Ayer. He starred as Deadshot, an incarcerated superhero assassin. He received top billing, and the film was a major box office success earning $746.8 million worldwide ("Suicide Squad—Box Office Mojo"). Critically panned (although Smith was not), the film nonetheless offered Smith an opportunity to challenge his image by playing a non-heroic character, yet one with a reserve of conscientiousness. Smith's participation in this project was a canny career move to capitalize on the superhero trend in contemporary movies. The role in the sequel was recast with Idris Elba.

2. "Obamacity," the essence of Obama, circulated widely in popular culture at the time of the 2008 presidential campaign, election, and after. For instance, male models who captured the sense of Obamacity were featured in ads and catalogues for aspirational, upscale fashion brands. Roman Watson was cast as Obama in a fashion spread in the September 2008 issue of *Harper's Bazaar*. Actor Dennis Haysbert invoked a sense of Obamacity when he claimed that his turn as President Palmer on the television series *24* may have helped to prepare America for its first Black president.

3. Smith seems to have achieved a comfort level in his star position that allows his screen characters to engage in interracial relationships. In *Bright*, he has a white wife without comment within the world of the film or among Netflix viewers. However, true to the Smith formula for the treatment of women, she appears in the opening scene and then vanishes for the rest of the film. This is the disappearing woman syndrome. Usually Black women cast as his wives or significant others disappear; here, the white woman vanishes as well, demonstrating a kind of equal opportunity sexism.

4. Although Smith's performance in *Concussion* was widely praised, he did not receive an Academy Award nomination. That year he, along with his wife, Jada Pinkett-Smith, boycotted the Oscar ceremony to protest the lack of diversity among the nominees. This was his participation in the Oscars-SoWhite movement, one of the few times Smith has taken a public position on a race-related issue.

5. A similar disjuncture between generations of Black male identities was evident in Sean Combs's performance of Walter Lee in the 2004 revival of Lorraine Hansberry's *A Raisin in the Sun*. Combs had never taken on such a substantive and challenging role before and expressed difficulty with aspects of the character, especially those scenes that depict Walter Lee's defeat in the face of his financial failure. Susan Batson, Combs's acting coach reveals the following: "Failure is not in his vocabulary—and that's his problem.... When I'd say 'What if someone came in and said they'd run off with your money,' he said: 'Oh, no, no, no. It wouldn't happen. You can't ask someone like me to imagine that because I won't allow it'" (Zinoman). When young Black men cannot relate to historic Black male despair, does this mean that we have arrived at a genuine postmodern, Post-Black moment?

Conclusion

1. For a full discussion of the challenges faced by Black stars in global film markets, see Cieply. The Black international glass ceiling was shattered by the phenomenon of *Black Panther* (2018). Although it remains to be seen if this was a singular achievement, it surpassed even Smith's international box-office records. More interesting is that Smith's post-racial star persona and aura would be incongruent with the profoundly Black and African world of *Black Panther*.

2. Julie Lobalzo Wright in *Crossover Stardom* configures such a line of succession of multi-media male stars.

3. While many white male stars excel in only one genre, Smith's scope extends to multiple genres, including science fiction, the buddy film, action, drama, romantic comedy, and even animation. Smith's animated features, showcasing his voice, 2004's *Shark Tale* and 2020's *Spies in Disguise*, have not been given critical attention here, being outside the parameters of this study.

4. As with any major star, Smith has generated his share of tabloid worthy narratives concerning, among other things, statements about Hitler, open marriage, divorce rumors, gay bromances, and Scientology.

5. During the coverage of the Black Lives Matter protest marches in June of 2020 in response to the police killing of George Floyd, which was captured on a bystander's cellphone, some television news reporters invoked words spoken by Smith on a talk show interview in 2016: "Racism isn't getting worse, it's getting filmed" (THR Staff). It might be added that Smith made this remark in the context of commenting about racism in America: "'When I hear people say it's worse than it's ever been I disagree completely.' Smith said race relations are not as bad as they were in the 1960s or the 1860s" (THR Staff).

6. Like Smith, Vin Diesel has expertly maneuvered around the obstacles confronting actors of color in Hollywood. In fact, he has gone Smith one better by avoiding race altogether. He deliberately trades upon his racial ambiguity for a major Hollywood career, and the rewards have been

tremendous. His twenty-two films, including the *Fast and Furious* franchise, have grossed a total of $11 billion, which eclipses even Smith's box office record. Though biracial, he never talks about his racial identity nor does he play characters that are racially categorized. At most, his characters will be Italian, Cuban, or Jewish. With the science fiction film *Pitch Black* (2000), the spy action thriller *XXX* (2002), and the drug revenge drama *A Man Apart* (2003), he established himself as "the perfect multiracial and multicultural hero" that Hollywood needed "to sell the myth of a raceless America" ("Vin Diesel").

7. Coincidentally, *Bad Boys for Life* reproduces this situation. At the end of the film, Mike Lowery (Smith) is almost killed by a younger version of himself, this time literally his long-lost son, Armando, played by Guyanese British actor Jacob Scipio.

8. Scott Mendelson offers an incisive analysis of this inflection point in Smith's career. He sees his last three films (*Gemini Man*, the animated *Spies in Disguise*, and *Bad Boys for Life*) as texts for the assessment of his achievement. What these films all have in common is a protagonist who, like Smith himself, is coming to terms with growing older and with the meaning of his life's work. Mendelson argues that these films all feature older men learning from younger men and questioning the morality of their lives of violence in the service of existing structures of power. They wonder if they have lived on the wrong side of justice and recognize the reward of such service: loneliness and emptiness. The other shortcoming of Smith's legacy is political. He rose to fame in a series of films during the 2000s that offered large-scale blockbuster entertainment in the aftermath of 9/11. Mendelson sees Smith "as a former mega-star reckoning with the entertainment (and implied messaging) he put out in the world during a crucial moment in history" (Mendelson). In addition to the implications of promulgating violence as entertainment, one might add there are other reckonings for Smith: the price paid for success in terms of artistic integrity and racial consciousness. For a more detailed assessment of Smith's legacy, see Mendelson.

Works Cited

Abramowitz, Rachel. "'Seven Pounds'? It's 'Adrenalic." *The Los Angeles Times,* 22 Dec. 2008, www.latimes.com/archives/la-xpm-2008-dec-22-et-muccino22-story.html.

Alexander, Amy. "Reading Between the Lines: Reviewing the Reviewers." *Africana,* 15 Nov. 2000, www.africana.com/columns/alexander/bl_lines_08.asp.

Alexander, Elizabeth. "'We're Gonna Deconstruct Your Life!': The Making and Un-Making of the Black Bourgeois Patriarch in Ricochet." *Representing Black Men,* edited by Marcellus Blount and George P. Cunningham, Routledge, 1995, pp. 157–71.

Amadou, Christina. "Evolving Potrayals of Masculinity in Superhero Films: *Hancock." The 21st Century Superhero: Essays on Gender, Genre and Globalization in Film,* edited by Richard J. Gray and Betty Kaklamanidou, Kindle ed., McFarland, 2011.

Andrews, David L. "The Fact(s) of Michael Jordan's Blackness: Excavating a Floating Racial Signifier." Andrews, pp. 197–152.

Andrews, David L., ed. *Michael Jordan, Inc.: Corporate Sport, Media Culture, and Late Modern America.* State U of New York, 2001.

Arnold, Gina, et al., editors. *Music/Video: Histories, Aesthetics, Media.* Bloomsbury, 2017.

Ashe, Bertram D. "Theorizing the Post-Soul Aesthetic: An Introduction." *African American Review,* vol. 41, no. 4, Winter 2007, pp. 609–623.

Ashe, Bertram D., et al. "These-Are-The 'Breaks': A Roundtable Discussion on Teaching the Post-Soul Aesthetic." *African American Review,* vol. 41, no. 4, Winter 2007, pp. 787–803.

Bacal, Edward D. "On the Obama-ization of Will Smith." *CineAction,* no. 77, 22 June 2009, p. 50+. *Gale Academic OneFile,* Accessed 8 June 2020.

Baldwin, James. *The Fire Next Time.* 1963. Vintage, 1993.

Barnes, Brooks. "Race and the Safe Hollywood Bet." *The New York Times,* 18 Oct. 2008, www.nytimes.com/2008/10/19/weekinreview/19barnes.html.

Baron, Cynthia. "Denzel Washington: Notes on the Construction of a Black Matinee Idol." *The Cine-Files,* vol. 6, Spring 2014, www.thecine-files.com/denzel-washington-notes-on-the-construction-of-a-Black-matinee-idol/.

_____. *Denzel Washington.* BFI/Palgrave, 2015.

Barry, Dan. "About New York; He Conned the Society Crowd but Died Alone." *The New York Times,* 19 July 2003, p. A1, www.nytimes.com/2003/07/19/nyregion/about-new-york-he-conned-the-society-crowd-but-died-alone.html.

Beale, Lewis. "A Variation on Vampire Lore That Won't Die." *The New York Times,*14 Jan. 2007, www.nytimes.com/2007/01/14/movies/14beal.html.

Bean, Travis. "Will Smith's Box Office History." *Forbes,* 22 Jan. 2020, https://www.forbes.com/sites/travisbean/2020/01/22/will-smiths-box-office-history-where-does- bad-boys-3-land/#6ad38e646120.

Bennett, Anita. "Will Smith Wears Drag to Remind Fans Aladdin Is Still In Theaters." *Deadline,* 15 June 2019, https://deadline.com/2019/06/will-smith-wears-drag-to-remind-fans-aladdin-is-still-playing-1202633273/.

Berardinelli, James. "After Earth (United States, 2013)." *Reelviews,* 31 May 2013, www.realviews.net/reelviews/after-earth.

Bogle, Donald. *Toms, Coons, Mulattoes, Mammies and Bucks: An Interpretive History of Blacks in American Films.* 1993. Continuum, 1996.

Bonilla-Silva, Eduardo, and Austin Ashe. "The End of Racism? Colorblind Racism and Popular Media." *The Colorblind Screen: Television in Post-Racial America,* edited by Sarah E. Turner, New York UP, 2014, pp. 57–80.

Bonilla-Silva, Eduardo, and Tyrone A. Forman. *Racism Without Racists.* Rowman and Littlefield Publishers, 2003.

Bonin, Liane. "Is the Wild Wild West Racist?" *Entertainment Weekly,* 1 July 1999, ew.com/article/1999/07/01/wild-wild-west-racist/.

Bordwell, David, and Kristin Thompson. *Film History: An Introduction,* 3rd ed., McGraw-Hill, 2009.

Bowen, Sesali. "The Weirdest Part of Netflix's Bright is the Racial Politics." *The Refinery 29,* 22 Dec. 2017, www.refinery29.com/en-us/2017/12/186181/netflix-bright-movie-racist-theme-orc-elf-species.

Brackett, David. "Black or White? Michael Jackson and the Idea of Crossover." *Popular Music and Society,* vol. 35, no. 2, May 2012, pp. 169–85.

Braithwaite, Les Fabian. "We Need to Talk About Jaden Smith's 'Gay Kiss' on The Get Down." *Out,* 17 Aug. 2016, www.out.com/popnography/2016/8/17/we-need-talk-about-jaden-smiths-gay-kiss-get-down.

Brantley, Will. *Conversations with Pauline Kael.* UP of Mississippi, 1996.

Brayton, Sean. "The Post-White Imaginary in Alex Proyas's *I, Robot.*" *Science Fiction Studies,* vol. 35, 2008, pp. 72–87.

_____. "The Racial Politics of Disaster and Dystopia in *I Am Legend.*" *The Velvet Light Trap,* No. 67, 2011, pp. 66–76.

Brody, Richard. "'Men in Black 3': The Uses of the Past." *The New Yorker,* 25 May 2012, www.newyorker.com/culture/richard-brody/men-in-Black-3-the-uses-of-the-past.

Browne, David. "Michael Jackson's 'Black or White.'" *Entertainment Weekly,* 25 June 2009, www.ew.com/article/2009/06/25/michael-jacksons-Black-or-white.

Burke, Frank. "Frank Burke on *Rome, Open City, Bicycle Thieves,* and Their Changing Places in the Anglo Cinephile Pantheon." The Screening Room, 10 Nov. 2015, https://screeningroomkingston.com/cinematica/features/rome-open-city/.

Burnett, Robert, and Bert Deivert. "Black or White: Michael Jackson's Video as a Mirror of Popular Culture. *Popular Music and Society,* vol.19. no. 3, 1995, pp. 19–40.

Burns, Lori A., and Stan Hawkins, editors. *The Bloomsbury Handbook of Popular Music Video Analysis.* Bloomsbury, 2019.

Butler, Judith. *Gender Trouble: Feminism and Subversion of Identity.* 1990. Routledge, 2006.

Calhoun, John. "I'll Take Manhattan." *TCI,* Feb. 1994, p. 9.

Carby, Hazel. *Race Men.* Harvard UP, 1998.

Carson, Tom. "Skin Flicks." *Gentlemen's Quarterly,* June 2005, pp. 119–22.

Cashmore, Ellis. *Beyond Black: Celebrity and Race in Obama's America.* Bloomsbury Publishing, 2012.

Chambers, Veronica. "Willing." *Premiere,* Jan. 1994, pp. 74–77.

Chin, Elizabeth. "Michael Jackson's Panther Dance: Double Consciousness and the Uncanny Business of Performing While Black." *Journal of Popular Music Studies,* vol. 23, no. 1, 2011, pp. 58–74.

Cieply, Michael. "Films with Black Stars Seek to Break International Barriers." *The New York Times,* 28 Feb. 2007, www.nytimes.com/2007/02/28/movies/28color.html.

Clarey, Christopher. "ATLANTA: DAY 4—GYMNASTICS; Russians Dazzle and Take the Gold." *The New York Times,* 23 July 1996, p. B15, https://www.nytimes.com/1996/07/23/sports/atlanta-day-4-gymnastics-russians-dazzle-and-take-the-gold.html.

Clark, Travis. "19 of the Highest-Paid Movie Roles of All Time, Including $100 Million for a Single Film." *Business Insider,* 20 Jan. 2020, www.businessinsider.com/16-of-the-highest-paid-movie-roles-of-all-time-2018–5.

Clum, John. *Acting Gay: Male Homosexuality in Modern Drama.* Columbia UP, 1992.

Coleman, Robin R. Means. *African American Viewers and the Black Situation Comedy.* Garland, 2000.

_____. "Elmo is Black! Black Popular Communication and the Marking and Marketing of Black Identity." *Popular Communication,* vol. 1, no. 1, 2003, pp. 51–64.

_____. *Horror Noir: Blacks in American Horror Films from the 1890s to Present.* Routledge, 2011.

Collins, Patricia Hill. *Black Feminist Thought,* 2nd ed., Routledge, 2000.

Colombe, Audrey. "White Hollywood's New Black Boogeyman." *Jump Cut,* vol. 25, 2002, www.ejumpcut.org/archive/jc45.2002/colombe.

"Coming out as a gay actor ruined my career, says actor Rupert Everett." *The Daily Mail Online,* 2 Dec. 2009, www.dailymail.co.uk/tvshowbiz/article-1232588.

Condon, Bill, director. *Gods and Monsters.* 1998. DVD Director's Commentary. Universal, 1999.

Copeland, H., and H.G. Copeland II. "Post/Black/Atlantic: A Conversation with Thelma Golden and Glenn Ligon. *Afro-Modern: Journeys in the Black Atlantic,* edited by T. Barson and P. Gorschlüter, Tate, 2010.

Corliss, Richard. "July 4: Will Smith's Holiday." *Time,* 1 July 2008. content.time.com/time/arts/article/0,8599,1819466,00.html.

Cornelius, Ray. "Will Smith's Message to the Haters: I'm Indestructible." Raycornelius.com, 6 May 2012, ray-cornelius.com/will-smiths-message-to-the-hatersim-indestructible/.

Cronin, Melissa, et al. "Will and Jada: The Man Who Came Between Them." *Star,* 19 Mar. 2012, pp. 36–39.

Crowdus, Gary, and Dan Georgakas. "Thinking About the Power of Images: An Interview with Spike Lee." *Cineaste,* vol. 26, no. 2, 2001, pp. 4–9.

Dargis, Manohla. "Able to Leap Tall Buildings, Even if Hung Over." Review of *Hancock. The New York Times,* 2 July 2008, www.nytimes.com/2008/07/02/movies/02hanc.html.

Dauphin, Gary. "Smith's Rules for Global Domination." *The Root,* 11 July 2008, www.theroot.com/smiths-rules-for-global-domination-1790900003.

"Dave Chappelle Doesn't Wear Dresses." *The St. Louis American.* 20 Apr. 2006, http://www.stlamerican.com/

news/editorials/dave-chappelle-doesn-t-wear-dresses/article_0a39c6e2-bbe7–5582-b7c-8c4d331406b5. html.

Davis, Nick. "*The Legend of Bagger Vance*." Review. NicksFlickPicks, Oct. 2000, www.nicksflickpicks.com/bagvance.html.

de Cuir, Greg, Jr. "'The Message is the Medium': Aesthetics, Ideology, and the Hip Hop Music Video." Arnold, pp. 53–65.

Deggans, Eric. "TV Review: Jay Pharoah in 'White Famous.'" *National Public Radio,* 13 Oct. 2017, www.npr.org/2017/10/13/557520604/tv-review-jay-pharoah-in-white-famous.

Denby, David. "Desperate Men." Review of Hancock. The New Yorker, 30 June 2008, www.newyorker.com/magazine/2008/07/07/desperate-men.

Denham, Jess. "Will Smith Has Spoken to Barack Obama About Playing Him in a Biopic." *The Independent,* 4 Aug. 2016, www.independent.co.uk/arts-entertainment/films/news/will-smith-spoken-barack-obama-playing-him-biopic-film-president-a7171291.html.

Dennis, David, Jr. "'Fate of the Furious' Dwayne Johnson Has Been Wrestling for Years With the Politics of Race, Pro Wrestling and Hollywood." The Undefeated, 31 Mar. 2017, theundefeated.com/features/the-rock-wwe-dwayne-johnson/.

"Denzel Washington—The Numbers." *The Numbers,* https://www.the-numbers.com/person/1660401-Denzel-Washington#tab=acting. Accessed 29 May 2020.

Denzin, Norman K. "Representing Michael." Andrews, pp. 3–14.

Devlin, Dean, and Roland Emmerich. *Independence Day. Scribd,* www.Scribd.com/doc/2164727/Independence_Day_Script. Accessed 6 Sept. 2010.

Devlin, Martina. "Hot and Cold, Sweet and Sour, Obama and Hilary." *The Irish Independent,* 10 Jan. 2008, p. 33.

Doherty, Thomas. "WWW: The Movie." *Cinefantastique,* vol. 31, no. 8, Oct. 1999, p. 50.

Donaldson, Melvin. *Masculinity in the Interracial Buddy Film.* McFarland, 2006.

Douglas, Orville Lloyd. "Why I Hate Being a Black Man." *The Guardian.* 9 November 2013, https://www.theguardian.com/commentisfree/2013/nov/09/i-hate-being-a-Black-man#comment-28716473.

Douglass, Frederick. *Narrative of the Life of Frederick Douglass, An American Slave.* 1854. Penguin, 1986.

Doyle, Kegan. "Muhammad Goes to Hollywood: Michael Mann's *Ali* as Biopic." *The Journal of Popular Culture,* vol. 39, no. 3, 2006, pp. 383–406.

Dreisinger, Baz. "Marching On." Review of *The Good Lord Bird,* by James McBride. *The New York Times,* 15 Aug. 2013, www.nytimes.com/2013/08/18/books/review/james-mcbrides-good-lord-bird.html.

Du Bois, W.E.B. *The Souls of Black Folk.* 1903. Penguin, 1989.

Duca, Lauren. "Everyone Is Saying That Will Smith Is Over." *The Huffington Post,* 4 Mar. 2015, www.huffpost.com/entry/will-smith-over_n_6800882.

"Dwayne Johnson The Numbers." *The Numbers,* https://www.the-numbers.com/person/72720401-Dwayne-Johnson#tab=acting. Accessed 1 May 2020.

Dyer, Richard. *Heavenly Bodies: Film Stars and Society.* 2nd ed. New York: Routledge, 2004.

Dyson, Michael Eric. "Tour(é)ing Blackness." Foreword. *Who's Afraid of Post-Blackness: What It Means to Be Black Now,* Free Press, 2011.

Ebert, Roger. "A Superhero With a Hangover." Review of *Hancock. Rogerebert.com,* 30 June 2008, www.rogerebert.com/reviews/hancock-2008.

_____. "The Taxman Cometh." Review of *Seven Pounds. RogerEbert.com,* 17 Dec. 2008, www.rogerebert.com/reviews/seven-pounds-2008.

"Eddie Murphy The Numbers." *The Numbers,* www.the-numbers.com/person/700401-Eddie-Murphy#tab=acting. Accessed 10 June 2020.

Ehrenstein, David. "Obama the Magic Negro." *The Los Angeles Times*, 19 Mar. 2007, www.latimes.com/la-oe-ehrenstein19mar19-story.html.

Ehrlich, David. "'Bright' Review: Netflix's First Blockbuster is the Worst Movie of 2017." *IndieWire,* 20 Dec. 2017, https://www.indiewire.com/2017/12/bright-review-netflix-will-smith-max-landis-david-ayer-worst-movie-2017–1201909960/.

Ellis, Trey. "The New Black Aesthetic." *Callaloo,* no. 38, Winter 1989, pp. 233–243, www.jstor.org/stable/2931157. Accessed 20 June 2018.

_____. "Response to NBA Critiques." *Callaloo,* no. 38, Winter 1989, pp. 250–51. *JSTOR,* www.jstor.org/stable/2931160. Accessed 16 May 2020.

Erigha, Maryann. *The Hollywood Jim Crow: The Racial Politics of the Movie Industry.* New York UP, 2019.

Evans, Bradford. "The Lost Roles of Chris Tucker." *Vulture.com,* 28 Jul. 2011, www.vulture.com/2011/07/the-lost-roles-of-chris-tucker.html.

Fanon, Frantz. *Black Skin, White Masks.* 1952. Grove Press, 2008.

Farber, Stephen. "Film Review: Hancock." *The Hollywood Reporter,* 24 June 2008, www.hollywoodreporter.com/review/film-review-hancock-125025.

_____. "Sex and Death." *Movieline,* Jan.-Feb. 1994, pp. 32–33.

Farley, Christopher John. "That Old Black Magic." Time, vol.156, no. 22. 27 Nov. 2000, p. 14. content.time.com/time/magazine/article/0,9171,998604,00.html.

Favor, J. Martin. "'Ain't Nothing Like the Real Thing, Baby': Trey Ellis' Search for New Black Voices." *Callaloo,* vol. 16, no. 3, Summer 1993, pp. 694–705.

Feinberg, Scott. "Awards Chatter' Podcast—Will Smith ('Concussion')." *The Hollywood Reporter,* 25 Nov. 2015, https://www.hollywoodreporter.com/race/will-smith-talks-going-politics-843527.

Fiedler, Leslie. "Come Back to the Raft Ag'in, Huck Honey!" *Partisan Review.* June 1948. *Mark Twain Adventures of Huckleberry Finn. A Case Study in Critical Controversy.* 2nd ed., edited by Gerald Graff and James Phelan, Bedford/St. Martin's, 2004, pp. 519–525.

Fisher, Mark. "'I, Robot': What Do Robots Dream Of?" Film Quarterly, 2 July 2012, filmquarterly. org/2012/07/02/i-robot-what-do-robots-dream-of/.

Fleming, Maria, ed. Introduction. *A Place at the Table: Struggles for Equality in America.* Oxford UP, 2001.

Fleming, Mike, Jr. "Michael Mann On Muhammad Ali, Will Smith & His New Cut Of 'Ali.'" *Deadline,* 17 Jan. 2017, https://deadline.com/2017/01/ali-movie-directors-cut-michael-mann-will-smith-muhammad-ali-1201887992/.

_____. "Mr. Smith Goes to the Future: The Fade In Interview." *Fade In,* vol. 8, no.1, 2004, pp. 32–39.

"Focus—Box Office Mojo." *Box Office Mojo,* www.boxofficemojo.com/release/rl189957633/. Accessed 6 June 2020.

Friedman, David M. *A Mind of Its Own: A Cultural History of the Penis.* Simon & Schuster, 2001.

Friedman, Vanessa. "Jaden Smith for Louis Vuitton: The New Man in a Skirt." *The New York Times,* 6 Jan. 2016, www.nytimes.com/2016/01/07/fashion/jaden-smith-for-louis-vuitton-the-new-man-in-a-skirt.html.

Fuchs, Cynthia. "The Buddy Politic." *Screening the Male: Exploring Masculinities in Hollywood Cinema,* edited by Steven Cohan and Ina Rae Hark. Routledge, 1993, pp. 194–210.

_____. "Don't Think About It." Review of *The Legend of Bagger Vance. PopMatters,* www.popmatters.com/film/reviews/1/legend-of-bagger-vance.shtml. Accessed 28 Jan. 2005.

Fuss, Diana. *Inside/Out: Lesbian Theories, Gay Theories.* Routledge, 1991.

Fuster, Jeremy. "3 Reasons Why 'Bad Boys for Life' Blew Up the Box Office." *The Wrap,* 19 Jan. 2020, https://www.thewrap.com/3-reasons-why-bad-boys-for-life-blew-up-the-box-office/.

Gamman, Lorraine. "Watching the Detectives: The Enigma of the Female Gaze." *The Female Gaze: Women as Viewers of Popular Culture,* edited by L. Gamman and M. Marshment. Seattle, Real Comet Press, 1989, pp. 8–26.

Gates, Philippa. "Always a Partner in Crime: Black Masculinity in the Hollywood Detective Film." *Journal of Popular Film and Television,* vol. 32, no.1, 2004, pp. 20–29.

Giannini, Melissa. "The Art of Being Jaden." *Nylon,* 6 July 2016, www.nylon.com/articles/jaden-smith-nylon-august-cover.

Gilchrist, Todd. "I, Robot: An Interview with Will Smith." *Blackfilm,* 9 July 2004, www.Blackfilm.com/20040709/features/willsmith.shtml.

Gillan, Jennifer. "'No One Knows You're Black!': 'Six Degrees of Separation" and The Buddy Formula." *Cinema Journal,* vol. 40, no.3, 2001, pp. 47–68.

Gilligan, Sarah. "Fragmenting the Black Male Body: Will Smith, Masculinity, Clothing, and Desire." *Fashion Theory,* vol.16, no. 2, 2012, pp. 171–92.

Glenn, Cerise L., and Landra J. Cunningham. "The Power of Black Magic: The Magical Negro and White Salvation in Film." *Journal of Black Studies,* vol. 40, no. 2, Nov. 2009, pp. 135–52. *JSTOR,* www.jstor.org/stable/40282626.

Golden, Thelma. *Black Male: Representations of Masculinity in Contemporary American Art.* Whitney Museum of American Art, 1994.

_____. Introduction. *Freestyle.* The Studio Museum in Harlem, 2001, pp. 14–15.

Goodman, Dean. "The Legend of Bagger Vance." Review. *John L.'s Kickin' Box Office Reports,* 8 Nov. 2000, http://jldmoox.tripod.com/nov082000.htm.

Gordon, Geoff. "Six Degrees of Trepidation: Will Smith Plays Gay With Apprehension." *The Advocate,* 8 Feb. 1994, pp. 54–56.

Graff, Gerald, and James Phelan, editors. *Mark Twain Adventures of Huckleberry Finn. A Case Study in Critical Controversy.* 2nd ed., Bedford/St. Martin's, 2004.

Gray, Herman. "Black Masculinity and Visual Culture." Golden, 175–80.

_____. "Television, Black Americans, and the American Dream." *Critical Studies in Mass Communication,* vol. 6, pp. 376–386.

Guare, John. *Six Degrees of Separation.* Vintage, 1990.

Guerrero, Ed. "The Black Image in Protective Custody: Hollywood's Biracial Buddy Films of the Eighties." *Black American Cinema,* edited by Manthia Diawara, Routledge, 1993, pp. 237–46.

Gumbel, Andrew. "Black Prince of Hollywood—Profile: Will Smith." *The Independent,* 14 Aug. 1999, www.independent.co.uk/arts-entertainment/Black-prince-of-hollywood-profile-will-smith-1112524.html.

Hall, Stuart. *Representations: Cultural Representations and Signifying Practices.* Sage, 1997.

_____. "The Spectacle of the 'Other.'" *Representation,* 2nd ed., edited by Stuart Hall, Open University, 2013, pp. 215–287.

Halligan, Benjamin. "Liquidities for the Essex Man: The Monetarist Eroticism of British Yacht Pop." Arnold, 97–108.

Han, Karen. "Netflix's 'Bright' Is a $90 Million Steaming Pile of Orc Sh*t." *The Daily Beast,* 22 Dec. 2017, www.thedailybeast.com/netflixs-bright-is-a-dollar90-million-steaming-pile-of-orc-shit.

"Hancock—Box Office Mojo." Box Office Mojo, www.boxofficemojo.com/release/rl746030593/. Accessed 6 June 2020.

Hardin, Michael. "Ralph Ellison's Invisible Man: Invisibility, Race and Homoeroticism From Frederick Douglass to E. Lynn Harris." *The Southern Literary Journal,* vo. 37, no. 1, 2004, pp. 96–120.

Harper, Phillip Brian. "Walk-On Parts and Speaking Subjects: Screen Representations of Black Gay Men." Golden, 141–148.

Harris, Paul. "The Observer Profile: Will Smith—Crown Prince." *The Observer,* 8 Aug. 2004, www.guardian.co.uk/film/2004/aug/08/comment.features/print.

Harris, Trudier. *Exorcising Blackness: Historical and Literary Lynching and Burning Rituals.* U of Indiana P, 1984.

Hemphill, Essex. "Does Your Mama Know About Me?" *Ceremonies: Prose and Poetry,* Plume, pp. 37–42.

Hicks, Heather. "Suits vs. Skins: Immigration and Race in *Men in Black.*" *Arizona Quarterly,* Vol. 63, no. 2, 2007, pp.109–53.

Hirschberg, Lynn. "How Black Comedy Got the Last Laugh." The New York Times, 3 Sept. 2000, Section 6, p. 35+, www.nytimes.com/2000/09/03/magazine/how-Black-comedy-got-the-last-laugh.html.

Holson, Laura M. "Will Smith, as Film Executive, Sets Out to Conquer the World." *The New York Times,* 21 Aug. 2006,www.nytimes.com/2006/08/21/business/worldbusiness/21iht-smith21.2547986.html

Howard, Gregory Allen. *Ali: The Movie and the Man.* Newmarket Press, 2001.

Howell, Peter. "Smith's 'Just Hyped' About Obama." *The Toronto Star,* 13 Dec. 2008, p. E07, www.thestar.com/entertainment/movies/2008/12/13/smiths_just_hyped_about_obama.html.

Huang, Echo. "Why Audiences in China Are Loving Green Book." *Quartz,* 9 Mar. 2019, qz.com/quartzy/1567028/why-chinas-loving-green-book-so-much/.

Hughes, Langston. *Selected Poems of Langston Hughes.* 1959. Vintage, 1990.

Hughey, Matthew. "Cinethetic Racism: White Redemption and Black Stereotypes in 'Magical Negro' Films." Social Problems, vol.56, no. 3, 2009, pp. 543–77. *JSTOR,* www.jstor.org/stable/10.1525/sp.2009.56.3.543.

Iannucci, Lisa M. *Will Smith: A Biography.* Greenwood Press, 2010.

Ifeanyi, KC. "The Last Taboo: Will Smith, 'Focus,' and Hollywood's Interracial Couples Problem." *Fast Company,* 2 Mar. 2015, www.fastcompany.com/3043046/the-last-taboo-will-smith-focus-and-hollywoods-interracial-couples-problem.

"Independence Day (1996)." *Box Office Mojo,* www.boxofficemojo.com/year/world/1996/. Accessed 3 June 2020.

Jackson, Cassandra. *Violence, Visual Culture, and the Black Male Body.* Routledge, 2011.

Jackson, Michael. "Black or White." Directed by Michael Landis, 14 Nov. 1991, official video, *YouTube,* uploaded by michaeljackson VEVO, 14 Nov. 2016, www.youtube.com/watch?v=pTFE8cirkdQ.

Jackson, Sandra, and Julie E. Moody-Freeman. *The Black Imagination: Science Fiction Futurism and the Speculative.* Peter Lang, 2011.

Jeffords, Susan. *Hard Bodies: Hollywood Masculinity in the Reagan Era.* Rutgers UP, 1994.

Jersey Girl. Directed by Kevin Smith, performances by Ben Affleck, Liv Tyler, and Jennifer Lopez, Miramax, 2004.

John-Hall, Annette. "Race Still Matters in Obama's Post-Racial America." The Philadelphia Inquirer, 26 Jan. 2009, www.philly.com/philly/hp/news_update/20090126_Annette_John-Hall_Race_Stills_Matters in Obama_s_post-racial_U_S_html.

Johnson, Roy S. "Lord of the Ring." *Savoy,* Dec. 2001/Jan. 2002, pp. 56–61.

Jones, Ralph. "The Inside Story of How 'Wild Wild West' Spun Out of Control." *Melmagazine.com,* melmagazine.com/en-us/story/wild-wild-west-inside-story. Accessed 10 Apr. 2021.

Kac-Vergne, Marianne. "White Folks Ain't Planning for Us to be Here." *Masculinity in Contemporary Science Fiction Cinema: Cyborgs, Troopers, and Other Men of the Future.* I.B. Tauris, 2018, pp. 121–55.

Kakoudaki, Despina. "Spectacles of History: Race Relations, Melodrama, and the Science Fiction/Disaster Film." *Camera Obscura,* vol. 17, no. 2, 2002, pp. 108–153. *Project Muse,* www.muse.jhu.edu/article/7993.

Kasindorf, Jeanie. "Six Degrees of Impersonation." *New York,* 25 Mar. 1991, pp. 40–46.

Katz, Brandon. "Will the Real Will Smith Please Stand Up?" *The Observer,* 24 May 2019, observer.com/2019/05/aladdin-disney-genie-will-smith-box-office-movies/.

Kauffmann, Stanley. "The Hustlers." *The New Republic,* 27 Dec. 1993, pp. 24–5.

Kellner, Douglas. "The Sports Spectacle, Michael Jordan, and Nike: Unholy Alliance." Andrews, pp. 37–63.

Killian, Kyle. "Border Crossings in Hancock: Hollywood's Racial Logics Redux." *Psychologytoday.com.,* 30 April 2014, www.psychologytoday.com/us/blog/intersections/201404/border-crossings-in-hancock-hollywood-s-racial-logics-redux.

King, Claire Sisco. "Car Crashes and Crosses to Bear: Trauma and Masculinity in *Seven Pounds.*" The Northwest Journal of Communication, vol. 40, no. 1, Winter 2012, pp. 13–40.

_____. "Hitching Wagons to Stars: Celebrity, Metonymy, Hegemony, and the Case of Will Smith." *Communication and Critical/Cultural Studies,* vol. 14, no. 1, 2017, pp. 83–102. doi: 10.1080/14791420.2016.1202422.

_____. "Legendary Troubles: Trauma, Masculinity, and Race in *I Am Legend*." *Millennial Masculinity: Men in Contemporary American Cinema*, edited by Timothy Shary, Wayne State UP, 2013, pp. 243–64.

King, Geoff. "Stardom in the Willennium." *Contemporary Hollywood Stardom*, edited by Martin Barker and Thomas Austin, Arnold, 2003, pp. 62–73.

King, Jamilah. "'The Get Down' Is the Queer Hip-Hop History We've Been Waiting For." *Mic.com*, 15 Aug. 2016, https://www.mic.com/articles/151515/the-get-down-is-the-queer-hip-hop-history-we-ve-been-waiting-for#.pIX30GbqC.

Larrieux, Stephanie. "Toward a Black Science Fiction Cinema: The Slippery Signifier of Race and the Films of Will Smith." *The Black Imagination: Science Fiction, Futurism and the Speculative*, edited by Sandra Jackson and Julie E. Moody-Freeman. Peter Lang, 2011, pp. 204–219.

Lawrence, Derek. "Why Hitch is the Greatest Rom-Com of All Time: Opinion." *Entertainment Weekly*, 11 Feb. 2020, https://ew.com/movies/2020/02/11/hitch-greatest-rom-com-all-time/.

Leader-Picone, Cameron. "Post-Black Stories: Colson Whitehead's Sag Harbor and Racial Individualism." *Contemporary Literature*, vol. 56, no. 3, 2015, pp. 421–49.

Lehman, Peter. "In an Imperfect World, Men With Small Penises Are Forgiven: The Presentation of the Penis/Phallus in American Films of the 1990s." *Men's Lives*, edited by M. Kimmel and M. Messner, Allyn & Bacon, 2001, pp. 494–504.

Lewis, Shantrelle. *Dandy Lion: The Black Dandy and Street Style*. Aperture, 2017.

Loinaz, Alexis L. "News/Will Smith Speaks Out About Red-Carpet Kiss Attack: 'It Was Just Was Just Awkward.'" E! Online, 23 May 2012, https://www.eonline.com/de/news/318395/will-smith-speaks-out-about-red-carpet-kiss-attack-it-was-just-awkward.

Longsdorf, Amy. "Spotlight on Will Smith: He Takes a Swing at 'Bagger Vance' and Finds the Role Fits Him to a Tee." *The Morning Call*, 4 Nov. 2000, www.mcall.com/news/mc-xpm-2000-11-04-3334231-story.html.

Longwell, Todd. "Weight of the World." *The Hollywood Reporter*, 9 Dec. 2008, www.hollywoodreporter.com/news/weight-world-124140.

Looby, Christopher. "'Innocent Homosexuality': The Fiedler Thesis in Retrospect." Graff and Phelan, 526–541.

Lothery, Todd. "FILM ROLES: African Americans Left Out in the Cold." *Raleigh News & Observer*, 9 Mar. 2001, products.kitsapsun.com/archive/2001/03–09/0067_film_roles__african_americans_lef.html.

Lott, Eric. "The Aesthetic Ante: Pleasure, Pop Culture, and the Middle Passage." *Callaloo*, vol. 17, No. 2, Spring 1994, pp. 545–55.

_____. "Response to Trey Ellis's: 'The New Black Aesthetic.'" *Callaloo*, no. 38, Winter 1989, pp. 244–46.

Lyle, Timothy. "'Check With Yo' Man First; Check With Yo' Man': Tyler Perry Appropriates Drag as a Tool to Re-Circulate Patriarchal Ideology." Callaloo, vol.34, no. 3, Summer 2011, pp. 943–48. *JSTOR*, www.jstor.org/stable/4124320/.

Magee, Lenox. "Post-Race USA—Are We There Yet?" *N'Digo*, 19 Feb. 2009, Squires 216.

Magill, David. "Celebrity Culture and Racial Masculinities: The Case of Will Smith." *Pimps, Wimps, Studs, Thugs and Gentlemen: Essays on Media Images of Masculinity*, edited by Elwood Watson, McFarland, 2009, pp. 126–37.

Malinowski, Jamie. "Colorblind Buddies in Black and White." *The New York Times*, 10 Nov. 2002, Section 2, pp.1+.

Manghani, Sunil. "The Pleasures of (Music) Video." Arnold, pp. 21–40.

Mapes, Marty. "The Legend of Bagger Vance." Review. *Moviehabit*, 2 Nov. 2000, www.moviehabit.com/reviews/leg_j000.shtml.

Mapplethorpe. Directed by Ondi Timoner, performances by Matt Smith and McKinley Belcher III, Samuel Goldwyn Films, 2018.

Marriott, David. *On Black Men*. Columbia UP, 2000.

Marshall, P. David. *Celebrity and Power: Fame in Contemporary Culture*. U of Minnesota P, 1997.

Mask, Mia. "Who's Behind That Fat Suit? Momma, Madea, Rasputia and the Politics of Cross-Dressing." *Contemporary Black American Cinema: Race, Gender and Sexuality at the Movies*, edited by Mia Mask, Routledge, 2012.

Maslin, Janet. "'Wild, Wild West': Gadgets, Bond Girls and Men in Chaps." *The New York Times*, 30 June 1999, https://archive.nytimes.com/www.nytimes.com/library/film/063099west-film-review.html.

Masters, Kim. "Will Smith's *After Earth* Apocalypse: Who Loses Most." *The Hollywood Reporter*, no. 21, 14 June 2013, pp. 15–16.

McCarthy, Todd. "Seven Pounds." Review. *Variety*, vol. 413, no. 6, 17 Dec. 2008, pp. 23–26. www.variety.com/2008/film/awards/seven-pounds-2–1200472723/.

McClintock, Pamela. "'Hancock' Solidifies Smith's Star Power." *Variety*, 11 July 2008, variety.com/2008/film/box-office/hancock-solidifies-smith-s-starpower-1117988837/.

McDonald, Mary. "Safe Sex Symbol? : Michael Jordan and the Politics of Representation." Andrews 153–174.

McDonald, Paul. "Reconceptualising Stardom." *Stars*, by Richard Dyer. British Film Institute, 1998, pp. 175–211.

_____. *The Star System: Hollywood's Production of Popular Identities*. Wallflower, 2000.

_____. "The Will Smith Business." *Hollywood Stardom*. Wiley-Blackwell, 2013, pp. 155–77.

McFarland, Melanie. "'White Famous': If It Weren't So Funny, We'd Weep." *Salon,* 14 Oct. 2017, www.salon.com/2017/10/14/white-famous-if-it-werent-so-funny-wed-weep/.

McFeely, William S. *Frederick Douglass.* Norton, 1995.

"Men in Black (1997)." *Box Office Mojo,* www.boxofficemojo.com/title/tt0119654/?ref_=bo_se_r_1. Accessed 4 June 2020.

Mendelson, Scott. "'Bad Boys 3' Confronts Will Smith's Legacy as Hollywood's Biggest Post-9/11 Movie Star." *Forbes,* 22 Jan. 2020, www.forbes.com/sites/scottmendelson/2020/01/22/bad-boys-for-life-shows-will-smith-at-war-with-his-movie-star-image/#28fa7a11f545.

Mercer, Kobena. "Just Looking for Trouble: Robert Mapplethorpe and the Fantasies of Race." *Black British Cultural Studies: A Reader,* edited by Houston Baker, Jr., et al., U of Chicago P, 1996, pp. 278–292.

_____. "Skin Head Sex Thing: Racial Difference and the Homoerotic Imaginary." *How Do I Look? Queer Film and Video,* edited by Bad Object-Choices, Bay Press, 1991, pp. 169–210.

Mercer, Kobena, and Isaac Julien. "True Confessions." *Black Male: Representations of Masculinity in Contemporary American Art,* edited by Thelma Golden, Whitney Museum of Modern Art, 1994.

Miller, Julie. "Why Will Smith Regrets Wanting to Be the World's 'Biggest Movie Star.'" *Vanity Fair,* 22 June 2016, www.vanityfair.com/style/2016/06/will-smith-movie-star-regret.

Milvy, Erika. "How Playwright Turned 'Six Degrees.'" *New York Post,* 7 Dec. 1993, p. 34.

Mishan, Ligaya. "The Distinctly American Ethos of the Grifter." *The New York Times Style Magazine,* 22 Sept. 2019, www.nytimes.com/2019/09/12/t-magazine/the-distinctly-american-ethos-of-the-grifter.html.

Modleski, Tania. "In Hollywood, Racist Stereotypes Can Still Earn Oscar Nominations." *The Chronicle of Higher Education.* 20 Mar. 2000, pp. B9-B10.

Morris, Wesley. "Landing with a Thud." Review of *Hancock. The Boston Globe,* 1 July 2008, archive.boston.com/ae/movies/articles/2008/07/01/landing_with_a_thud/.

_____. "The Last Taboo: Why Pop Culture Just Can't Deal with Black Male Sexuality." *New York Times,* 27 Oct. 2016, www.nytimes.com/interactive/2016/10/30/magazine/Black-male-sexuality-last-taboo.html.

Morrison, Mark. "I'm Extremely Confident in Who I Am." *USA Weekend,* 3–5 Dec. 1993, pp. 4–5.

Morscheck, Peter. "Why Was Will Smith Called 'The Most Powerful Actor in Hollywood' by Newsweek in 2007?" *Quora,* 25 Sept. 2018, www.quora.com/Why-was-Will-Smith-called-the-most-powerful-actor-in-Hollywood-by-Newsweek-in-2007.

Mozaffar, Omer. "Happiness Is a Good Father." *RogerEbert.com,* 9 June 2011, www.rogerebert.com/far-flung-correspondents/happiness-is-a-good-father.

Muchnic, Susan. "Making the Case for the 'Post-Black' School of Art." *The Los Angeles Times,* 29 Sept. 2001, www.articles.latimes.com/2001/sep/29/entertainment/ca-51175/2.

Murphy, Mekado. "Dwayne Johnson: Saving the World, Film by Film." *The New York Times,* 24 May 2019, www.nytimes.com/2019/05/24/movies/dwayne-johnson-hobbs-shaw.html.

"My Favorite Scene: Glory (1989) 'One Tear.'" *Killing Time,* 20 Sept. 2016, www.justkillingti.me/2016/09/20/my-favorite-scene-glory-1989-one-tear.

Nadkarni, Rohan. "Will Smith is Still Sorry About *Wild Wild West.*" *GQ,* 22 June 2016, www.gq.com/story/will-smith-sorry-about-wild-wild-west.

Nama, Adilifu. *Black Space: Imagining Race in Science Fiction Film.* U of Texas P, 2008.

_____. *Super Black: American Pop Culture and Black Superheroes.* U of Texas Press, 2011.

Nashawaty, Chris. "The *Kid* Kicks Butt." *Entertainment Weekly,* 25 June 2010, pp. 14–15.

Naughton, Jim. *Taking to the Air: The Rise of Michael Jordan.* Warner, 1992.

Nelson, Josh. "ANALYSIS: Neuralysing History, Race, Time, and Fatherhood in 'Men in Black 3.'" Philmology, 16 July, www.philmology.com/?p=1886. Accessed 10 December 2019.

Nelson, Steffie. "Quest for Salvation: 'Pounds' Carries the Weight of a Devastating Burden." *Variety,* 15–21 Dec. 2008, pp. 8+.

Nesenholtz, Seth. "Unintentional Camp and the Image of Will Smith." *Bright Lights Film Journal,* May 2003, www.brightlightsfilm.com/40/willsmith.htm.

Nickson, Chris. *Denzel Washington.* St.Martin's, 1996.

_____. *Will Smith.* St. Martin's, 1999.

Nolfi, Joey. "Domestic Box Office Down Nearly $400 Million Since Coronavirus Closures." *Entertainment Weekly,* 2 April 2020, https://ew.com/movies/domestic-box-office-down-400-million-coronavirus/.

Norton, Chris. "Black Independent Cinema and the Influence of Neo-realism: Futility, Struggle, and Hope in the Face of Reality." *Images Journal: A Journal of Film and Popular Culture,* No.5, 1997, www.imagesjournal.com/issue05/features/Black.htm.

O'Brien, Daniel. "Saving the World for White Folks? Will Smith Racialises Science Fiction as Black Man and Man in Black." *Black Masculinity on Film: Native Sons and White Lies,* Palgrave Macmillan, 2017, pp. 177–95.

Ojuma, Akin. "The Observer Profile: Denzel Washington- Will Talent Out This Time." *The Guardian,* 24 March 2002, p. 27.

Onwuachi-Willig, Angela. "There's Just One Hitch, Will Smith: Examining Title VII, Race, and Casting Discrimination on the Fortieth Anniversary of Loving v. Virginia." *Wisconsin Law Review,* no. 2, 2007, pp. 319–43.

Osayande, Ewuare X. "An Open Letter to Will Smith." *Weallbe,* 11 Feb. 2009, weallbe.blogspot.com/2009/02/open-letter-to-will-smith.html.

Osumare, Halifu. *The Africanist Aesthetic in Global Hip Hop: Power Moves.* Palgrave Macmillan, 2007.

O'Toole, Lesley. "An Interview with Will Smith." Daily Express, 13 Jan. 2009, https://www.express.co.uk/entertainment/films/79786/An-interview-with-Will-Smith.

Page, Jennifer Renee. "'And he shall be called woman'": Behind the Mask of Selected Black Male Actors Cross-Dressing in Entertainment." M.A. Thesis, Clark Atlanta U, 2009.

Palmer, Lorrie. "Black Man/White Machine: Will Smith Crosses Over." *The Velvet Light Trap,* no. 67, Spring 2011, pp. 28–40.

Park, Ji Hoon et al. "Naturalizing Racial Differences Through Comedy: Asian, Black, and White Views on White Views on Racial Stereotypes in Rush Hour 2." *Journal of Communication,* vol. 56, 2006, pp. 157–77. *International Communication Association,* doi:10.111/j.1460.2006.00008.x.

Pharoah, Jay. "Will Smith & Denzel Washington Spoof Behind the Actor 'Why' Denzel & Will Smith Impressions." *YouTube,* 6 Feb. 2010, www.youtube.com/watch?v=EqZGGqO6euO.

Pinckney, Darryl. "Big Changes in Black America." The New York Review of Books, 24 May 2012, www.nybooks.com/articles/2012/05/24/big-changes-Black-america/?pagination=false.

Pinkney, Larry. "Internalizing Our Own Oppression." *Black Commentator,* no. 508, 14 Mar. 2013, www.Blackcommentator.com/508/508_kir_internalizing_oppression_share.html.

Portwood, Jerry. "Standing Ovation: Will Smith in Six Degrees of Separation." *Backstage,* 10 Feb. 2014, www.backstage.com/magazine/article/standing-ovation-will-smith-six-degrees-separation-11984/.

Poulson-Bryant, Scott. "Dreaming Cinema: Acting Out." *Vibe,* Feb. 1994, p. 96.

Precious. Directed by Lee Daniels, performances by Gabourey Sidibe and Mo'Nique. Lionsgate, 2009.

"The Pursuit of Happyness—Box Office Mojo." Box Office Mojo, www.boxofficemojo.com/release/rl1349158401/. Accessed 7 June 2020.

Quinn, Eithne. "Black Talent and Conglomerate Hollywood: Will Smith, Tyler Perry, and the Continuing Significance of Race." *Popular Communication,* vol. 11, no. 3, 2013, pp. 196–210. doi: 10.1080/15405702.2013.810070.

Raab, Scott. "Will Smith on Kids, His Career, Ferguson, and Failure." *Esquire,* 12 Feb. 2015, www.esquire.com/entertainment/interviews/a9938/will-smith-interview-0315/.

Raferty, Brian. "It's Time to Revisit *Ali,* Will Smith's Knockout Boxing Biopic." *Wired,* 6 June 2016, www.wired.com/2016/06/revisiting-ali-will-smith-michael-mann/.

Ransom, Amy. I Am Legend *as American Myth: Race and Masculinity in the Novel and Its Film Adaptations.* McFarland, 2018.

Reed, Justin Phillip. "The Double Agency of Will Smith in Sci-Fi." *The Rumpus,* 3 Mar. 2016, www.therumpus.net/2016/03/the-double-agency-of-will-smith-in-sci-fi/.

Reed, Wornie L., and Bertin M. Louis, Jr. "'No More Excuses': Problematic Responses to Barack Obama's Election." *Journal of African American Studies,* vol. 13, 2009, pp. 97–109. Springer, doi: 10.1007/s12111-009–9088–3.

Report to the Commissioner. Directed by Milton Katselas, performances by Michael Moriarty, Tony King, and Susan Blakely, United Artists, 1975.

Rex, Kasai. "'Bad Boys II' is a Transformative Piece of Black Cinema." *Vice.com,* 30 Mar. 2015, www.vice.com/en_uk/article/ppxpby/bad-boys-ii-saved-my-life-327.

Rich, Frank. "American Pseudo—The All-American Imposter." *The New York Times Magazine,* 12 Dec. 1999, pp. 80–87, 98+.

Ricochet. Directed by Russell Mulcahy, performances by Denzel Washington and John Lithgow, Warner Bros., 1991.

Rizov, Vadim. "Seven Pounds." *Sight & Sound,* vol. 19, no. 2, Feb. 2009, pp. 72–73. EBSCOhost,search.ebsco-host.com/login.aspx?direct=true&AuthType=ip,shib&db=f3h&AN=36125833&site=ehost-live&scope=site.

Robb, Brian J. *King of Cool: Will Smith.* Plexus, 2000.

Roberts, Tamara. "Michael Jackson's Kingdom: Music Race, and the Sound of the Mainstream." *Journal of Popular Music Studies,* vol. 23, no. 1, 2011, pp.19–39.

Rodriguez, Ashley. "Highest Grossing Romantic Comedies Released in the U.S." *The Atlas,* theatlas.com/charts/ryO7ICIZm. Accessed 25 Feb. 2020.

Rodriguez, Hansel. "Bright (2017): Corporate Worldmaking, Racial Allegory and the Netflix Blockbuster." *Film Matters,* vol. 9, no. 9, Winter 2018, pp. 122–131. doi: 10.1386/fm.9.3.122_1.

Rogin, Michael. *Independence Day, or How I Learned to Stop Worrying and Love the Enola Gay.* BFI, 1998.

Roman, David. "Fierce Love and Fierce Response: Intervening in the Cultural Politics of Race, Sexuality, and AIDS." *Critical Essays: Gay and Lesbian Writers of Color,* edited by Emmanuel S. Nelson, Haworth, 1993, pp. 195–219.

Rose, Steve. "Bright Review: Will Smith's Sci-Fi Is a True Original …For Better or Worse." *The Guardian,* 20 Dec. 2017, www.theguardian.com/film/2017/dec/21/bright-review-netflix-will-smith-joel-edgerton.

_____. "Make Will Smith Great Again!" *The Guardian,* 22 Dec. 2016, www.theguardian.com/film/2016/dec/22/make-will-smith-great-again-collateral-beauty.

_____. "Will Smith's Bright: Racial Allegory or Straight Up Racism?" *The Guardian,* 27 Jan. 2018, www. theguardian.com/culture/2018/jan/27/will-smiths-bright-racial-allegory-or-straight-up-racism.

Rose, Tricia. "Rap Music and the Demonization of Young Black Males." Golden, 149–157.

Rotello, Gabriel. "Will Smith, Hitler and the Holocaust's Unanswerable Question." *The Huffington Post,* 27 Dec. 2007, https://www.huffpost.com/entry/will-smith-hitler-and-the_b_78481.

Rottenberg, Catherine. "Passing: Race, Identification, and Desire." *Criticism,* vol. 45, no.1, 2003, pp. 435–52.

Rus, Mayer. "Will and Jada Pinkett Smith's Malibu Home." *Architectural Digest,* Sept. 2011, www. architecturaldigest.com/story/will-and-jada-pinkett-smith-home-article.

Ryan, Joal. "Men in Black 3 Beats The Avengers, but Did Will Smith Sequel Lose to History?" Eonline, 28 May 2012, https://www.eonline.com/news/319337/men-in-Black-3-beats-the-avengers-but-did-will-smith-sequel-lose-to-history.

Sager, Mike. "The Fresh King." *Vibe,* vol.6, no. 7, 1998, pp. 130–36.

"Samuel L. Jackson The Numbers." *The Numbers,* www.the-numbers.com/person/670401-Samuel-L-Jackson#tab=acting. Accessed 10 June 2020.

Sanchez, Tani Dianca. "Neo-Abolitionists, Colorblind Epistemologies and Black Politics: The Matrix Trilogy." *The Persistence of Whiteness: Race and Contemporary Hollywood Cinema,* edited by Daniel Bernardi, Routledge, 2008, pp. 102–24.

Schatz, T. "The New Hollywood." *Film Theory Goes to the Movies,* edited by J. Collins, H. Radner and A. Preacher Collins. Routledge, 1993. pp. 8–36.

Schneider, Sven Raphael. "Dressing Gowns & Robes for Men." Gentleman's Gazette, 3 Feb. 2011, www. gentleman'sgazette.com/dressing-gown.

Scott, A. O. "An I.R.S. Do-Gooder and Other Strangeness." Review of *Seven Pounds.* The New York Times, 18 Dec. 2006, www.nytimes.com/2008/12/19/movies/19seve.html.

Seitz, Matt Zoller. "White Famous Is a Stale, Pandering Look at Hollywood." *Vulture,* 15 Oct. 2017, www. vulture.com/2017/10/white-famous-showtime-jay-pharoah-review.html.

Sen, Raja. "Meet Will Smith, the Racist." Livemint, 19 Dec. 2017, www.livemint.com/Consumber/BjHB3UG74lOiyPmZlWJ4mN/Meet-Will-Smit-the-racist.html.

Serjeant, Jill. "Will Smith voted 2008's top money-making movie star." *Reuters,* 2 Jan. 2009, www. reuters.com/article/us-moneymaking/will-smith-voted-2008s-top-money-making-movie-star-idUSTRE5013DY20090102.

"Seven Pounds—Box Office Mojo." *Box Office Mojo,* www.boxofficemojo.com/release/rl1148093953/. Accessed 29 May 2020.

Siegel, Tatiana. "How Will Smith Cracked the Code on Making Real Money in Hollywood." *The Hollywood Reporter,* 10 Oct. 2019, www.hollywoodreporter.com/features/how-will-smith-cracked-code-making-real-money-hollywood-1246035.

Simpson, Richard. "Will: Ask Your Wife Before You Cheat on Her." *DailyMail.com,* 8 Feb. 2005, https://www. dailymail.co.uk/tvshowbiz/article-337032/Will-Ask-wife-cheat-her.html.

Sims, David. "The Shadow That's Haunting Will Smith." *The Atlantic,* 25 Jan. 2020, www.theatlantic.com/culture/archive/2020/01/will-smiths-movie-stardom-will-live-forever/605437/.

Singh, Anita. "Will Smith tops Hollywood power list." *The Telegraph.* 10 Feb, 2009, https://www.telegraph.co.uk/news/celebritynews/4583577/Will-Smith-tops-Hollywood-power-list.html.

Siquig, Alex. "An Oral History of Will Smith's 'Miami.'" *GQ,* 24 Mar. 2016, www.gq.com/story/will-smith-miami-oral-history.

Six Degrees of Separation. By John Guare, directed by Jerry Zaks, performances by Stockard Channing, John Cunningham, and James McDaniel, 28 June 1990, Lincoln Center Theater, Mitzi E. Newhouse Theater, New York.

_____. By John Guare. Directed by Jerry Zaks, performances by Stockard Channing, John Cunningham, and Courtney Vance, 10 Nov. 1990, Lincoln Center Theater. Vivian Beaumont Theater, New York.

Smith, Sean, "The $4 Billion Man." *Newsweek,* 9 Apr. 2007, pp. 82–84.

Smith, Will. "Personal Reflections on a Historic Moment." *USA Today,* 21 Jan. 2009, www.usatoday.com/news/opinion/personal-reflecions.htm.

Sperling, Nicole. "Will Smith's Production Pulls Out of Georgia, Citing the State's Voting Law." The New York Times, 12 April 2021, https://www.nytimes.com/2021/04/12/business/will-smith-emancipation-georgia.html.

Squires, Catherine R. *The Post-Racial Mystique: Media and Race in the Twenty-First Century.* New York UP, 2014.

Stables, Kate. "The Pursuit of Happyness." Review. *Sight and Sound,* vol. 17, no. 3, Mar. 2007, p. 71.

Stanfill, Francesca. "Living Well Is Still the Best Revenge." *The New York Times Magazine,* 21 Dec. 1980, pp. 20+.

Stephens, Charles. "Sexual Objectification of Black Men, From Mapplethorpe to Calvin Klein." *The Advocate,* 17 May 2017, www.advocate.com/current-issue/2017/5/17/sexual-objectification-Black-men-mapplethorpe-calvin-klein.

Story, Richard David. "Six Degrees of Preparation." *New York,* 7 June 1993, pp. 38–43.

Strohmeyer, Robert. "The Legend of Bagger Vance." Review. *FilmCritic.com,* www.filmcritic.com/misc/emporium.nsf/0/b2211fdf1499788f8825698b000871a1?OpenDocument.

Subramanian, Janani. "Alienating Identification: Black Identity in The Brother From Another Planet and I Am Legend." *Science Fiction Film and Television,* vol. 3, no. 1, 2010, pp. 37–56. doi: 10.3828/sfftv.2010.3.

"Suicide Squad—Box Office Mojo." *Box Office Mojo,* www.boxofficemojo.com/release/rl1145865729/. Accessed 14 Apr. 2020.

Sussler, Betsy. "Thelma Golden by Glenn Ligon." Interview. *Bomb Magazine,* 4 Apr. 2004, www.bomb magazine/org/articles/thelma-golden/.

Taubin, Amy. "Playing It Straight: R.E.M. Meets a Post-Rodney King World in *Independence Day.*" *Sight and Sound,* vol.6, no. 8, 1996, pp. 6–8.

Thai, Xuan, and Ted Barrett. "Biden's Description of Obama Draws Scrutiny." *CNN.com,* 9 Feb. 2007, https://www.cnn.com/2007/POLITICS/01/31/biden.obama/.

THR Staff. "Will Smith: 'Racism Is Not Getting Worse, It's Getting Filmed.'" *The Hollywood Reporter,* 3 Aug. 2016, www.hollywoodreporter.com/news/will-smith-colbert-race-relations-obama-politics-sings-summertime-916816.

Touré. *Who's Afraid of Post-Blackness? What It Means to Be Black Now.* Free Press, 2011.

Travers, Ben. "'White Famous' Review: Jay Pharoah's 'Californication' Knock-Off Is Shallower and Less Funny." *Indie Wire,* 12 Oct. 2017, www.indiewire.com/2017/10/white-famous-review-jamie-foxx-showtime-bad-californication-1201886532/.

Uschan, Michael V. *Will Smith.* Greenhaven Publishing, 2009.

Valby, Karen. "Will Slaps Reporter: Vitalii Sediuk Strikes Again." *Entertainment Weekly,* 19 May 2012, https://ew.com/article/2012/05/19/will-smith-smacks-reporter-vitalii-sediuk/.

VanArendonk, Kathryn. "Why *Westworld*'s Throwaway Scene of Black Male Nudity Felt So Dehumanizing." *Vulture,* 31 Oct. 2016, www.vulture.com/2016/10/westworld-Black-male-nudity-anatomy-of-a-scene.html.

Vernallis, Carol. *Experiencing Music Video: Aesthetics and Cultural Context.* Columbia UP, 2004.

"Vin Diesel: A Colorless Actor for a Colorblind America." *Africultures.com,* 3 Apr. 2005, africultures.com/vin-diesel-a-colorless-actor-for-a-colorblind-america-3781/.

"Vin Diesel The Numbers." *The Numbers,* www.the-numbers.com/person/39880401-Vin-Diesel#tab=acting.

Voss, Brandon. "Sibling Revelry." *The Advocate,* 22 Dec. 2010, www.advocate.com/Arts_and_Entertainment/Television/Sibling_Revelry.

Wallace, Maurice. *Constructing the Black Masculine: Identity and Ideality in African American Men's Literature and Culture 1775–1995.* Duke UP, 2002.

Washington, Laurence. "Celebrity Interviews: Will Smith." *Blackflix,* www.Blackflix.com/interview/smith_will.html. Accessed 5 Jun. 2020.

Watson, Margeaux. "Hollywood's Lack of Black Leading Ladies." *EW.com,* 11 July 2008. https://ew.com/article/2008/07/11/hollywoods-lack-Black-leading-ladies/.

Weiss, Josh. "'Wild Wild West' at 20: Revisiting An Alt-History, Steampunk Masterpiece." *Forbes.com,* 1 July 2019, www.forbes.com/sites/joshweiss/2019/07/01/wild-wild-west-at-20-revisiting-an-alt-history-steampunk-masterpiece/?sh=61f960a211a0.

White, Adam. "How Will Smith's Box Office Woes Reflect a Hollywood in Crisis." *The Independent,* 10 Jan. 2020, www.independent.co.uk/arts-entertainment/films/features/will-smith-career-box-office-bad-boys-gemini-man-a9269521.html.

White, Armond. "The Invincible Man." Review of *I Am Legend,* directed by Francis Lawrence. *New York Press,* 11 Nov. 2014, www.nypress.com/news/the-invincible-man-ICNP1020071219312199990.

_____. "The Pursuit of Crappyness." Review of *Hancock,* directed by Peter Berg, *New York Press,* 9 July 2008, www.nypress.com/news/the-pursuit-of-crappyness-KINP1020080709307099997.

_____. Review of *I, Robot,* directed by Alex Proyas. *New York Press,* 20 July 2004.

Wiegman, Robyn. "The Anatomy of Lynching." *Journal of the History of Sexuality,* vol. 3, no.3, Jan. 1993, pp. 445–67. *JSTOR,* www.jstor.org/stable/3704016.

"Will Smith Censored in *I, Robot.*" *Breaking News,* 21 Jul. 2004, www.breakingnews.ie/showbiz/smith-censored-in-i-robot-158106.html.

"Will Smith Stars As Mysterious Golf Caddy in 'The Legend of Bagger Vance.'" *Jet,* vol. 98, no. 24, 20 Nov. 2000, pp. 60–64.

"Will Smith Talks 'I, Robot' Nude Scene." *KillerMovies,* 12 July 2004, www.killermovies.ccom/i/robot/articles/4205.html.

"Will Smith Talks Gemini Man and Being His Own Competition." *The Daily Show,* 10 Oct. 2019, *You Tube,* uploaded by Comedy Central Africa, Oct. 2019, www.youtube.com/watch?v=dRk02XLEYH4.

"Will Smith The Numbers." *The Numbers,* www.the-numbers.com/person/770401-Will-Smith#tab=acting. Accessed 29 May 2020.

"Will the Real Will Smith Please Stand up?" *The Guardian,* 24 June, 2008, www.theguardian.com/film/filmblog/2008/jun/24/willtherealwillsmithpleasestandup.

Williams, Kam. "Movie Review: The Legend of Bagger Vance." *The Black World Today,* 5 Nov. 2000, *Marxism-Thaxis Movie Review,* 7 Nov. 2000, lists.econ.utah.edu/pipermail/Marxism-thaxis/2000-November/016803.html.

Williams, Roland Leander, Jr. *Black Male Frames: African Americans in a Century of Hollywood Cinema, 1903–2003.* Syracuse UP, 2018.

Wilson, S.S. et al. *Wild Wild West.* Script, 15 June 1998, imsdb.com/scripts/Wild-Wild-West.html. Accessed 17 April 2021.

Wolfe, Tom. *The Bonfire of the Vanities.* Farrar, 1987.

Wong, Victor. "Man in Black: Does Will Smith's Race Matter." *Alternate Takes,* 21 July 2005, www.alternatetakes.co.uk/?2005,7,6,print.

Woods, Amy Louise. *Lynching and Spectacle: Witnessing Racial Violence in America.* U of North Carolina P, 2009.

Wright, Julie Lobalzo. *Crossover Stardom: Popular Male Music Stars in American Cinema.* Bloomsbury, 2018.

Yarborough, Gerry. Letter. *Premiere,* Mar. 1994, p. 16.

Young, Elizabeth. *Black Frankenstein: The Making of an American Metaphor.* NYU Press, 2008.

Zacharek, Stephanie. "Hancock." Review. *Salon,* 1 July 2008, www.salon.com/2008/07/01/hancock/.

_____. "The Legend of Bagger Vance." Review. *Salon,* 4 Nov. 2000, www.salon.com/2000/11/03/bagger/.

_____. "Wild, Wild West." Review. *Salon,* 30 June 1999, www.salon.com/ent/movies/review/1999/06/30/wild_west.

Zinoman, Jason. "Theater; P. Diddy's Broadway Crash Course." *The New York Times,* 25 Apr. 2004, www.nytimes.com/2004/04/25/theater/theater-p-diddy-s-boradway-crash-course.html.

Index